Common Good

Review 3
Common Good

Tulane School of Architecture
and Built Environment
Tulane University

Published by
Actar Publishers,
New York, Barcelona
www.actar.com

Editor
Patricia Fraile Garrido

Publication Assistants
Emily Brandt
Asha Hokanson

Copy editing and proofreading
Emily Capdeville

Printing and binding
Arlequin & Pierrot

Distribution
Actar D, Inc. New York, Barcelona.

New York
440 Park Avenue South, 17th Floor
New York, NY 10016, USA
T +1 2129662207
salesnewyork@actar-d.com

Barcelona
Roca i Batlle 2
08023 Barcelona, Spain
T +34 933 282 183
eurosales@actar-d.com

Indexing
English ISBN: 978-1-63840-181-0
Library of Congress Control Number: 2025941347

Printed in Spain

Publication date: December 2024

Cover image: © Common Good, *Olga Pipnik*

HOW TO USE THIS BOOK

THIS IS NOT A YEARBOOK

Indeed, like a yearbook, this book is composed of the materials produced by students and professors during two academic years, spanning five semesters: 2023-2024. However, its ambition goes beyond presenting the work being done at Tulane School of Architecture and Built Environment. It is designed to spark conversation about potential opportunities within the built environment.

You don't have to read it in order.

You can use it as a compilation of sheets, organized to explain the school's research in the context of real-world application. The topics are created to orient the work, categorizing them by variations of affordability.

You can use it to understand the physics of Tulane School of Architecture and Built Environment. Explore it in its entirety. Look at the work our professors do, the courses we develop, or the final theses that students present as a culmination of their journey here.

The following captions are guides to help you navigate this document.

KEY

Whose work

s>	**i>**	**UG**	**GR**	**UG + GR**
student	instructor	undergraduate	graduate	both

When: year and semester

FA	**SP**	**SU**
Fall	Spring	Summer

Programs

arch	**desg**	**pres**	**sred / msred**
architecture	design	preservation	real estate

CONTENTS

8 / DIALOGUE AS COMMON GOOD /

9 / MISSISSIPPI AS COMMON GOOD /

10 / WATER AS COMMON GOOD /

11 / LANDSCAPE AND TERRITORY AS COMMON GOOD /

12 / CONTEXT AND PLACE AS COMMON GOOD /

13 / INFRASTRUCTURES AS COMMON GOOD /

14 / REPRESENTATION AND NARRATIVES AS COMMON GOOD /

FOREWORD

Iñaki Alday
Dean of Tulane School of Architecture and Built Environment

"Remember to imagine and craft the worlds you cannot live without, just as you dismantle the ones you cannot live within."

Ruha Benjamin

Architects, designers, urbanists, preservationists, developers, landscape architects and engineers are tasked with developing desired futures, the environment we and the following generations will live in. This embodies the idea of 'transformation'. Transformation is what Ruha Benjamin describes as: the double action of dismantling and imagining and crafting. What we cannot longer live within and what we cannot live without.

Creative fields often focus on subjectivity and personal expression. However, this is not the meaning of 'we' in the fields of the built environment. Paraphrasing Margarita Jover, when she states that "the landscape is not to be drawn, it is the result of generations of its inhabitants shaping the territory", the built environment is the physical expression of a society, a time, a culture. And our fields are tasked to materialize it, in an aspirational way: creatively, innovatively, empathically, caringly, lovingly, beautifully.

In our daily work, architecture and the fields of the built environment have drifted towards a position of service providers, although it can be argued that this has always been the case as far as the concept of "client" has been involved for centuries and since the professions and disciplines were formulated. The real question is 'who we serve'. Our work for private clients consumes planetarian resources. Public clients are imperfect representatives of their constituencies. Communities are never homogeneous and include conflicting interests. The answer to the question of 'who we serve', thus, is far from simple. Our ultimate goal is to serve our peoples and societies in their betterment, and what they share: the commons.

Aware of this complexity, we address in this volume the notion of our role for the 'public good' as professionals and, especially, as the community of learners that our school is. Our globalized neo-liberal society is showing a crisis of the idea of the commons, materialized in dissents about infrastructures, education, health and even the basic principles of democracy. Meritocracy -as described by Sandel-, post-colonial effects, competitiveness -'winners take all'- and different contemporary dynamics are eroding the very idea of the common good. With the irruption of the digital society, an additional question 'what a good digital society looks like?' emerges among philosophers and social scientist. Sandel questions the role or even the commitment of academic institutions in the education for the common good.

At this point, at Tulane School of Architecture and Built Environment, we have no doubts about our mission in educating future professionals who will have the public good in the very core of any endeavor. Working from New Orleans, we perceive the climate crisis and the exacerbated social inequality as existential challenges for a good society and its built environment. And, as educators, we want everyone entering through the doors of the school to succeed in becoming a well-prepared, thoughtful professional, without leaving anyone behind. With these aspirations, are we effectively tackling the public good? How are we doing it? This volume is both a self-examination and a vehicle to share with others towards a collective action for the future.

INTRODUCTION

Patricia Fraile Garrido
The ReView editor

We are very fortunate to belong to an institution like this one and to be able to view the world through our unique lens. We are keenly aware that if we have made it this far—whether as students, faculty, or staff at the Tulane School of Architecture and Built Environment in New Orleans—it is more due to luck than merit. Michael Sandel has helped illuminate this for us, and it shapes a distinctive attitude toward our disciplines, our professions, and our work as educators.

In *The Tyranny of Merit*, Sandel questions universities' neglect of understanding and pursuit of the common good, and his book—as part of the current debate about our democracy and our societal concerns—has sparked critical discussions at TuSABE about credentialism, the collective versus the individual, and our role as educators, researchers, and practitioners in the realm of the common good:

> *"Governing well requires practical wisdom and civic virtue - an ability to deliberate about the common good and to pursue it effectively. But neither of these capacities is developed very well in most universities today, even those with the highest reputations."*
>
> Sandel, The Tyranny of Merit, p.99

If we have reached this point thanks to luck and the circumstances of our capital—whether cultural, economic, or social—anyone else with the same starting conditions could have been in our place. Success, therefore, is not so much about us as it is about the foundational opportunities we've had. This realization allows us to distance ourselves from ego, from the notion of individual merit, and to adopt a sense of detachment toward what we produce. More importantly, it inspires in us a desire to give back—not in a paternalistic sense, but to contribute meaningfully to society. It drives us to serve others and work for *the common good.*

Understanding the common good is a challenge in a world dominated by segregation, individualism, capitalism, and meritocracy. Yet, recognizing that fortune has brought us here makes it easier to empathize with lives far removed from our own and with perspectives vastly different from ours. Architecture and the built environment have a lot to say in that regard. The commons—the public spaces that bring us together as citizens—are critical to sustaining and nurturing a democratic society. However, for a variety of reasons, we are now witnessing the erosion of these commons, leading to increasing separation between people of different backgrounds and diminishing opportunities for meaningful encounters. This decline of the commons contributes to growing inequality and the fragmentation of our collective life. Addressing the crisis of the commons is, therefore, a step toward revitalizing our shared existence, and by enhancing our built environment, we can also strengthen the bonds and values that hold our communities together.

At TuSABE, our work for the common good takes on multiple angles, some of which are captured in this book and inform the content and structure of this publication. We address the pursuit of the common good across various scales (infrastructures, landscape and territory), bridging the past (history and heritage) and the future (development), tackling pressing concerns (climate adaptation), and finding solutions deeply rooted in localism (context and place). We focus on building common human bonds (dialogue, community networks, communal living), spanning from the abstract (creativity) to the tangible and built (technology and making). Located in New Orleans, on the Gulf Coast, we are grounded in the unique challenges and considerations of this region—our foundation and identity (water, the mighty Mississippi River). Each of these concepts is articulated by a faculty member whose expertise and perspective illuminate the topic and set the stage for the subsequent teaching, projects, and work featured in the chapters that follow.

Thus, **Eisa Esfanjary, in "History and Heritage as common good"** discusses the importance of preserving cultural and natural heritage in order to foster community identity and promote environmental sustainability. **Will Bradshaw, in "Development for the common good,"** focuses on Leonard Riggio's family-to-family philanthropic approach to post-Katrina recovery in New Orleans. **Margarita Jover, in "Communal Living as common good,"** proposes a housing redevelopment project in New Orleans, advocating for a community-led, architect-supported model that enhances social equity, ecological performance, and collective well-being. **Ann Yoachim, Nick Jenisch, and Emilie Taylor-Welty, in "Community Networks as common good,"** showcase how collaborative design processes build trust, equity, and innovation while addressing human and environmental challenges at all scales. In the same vein, **Wes Michaels** explores the critical need to rigorously assess the impact of civic design projects on the public good, and offers methodologies for evaluating their outcomes. **Tiffany Lin, in "Creativity as common good,"** explains how design education cultivates curiosity, intellectual agility, and empathy, equipping students with the skills to tackle complex problems in a complex reality. **Jesse Keenan, in "Climate Adaptation for the common good,"** emphasizes the need to design buildings with future programmatic adaptability to combat climate-driven obsolescence.

Adam Marcus, in "Technology and Making as common good" examines how an integrated and critical application of technology in architecture—spanning design, fabrication, construction, and building performance—can address climate change, reduce carbon emissions, and promote ecological and social engagement beyond traditional siloed approaches. **Edson Cabalfin, in "Dialogue as common good,"** stresses the importance of transforming architecture and the built environment into practices rooted in empathy, compassion, and dialogue. Within this same theme, I explore the growing movement of participatory architecture as a means of reclaiming civic agency, challenging corporate-driven urbanism, and redefining architectural education to serve the common good through collaboration. **Richard Campanella, in "Mississippi as common good,"** considers the historical and ongoing tension between public access and private ownership of the terrain created by rivers, using the case of the St. Mary Batture in New Orleans as a key example. **Iñaki Alday, in "Water as common good,"** speaks to the critical importance of water as a universal public good, essential for life, health, equity, and ecological balance, while advocating for a paradigm shift in how we manage, preserve, and integrate water systems into sustainable urban and architectural practices amidst the challenges of climate change and societal inequities. **Liz Camuti, in "Landscape and Territory as common good,"** assesses the urgent need to reimagine coastal infrastructure to address climate challenges, advocating for the transformation of historically inequitable and extractive systems into life-giving designs.

In **"Context and Place as common good," Iñaki Alday** also discusses how architects can navigate the tensions between private clients, public interests, and equity, using the Zaragoza tram project to illustrate how thoughtful public space design can promote democracy and equity. **Liz Russell, in "Infrastructures as common good,"** imagines infrastructures as a tool for transformation, addressing the challenges that population growth and ecology pose to our infrastructure systems and highlighting the urgent need to rethink infrastructure as a dynamic, shared investment. Finally, in **"Representation and Narratives as common good," Austin Lightle** examines the environmental impact of digital data in architecture, highlighting the ecological consequences of data centers and exploring how architects can use digital tools to raise awareness and drive climate activism through their designs.

"The ReView: Common Good" showcases a rich tapestry of academic coursework, faculty professional practice, student capstone projects, research initiatives, and events from the 2023-2024 academic year at Tulane School of Architecture and Built Environment in New Orleans. It responds to two essential questions: *What is the school's ethical, social, and intellectual commitment to the common good?* and *What does it mean to educate and practice for the common good?* And it does so transdisciplinarily across our diverse programs—Architecture, Design, Real Estate, Historic Preservation, Landscape, and Social Innovation. Our courses often defy categorization; many of them could easily fit into multiple categories at once. This interconnectedness reflects our broader commitment to serving the public good in a way that transcends traditional boundaries.

In a time defined by global challenges, widening social disparities, and a growing need for empathetic, multidisciplinary approaches, TuSABE reaffirms its commitment to advancing the common good in the built environment. We invite readers to join us in this ongoing endeavor—to reimagine the contours of the common good as not merely a theoretical construct, but as a call to action for shaping a better future.

COMMON GOOD - The Review 2023-2024 -
PATRICIA FRAILE, IÑAKI ALDAY, EMILY BRANDT, ASHA HOKANSON
Tulane School of Architecture and Built Environment
Patricia Fraile
HISTORY AND HERITAGE as common good
ARCH 2930/6930 - ARCH 6990 - ARCH 4937/6937
Eisa Esfanjary
Will Bradshaw
DEVELOPMENT for the common good
SRED2050 - ARCH 6990 - Alexandria Housing Study
Vela & García - Todd Erlandson
Margarita Jover
COMMUNAL LIVING as common good
SRED 6740 - ARCH 2022/6022 - ARCH 3032/6032 - ARCH 5990
Aldayjover - ARCH 4937/6937 - Sergi Serrat
Juan Medina
A.Yoachim, N. Jenisch,
E. Taylor-Welty
Wes Michaels
COMMUNITY NETWORKS as common good
Smith Marks - ARCH 5990 - Engaged Urban Design
Design in the Public Interest
Tiffany Lin
CREATIVITY as common good
Digital & Tactile Design - Discover - Digital media
Jill Stoll - Textiles & Typographic Specimens - Tiffany Lin
Visual Communication and Advocacy
Jesse Keenan
CLIMATE ADAPTATION for the common good
Ecological Tectonics - Domesticating Bigness
Building, Climate, Comfort
Adam Marcus

DIALOGUE
ARCH 6031
Play It Louder
Richard Campanella
MISSISSIPPI
The New Orleans Public Space Project
as common good
Iñaki Alday
WATER
ARCH 5990 - ARCH 6990 - SRED 4932
as common good
LANDSCAPE AND TERRITORY
ARCH 5990 - ARCH 2021/6021 - Gulf Research Studio
Austin Lightle
as common good
Liz Camuti
Iñaki Alday
CONTEXT AND PLACE
as common good
URBAN Studio - Swiss Models of Regeneration of Buildings
Dumez & Marcano - Mouton - Bardón de Tena
Liz Russell
INFRASTRUCTURES
SRED 6740 - ARCH 5990
as common good
Austin Lightle
REPRESENTATION AND NARRATIVES
ARCH 6990 - ARCH 1012 - Culture - MAateriality - Common Objects
Adam Marcus - Creating Value Through Productization
as common good

Students in the Conservation Technology course view the truss structure within the attic of an early 19th-century French Quarter residence.

1

HISTORY & HERITAGE

AS COMMON GOOD

HISTORY AND HERITAGE AS COMMON GOOD

Preserving Heritage, Sustaining Futures

By Eisa Esfanjary
Incoming Associate Director of the Historic Preservation Program
Tulane School of Architecture and Built Environment

As the world struggles with complex environmental, social, and civilizational crises, Michael Sandel critiques the neglect of universities in understanding and pursuing the common good. However, there are compelling reasons to believe that the historic preservation cares for the common good. Preserving cultural and natural heritage not only strengthens national identity and fosters cultural and communal values but also plays a crucial role in advancing environmental and social sustainability. In doing so, it significantly contributes to the common good, providing invaluable benefits for future generations. The Historic Preservation Program, with its focus on the history and heritage of places, is an integral part of TuSABE's identity and mission, particularly in its commitment to the common good.

Historically, the concept of the common good has been a cornerstone of design, construction, and social life in diverse cultural and geographic contexts. Traditionally, the idea of the common good has been deeply embedded in building typologies, often shaped by society and rooted in earlier forms. The idea that at any given time there is a common "type" of building, the so-called "leading type," which is shared by a society and which in turn has its roots in the preceding type and, retrospectively, in an earlier elementary cell or *cellula elementare*.[1]

This concept contrasts sharply with some of today's design trends, where individuality of the designers or clients often take precedence. What is needed now is an understanding of how communal identity can inform architecture and urbanism. The common good has thus been a guiding principle of the built environment throughout history, and heritage conservation plays an essential role in preserving this collective cultural legacy.

Today, history and heritage are widely regarded as resources that benefit society as a whole. The idea of cultural heritage is central to the common good, as outlined in the 1972 UNESCO Convention.[2] This document establishes heritage as a shared global resource, emphasizing that cultural resources do not belong to individuals or particular communities alone, but to all humanity. In this context, heritage sites serve as symbols of shared history and collective memory.

Cultural heritage is, in itself, a shared common good. Cultural heritage encompasses both tangible and intangible elements. Tangible heritage includes physical assets such as monuments, ancient sites, historic buildings, artifacts, common spaces, cultural landscapes, industrial sites, gardens, and green spaces. Intangible heritage, on the other hand, "refers to the practices, representations, expressions, knowledge, and know-how, that are transmitted from generation to generation within communities, ccreated and continuously transformed by them in response to their environment and their interaction with nature and history."[3]

Many of the structures preserved—whether tangible or intangible—are public in nature, such as public buildings, communal spaces, and cultural landscapes. Even private properties are often maintained, adapted, or preserved in ways that serve the broader interests of the community. These elements, as both natural and cultural heritage, not only safeguard historical and cultural identities but also stimulate sustainable development.

One of the primary objectives of the Historic Preservation Program at Tulane is to foster a sense of belonging and community attachment to specific places, histories,

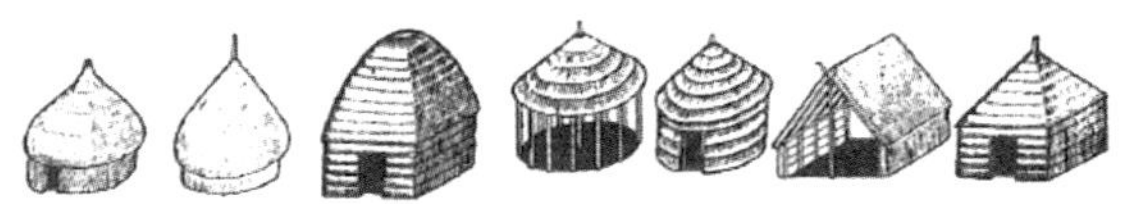

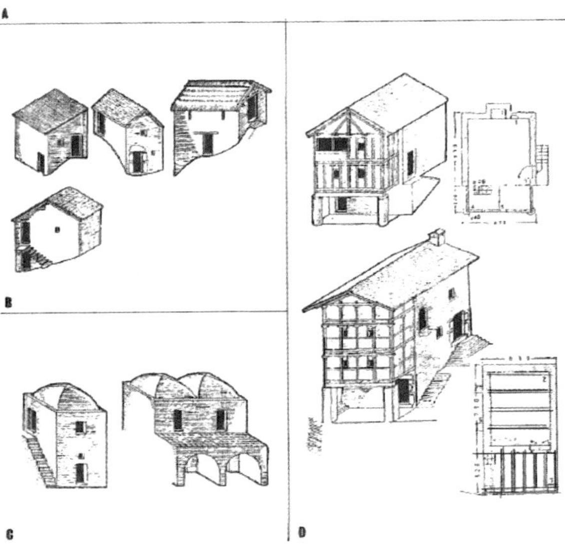

A: basic types;
B, C, D: subsequent doublings (after Gianfranco Caniggia and Gian L. Maffei, Composizione Architettonica e Tipologia Edilizia: 2. Il Progetto Nell'ediliziaa di Base, Venice, 1984)

and heritage. As Sandel states, "We cannot deliberate about common purposes and ends without a sense of belonging."[4] Only when individuals recognize that they are part of a place—and feel a connection to its history and meaning—will they act responsibly toward it. Without this connection, no matter how much money or resources are invested, preservation efforts are unlikely to be truly effective. Thus, the past built environment was characterized by a deep consideration of the common good, and current preservation efforts continue to champion collective benefits.

There is no doubt that significant historic places and monumental structures should be preserved for the benefit of present and future generations. The question remains, however, why are the principles of historic preservation primarily applied to historic places, but not extended to contemporary and future design practices? The short life cycle of many modern buildings, combined with the pressure to demolish structures deemed obsolete, places a heavy burden on the environment. Demolishing buildings not only wastes embodied energy and resources, but also restarts the cycle of resource extraction and energy consumption, leading to further environmental degradation. This ultimately undermines the very concept of the common good.

To minimize carbon emissions and environmental damage, it is essential to keep the demolition of buildings—whether historic or contemporary—to an absolute minimum. We need to prioritize preservation, retrofitting and, in some cases, contextual improvements over new construction.

There is an urgent need to rethink current design and development practices to ensure that they are fit for purpose. The principles of conservation as outlined in national and international conventions, including UNESCO and ICOMOS recommendations, should be applied beyond the specialized field of heritage conservation. These principles can and should inform sustainable design, development planning and decision-making processes.

These principles include, but are not limited to, adaptability, reversibility, legibility, distinguishability, authenticity, integrity, irreplaceability, simplicity, flexibility, compatibility, locality, community, identity, continuity, longevity, holistic, responsibility, efficiency, and sustainability. By adopting these principles, we can achieve a sustainable balance between the needs of present and future generations, avoid wasting valuable resources, and preserve shared cultural identity, environmental health, and sustainable development.

Thus, the Historic Preservation Program is dedicated not only to preserving our past, but also to promoting the common good for present and future generations.

[1] Kropf, 'An enquiry into the definition of built form in urban morphology', p. 99
[2] https://whc.unesco.org/en/conventiontext/
[3] 2003 UNESCO Convention for the Safeguarding of the Intangible Cultural Heritage https://ich.unesco.org/doc/src/18440-EN.pdf
[4] Sandel, *The Tyranny of Merit*, p. 222.

PRESERVATION STUDIO II

Heather Veneziano
Mark Rabinowitz

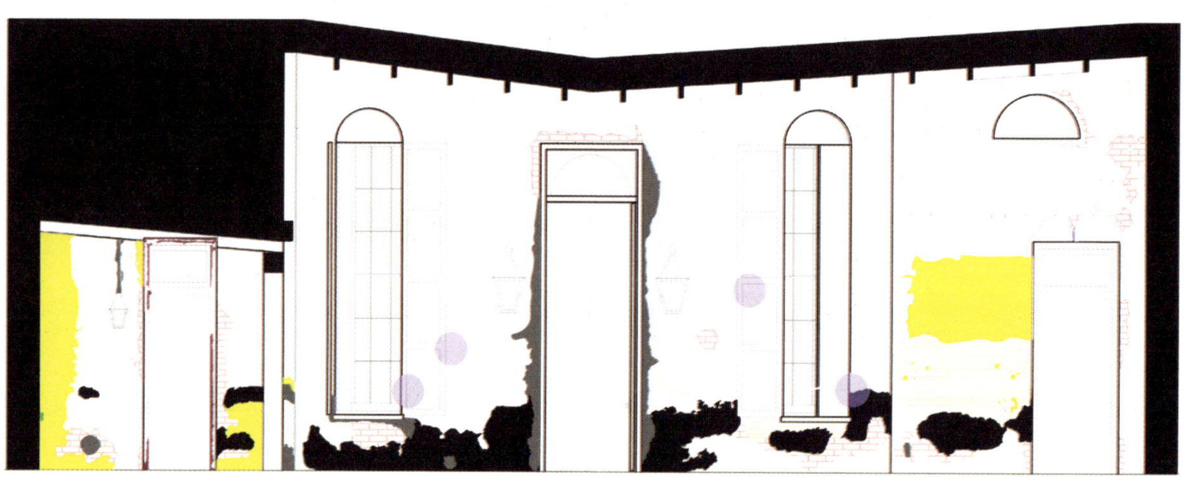

In the fall of 2023, the Tulane School of Architecture and Built Environment was approached by the management of Latrobe's on Royal, located at 707 Conti Street. They showed interest in gaining a greater understanding of the architectural history and significance of the site.

The Fall 2023 Preservation Studio I class conducted initial research and documentation of the property. Their work continued into the Spring 2024 Preservation Studio II, led by Heather Veneziano and Mark Rabinowitz, to create a Historic Structure Report (HSR), along with thirteen Tulane School of Architecture graduate students who participated in group and individual work to construct a detailed history and current conditions of Latrobe's on Royal.

The intention of the Preservation Studio II course is to concentrate on documenting, analyzing, and planning the preservation of the built environment as a basis for understanding the technical, theoretical and procedural aspects of urban conservation.

Students:
Allyson Hinz
Bailey Godwin
Catherine Restrepo
Dang Doan
Eileen Tomczuk
Emily Stood
Isabel Coletti
Jenna Voss
Jessica Triche
Katherine Schqwab
Kristian Carroll
Lauren Vagts
Lisa Black
Madeline Wilson
Maria Gabriela Arrieta Vallerino
Parker Heitzmann
Rachel Shannon
Sam Crowley
Tahlor Cleveland

Latrobe's on Royal is a contributing structure listed on the National Register of Historic Places, listed as Louisiana State Bank. The structure is also designated by the Vieux Carre Commercial District. Its significance is due to its contributed architect, Benjamin Henry Latrobe, also coined "The father of American Architecture." In addition, its architectural style, contribution to the French Quarter urban fabric, and role in the formation of the "Bank" typology lend itself towards noteworthy. The HSR provides documentary, graphic, and physical information about a property's history and existing conditions. The report also serves as an important guide for all changes made to such a historic property over time with information regarding recommended repair, rehabilitation, and restoration procedures.

There is apparent warping in the Royal Street façade towards the roof and parapet of the building. It is advised to consult an engineer about what is happening to the structure underneath the finishes. It is likely that the brick infill of the carriageway is made of soft brick. It could be useful to seek further testing to determine if the current paint allows the brick to breathe. A mineral silicate paint would be recommended. It may be prudent to seek further documentation on the roof of the carriageway. The dip in roof lines has the potential to hold water if current draining processes are not functioning properly. Paint analysis concludes that the current paint color is not accurate to what may have originally been painted. Consider repainting to a shade that is more historically accurate.

Much of the paint on the window and door frames is peeling or otherwise damaged. Repairing this would require a professional painter with experience working on historic wooden windows, who can propely ensure the paint's application. Millwork around windows and doors

is also damaged in some areas. This would require the advice of a professional with experience working with wooden windows and doors to patch or repair. In some cases, cracking at the door headers would require consultation with a structural engineer.

Conditions in the entire structure indicate moisture, cracking, and losses due to foundational shifts. It is essential to consult with a structural engineer trained in the Secretary of Interior Standards to evaluate the foundation of the building and any historically appropriate repairs it may need. Following this, a masonry expert would be required for repairs both structural and cosmetic to the walls, with a special focus on reversing and defending against further water damage. The work of the masonry expert would require removal of Portland cement, repointing and cleaning brick, and some testing to discover any unknown effects of the iron components or modern additions to the walls. Removing the Portland cement is especially important for avoiding further water damage, but should only be performed by a professional due to the risks this removal poses to the original masonry. The plaster may be removed and reapplied by a plaster professional. It is necessary to consult with a plasterer trained in conservation to test the aggregate compound of the historic plaster to determine the ratio of lime to fiber to water as well as makeup of the aggregate.

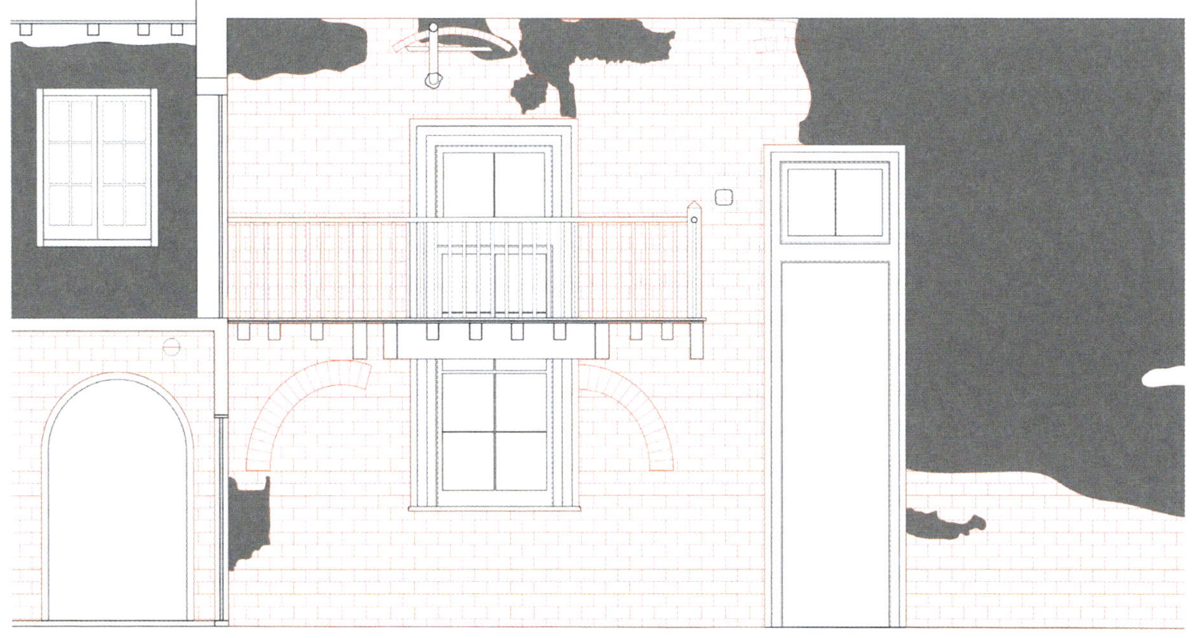

Some fixtures and hardware have been updated with improper replacements. Replacing these with historic recreations would bring some historic character back to the property. Since construction, HVAC and other modern additions have been made to the property. The HVAC especially has a huge effect on the behavior of water throughout the building. This should be kept in mind when doing any work. While the HVAC cannot be removed due to the needs of the venue and climate of New Orleans, it alters the interior temperature and the way condensation moves throughout the walls.

With continued restoration and conservation efforts, Latrobe's on Royal may continue as a core component to the architecture of the historic French Quarter of New Orleans, Louisiana.

ARCH 2930 + 6930 | **Elective** | UG + GR | **SP24**

THE ARSENAL OF OBSERVATION

Andrew Liles [C]

This course articulates the power of in situ sketching for recording both the logos and pathos of place. More than observation, this pattern of documentation will be taught as a method of field work, or onsite data collection. The sketchbook is your arsenal for observation, and this arsenal equips you to see.

Composition, catalog and collage will be employed to not only articulate tangibles but to perhaps also capture an ethos. The media by which the explorations will occur will be largely graphite, ink and watercolor and at a scale commensurate with nimble in-situ observation, the sketchbook. Precedent research will occur through analysis of the field work of notable architects. As the course instructs in the cataloging of place and less in the fundamentals of sketching, some freehand drawing aptitude is expected.

The first section of the semester parses the city through the lens of Kevin Lynch's Image of the City: students must mine the districts, edges, paths, nodes and landmarks of the city for evidence of place. They subsequently record it in the sketchbook through proportion, depth and scale. The second section of the semester narrows to a chosen focus of reportage illustration yet still simply is probing the city and not proving.

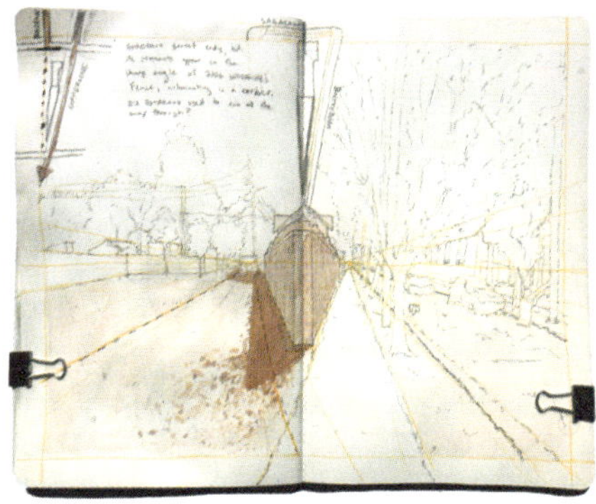

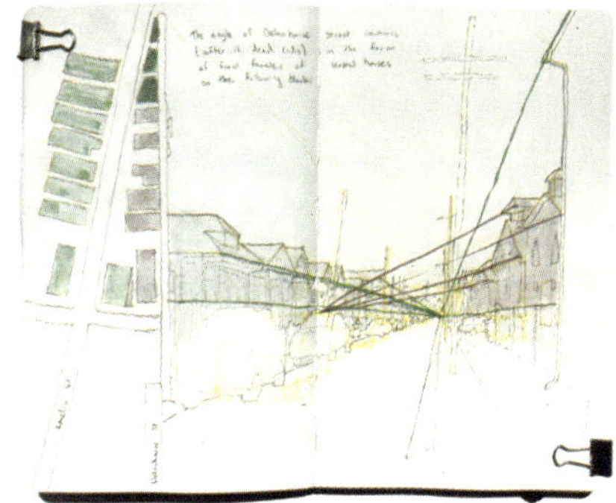

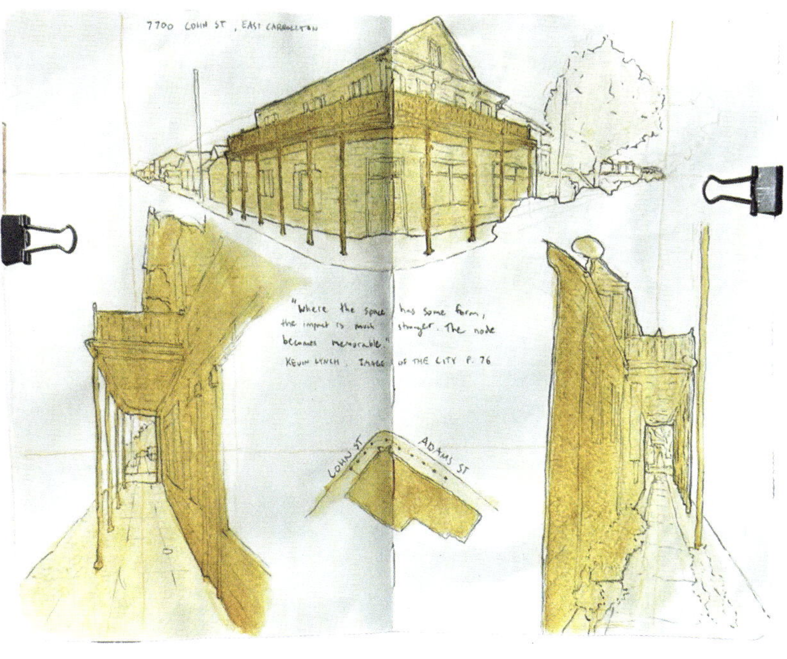
7700 COHN ST, EAST CARROLLTON
"Where the space has some form, the impact is much stronger. The node becomes memorable."
KEVIN LYNCH, IMAGE OF THE CITY P. 76
COHN ST
ADAMS ST

SAINT PHILIP ST
DECATUR ST
N PETERS ST
JOAN OF ARC STATUE
FRENCH QUARTER 4/21/24
• The French Market Building twists in plan as N Peters St merges with Decatur St
• Because of the twist, the Joan of Arc statue, on a narrow, wedge shaped block, appears through the colonnade.

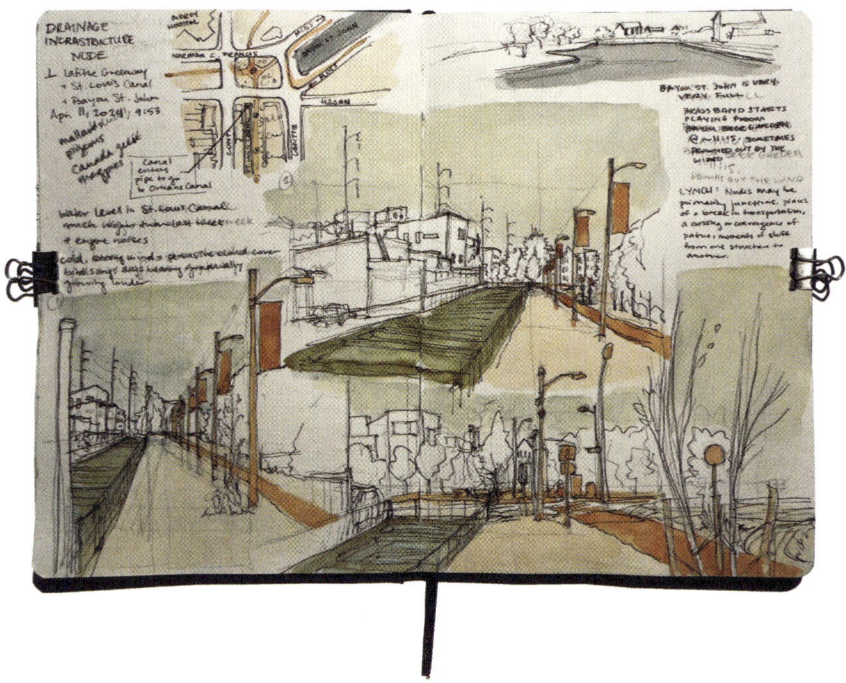
DRAINAGE
INFRASTRUCTURE
NODE
1 Lafitte Greenway
+ St. Louis Canal
+ Bayou St. John
Apr. 11, 2024; 9:53
mallards
pigeons
Canada geese
magpies
Canal
empties
pipe to go
to Orleans Canal
Water level in St. Louis Canal
engine noises
BAYOU ST. JOHN IS VERY, VERY FULL
BRASS BAND STARTS PLAYING FROM
SOMETIMES
OUT BY THE WIND
LYNCH: Nodes may be primarily junctions, places of a break in transportation, a crossing or convergence of paths, moments of shift from one structure to another.

LYNCH: edges may (like paths) have directional qualities
(river: levee: rail: road: neighborhood)
(neighborhood: avenue/boulevard)
CAR STOP
HILLARY &
ST. CHARLES
toward levee 15:25
levee

s> Alison Slomski

i> Andrew Liles

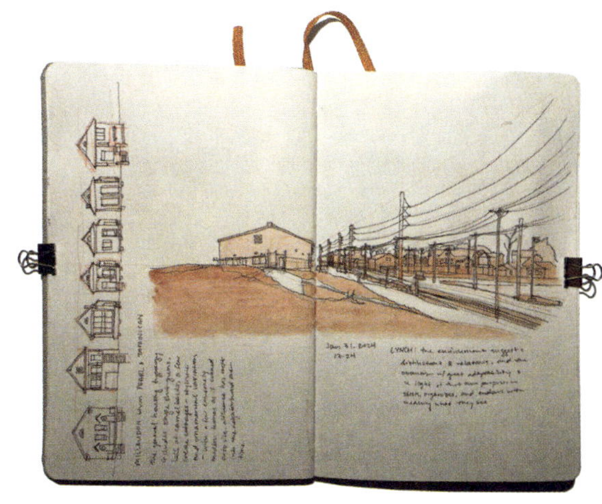

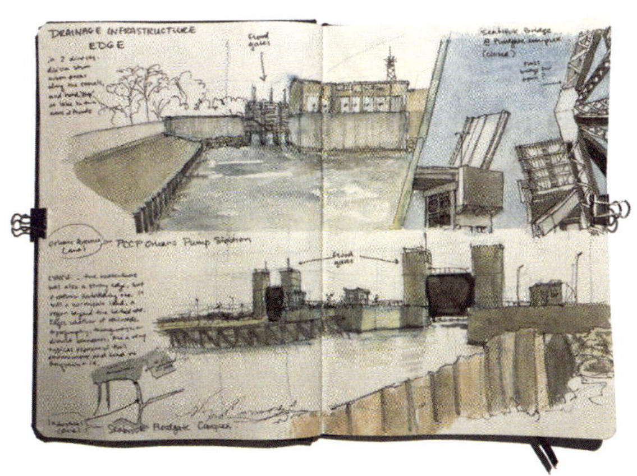

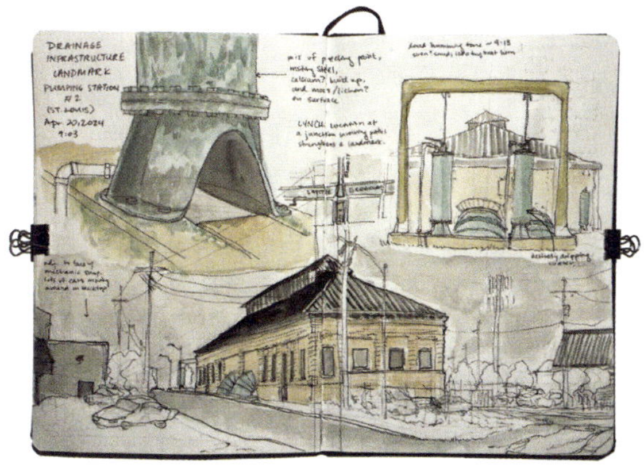

Kosta Sevic

TOWARDS ENERGY SOVEREIGNTY:

A Case for Retrofitting Modernist Block 23 in New Belgrade

ARCH 6990 Instructors:
Margarita Jover [D] + Jesús Meseguer [A]

s> Kosta Sevic

i> Margarita Jover + Jesús Meseguer

This thesis proposes a comprehensive, sustainable retrofit for Block 23 in New Belgrade, a key example of socialist-era modernist architecture in Serbia's capital. Faced with the pressures of commercial expansion, luxury developments, and a host of urban challenges—such as housing shortages, rising energy costs, and the neglect of communal spaces—this project seeks to preserve and revitalize the architectural heritage of New Belgrade by adapting it to contemporary needs. Rather than allowing real estate commodification to reshape this area, the project aims to retain its community-focused design while aligning with social and environmental imperatives.

The retrofit focuses on two primary objectives: energy sovereignty and increased housing capacity. Through a public-private energy partnership, the project will draw on regional and local renewable resources—geothermal, biomass, solar, and wind power—to reduce dependence on polluting fuels like coal and oil. This infrastructure promises not only to stabilize energy costs but also to improve resilience against energy supply issues linked to geopolitical instabilities. At the neighborhood scale, Block 23 serves as a testing ground for this model due to its distinctive layout and programmatic potential.

The intervention proposes both upgrading existing structures and introducing new typologies. Key changes include expanding floor areas, rectifying outdated building envelopes, and reintegrating balconies to improve spatial accommodations. The project also addresses informal building modifications by expanding residential units and offering diverse typologies to meet evolving housing demands. Additional public amenities and com-

munity spaces will be embedded within these structures, counteracting the often impersonal scale of modernist designs and reintroducing a more intimate, human-centered environment.

The deep retrofit will employ locally sourced mass timber, complementing the original concrete forms, to support sustainability. This design will support multi-generational living, fostering inclusivity and diversity while integrating recreational and communal spaces that align with Serbian cultural practices. By enriching social spaces and prioritizing energy autonomy, the project advocates for a transformed urban fabric that is environmentally conscious, socially equitable, and community-oriented.

Ultimately, this thesis proposes a paradigm shift in urban planning that combines energy resilience, housing diversity, and social equity. It envisions a sustainable future where urban development supports not only environmental goals but also the well-being of residents, fostering a vibrant and resilient community within a historic modernist framework.

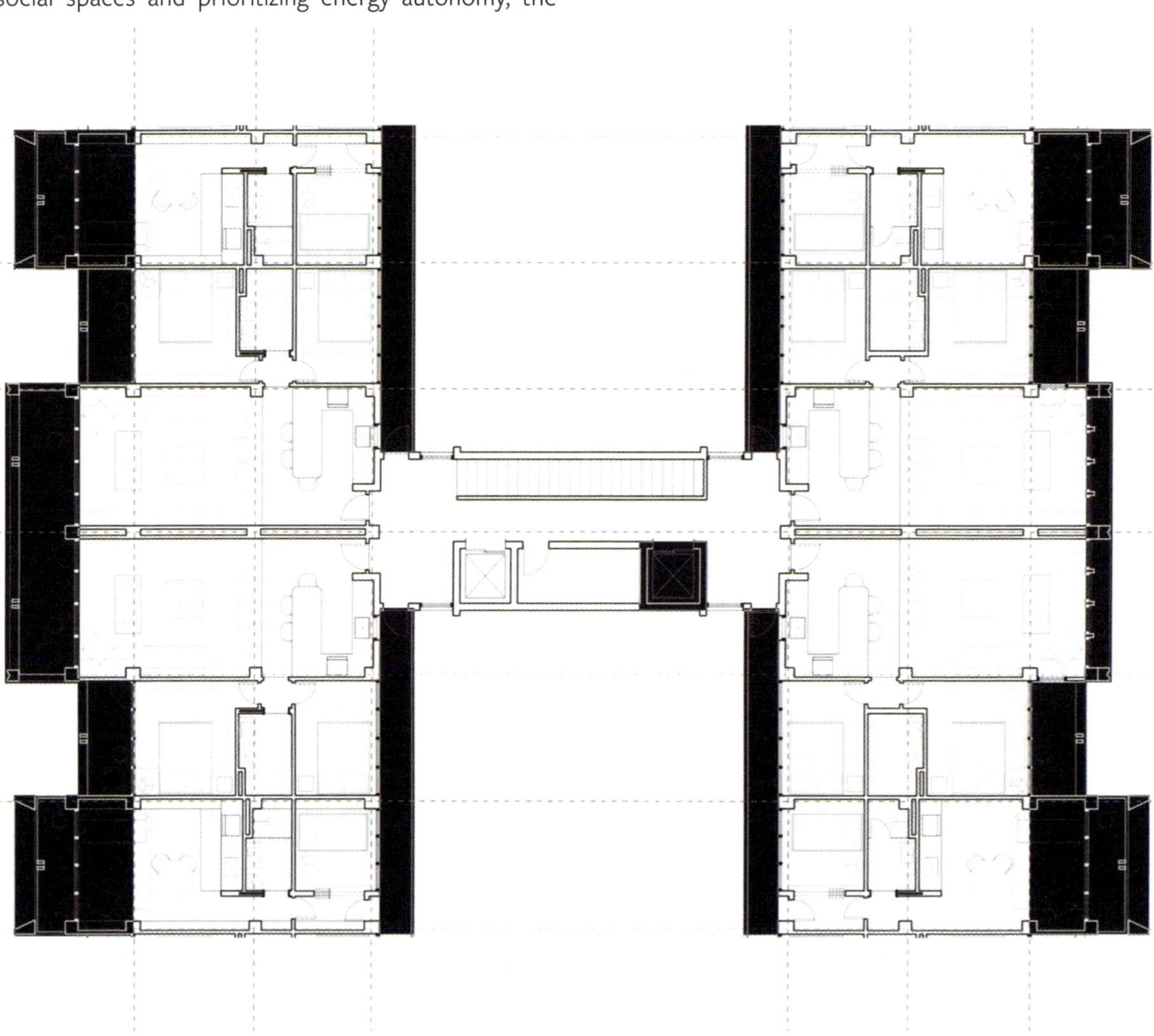

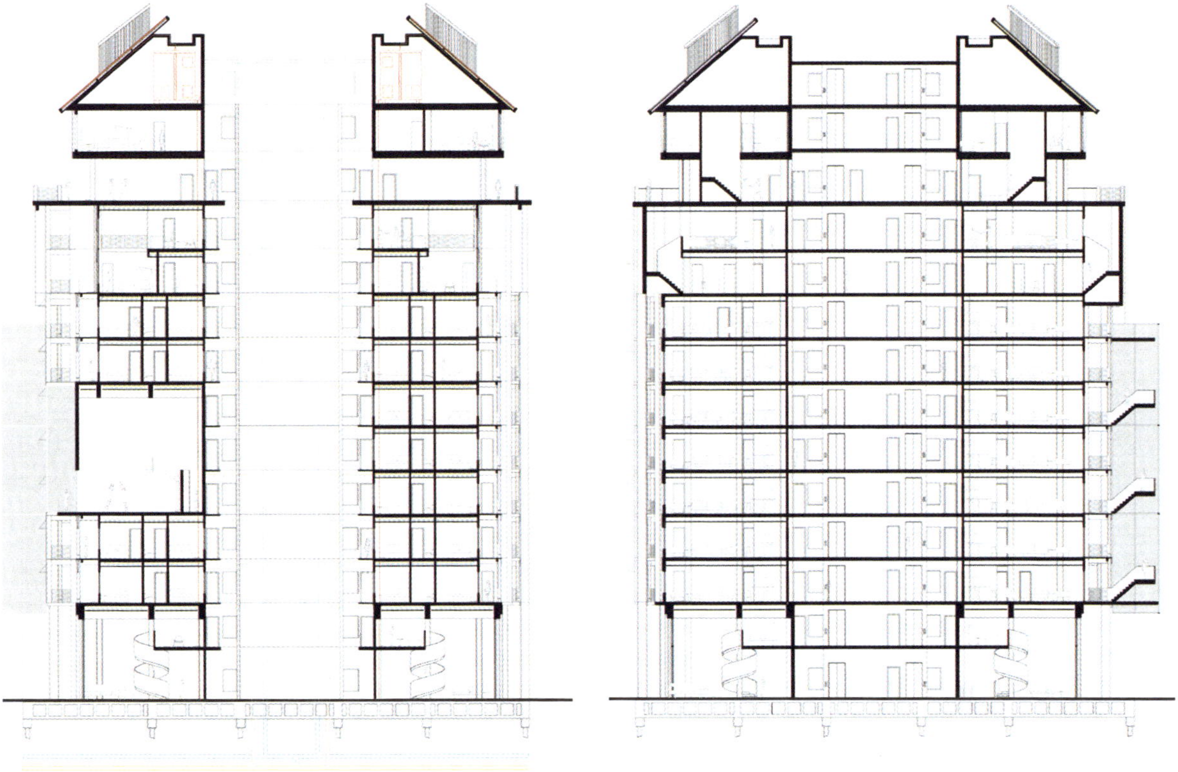

s> Kosta Sevic

i> Margarita Jover + Jesus Meseguer

Don't Stand Alone

The Albert and Tina Small Center for Collaborative Design

Curated by Jose Cotto

New Orleans has a rich history of Black labor organizing, marked by significant contributions to the fight against white supremacy and economic justice. Black workers have long engaged in collective action, often forming interracial alliances, to demand fair pay, job equality, and better working conditions despite facing violent opposition. This resistance traces back to the 1811 slave uprising on River Road and the early craft unions formed by Black iron workers in the French Quarter. During the Civil War, many Black men from Louisiana joined the Union forces, and after Emancipation, Black New Orleanians founded the first African American daily newspaper and passed a progressive state constitution.

In the late 19th century, New Orleans became a focal point for the national labor movement. The Comité des Citoyens challenged segregation with the landmark Plessy v. Ferguson case, and the city witnessed a powerful general strike in 1892 involving workers from various industries. Throughout the 20th century, Black domestic workers, teachers, sex workers, and hospitality workers continued to push for fair wages and racial equality, often intertwining with civil rights movements.

The "Don't Stand Alone" exhibit traces this history, highlighting the crucial role of Black labor in shaping New Orleans' economy and public institutions. Initiated by Stand with Dignity, this project connects today's Black labor activism with its historical roots, aiming to inspire ongoing efforts for workplace democracy and social justice.

KAISER
CIVIL RIGHTS
AT WORK

WORKERS
NEED A
RAISE.

trip to DC & Philadelphia

Sustainable Real Estate and Design

The MSRED Field Study trip is designed to bring the summer's intensive academic knowledge to life, giving students a chance to bond with each other, but also to create some case studies that can be used as shared references throughout the fall and spring semesters. The schedule for most days is packed with early morning walking tours of development projects, meetings with established industry professionals, and occasionally evening networking events with MSRED alumni and program partners. The summer 2023 trip included visits to the DC Office of Planning, STUDIOS Architecture, Citadel DCA, JLL, Reinvestment Fund, the Delaware Waterfront Redevelopment Authority, and Stantec, among others. Our trip also coincided with an exhibit and reception at the National Building Museum honoring the work of Tulane alum Alan Karchmer (A '78).

HFA
HFA
HFA

Thank you.

trip to Puerto Rico

Masters of Historic Preservation

Graduate students from Tulane School of Architecture and Built Environment's Historic Preservation program traveled to Puerto Rico for a seven-day academic trip during their spring break, accompanied by renowned Puerto Rican architect and historian Jorge Rigau, Interim Director of the Historic Preservation program Mark Rabinowitz, and faculty member Alex Lopez. The trip allowed students to explore Puerto Rico's rich history and cultural heritage through guided tours, studio visits, and lectures. The trip aimed to expose students to the challenges and opportunities faced by preservationists in a different cultural context, serving as an invaluable learning experience for the Historic Preservation graduate students.

NO

Renovation of 4304-06 Magazine Street, New Orleans, LA
By Professor John Huppi

2

DEVELOPMENT

FOR THE COMMON GOOD

LEADERSHIP IN THE BUILT ENVIRONMENT

When Leadership Transcends Protocols: A Family-to-Family Rebuilding in New Orleans.

By Will Bradshaw
Professor of Practice in Real Estate Development
Tulane School of Architecture and Built Environment

In the darkest of times, true leadership is always personal. Family to family. From the very beginning, Len knew what mattered most.

A house from Project Home Again. Image courtesy of Will Bradshaw.

My time in New Orleans began with Hurricane Katrina and the federal levee failures that followed. I was an overconfident 28-year-old just starting a PhD programme at MIT. I had just finished a successful stint running a small housing nonprofit in North Carolina and had been awarded a National Science Foundation fellowship. I was sure I knew what I was doing.

One day my thesis supervisor, Phil Thompson, asked me to accompany him to a meeting in the offices of Barnes and Noble chairman Leonard Riggio, who was planning a major response to the disaster in New Orleans. I agreed.

In retrospect, I had no business being there. The other participants were the CEO of Neighborworks America, the head of the Clinton-Bush Katrina Fund, the head of the Children's Defense Fund, a couple of tenured MIT faculty, a former deputy mayor of New York, and our host, the CEO of the largest bookseller of all time.

As the meeting continued, Len listened while everyone pitched him on their approach to recovery. But he kept asking something. How are you going to help the families? He wanted to make a gift from his family to theirs, but that's not how large-scale disaster recovery is set up. Finally, he turned to me and said, "Move to New Orleans for me." I said yes.

Len had a clear vision of what he wanted to do, even if it didn't fit into the established protocols for recovery. He wanted his resources to go directly from his family to a displaced family, where his gift would restore the equity that people had lost as the floodwaters rose. Almost every community development professional we talked to would bristle at this idea. He could do so much more, if he better leveraged his philanthropy.

Instead of listening to this critique, he built houses and gave them away. Those houses were concentrated in neighborhoods where our work pushed the percentage of recovered houses over 50%.

Hitting this 50% mark gives confidence to skittish residents wondering whether they should rebuild in a once-abandoned neighborhood. Almost five homeowners in the block around every Project Home Again house decided to return. Len's family-to-family gift of 171 homes leveraged nearly 1,000 more restored homes across Gentilly.

Qualifying families had to swap their storm-damaged home for a new one and were given a five-year forgivable mortgage. They didn't have to make any payments on the note, but they did have to live in the house for five years, at which point their equity would be restored.

Our first houses were handed over in 2008. In 2013, Project Home Again threw a party. The first group of homeowners gathered in a courtyard and took turns burning these mortgages. I don't think I'll ever be at a more hopeful event or be part of a more generous effort.

But now I am most struck by something else. Len left behind an infrastructure. A construction company that built its local reputation on this project. A career hospitality worker who became an extraordinary non-profit leader. A group of built environment professionals who started with Project Home Again and built a life here. An entire organisation, Home By Hand, that grew into People's Housing Plus, leading the charge for a more just New Orleans.

And me. I've helped invest over $100 million here. I've started four businesses. I was a founding faculty member of Tulane's Sustainable Real Estate Development programme, and we have trained nearly 300 professionals. Most importantly, I met my wife because of Len. We're raising three more native New Orleanians.

On August 27, 2024, Len passed away at the age of 83. He left an indelible mark on this city and on so many of us. Along the way, he reminded us all of something we know, but too often forget when we're doing things the "right" way. In the darkest of times, true leadership is always personal. Family to family. From the very beginning, Len knew what mattered most. ■

BAY AREA CHILDREN'S CENTER

EDUCATIONAL
San Francisco, 2020

Credits
Architects: March Studio
Collaborators: Terremoto landscape

This biotechnology company is revolutionizing healthcare by helping people to live happier, healthier lives. March Studio designed a preschool that prioritizes nature and innovation and acts as a catalyst to improve the wellbeing of the children and the larger community through the lens of STEAM (Science, Technology, Engineering, Art, and Math). The result is flexible open classrooms in a natural palette that are punctuated by a lively spine connecting the indoor and outdoor laboratories. In collaboration with Terremoto Landscape, a natural playground rich with possibilities brings nature indoors making for a happy, healthy, and sensory environment for young explorers.

Honorable Mention, Architect's Newspaper Best of Design Awards, Interior Institutional 2020

Fig. 1 An open and airy classroom filled with natural light

Fig. 2 Outdoor play area and lab designed for hands-on exploration

SONSOLES VELA
& RUBEN GARCIA RUBIO

HEATED INDOOR SWIMMING POOL AND GYM

COMPETITION
Casar de Caceres, Spain

Credits
Architects: studioVRA (Rubén García Rubio & Sonsoles Vela Navarro)

The proposal aims to optimize the integration and use of natural resources. It includes a new plaza at the southwest entrance to connect and activate the secondary entrance to the sports pavilion. The building's shape harmoniously fits into this part of the city and allows for rainwater collection, solar panels, and skylights. Internally, large spaces are organized around a programmatic stripe with all small-scale components, while providing a coherent layout. A modular and prefabricated construction is proposed, using primarily timber and white corrugated sheet metal.

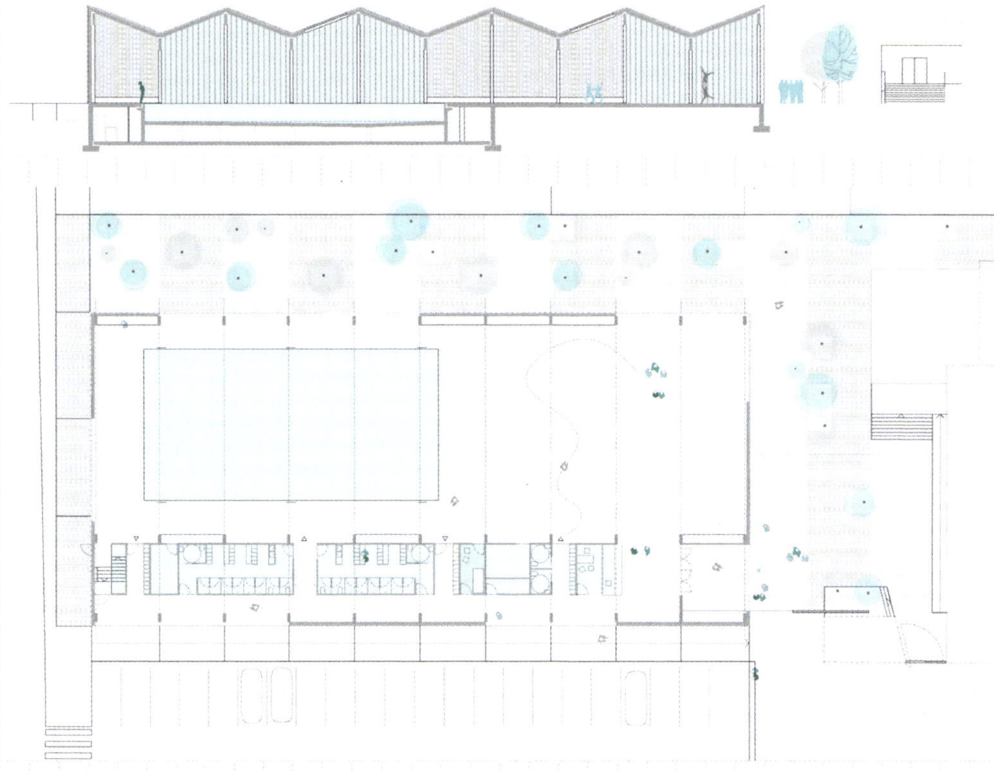

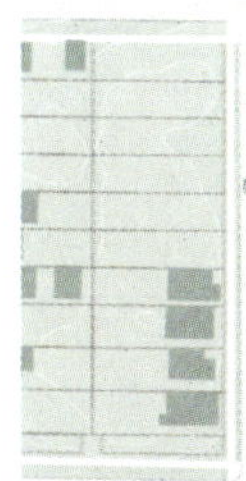
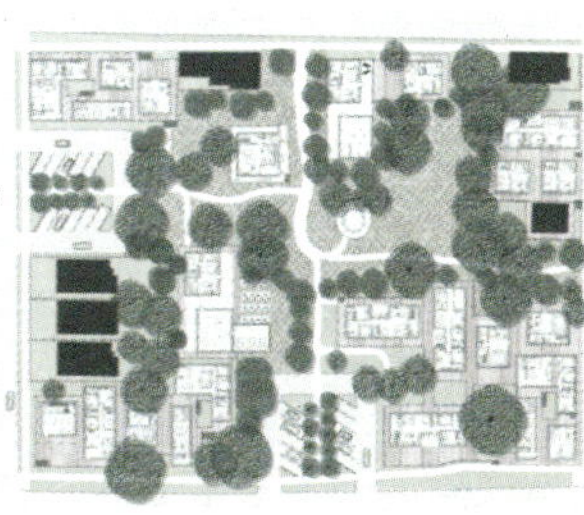
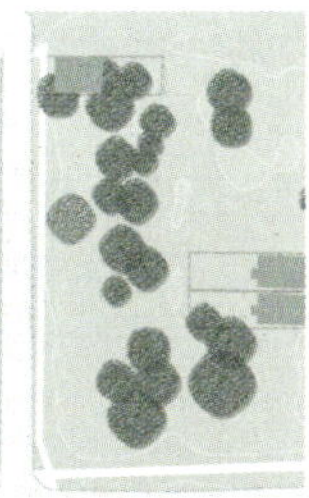

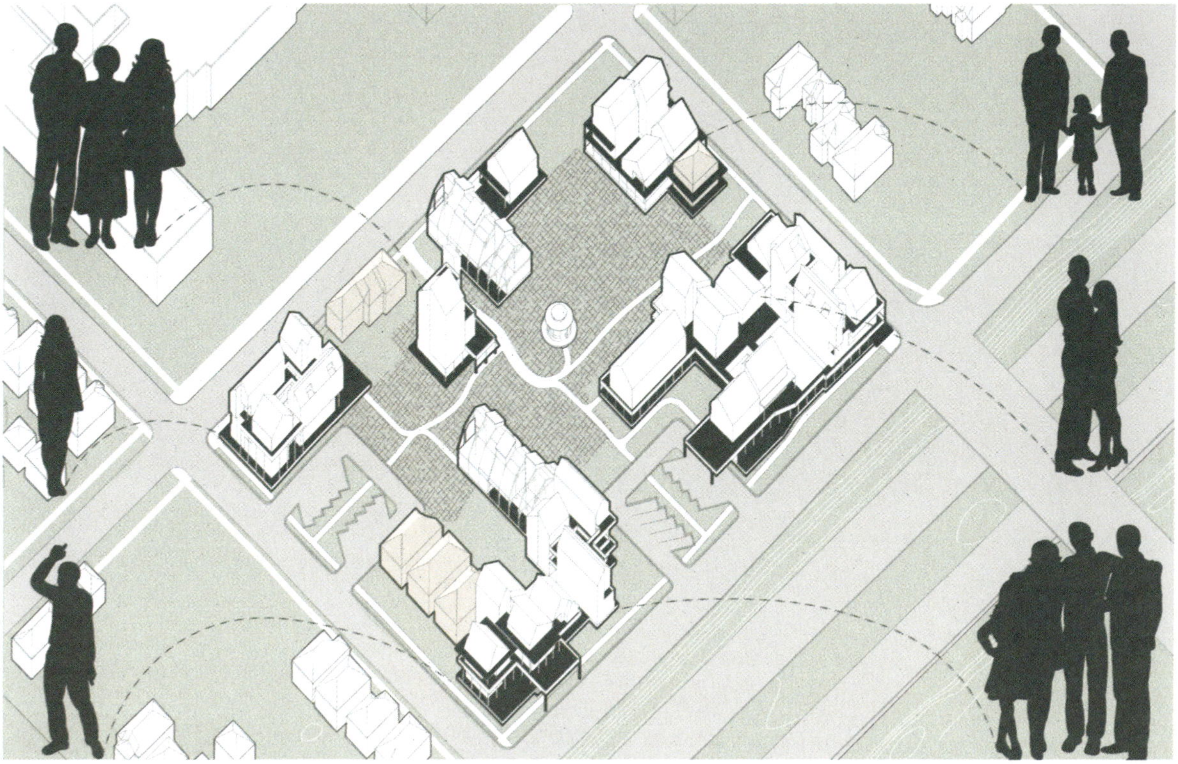

Brooke Mehney

COMMON ROOTS

Cultivating New Models for Intergenerational Development in Detroit

ARCH 6990 Instructors:
Margarita Jover [D] + Liz Camuti [A]

s> Brooke Mehney

i> Margarita Jover + Liz Camuti

Re-inhabitation of disinvested city centers, such as those in the Rust Belt of the American North, becomes a point of entry into the reimagination of land stewardship. By examining the parcellation and privatization of land, along with the history of land use and city development as a real estate investment, the existing urban fabric of Detroit can be analyzed and altered to provide a new methodology for living that responds to both ecological and social demands and poses a possibility for the future inhabitation of the city. This future inhabitation is grounded in community land trusts as a method of collective land ownership along with cooperative investment to oppose traditional development methods and gentrification caused by "revitalization."

Detroit, with a rapidly declining population since 1950 and declining industry, has significant parcel vacancies, totaling 114,239 properties. This project puts forward a design framework for imagining how the fallow land of Detroit can be redeveloped using community land trusts and collective investment to generate both an urban plan and site-specific architectural output through active scenario planning. Collective organization by a community-through-community land trusts allows for neighborhood scale development that generates opportunities for the return and renewal of previous familial networks that have departed from the city. The CLT serves as a mechanism to prevent displacement, while the development of the site allows for a return to community control over neighborhood systems. The inhabitation of the community, centered around community inputs and investment, orients itself around the enhancement of green space and spatial connections, while accommodating for an increase in neighborhood population to support community goals. In doing so, this project cultivates a lineage of land, people, material, capital and knowledge, while encouraging additional inhabitation of former familial networks.

Through the established framework, the Fitzgerald/Marygrove neighborhood is developed to experience community organization with individual's property investment to reorganize the neighborhood based on site conditions such as topography, non-investors, tree canopy, and the existing road network. In doing so, this project works to establish a new model for intergenerational living within a neighborhood while right-sizing development to accommodate future economic climate realities and dynamic ecosystems. The ground up community development mechanisms center community control to allow for urban vitalization that prevents displacement while providing opportunities for neighborhood growth.

DESIGN & REAL ESTATE

Javier Marcano [C]

The main objective of this class is to introduce Sustainable Real Estate students to design thinking with a focus on Architecture, Urbanism, Landscape Architecture, and the built environment. As the Real Estate industry plays a pivotal role in urban development, this course emphasizes the responsibility of real estate professionals in creating sustainable cities and buildings. Students will explore basic design principles through a series of exercises and projects, enhancing their professional presentation skills and ability to articulate concepts related to design principles, architectural typologies, and zoning regulations.

Through five comprehensive projects, students will learn to think spatially, communicate ideas effectively on paper, and create both digital and physical models using techniques such as collaging, digital editing, reproduction, and 3D printing. The course is structured into two parts: lecture/discussion sessions and practical application through projects. In the lecture/discussion sessions, students will be introduced to fundamental design principles and zoning regulations. They will then apply this knowledge in their projects, working in "neighborhood teams" to develop design proposals for specific sites within their designated neighborhoods. These proposals must comply with the site's zoning regulations.

Want to see pictures of the final review?

This methodology ensures that students not only understand the theoretical aspects of sustainable real estate design but also gain hands-on experience in applying these principles in real-world scenarios.

s> Hadley Coldren + Riyana Wadhwani **i>** Javier Marcano

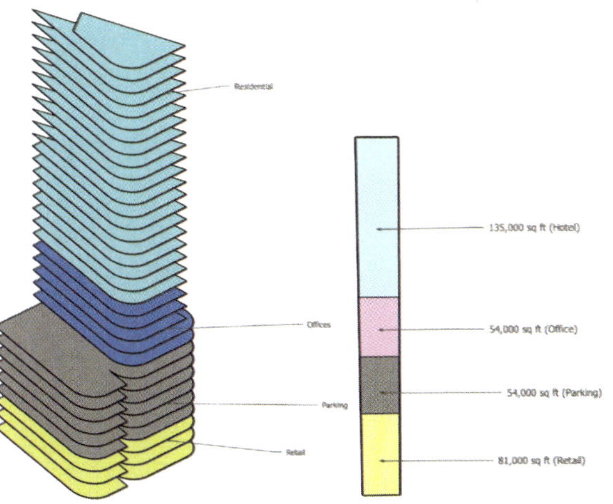

This project showcases a tower typology envisioning a mixed-use development on the 201 Canal St Block in downtown New Orleans. The students addressed the challenges and opportunities presented by a vertical composition, striving for a design that is both feasible and contextually responsive. The building height, governed by a Floor Area Ratio (F.A.R) of 14, allows for an intriguing intervention that integrates well within its urban setting.

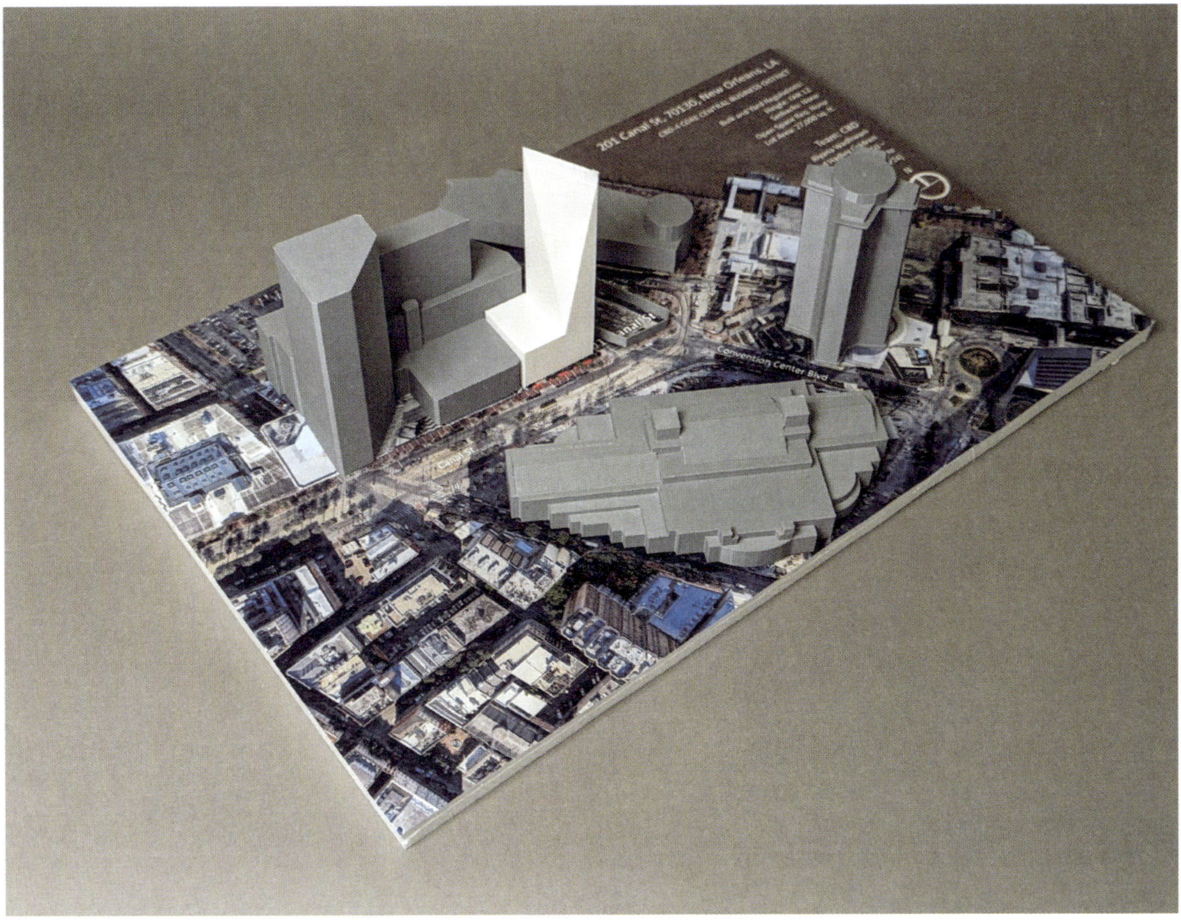

Alexandria Downtown Housing Study

The Albert and Tina Small Center for Collaborative Design

The Albert & Tina Small Center for Collaborative Design at Tulane School of Architecture and Built Environment has long worked with cities and towns internationally and here at home, engaging with mayors, neighborhood groups, and businesses to help them envision the future of their cities. In the Gulf South, Small Center has aided cities in reimagining their public spaces after disaster, preserving cultural landmarks, engaging residents around public art, and many more projects.

Small Center studied downtown Alexandria, LA in response to a market study calling for infill housing in the downtown, and as a follow-up to the City's participation in the Mayors' Institute on City Design.

Work included planning analysis, site selection, and schematic designs sensitive to historic context, scale, and potential to serve commerce centers and achieve river views. The goal of the study is to demonstrate the possibility for modestly-scaled apartments and/or condos that would blend in with the scale of the historic core while taking advantage of unique assets such as the riverfront, and serving known markets including hospital workers.

Roadways and networks were analyzed to understand gateways and access to the Downtown core, wayfinding, traffic patterns, and parking. The number of on-street, lot, and structured parking spaces far outstrips need as observed at various times of the workday, and increasingly so on weekends. This represents an opportunity to develop new buildings on former parking lots in the downtown without disrupting the functionality of existing businesses.

Small Center staff and students visited Alexandria and performed on-site and remote analysis to determine key areas within downtown and to understand its key urban design characteristics: historic context, scale, existing commercial development, educational and other institutions, green space, light industrial facilities, and more.

Four sites are proposed for developing housing to demonstrate the variety of possible areas, immediate contexts, building massing and styles throughout Downtown. Sites were chosen in response to several criteria including the possibility of enough density of units to attract developers, and adjacency to historic and active commercial contexts.

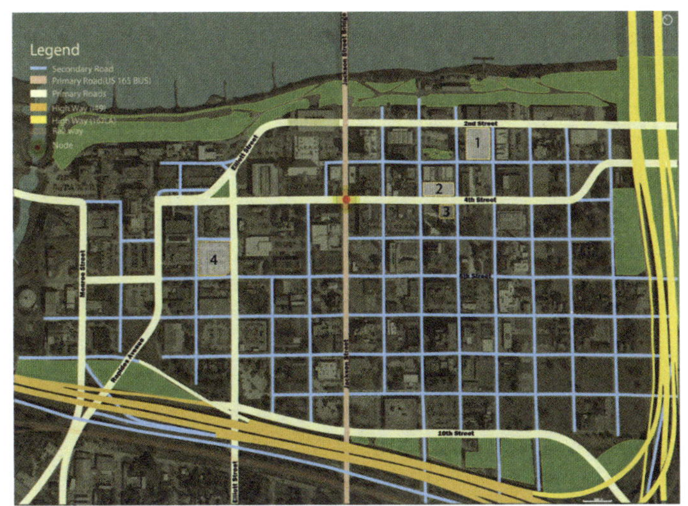
Legend
Secondary Road
Primary Road (US 165 BUS)
Primary Roads
Node
2nd Street
4th Street
20th Street
Monroe Street
Elliott Street
Jackson Street
1
2
3
4

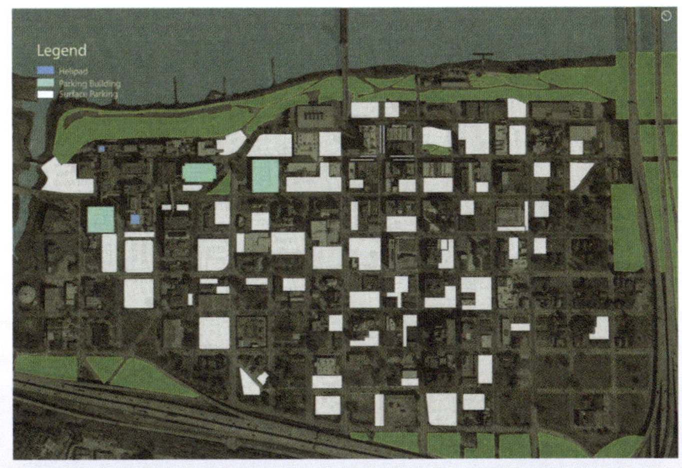
Legend
Helipad
Parking Building

Legend
Hospital Zone
Hospital Buildings
Business Core
Light Industrial
Arts & Education Zone

By Brooks Barrios

3

COMMUNAL LIVING

AS COMMON GOOD

META-HOME AND THE COMMON GOOD

A Vision for Intentional Housing Redevelopment

By Margarita Jover
Professor in Architecture and Program Co-Director of Landscape + Engineering
Tulane School of Architecture and Built Environment

Resident owners can co-design their future lifestyle following climate adaptation, mitigation, and regeneration guidelines while leveraging profits from a densification scheme. This transformation is the seed of a bottom-up urban revolution.

Existing Multiparcel Urban block in the Garden District

This text describes a hypothetical but site-specific housing redevelopment project in the Garden District of New Orleans. It argues that democratizing access to financial means and providing assistance in legal and urbanistic mechanisms can empower resident-owners of an urban block to self-develop if they wish to. Resident owners can co-design their future lifestyle following municipal climate adaptation, mitigation, and regeneration guidelines while leveraging profits from a densification plan.

This redevelopment project advocates for alternative leadership, one led by others rather than the one who can easily borrow significant capital and does not live in a place. While this ideology takes a straightforward real estate business out of the market for a big part of the contemporary "status quo," this alternative, redevelopment mechanism driven by resident owners can readily diversify housing types, boost collective belonging to a location, avoid gentrification, and provide agency over lifestyle. With the necessary support of public institutions (municipality), clarity of urbanistic regulations (for social and ecological flourishing), and a fair banking system (providing loans at low interest rates), this redevelopment plan can benefit the many who already inhabit a place.

In this specific urban block, twenty-four owners live in detached homes. Twenty-two—hypothetically—decide to work together to form an intentional community and transform the place according to their specific ideals of well-being. To be a plausible scenario for redevelopment, two residents do not participate in the redevelopment plan.

Intentional communities are American legal entities entrusted with the right to self-develop. There are about four hundred different intentional communities in the United States. This intentional community of twenty-two owners hires an architect to study a series of scenarios for increased density and complexity, allowing each to own more than one home. The range of densification proposed by the municipality in this context is—hypothetically—between 3 and 5 times the current number of homes. The reason for this guideline stems from the observation that the Garden District has not only single-family homes, but also other morphologies of larger scale, such as schools, churches, shops, small businesses, clinics, hospitals, and warehouses for light industry. This complexity in programs and morphologies gives a contextual opportunity for housing redesign to scale up on the urban block as a big home containing several

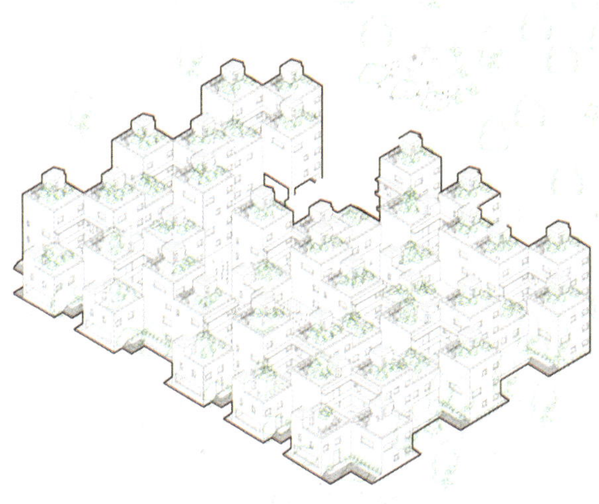

Drawing by Minh Hoang

houses of different sizes. This essay describes a meta-home as a new spatial arrangement of housing at the urban block scale.

Once the densification scenario is defined for this meta-home, each homeowner could have up to 5 homes instead of one. The owners, who are the clients of the architects, could keep two houses for themselves to live in, rent a third—at a rent controlled by the municipality—and sell one or two to pay the "urban operation" (construction company, architects, etc.). The urban operation can be organized as a for-profit or nonprofit enterprise, depending on the mission of the intentional community. The economic benefit to the resident owners will come from becoming landlords. The state will provide a low-interest line of credit to help low- to moderate-income owners access the economic benefits of this redevelopment program.

Residents will increase their quality of life and financial situation, while improving the neighborhood and the city. A better quality of life comes from organizing access to larger green space and amenities in a collective membership regime. A better neighborhood comes from improving the ecology, the energy performance, the structure of public spaces and livability, and the diversity of programs, including essentials for the daily life of a diverse array of people.

With this redevelopment project, the neighbors move from owning a plot of land of about 5000 ft2 (500m2) and a house of about 3000 ft2 (300m2) to a scenario of membership in collective spaces and a house two to three times larger. This transformation is the seed of a bottom-up urban revolution.

According to the mission of each intentional community, the project can improve the lives of residents. Driven by community policy, it can increase social wealth by providing different types of housing for students, seniors, and families, while stimulating economic activity with mixed-use programs such as small to medium sized businesses. In addition, redevelopment can serve climate change agendas such as climate adaptation, mitigation, and regeneration.

Overall, "climate adaptation" refers to strategies to adapt to the extreme weather events that are already occurring here. To prepare for heavier rainfall and more prolonged droughts, the urban block scale accommodates more extensive water storage easily than in individual properties. The urban block can provide a climate refuge of forested landscapes to prepare for longer heat waves. To be more resilient in the face of failing power supply infrastructure (due to hurricanes and tornadoes) or potable water infrastructures (due to lack of pressure or salinity intrusion), the urban block community can share its redundant power generation systems and water treatment. Contributing to "climate mitigation" means reducing CO_2 emissions while accommodating CO_2 absorption.

Mixed-use areas tend to reduce mobility and thus consume less energy than single-use areas. After reducing the need for mobility, the second most important energy cost is the energy lost in transmission lines. Microgrids based on renewable energy (solar, wind, and biomass) can add complexity and resilience to the energy system, especially if it is a system of interdependent microgrids between urban blocks and neighborhoods. A not-for-profit energy company owned by residents can ensure that profits go to maintenance and technological upgrades rather than to increasingly greedy stakeholders. Preparing for "climate regeneration" means that the metabolism of the urban block will, over time, bend toward the improvement of earth systems. The block's services can include water conservation, soil regeneration, carbon sequestration, reforestation, and biodiversity restoration, to name a few.

Public, collective, and private spaces are legally different categories. In the last centuries, public and collective spaces have reduced their presence in favor of private spaces. This urbanistic regulation aims to create collective space in any redevelopment project in the Garden District of New Orleans, with the aim of increasing social and ecological performances.

Public space is radically different from collective space. Public space—typically at ground level—can be used by anyone in the city or the world. Collective space is accessed through membership, which implies site-specific rights and responsibilities. In this redevelopment mechanism, the urban regulation makes outdoor or indoor collective space mandatory. The design and mission of these collective spaces are a core aspect of the intentional community's mission. It is easy to imagine a variety of proposals emerging. Some communities might want to focus on gardening, while others focus on sports or a forested landscape. These collective spaces must comply with municipal regulations demanding a specific capacity for water storage. Regulations are already in place for the first few inches of rain, but this amount may require increasing amounts to be stored over time in the coming years. According to the intentional community's plans, redevelopment programs will also guarantee private ownership of homes and private property.

The policies embedded in this urban block scale redevelopment project aim to influence the future path of the city in facing the challenges of climate change. The plan can contribute to densifying the city where it is most needed, diversifying the level of social incomes living together opening the possibility of blurring historical redlining practices; hybridize programs that promote mixed-use housing, offices, and services, and even small-scale manufacturing; increase tax revenues for a city with more residents; empower existing site-specific communities—as economic developers—to combat and avoid gentrification while implementing larger agendas of climate adaptation, mitigation, and regeneration.

Architects are service providers who typically work for private clients or public agencies for a fee. Because they can visualize futures—through the reimagining of materials and the reassembly of systems—they can also make proposals that are discussed in the social and political spheres of society. Architects can promote alternative ways of living or alternative ways of redeveloping, perhaps even without a client paying for it. This small text aims to promote the capacity of architecture as service to the common good and society at large. ■

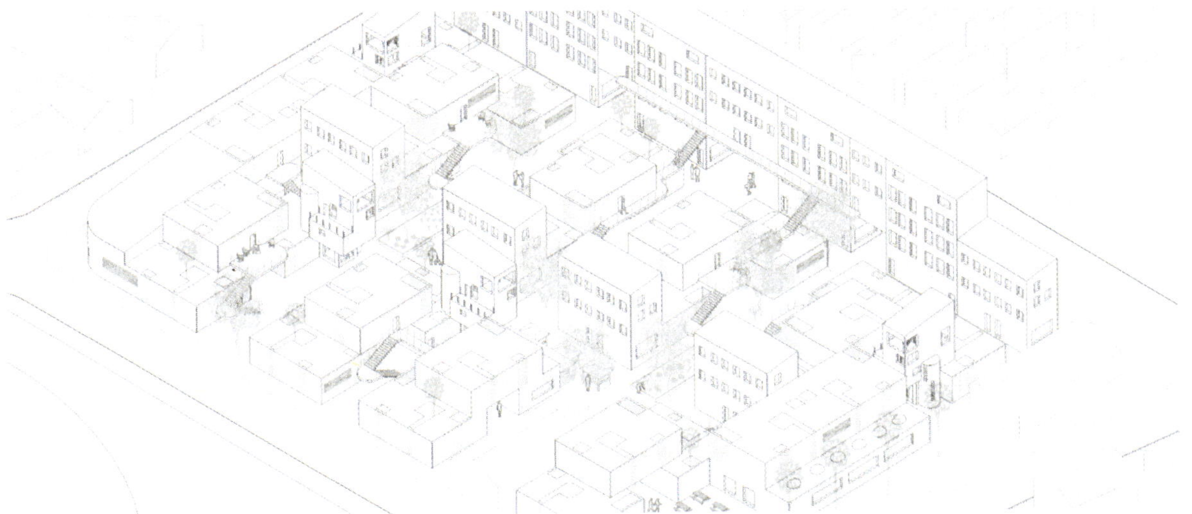

Drawing by Jack Morris

Credits:
Pedagogy, coordination, and faculty: Margarita Jover
Faculty: María Redondo for student Minh Hoang;
Faculty: Jesús Meseguer for student Jack Morris.

LAS ARMAS SOCIAL HOUSING

RESIDENTIAL
Zaragoza, Spain

Credits
Architects: aldayjover architecture and landscape
Photos: José Hevia

The project is located in Zaragoza's San Pablo neighborhood, which was in decline as residents moved away and infrastructure deteriorated. A regeneration program in the late 20th century revitalized the area with social housing, public spaces, and cultural activities. This initiative included a project to renovate one of the neighborhood's central blocks, which included a series of social housing developments, commercial space for young entrepreneurs, new public spaces, and a music school.

The commission included the design of three apartment buildings that would ultimately define the perimeter of the block. They would also determine the shape of the new public space, which, supported by the music school, new commercial spaces, and resident activism, is home to recurring cultural, recreational, and commercial activities, such as the Mercado de las Armas, a monthly event, or the urban art and graffiti festival "Asalto," which has helped decorate the blank walls around the courtyard and throughout the neighborhood.

The project engages with the historic environment to ensure a respectful renovation. On this basis, in addition to closing the perimeter of the block, building heights are limited and long continuous facades are avoided. In addition, the visual characteristics and identity of the neighborhood were considered very important, so an exhaustive study of textures and color qualities was undertaken. The final color scheme was defined after an analysis of the predominant palette and hues in the neighborhood.

The project places special emphasis on intermediate spaces—not public, not private—understood as areas for dialogue and social activity. Ground floors were opened up to create additional space for new businesses and workshops. Finally, in terms of the internal public space—the most remarkable and successful element of the project —access is provided through the opening of walkways underneath the apartment buildings. These walkways, which act as thresholds and transitional spaces between the interior of the block and the street, and which also house the entrances to the communication cores inside the apartment buildings, will function as an interlude between the private domestic space and the adjacent public space.

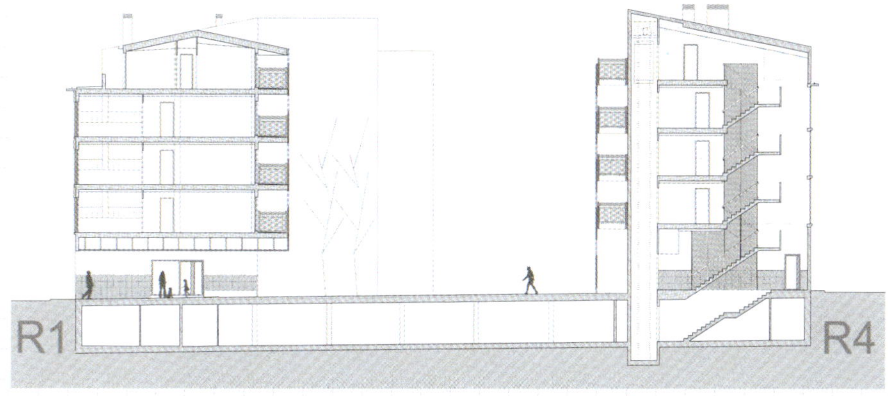

Fig. 1 Section

PETER PAN

R1
R2
R4

Fig. 2 Floor plan

Fig. 3 View from the courtyard

The “Shared Ground Floor” recognizes that the street is a cooperative space, a space of change, and that it should be used more. The street is everyone’s domestic space. We approach this project through a scalable implementation schedule, which operates in phases at different levels and requires the participation of numerous constituents—especially neighbors—for its implementation. The proposed format is open and flexible, and clearly expresses that the strategy to be followed will be tailored to adapt to new urban rituals and citizens’ needs. Our intention is that the proposal be understood as dense, fluid, accessible, integrative, changing and unexpected.

The street in ten years? It is an opportunity.

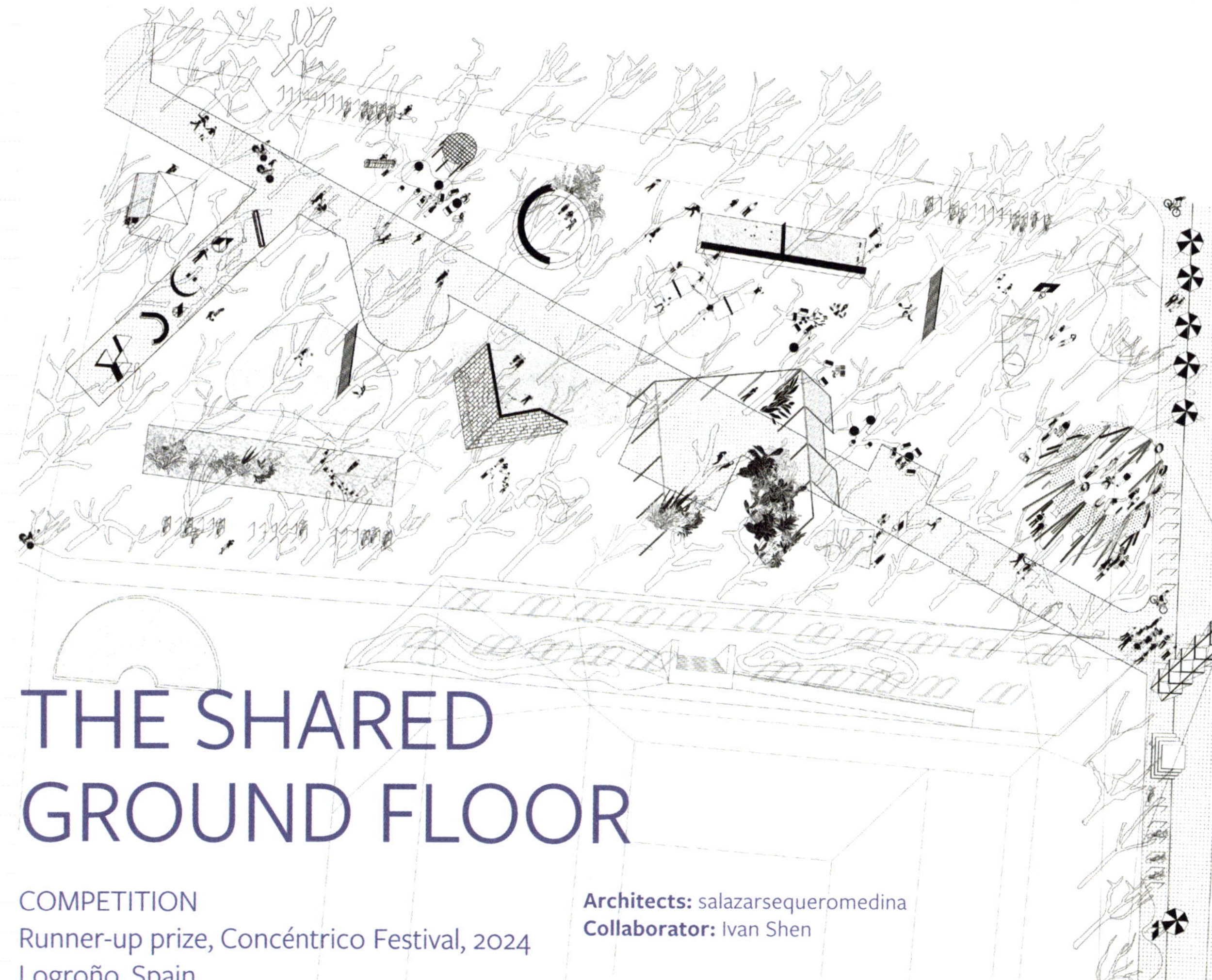

THE SHARED GROUND FLOOR

COMPETITION
Runner-up prize, Concéntrico Festival, 2024
Logroño, Spain

Architects: salazarsequeromedina
Collaborator: Ivan Shen

CAN TRAVI SENIOR HOUSING

RESIDENTIAL
Barcelona, Spain, 2010

Credits
Architect: Sergi Serrat GRND82
Collaborators: Cristina Garcia, Gines Egea, Carles Bima
Developer: Patronat Municipal de l'Habitatge

The building combines public housing with a community center for the neighborhood. This project relies on common sense and takes full advantage of the natural conditions of the site, including its impressive views over Barcelona, to turn all the homes into desirable vantage points. The topography is addressed with a horizontal plinth that houses the public programs, while the residential units are positioned above it, completing the surrounding urban sequence.

We capitalize on the Mediterranean climate by incorporating a spacious terrace into each home, which plays a central role in the transition between indoor and outdoor living. This terrace is designed as a large void, an excavation within the building's white mass. The scale of this negative space exceeds that of the individual unit, fostering a dialogue between the building and the city. The terraces alternate floor by floor, creating a staggered pattern of black and white reminiscent of a chessboard. This repetitive design forms a textured facade that defines and characterizes the building.

The terraces serve as focal points life, where both domestic and civic activities are carried out and visible to the city. They function like the central courtyards of Algerian kasbah houses, but arranged in a vertical plane. Each user personalizes their terrace, reflecting their unique lifestyle. The diverse activities and interactions of the users become part of the building's overall form, with the terraces' interior positioning integrating these everyday moments into the architecture. The building's white facade acts as a unifying backdrop, much like snow covering a landscape, highlighting and framing these daily life activities for the city to see.

Fig.1
View from a terrace

Fig.2
Floor plan

Figs. 4, 5
Exterior views

ARCH 4042 + 6022 | **Core** | UG + GR | **SP24**

INHABITATION

Margarita Jover[C]
Hannah Kenyon
Cristóbal Molina
MC Matucheski
Jesus Meseguer
Maria Redondo Perez

ARCH 2022-6022 Core studio is organized into two parts. The first 7 weeks are dedicated to designing 4 small quick projects: horizontal, vertical, and sectional homes and the inhabited stair. The second part of the course is dedicated to the design of the collective housing project that combines the previous designs.

The project is the design of collective housing with shared amenities and collective open spaces—it occurs densifying an existing urban block of 300 feet by 300 feet (100meters). The cultural challenge is to keep the 'suburban' lifestyle but with mixed-use, mixed-income and ecologically minded strategies. To that end the notion of the meta-home is put forward for exploration.

This core studio works with the hypothesis that the site has 21 owners—all except 2 agree to redevelop together. One of them decides to participate in the redevelopment and relocate its business. Owners are determined to redevelop themselves self-organizing as an "intentional community." They hire an architect to study the transformation from a group of homes to a meta- home that must generate collective usable space, hypothetical profits, and ecological benefits.

The three spheres of knowledge students get in this course are:

1. Visualization, that includes the consolidation of the universal language of "orthogonal projection".

2. The architectural theme of collective housing with its set of constraints; the methodology of the project as the main field for architectural thinking.

3. Critical thinking in relation to the way we live today and can live tomorrow if we were to do it in a more sustainable way.

Want to see pictures of the final review?

s> Nathan Rich

i> MC Matucheski

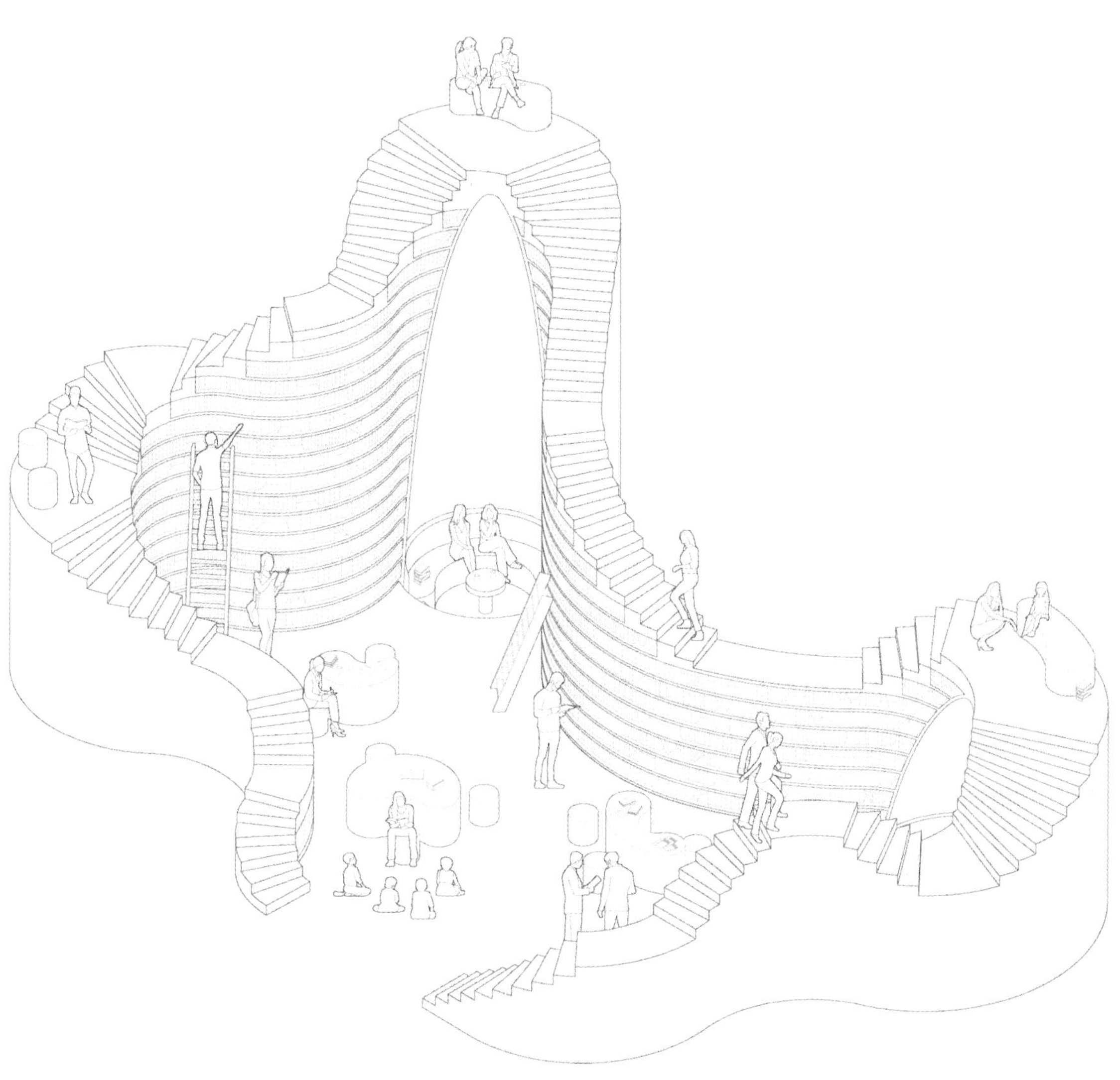

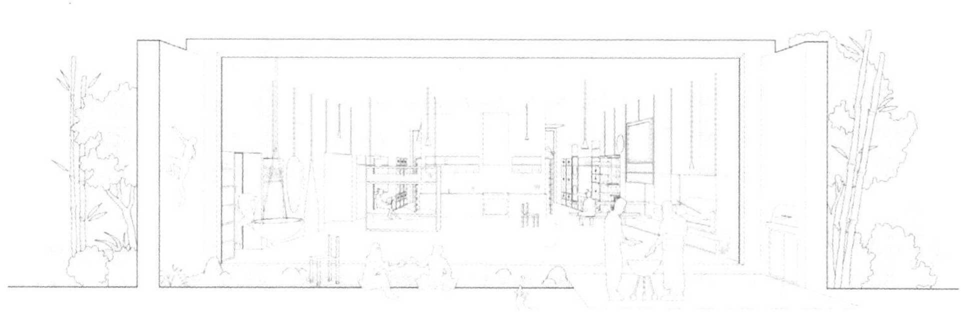

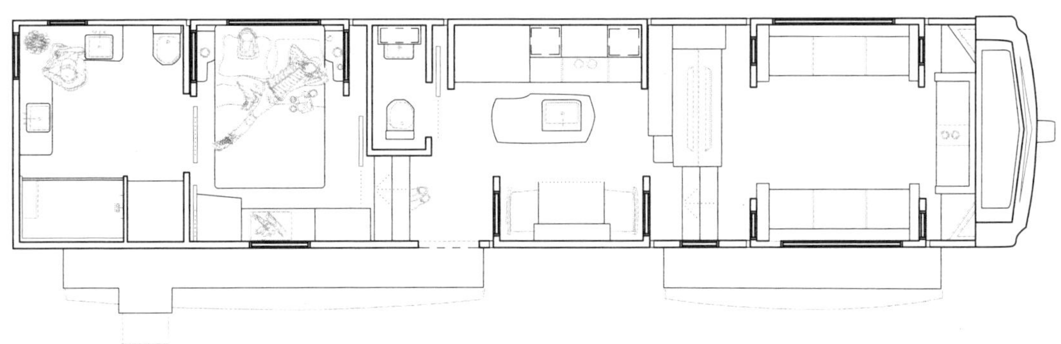

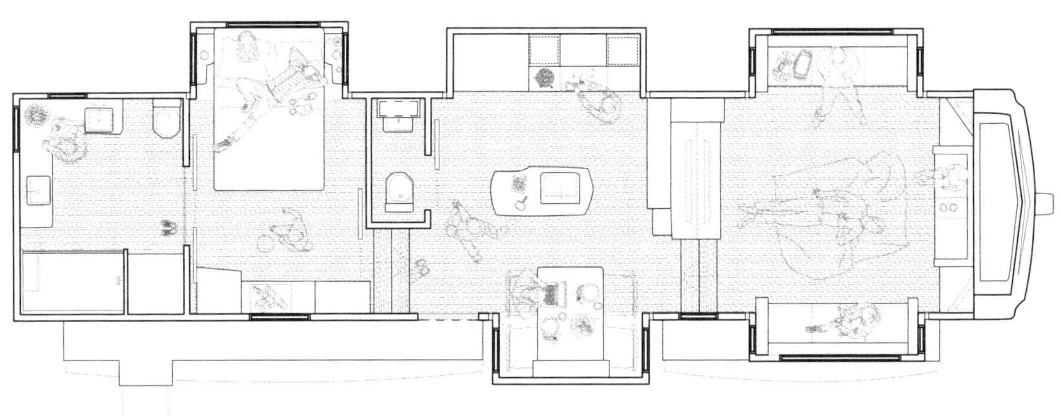

s> Brooks Barrios **i>** Margarita Jover

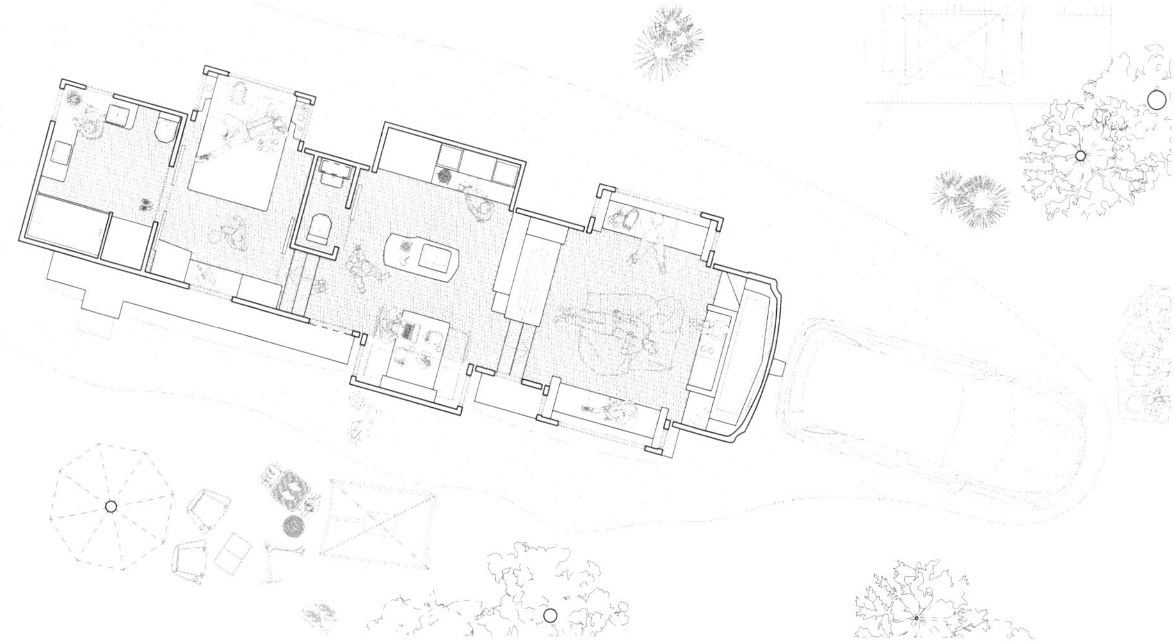

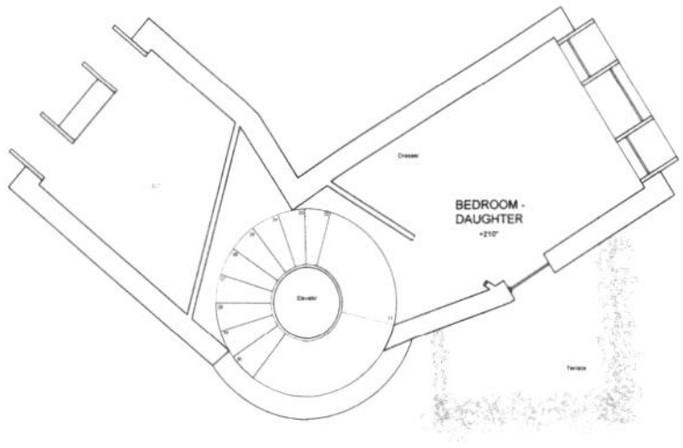

BEDROOM - DAUGHTER

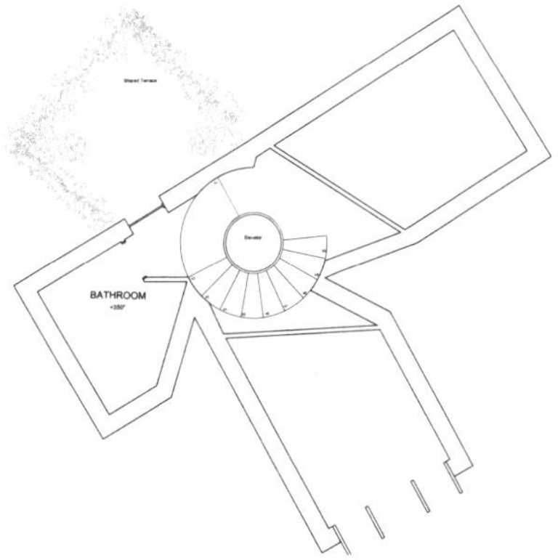

BATHROOM

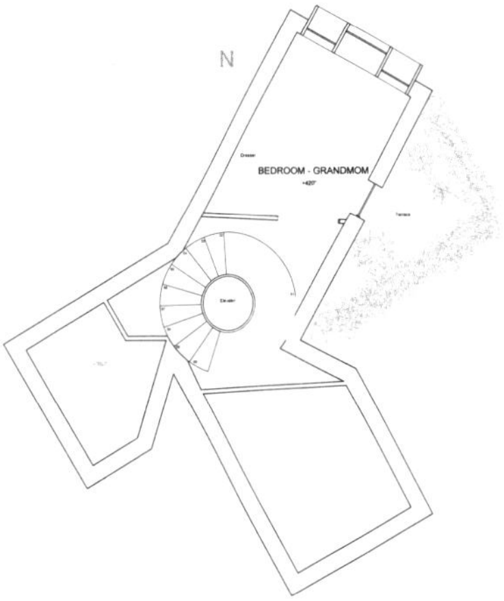

N

BEDROOM - GRANDMOM

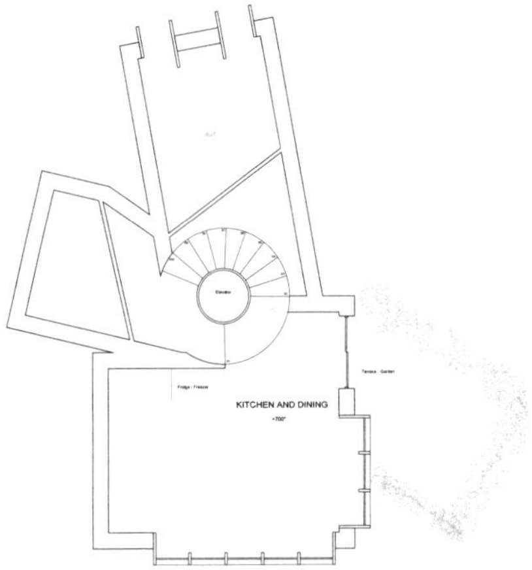

KITCHEN AND DINING

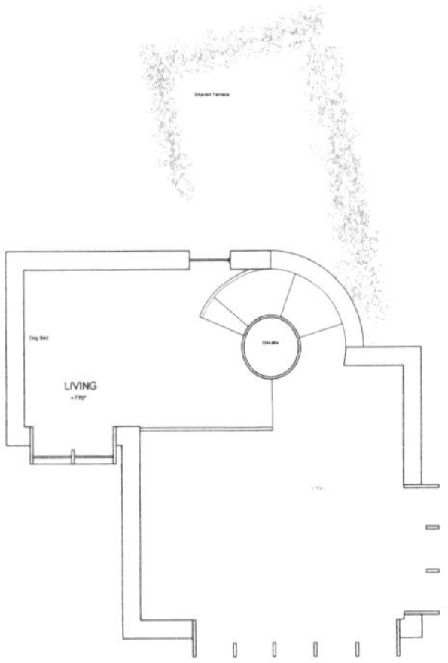

LIVING

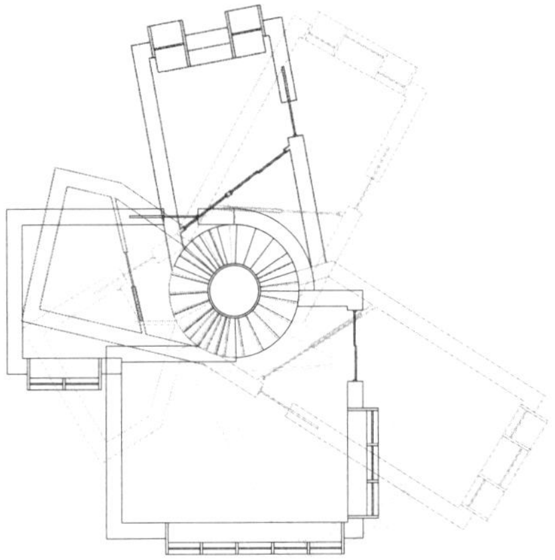

s> Kristina Huong

i> Maria Redondo Perez

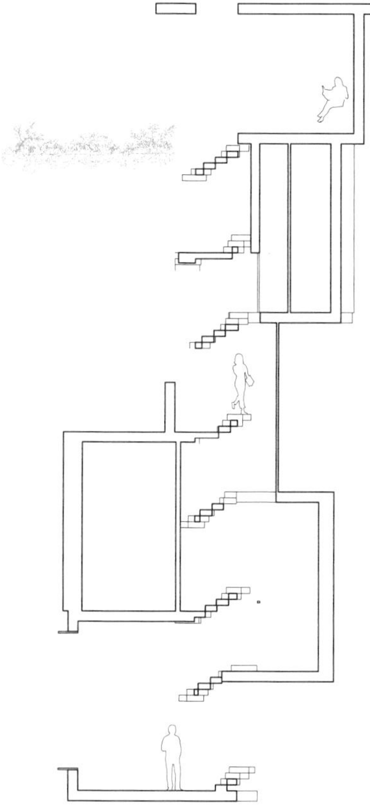

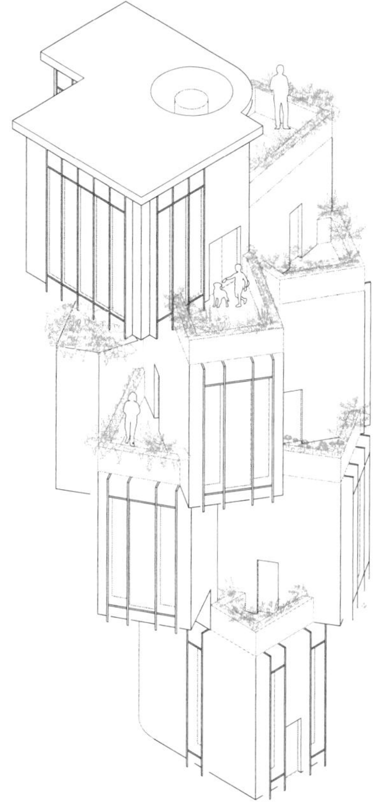

s> Harmon Kerrison

i> Hannah Kenyon

private units
public space
glass porch
mesh paths
vertical gardens

s> Kendra Johnson

i> Cristóbal Molina

ARCHITECTURE & SOCIAL INNOVATION

Kenneth Schwartz[C]

This seminar explores architecture and urban design in relation to the broad field of social innovation. Social justice issues engage many disciplines of academic inquiry as well as practice applications. The specific focus of this course involves Architecture inclusively considered as the built and natural environment (theories and practice). Architecture intersects with challenges, problems, and creative opportunities for positive social change. These will constitute major areas of research and speculation based on the readings for the course and individual student explorations.

Flor de Poblacion, Chile

Quinta Monroy

s> Ella Weeks

i> Kenneth Schwartz

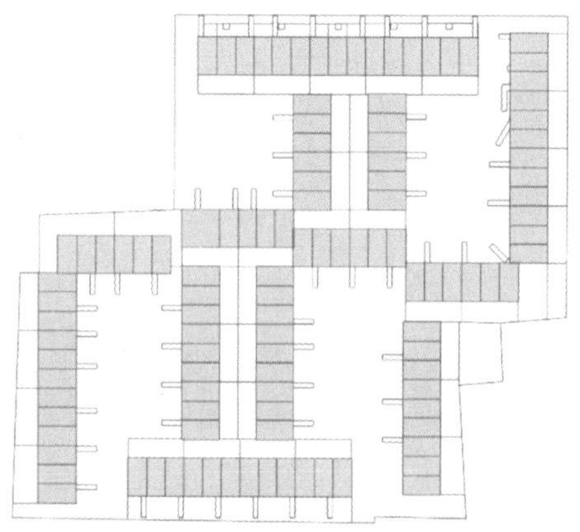

Site Plan as built, 2005

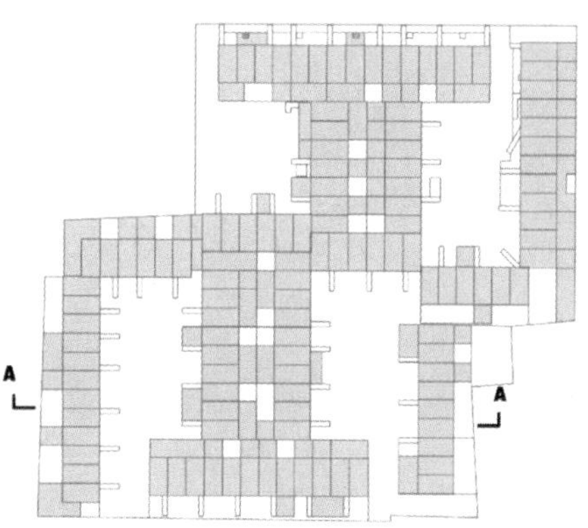

Site Plan, 2017

Ella Weeks' case study, "The Tension Between The Aesthetic & The Urgent," explores the capability of architecture to address the global low-income housing crisis through sustainable and lasting models. Weeks examines Elemental, a pioneering architectural initiative led by Alejandro Aravena, focusing on its innovative approach to low-income housing in Chile.

The global housing crisis is dire, with 1.8 billion people lacking access to adequate housing and basic services, a figure expected to rise to 3 billion by 2030. Housing costs have outpaced income growth globally, leading to a significant rise in homelessness and unsafe living conditions. Latin America exemplifies this crisis, with a 136% increase in housing deficits from 1990 to 2000.

Elemental's approach, recognized with multiple awards, including the Pritzker Prize, revolves around creating scalable and adaptable housing solutions. The firm's social housing program aims to develop model projects using best practices in various disciplines, offering a significant contribution to affordable housing.

The core philosophy of Elemental is "incrementality." This approach emphasizes building basic structures that residents can expand and personalize over time, empowering them to improve their living conditions gradually. Quinta Monroy, one of Elemental's notable projects, exemplifies this model. It transformed a self-built settlement into a structured yet adaptable housing community, allowing residents to expand their homes as needed.

Elemental's design thinking is human-centered, focusing on practical and emotional needs rather than theoretical assumptions. The firm's projects prioritize efficient land use, urban integration, and future proofing against potential expansions, ensuring long term sustainability and livability.

Weeks highlights Elemental's success in balancing aesthetic considerations with urgent housing needs, demonstrating that thoughtful, incremental design can provide durable solutions to the low-income housingcrisis. This case study underscores the potential for architecture to create meaningful social change by addressing one of the most pressing global issues of our time.

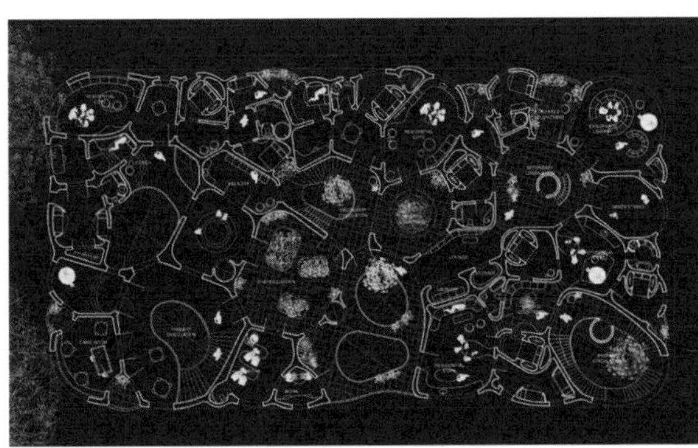

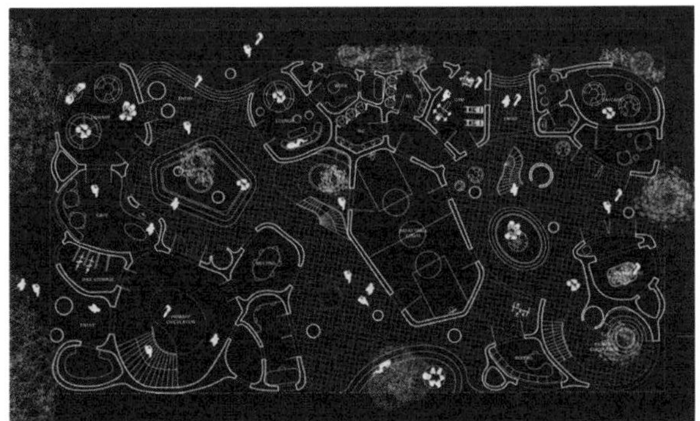

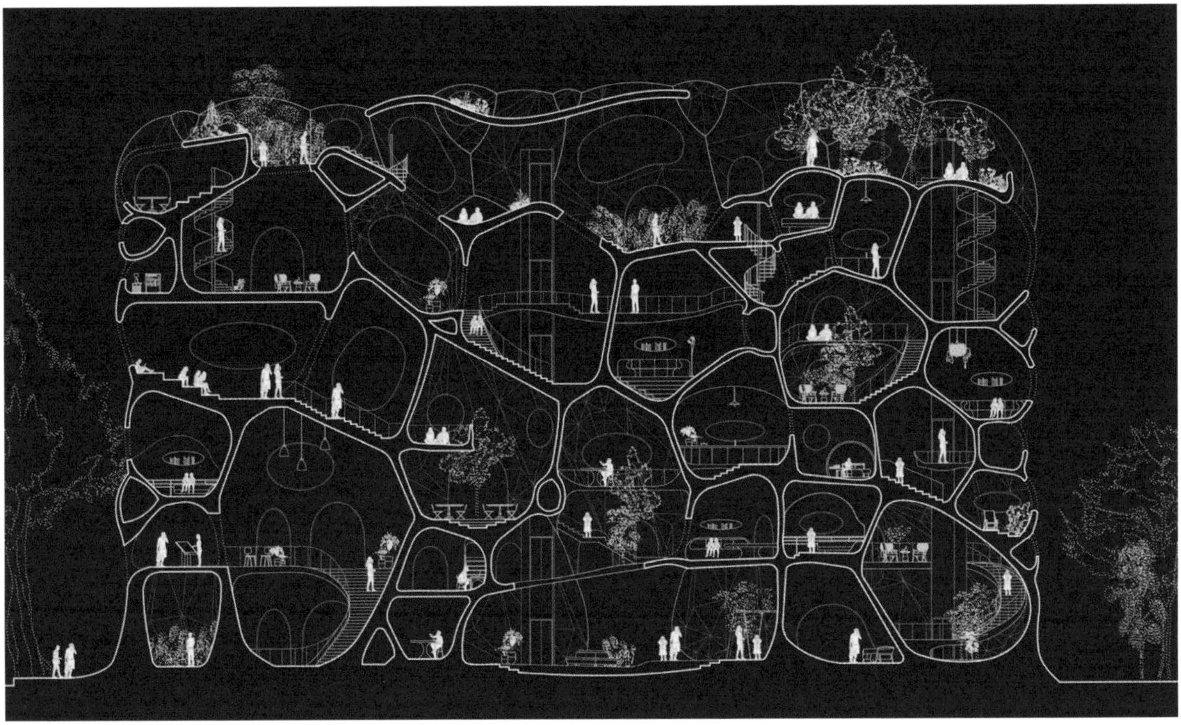

Ella Weeks + Britini Crawford

RECIPROCAL DWELLING:

A Neuroarchitectural Aspiration for Multi-Generational Cohousing, Inspired by Reciprocal Geometry

ARCH 5990 Instructors:
Cordula Roser Gray + Todd Erlandson

s> Ella Weeks + Britini Crawford

i> Cordula Roser Gray + Todd Erlandson

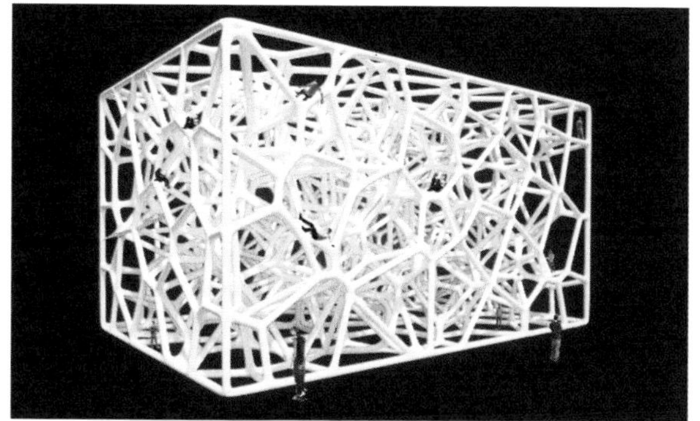

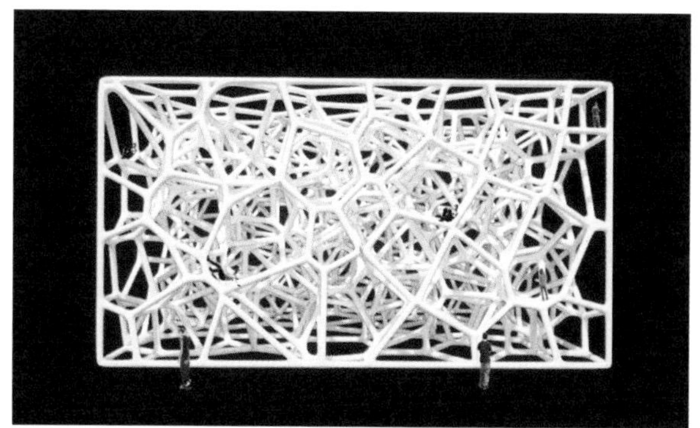

Modern, a priori approaches to public housing projects have proven themselves to be insufficient for the social and psychological health of the low-income American resident. This prolific low-income housing typology, often prescriptive and anonymous, neglects user centered experience and is therefore in need of critical redesign to alleviate psychological vulnerability belonging to populations at the poverty line. By prioritizing user autonomy and sense of place, agency-oriented design can accentuate a sense of empowerment, thus fostering psychological wellbeing and endurance in a low-income community.

The term public housing can be understood as dwellings funded by local government for low-income households who face both physical and financial strain. In urban studies, public housing is often interpreted as a means of controlling urban growth. Several studies have analyzed architectural successes and failure of public housing projects while others have investigated the economic and social status of public housing residents. Few investigations explore both topics concurrently in an attempt to understand how public housing design can create economic stability and social longevity while also boosting the neurological and sociological health of its dwellers. Statistically, psychological health suffers amongst low-income communities. Historically, low-income infrastructure does, too. In this thesis, we hope to reinvigorate a neglected typology.

Countless government housing projects endure extreme deterioration due to lack of maintenance. But these projects' failure extends beyond structural upkeep. Public housing projects are often poorly maintained and demolished due to the prioritization of wealthier sectors and privately-owned and funded developments. This priority is evident in the history of public housing legislation. Since the 1930s, ceilings have been placed on construction, quality materials have been disincentivized, and federal funding has been routinely capped. Sensational media has also muddied the reputation of public housing. Architecture itself has been directly blamed for the failure of projects like Pruitt-Igoe, and critics assert that modern design principles bred an impersonal , shameful environment. Finger-pointing has distracted from the importance of subsidized housing, especially given the current low-income housing crisis.

Through cognizance of the acquired research, a method of design can be created to develop a form of architecture that achieves the personal on the scale of the impersonal, withstands age, and responds to the low income user in a natural, empowering way. The goal of this research is to birth extremely intimate spaces from what are known to be the least intimate institutions–partially because of their monochromatic minimalist design. The proposal aims to combat the idea that good design should only be reserved for those who can afford its upkeep. It is intended for this proposal to illustrate what a contemporary, successfully-refocused affordable housing project could reflect.

ARCH 3032 + 6032 | **Core** | UG + GR | **SP24**

URBAN HOSTEL:

A Temporary Place for Nomads

Irene Keil [C]
Kentaro Tsubaki [C]
Emilie Taylor-Welty
Cynthia Dubberly
Patricia Fraile

The studio focuses on the development of an architectural project with regards to site relationships, historic context, structure, systems, materiality, and building codes, meeting the NAAB accreditation requirements of the integrated studio. "Integration" will be understood not only as a coordination of building systems during the project development, but as a constant reciprocal feedback between intent and material manifestation, a careful calibration of intent, form, system, material, and technology where relationships are never unidirectional but have inherent potentials and unanticipated possibilities.

The pedagogical objective of this studio is to lead the student through a design process in which architectural ideas, spatial planning, and building technologies are integrated. Students will be expected to understand and comply with all applicable building code regulations, such as life safety and egress while addressing and exploring the implications of construction techniques, building technologies and systems in their building proposal. Students work individually on one design project over the semester. Typically, the charge for the integrated studio is the design and resolution of a normative building program and building type—a mid-scale building in an urban context.

Want to see pictures of the UG final reviews?

The project is a hostel, a form of low-cost, short-term, shared sociable lodging where guests rent a bed—a bunk bed in a dormitory. All travelers have communal use of lounge(s) and kitchen areas and a variety of other social spaces determined by each student. The building is to be developed over a public ground level with some hostel functions and adjacent outdoor space.

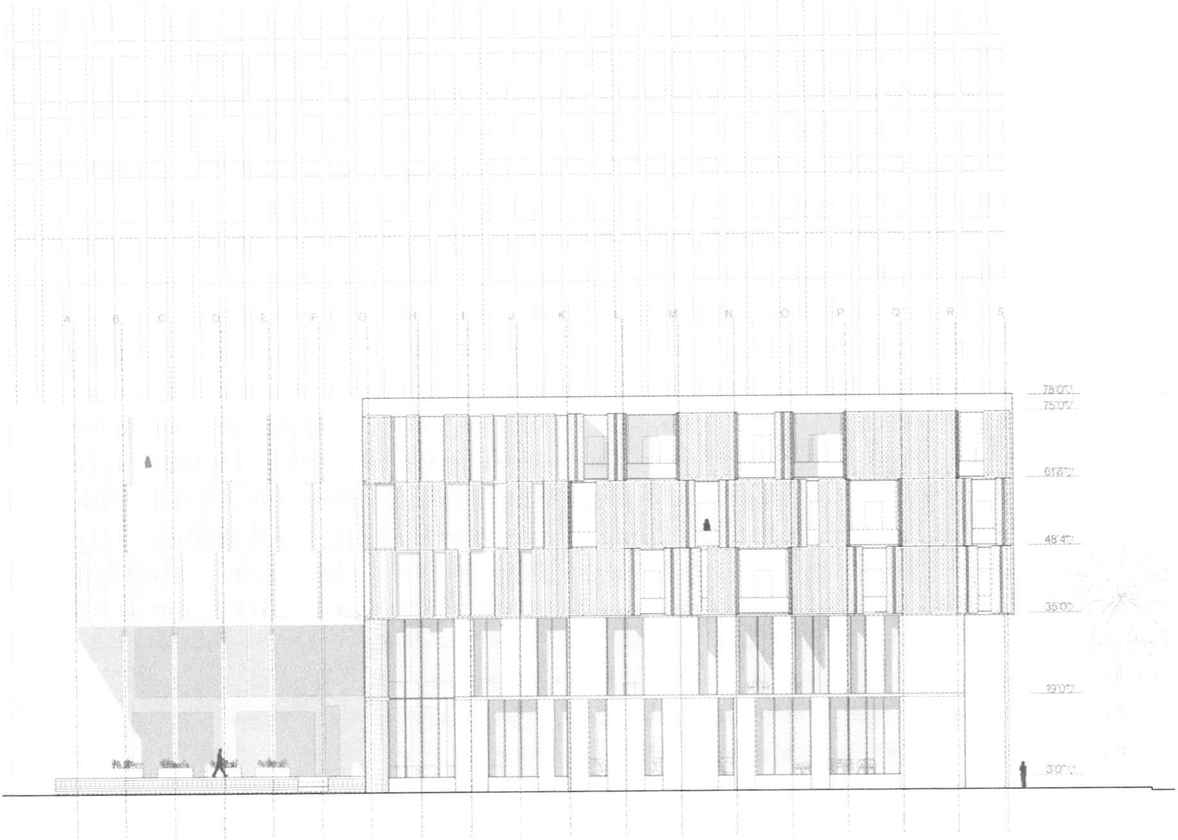

s> Alex Cohen **i>** Irene Keil

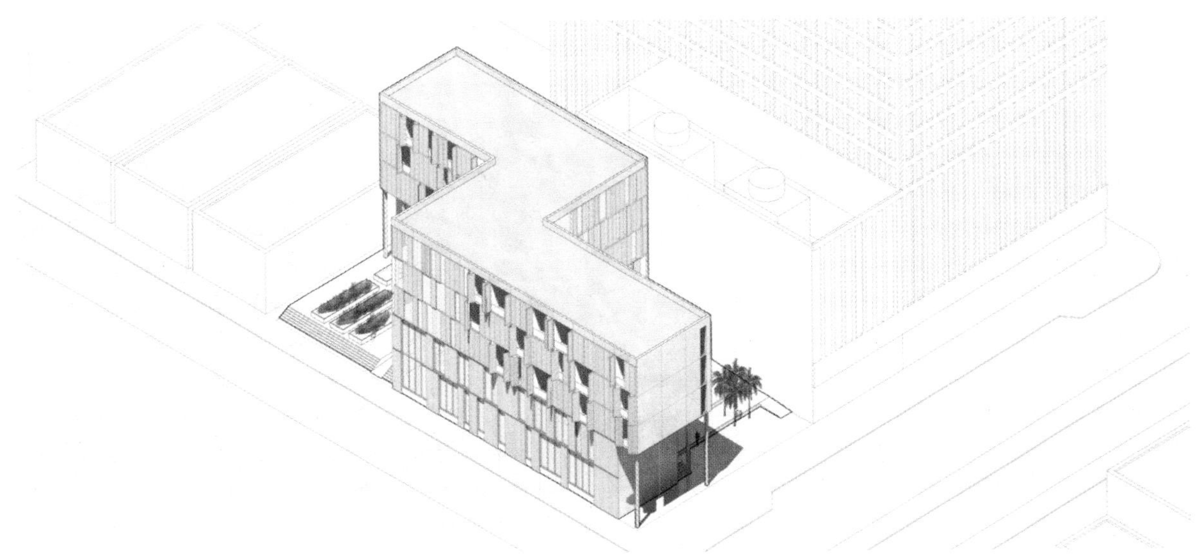

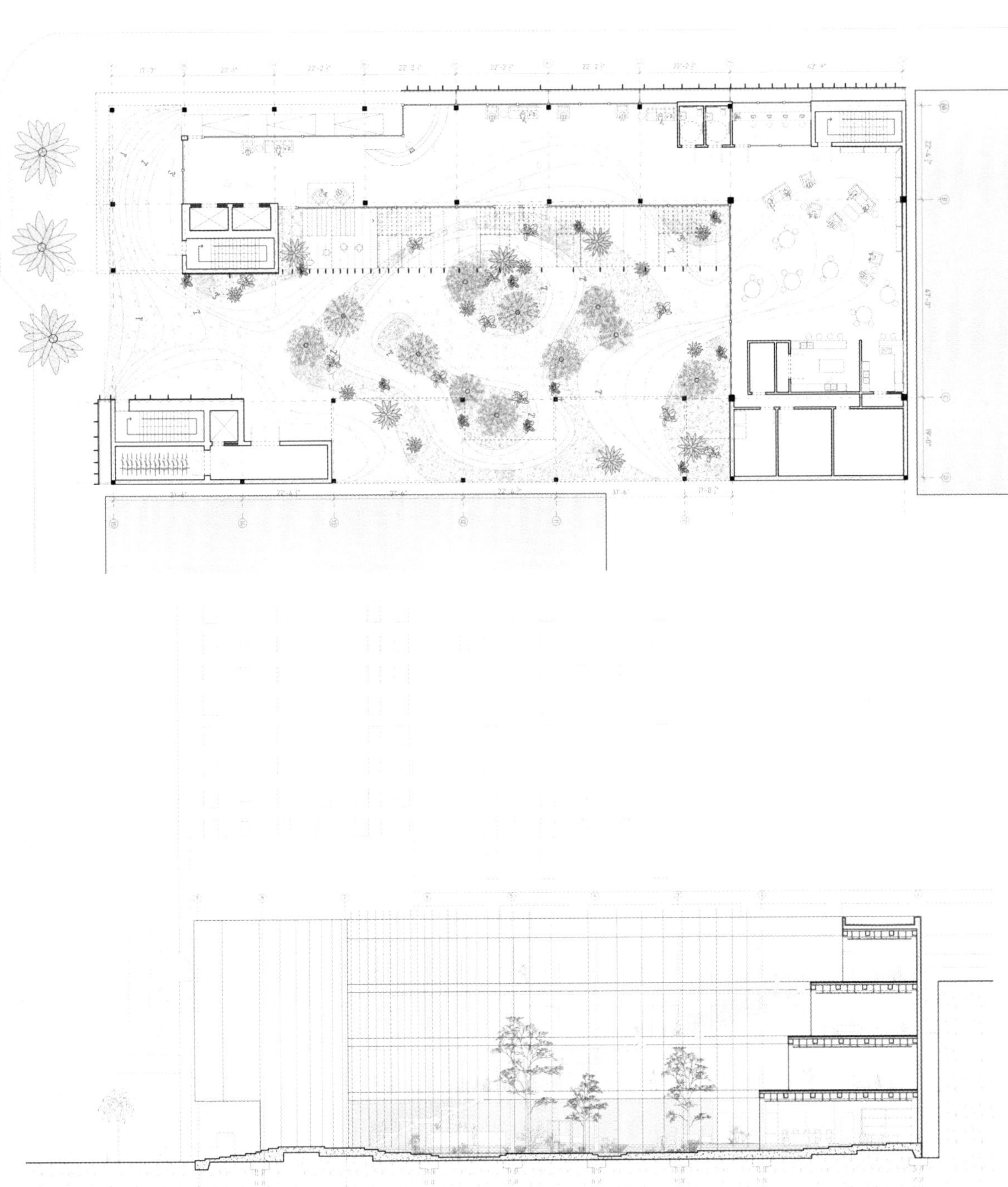

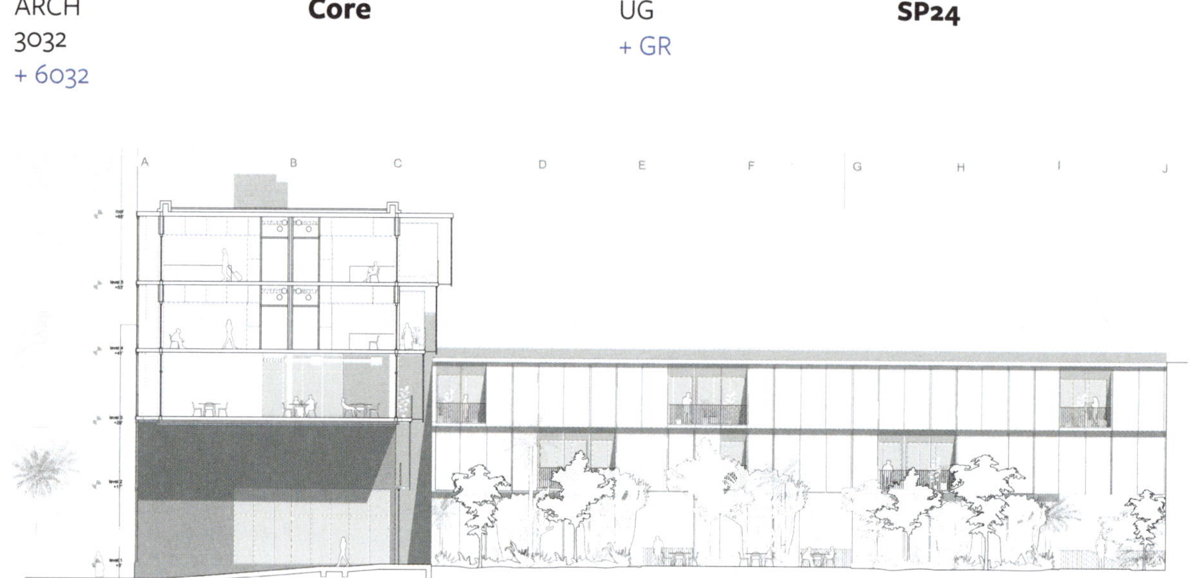
A
B
C
D
E
F
G
H
I
J

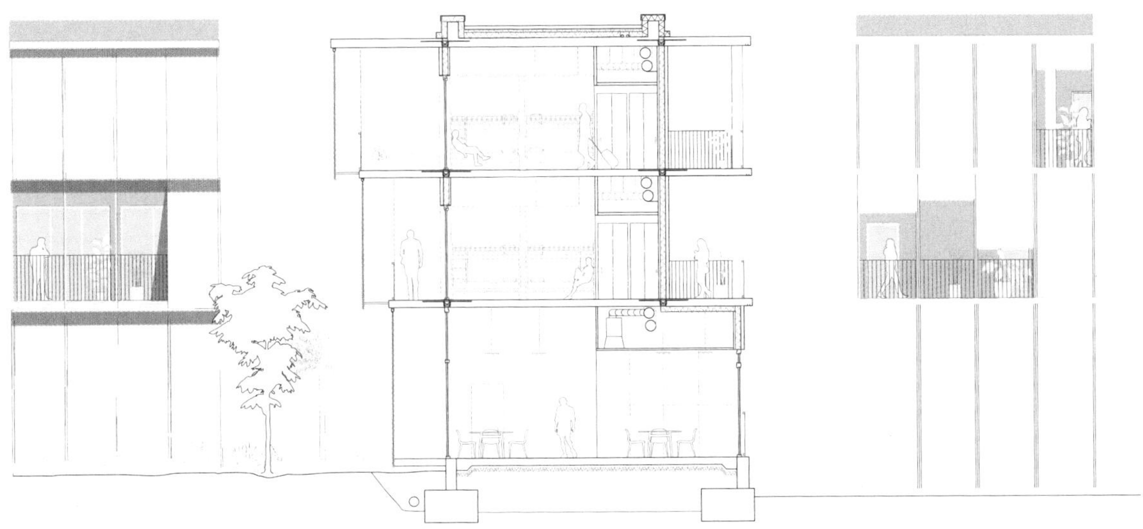

roof
+65'
level 5
+53'
level 4
+41'
level 3
+29'
level 2
+17'
level 1
+3'

ARCH
3032
+ 6032

Core

UG
+ GR

SP24

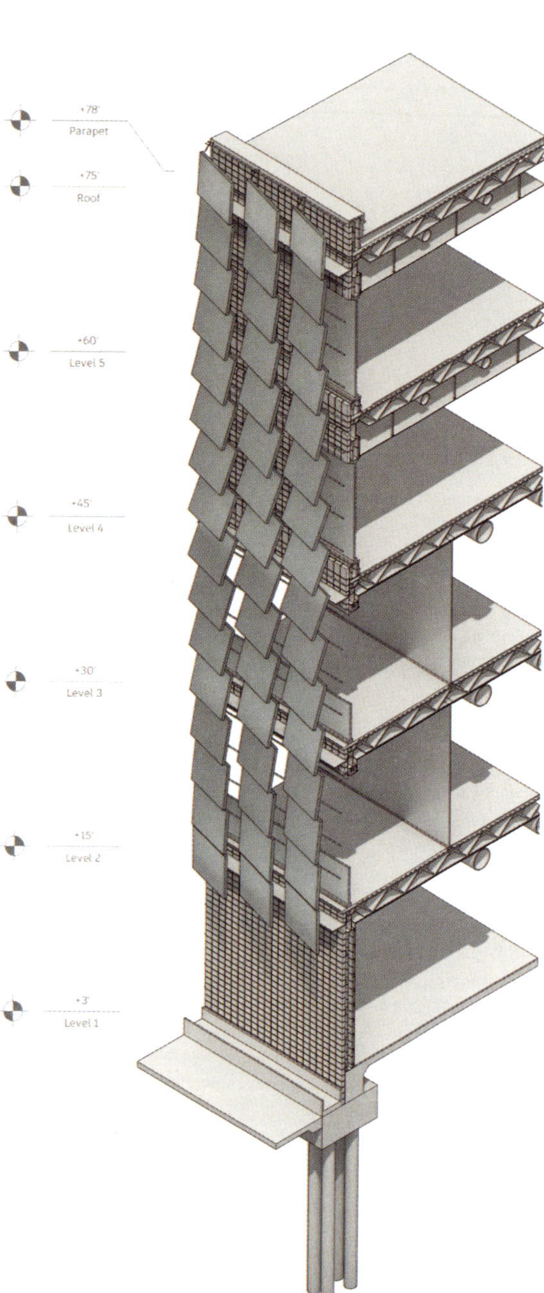

s> Asha Hokanson

i> Emilie Taylor-Welty

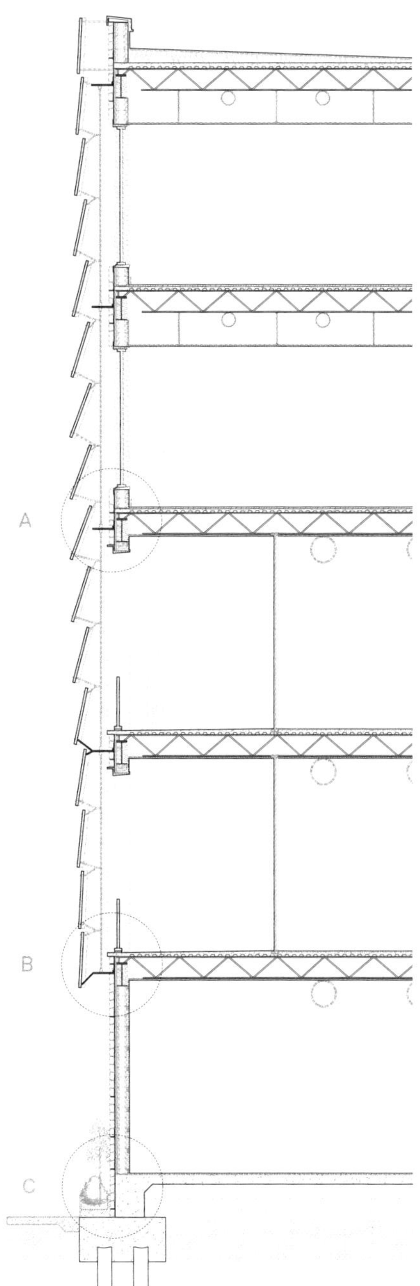

s> Camilla Greppi

i> Patricia Fraile

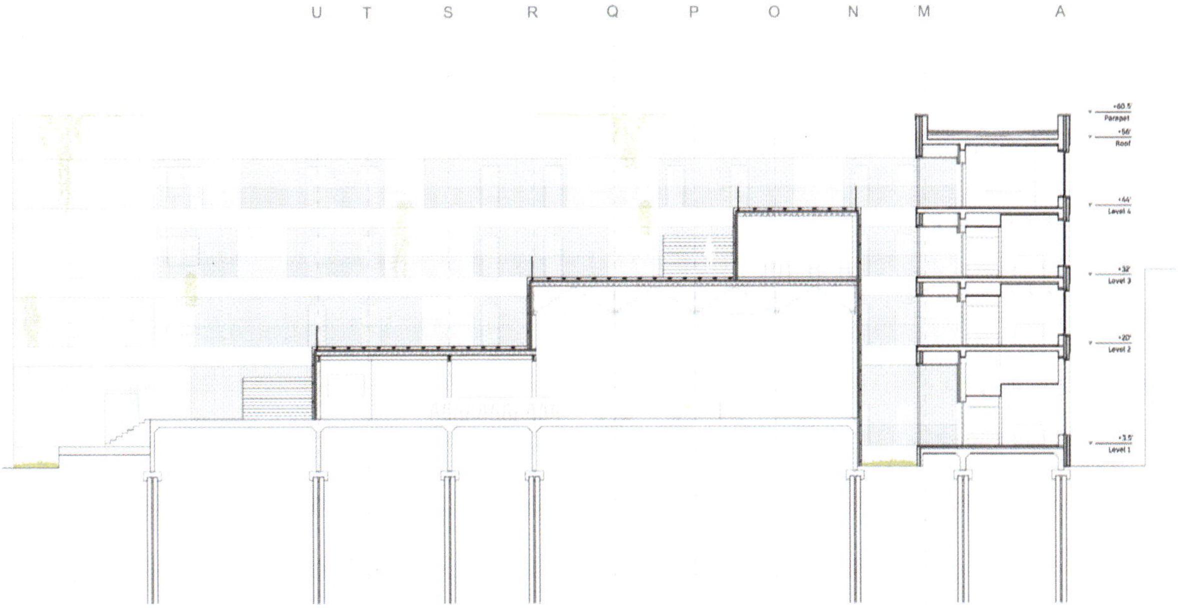

U T S R Q P O N M A

+60.5' Parapet
+56' Roof
+44' Level 4
+32' Level 3
+20' Level 2
+3.5' Level 1

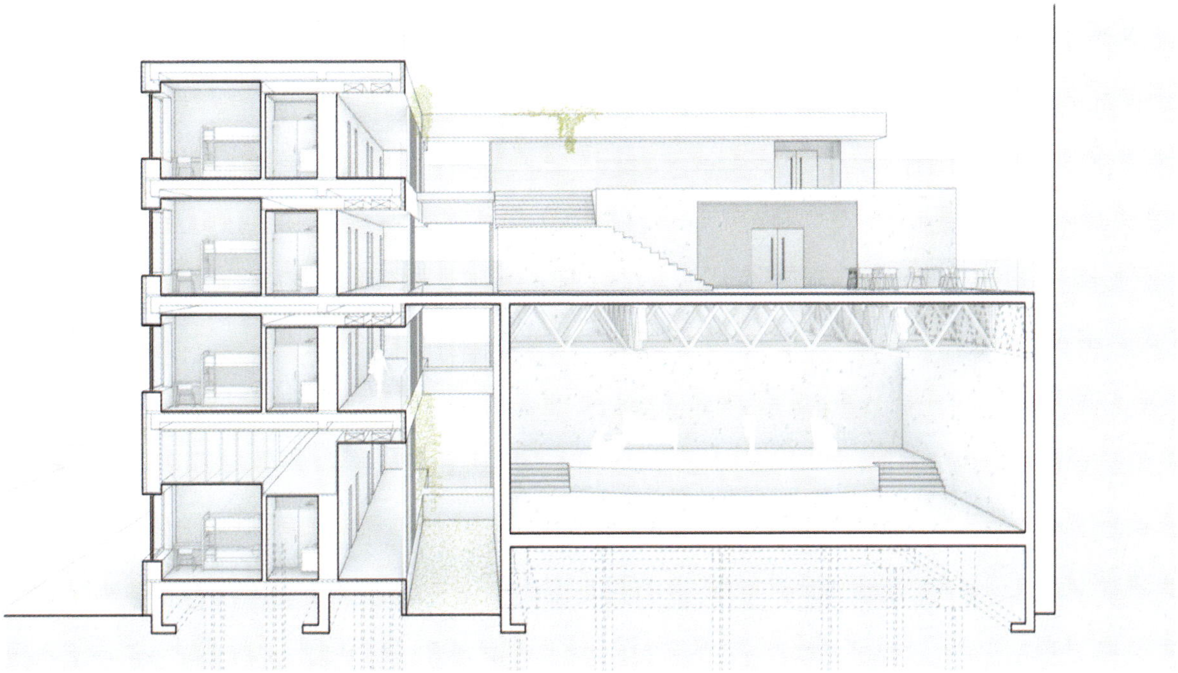

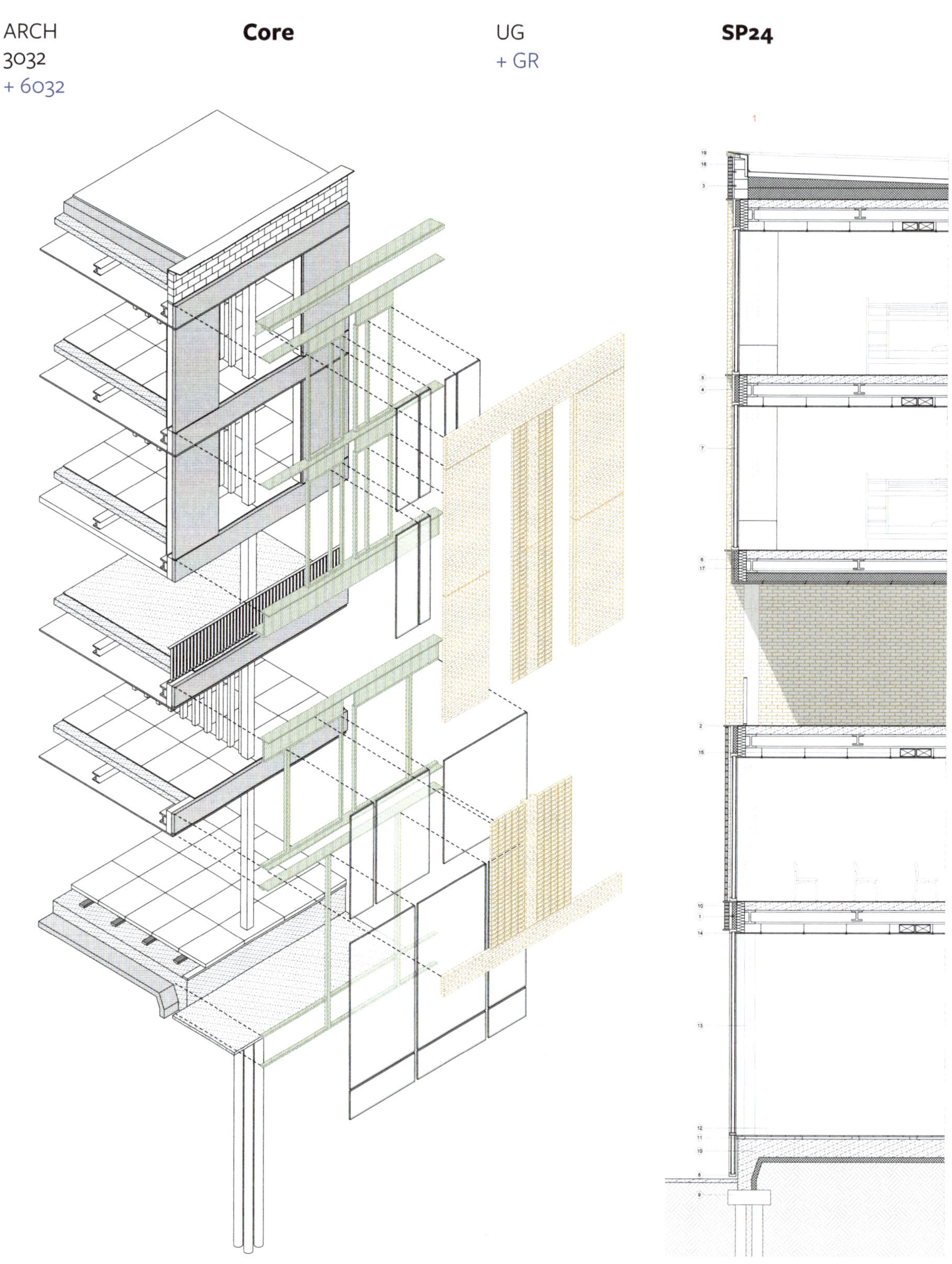

s> Susie Kresch, Evan Unruh

i> Irene Keil, Patricia Fraile

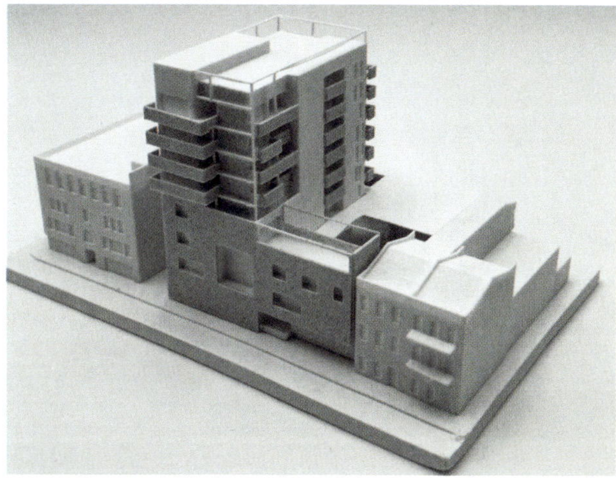

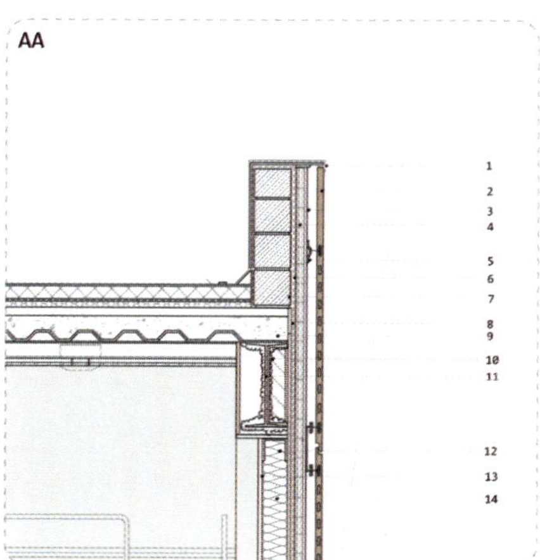

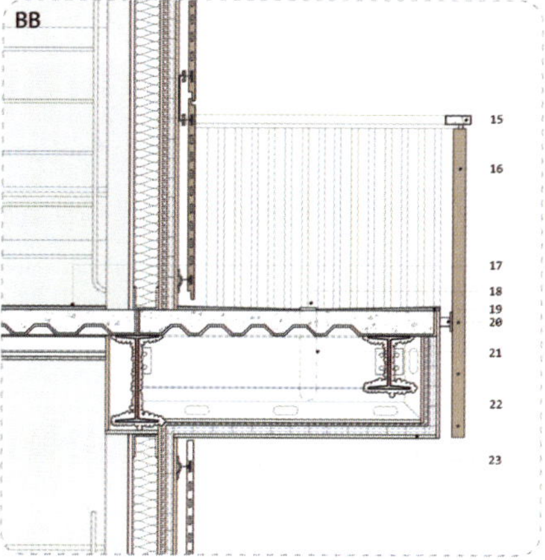

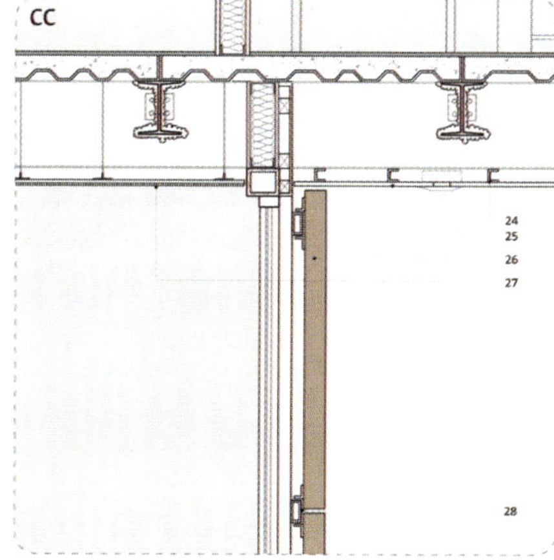

Want to see pictures of the GR final reviews?

s> Darby Hunter, Nikos Theoharis

i> Kentaro Tsubaki, Cynthia Dubberly

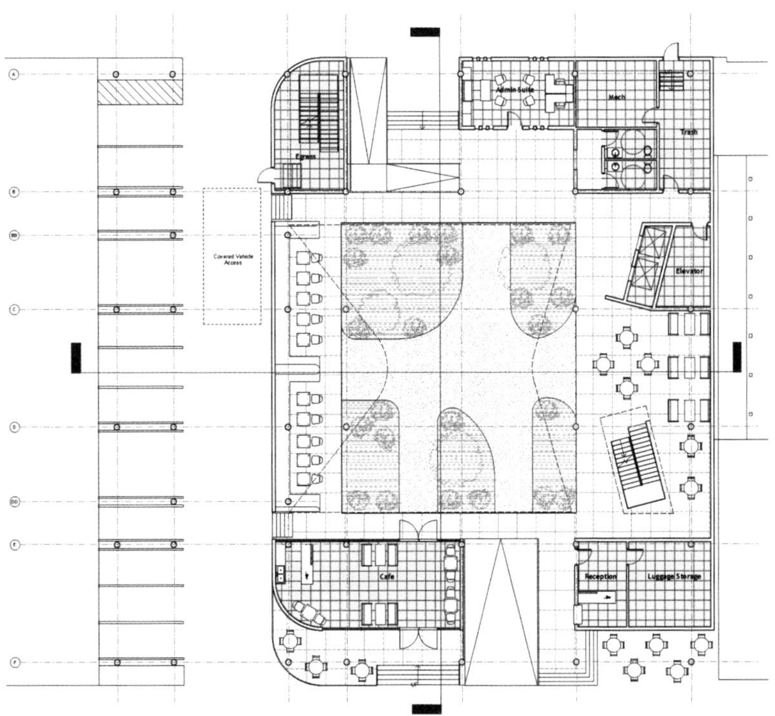

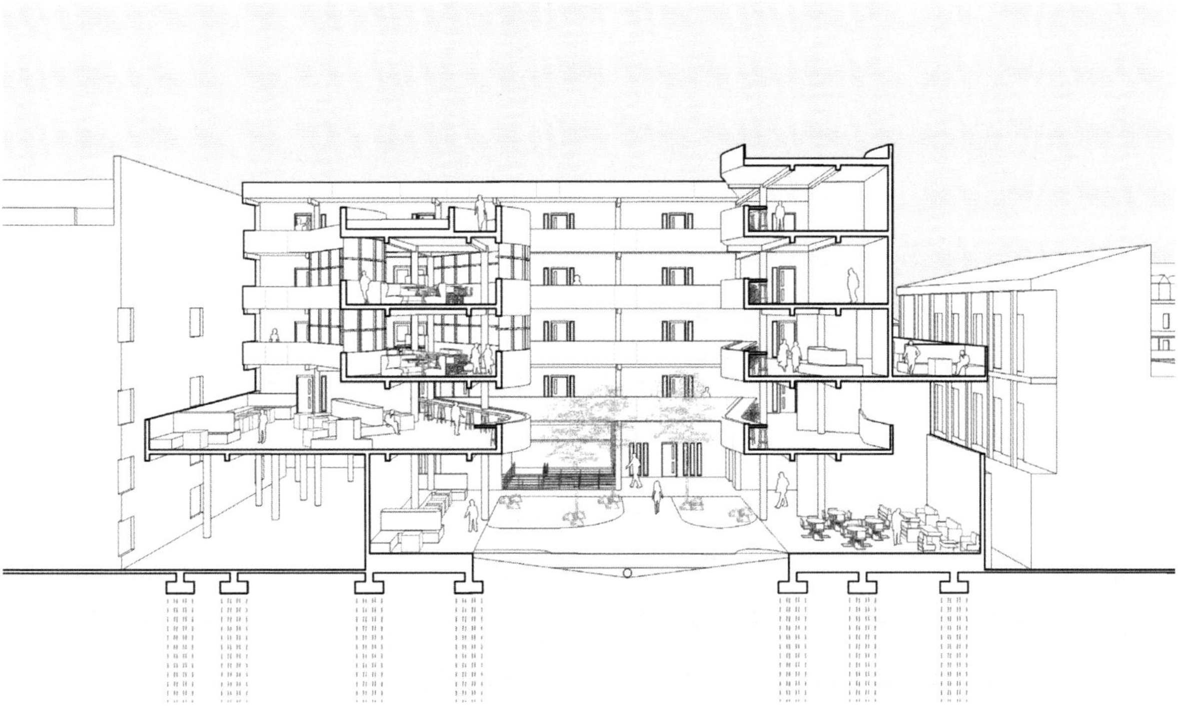

DIRECTED RESEARCH

Casius Pealer [C]

In this course students will conduct an original investigation in order to acquire new knowledge within a framework set by a client in practice. The primary goal of this research class is to deepen students' personal understanding of a particular topic or issue in real estate development. A key secondary goal is to build students' skills and confidence to make succinct public presentations of complex material. Students will be assessed both on your final work product (written and oral) as well as students' professional client communication along the way.

INSTITUTIONAL CAPITAL:

A "Blessing and a Curse"

Andrew Mann

Affordable housing is a pressing issue in the United States, with profound humanitarian and economic ramifications. Despite its critical nature, many Americans remain unaware of the severe shortage of affordable housing. This shortage hampers economic mobility and exacerbates childhood poverty. Access to affordable housing is essential for boosting homeownership, which in turn can help reduce intergenerational poverty. Furthermore, enhancing affordable housing access has been linked to potential GDP increases.

The primary problem is a lack of supply. According to the National Low Income Housing Coalition, no state or county in the U.S. allows a renter working full-time at minimum wage to afford a market-rate two-bedroom apartment. This highlights a systemic issue requiring urgent intervention.

Affordable housing exists in various forms, supported by numerous programs. However, these programs often fail to provide a pathway to homeownership. Tenants do not build equity regardless of how long they rent, and rising construction costs for traditional site-built housing make it more difficult to preserve existing affordable housing. Manufactured Home Communities (MHCs) and homes present a more cost-effective solution, as they are cheaper to develop and maintain, resulting in lower rents. With increasing material costs and supply chain issues, manufactured homes offer a more affordable option for both renters and investors.

Despite the benefits of MHCs, developing new communities is challenging due to financing, regulatory, and political obstacles. Existing MHCs also face threats to their affordability and supply, as larger capital markets are increasingly interested in these assets. This interest could impact the future of MHCs, their residents, and the development of new communities.

Parker Invest, founded by Tony Shu and James Parker, focuses on MHC investing, viewing these communities as recession-resistant investments with steady cash flow. Their investment strategy is based on the affordable housing shortage in the U.S. and the rising demand for MHCs. They foresee significant institutional capital entering this space, which could either preserve and expand MHC supply or lead to rent increases and the repurposing of these communities, worsening the affordable housing crisis.

The affordable housing shortage impacts all regions of the country, with over 10.8 million individuals living at or below 30% of the area median income and a shortage of more than 7 million affordable units. For example, Louisiana has only 41 affordable units available for every 100 needed for those earning 30% of the area median income. Between 1960 and 2016, median rent payments rose by 61%, while renter income increased by only 5%.

The shortage has significant economic effects. Housing is vital for economic mobility, stable childhoods, consistent education, and general health and safety. The lack of affordable housing reduces earning potential and slows GDP growth. Cities need diverse housing options to attract workers and new employers. The National Low Income Housing Coalition estimates the affordable housing shortage costs the U.S. economy $2 trillion annually in lower wages and productivity. Increasing the supply of affordable rental homes could add between $1.2 billion and $2.4 billion annually to local economies.

Investing in affordable housing supports job creation and increases tax revenue. One affordable housing unit produces an average of three jobs and $60,000 in local tax income. Every dollar invested in affordable housing creates $2.30 in economic activity. Building or rehabilitating two million units over two years could yield one million jobs annually.

The current system often perpetuates generational poverty by creating perpetual renters. Entry-level homes are becoming increasingly expensive, making it difficult for low earners to purchase. Manufactured homes, which cost significantly less than site-built homes, offer an attractive ownership opportunity. Their modular building process keeps prices low, providing immediate ownership opportunities for low-income families. These homes can also become income-producing assets if the owners' economic situation improves.

Despite their potential, the expansion of MHCs faces numerous challenges. Nonetheless, they remain one of the few viable forms of affordable housing. Manufactured homes, often referred to as mobile homes or trailers, are factory-built housing units mounted on a steel chassis, allowing for transportation. Unlike travel trailers, these homes are permanent residences typically not moved after initial placement. Their modular construction process is efficient and cost-effective, making manufactured homes an affordable housing option.

Over 20 million Americans live in manufactured homes, surpassing the number of people living in public or federally subsidized housing. There are over 50,000 MHCs in the U.S., with significant numbers in states like Texas, North Carolina, and Florida. In Louisiana, there are about 185,408 manufactured home units.

The demographic of manufactured home residents primarily consists of blue-collar workers, retirees, and unemployed individuals. Most residents identify as working-class or living on a fixed income. Interestingly, higher-educated low-income households are more likely to choose manufactured homes over single-family detached homes due to the lower costs.

Manufactured homes are significantly more affordable than other housing options, with the average monthly cost for a manufactured home renter at about $751, compared to $1,052 for other housing options. This affordability is particularly appealing in expensive urban areas where conventional housing rents are much higher. Though MHCs are often found in rural areas, 61% are located in metropolitan areas, with 14% of all manufactured home units in the top 15 metropolitan statistical areas.

Investing in MHCs can help address the affordable housing crisis, but it requires investors who understand the nuances of these communities. Federal funding and programs like Fannie Mae and Freddie Mac are beginning to support this sector more, but challenges remain in maintaining and developing new communities. Policymakers must take action to support the development and sustainability of MHCs, addressing both the humanitarian and economic aspects of the affordable housing crisis.

By Jose Cotto and Michael Wong

4

COMMUNITY NETWORKS

AS COMMON GOOD

REDEFINING DESIGN

From Individual Authorship to Collective Collaboration

By Ann Yoachim, Nick Jenisch and Emilie Taylor-Welty

Ann is Professor of Practice in Design and Director of the Albert and Tina Small Center for Collaborative Design.
Nick is Adjunct Lecturer in Architecture and Associate Director, Urban Design at the Albert and Tina Small Center for Collaborative Design.
Emilie is Director of the Architecture program, Design-Build Manager at the Albert and Tina Small Center for Collaborative Design, and Favrot III Associate Professor of Architecture.

Connection opens us up to new ways of knowing, and sustained engagement builds trust over time allowing us to envision new futures and bring ideas to fruition at scales large and small.

Photo credits: Jose Cotto

What is possible when architects and designers in practice and in academia see themselves as part of an interconnected web: moving from the individual to the collective, from 'hero' and sole authorship to valuing and integrating the expertise of others on an equal footing? Recognizing community networks as a common good allows us to move in this direction simply by providing opportunities to connect, listen and learn from each other. This act of connection opens us up to new ways of knowing, and sustained engagement builds trust over time. At their best, these networks allow us to envision new futures and bring ideas to fruition, addressing human and environmental concerns at scales large and small.

Simply put, relationships matter.

This broader ethos is manifested in Tulane School of Architecture and Built Environment's Albert & Tina Small Center of Collaborative Design (formerly the Tulane City Center). For nearly twenty years, the Center has served as a hub within New Orleans, actively collaborating with the existing robust networks of non-profits, professionals, artists, government officials and policy makers. Over time, the Center has become a trusted partner, facilitating the visions of partner organizations, serving as a convener and connector across networks, and providing high quality, responsive design services to those who don't have access. Trust is essential in wider efforts to address historical inequities. Engaged design processes and outcomes also allow organizations to gain legitimacy and build capacity in a variety of ways. From expanding their constituencies, supporters and funders, to building structures that serve as physical manifestations of their goals, organizations co-create new opportunities to serve the common good.

Equally important, through curricular and co-curricular experiences, the Center provides the next generation of architects and designers an opportunity to reimagine the possibilities of community networks as a common good by asking them to consider what design is, who design is for, and to assess their o w n roles and responsibilities.

Students engage with all facets of the Center's work including exhibitions and public programming, urban design and planning, design-build, graphic design advocacy and visioning projects. Deep engagement with all projects can include volunteering, prototyping on site, storytelling and photography, working with professionals beyond design, and gaining a clearer understanding of partner priorities. Students in semester-long design-build studios navigate design opportunities alongside our partners, and face constraints including material costs and project timelines. The Center's summer fellows gain an expansive view of design through projects ranging from design research, exhibition and public programming curation to site plans and renderings for partners.

Through this collaborative work, students and faculty from across the School of Architecture have completed over 150 projects including 45 structures in the Greater New Orleans area and shaped how others see themselves in the design process. Parisite, the city's only official skate park, is an example of what is possible when we embrace the power of community networks as a common good.

In 2010, a group of skaters approached the Small Center for technical assistance in protecting the nascent park and design assistance in continuing its build-out underneath an interstate. The Center leveraged Tulane University's networks and legal representation to legitimize a grassroots initiative. A master plan was developed through deep collaboration using both traditional engagement methods and the development of visual plans with neighbors and community leaders, as well as skating and clean-up days organized by Transitional Spaces, the skaters' nonprofit.

The results of the inclusive design process and organizational capacity building can be seen today in the diversity of the skating population that uses the park, the development of additional phases of the masterplan, and the continued existence of the organization itself. Trust built during the master planning process and resulting design-build studio in 2014 led to a continued partnership with Small Center in 2021, when summer fellows worked with the next generation of Transitional Space leaders to design the next phases in the evolution of the site. This newest public park space is visited by thousands of young people every year and has garnered national awards from the SEED and the Rudy Bruner Foundation, underscoring the power of design and collaboration to transform our cities. ■

MEASURING THE COMMON GOOD

Evaluating the Impact of Public Spaces on Community Well-being

By Wes Michaels
Associate Professor of Landscape Architecture
Tulane School of Architecture and Built Environment

Are we truly contributing to the common good, or are we mistaking intentions for outcomes? Assessing our impact on civic life demands a rigorous approach to understanding public spaces' roles in fostering community.

Perceptions of neighborhood change among residents (2017 vs 2023)

↑60% pts

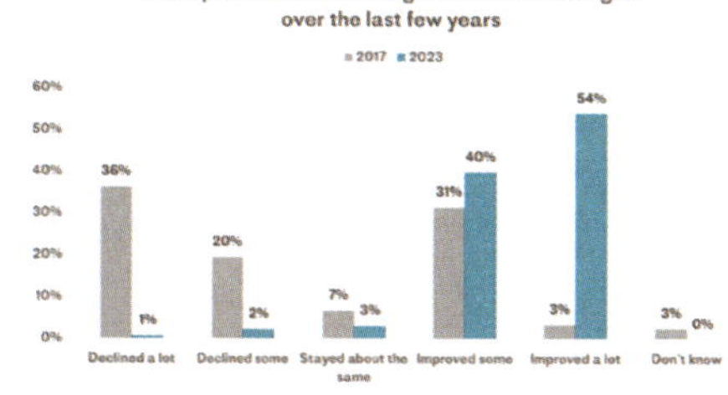

Photo credits: Wes Michaels

As design professionals and educators, we must ask ourselves a fundamental question when pursuing the common good: are we actually doing good? And if so, how do we know? Misguided civic virtue can be as detrimental as self-interest, and distinguishing between the two is often challenging. If good intentions pave the path to hell, our allied design professions have undoubtedly laid their share of bricks.

This question has sparked growing interest in developing methodologies to rigorously assess how civic spaces impact communities, and especially how they promote what might be called the common good. In just the past 3 years, two of our projects were evaluated using such methods, and a study of another project is getting underway. The most recent study, published in October 2024, examined our Fitzgerald Neighborhood project in Detroit (2016-2022), which featured two main interventions: a new neighborhood park and a revitalized commercial street.

The evaluation was conducted by Reimagining the Civic Commons, an initiative of four socially focused philanthropies, including the Kresge Foundation and the Knight Foundation. Their approach developed "a practical measurement system to analyze the impact of investments in public spaces and surrounding communities, and to track progress over time. This data-driven approach offers a new way to determine the multiple values of reinvesting in civic assets."

One of the provocations for this collection of work at TuSABE, the ReView, is the work of Michael Sandel and the ideas in his book The Tyranny of Merit: What's Become of the Common Good? While Sandel outlines the urgency of the issue, Reimagining the Civic Commons explores techniques for measuring its success. In the Fitzgerald report, they compared baseline data from 2017 with post-project data from 2023—through interviews, chance encounters, data collection, and observation—and measured four outcomes: civic engagement, socioeconomic mixing, environmental sustainability, and value creation.

In his book, Sandel observes the lack of socioeconomic mixing as a symptom of declining common good, noting that, "Those who are affluent and those of modest means rarely encounter one another in the course of the day. We live and work and shop and play in different places; our children go to different schools." The study in Fitzgerald looks at this very metric: how a public space improves or hampers the mixing of people from different income levels. The results revealed significant improvements in income mixing after the project was complete, scoring 75/80 on their index.

Sandel continues: "But if the common good can be arrived at only by deliberating with our fellow citizens about the purposes and ends worthy of our political community, then democracy cannot be indifferent to the character of the common life. It does not require perfect equality. But it does require that citizens from different walks of life encounter one another in common spaces and public places. For this is how we learn to negotiate and abide our differences. And this is how we come to care for the common good." The Reimagining the Civic Commons report on Fitzgerald studies these types of impromptu social interactions where people are close enough to have conversations. The report found, "along with gathering a wider mix of people, Ella Fitzgerald Park and McNichols have seen increases in opportunities for impromptu interactions. The park more than doubled (from 28% to 58%) the proportion of site visitors who are within conversational distance of one another." [1]

The report also found that people had gained trust in their local government, spent more time out of their homes, and had a vastly more optimistic forecast for the future of their neighborhood, among other findings. While the effort to measure the common good is far from perfect, these are promising first steps. As part of a Tier 1 research university with a significant liberal arts foundation, Tulane University School of Architecture and Built Environment is uniquely positioned to embrace a data-driven approach to promoting the common good, while also mining the civic lineage of our fields—architecture, landscape architecture, design, real estate, and preservation—as a theoretical foundation. We can better position ourselves to engage in meaningful research initiatives across the university as well as center the pursuit of the common good among our faculty and students. ■

[1] Reimagining the Civic Commons, p 77

NORTH CAROLINA FREEDOM PARK

PUBLIC SPACE
Raleigh, 2023

Architect: Perkins&Will
Collaborators: Holt Brothers Construction, MMSA (Structural), Sunderland Engineering (MEP), NV5 (Civil), Surface 678 (Landscape), Holt Brothers Construction, Demiurge (Specialty Fabricator)
Photos: Arsalan Abbasi + Keith Isaacs

"NC Freedom Park tells the story of slavery and freedom...tragedy and triumph, suffering and compassion, sadness and joy." - John Hope Franklin

A place of hope, memory, gathering, and reflection, North Carolina Freedom Park is a tribute to freedom as expressed through the African-American experience. Just as the oak tree relies on a root structure that is hidden from view, North Carolina's growth and prosperity has depended greatly on the unsung contributions of countless African American men and women. The Park expands on the state's history and brings the hidden roots of the Freedom story to life through four primary elements:

The Paths are carved into the site, bringing users below existing topography while preserving legacy tree root-zones. The Paths influence movement through the site while creating places to commemorate, learn, and gather.

The Walls express the stories of the hidden past. Twenty quotes attributed to North Carolinians are embedded in the walls, revealing the roots "of slavery and freedom, humanity and inhumanity, democracy and its denial."

The Beacon of Freedom emulates an eternal flame inspired by Lyda Moore Merrick's words, "My father passed a torch to me, which I have never let go out." The 43' tall, cantilevered centerpiece of the park gestures upwards towards the sky and characterizes the spirit of African Americans and all who have struggled for freedom.

The Brush Arbor is a place for thought, relaxation, prayer, and reflection. This passive, naturalized wooded garden is sheltered by the preserved oak trees and tells the story of the Park's founders, vision, and context.

Fig. 1
The Walls

Fig. 2
The Paths

Figs. 3, 4
The Walls

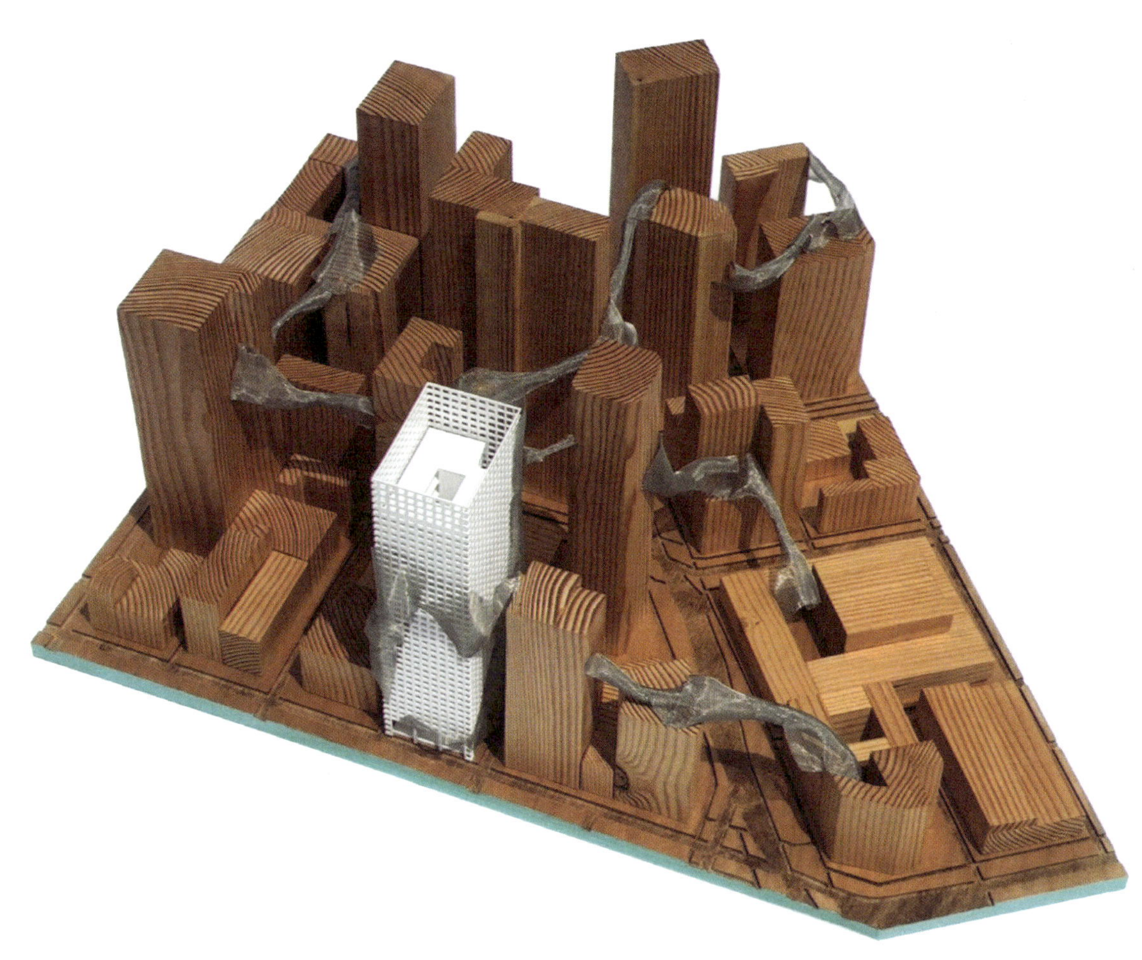

Fiona Alicandri + William Trotter

NOOSPHERE II:

A Battery for the Modern Metropolis

ARCH 5990 Instructors:
Cordula Roser Gray + Todd Erlandson

s> Fiona Alicandri + William Trotter **i>** Cordula Roser Gray + Todd Erlandson

Following the COVID-19 pandemic, cities across the globe saw steep decline in commercial office occupancy—a deficit that is still unresolved as reoccupation efforts have largely failed. With the initial reaction by developers and designers to convert these spaces into residential use being widely accepted, we argue that there are additional programmatic arrangements and opportunities not being exhausted or ideated at its present state of development.

Rather than contributing to existing proposals seeking to convert these spaces for residential use, this thesis aims to transform empty office buildings with a civic invigorator aimed to encourage social connection and ecological healing.

The thesis intends to address the environmental condition by connecting the multifaceted layers of the metropolis while also evoking a sense of responsibility and education in the issue of climate change. With a rise in work-from-home tendencies among members of the metropolitan workforce, a lack of social interaction ensues, prescribing a need for innovative solutions to maintain human engagement and foster community building through educational and environmental aids.

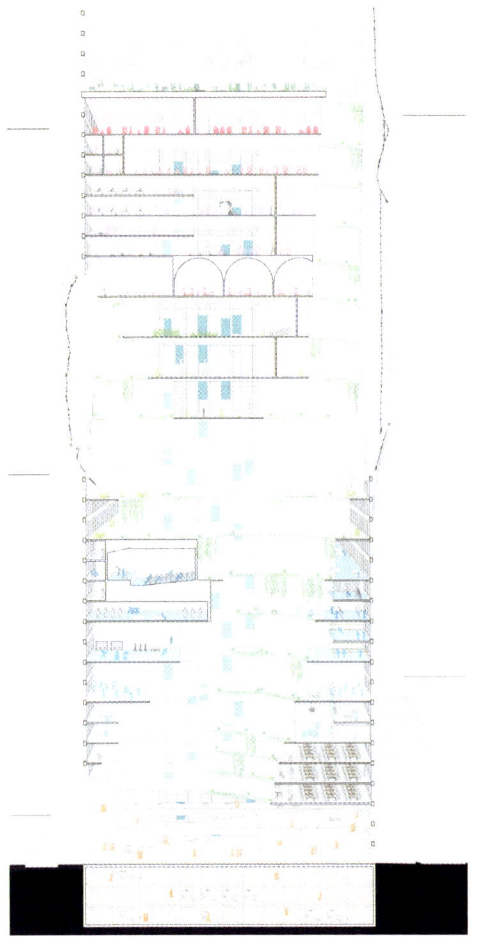

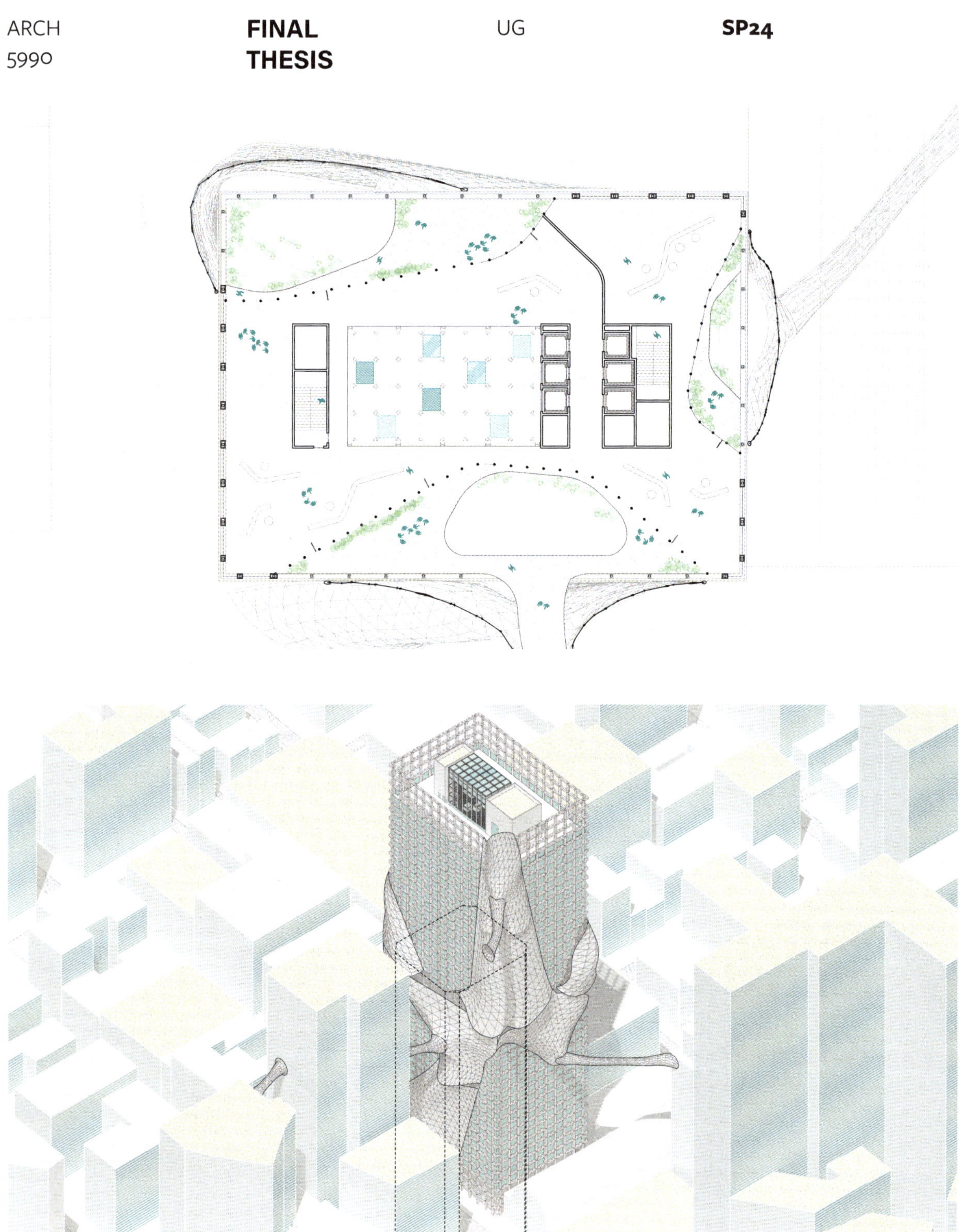

s> Fiona Alicandri + William Trotter

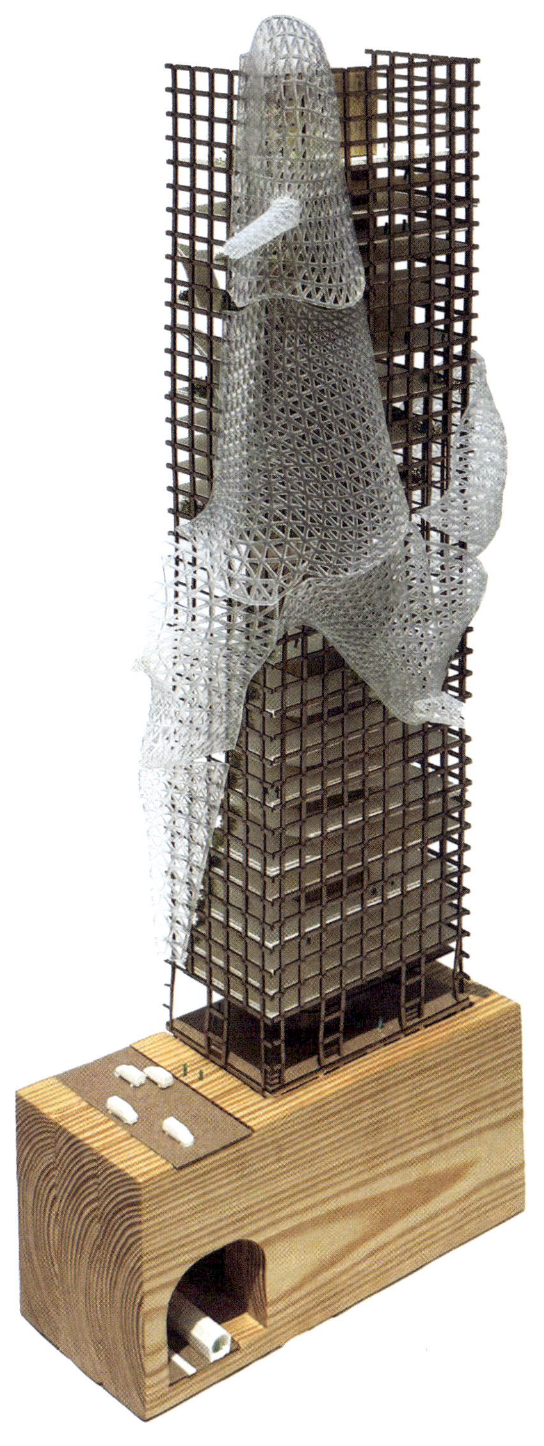

i> Cordula Roser Gray + Todd Erlandson

ARCH 4931 + 6931 | **Elective** | UG + GR | **FA23**

ENGAGED URBAN DESIGN

Nick Jenisch [C]

The Albert & Tina Small Center for Collaborative Design has long worked with cities and towns both globally and here at home, engaging with mayors, neighborhood groups, and businesses to help them envision the future of their cities. In the Gulf South, Small Center has aided cities in reimagining their public spaces after disaster, preserving cultural landmarks, engaging residents around public art, and many more projects. The seminar will center around real-time, engaged projects in collaboration with local residents, neighborhoods, and cities.

This semester we will work with Broad Community Connections, Sprout NOLA, businesses along the Broad and Bayou Rd. corridors, and fellow design professionals working to make the City of New Orleans more engaging and equitable. Student research and design will directly support local businesses and non-profits in promoting their corridors through pedestrian-friendly urban design, wayfinding, parks, community gardens, zoning changes, and more. This course will include readings, discussions, site visits and analysis, and design work in real-time alongside municipal and neighborhood group partners.

Students will study precedents from Livernois Avenue in Detroit to Oretha Castle Haley Blvd. in New Orleans, focusing on history, research, engagement, and creative design.

Throughout this course, we made sure to engage with the city committee members as well as business owners to ensure our work fit the needs and quality standards for Broad Street and the city of New Orleans. First, we met with city committee members and leaders to discuss our individual proposals for Broad Street. During this seminar, the class was categorized into groups based on interest and received feedback from reviewers in a rotational style. Towards the end of the semester, the class met with the business owners of Broad to talk about how to being more traffic to the businesses in the area. The class also shared their final proposal ideas with the Broad business owners as well.

THE
BLACK
SCHOOL

Along the Broad Street corridor, there are many vacant lots, abandoned buildings, and unused parking lots that are potential sites for future development that could act as catalysts for the communities. Looking at the Boston Ujima Project as an example of a democratic investment fund that allows community members to invest and be involved in redevelopment and revitalization in their communities, the intention of this plan is to identify potential sites for combating commercial displacement and promoting equitable economic development along Broad Street. The first step of this plan will be to create a system by which sites on or adjacent to Broad Street are identified as ideal locations for these new development nodes. Along with the redevelopment of existing structures, this plan also looks to introduce public green spaces that support climate sustainability, provide space for the community to gather, and consider good usable space by which new development can happen around. By engaging with the community owned real estate initiative and working through a few examples of how sites are identified, this plan hopes to provide a framework by which continuing redevelopment occurs. In doing so, we will consider federal, state, and local resources that might be leveraged when redeveloping historic buildings, creating new green spaces, and revitalizing buildings.

s> Kate Galvin + Marhaba Nigar + Elliot Slovis **i>** Nick Jenisch

ESPLANADE AVE
URSULINES AVE
LAFITTE GREENWAY
ORLEANS AVE
BIENVILLE ST
BANK ST
CANAL ST
VACANT LOTS
COMMERCIAL ENTERPRISES
RESIDENTIAL PROPERTIES
PUBLIC / HEALTHCARE / INSTITUTIONAL
RESIDENTIAL INTERVENTION
COMMERCIAL INTERVENTION
SCOPE OF ENTIRE INTERVENTION

s> Dang Doan + Riley Siltler + Joshua McDrew + Kailash Ramkhelawon

i> Nick Jenisch

The proposed intervention is to develop multi-functional zones along the corridor that engage the neutral ground as well as increase pedestrian circulation/accessibility to the surrounding institutions.

As you move along the corridor, the zones begin to transition as the level of engagement begins to shift from residential to commercial. The idea is to have these zones serve as a buffer between the current ideology of Broad St. being just a busy through way for cars just getting to work, or quick-stop errands. Engaging in urban development, and not allowing pedestrian through way and accessibility, takes away from the authenticity of the community and dismantles any sense of culture. Ecologically, these zones provide stormwater management, mitigating flood crisis, as well as canopies that challenges the "urban heat island" effect that has a hold on the city of New Orleans. To mitigate the effect of carbon emissions exposure, facades of CO_2 tolerant vegetation will inhabit the zones of engagement.

This engagement with the various zones and inhabitants along the corridor creates an interlacing connection with the residents and the businesses of the neighborhood.

ARCH 3742 6742 | **Elective** | UG + GR | **SP24**

DESIGN IN THE PUBLIC INTEREST

Jose Cotto [C]

In 2008, community members along the Broad Street neighborhoods of Treme, the Seventh Ward, the Fair Grounds, Mid-City, Lower Mid-City and Faubourg St. John came together to form Broad Community Connections (BCC) with a goal to imagine a commercial corridor where people from various racial, cultural, and socio-economic backgrounds could work together towards common goals. They desired to close the 20-year racial life expectancy disparity, increase economic development, create a healthy + thriving corridor, and honor its rich history and culture. 15 years later, BCC continues this charge—organizing and supporting over 120 small businesses from Tulane Ave. to St. Bernard Ave.

In partnership with BCC, this semester we will work with businesses and organizations along the Broad Street corridor to visualize and communicate stories of the past, present, and future. We'll end the semester seeding design ideas that amplify the intersections of community, culture, and commerce and imagine a more pedestrian friendly corridor.

Over the course of the semester, students can expect to meet with partners and guest artists, participate in photo walks and critiques, contribute to group discussions (grounded with articles, videos, podcast, etc.), engage in workshops that cover technical skills, and collaboratively explore how tapping into our senses can inspire and ground design ideas.

Below is a snapshot of some of the "lenses" through which we will approach our learning/work and what we will be up to throughout the semester.

partners_break bread with community partners to outline needs, aspirations, and goals.
people_connect and engage with people that call Broad Street home and amplify their stories.
place_create visuals that help us better understand and appreciate the places that make up Broad Street.
periphery_zoom out to understand and contextualize broader neighborhood contexts and histories.
possibility_explore possibilities to questions, concerns, and desires identified through engagement.

At the Albert and Tina Small Center for Collaborative Design, we are working to expand the role of designers and the impact of good design in our home, New Orleans, by creating a space for more voices in the design process. Collaboration will be critical to a successful semester and engagement process with our partners. We hope you each will bring your own perspectives, interests, and skill sets to the table, and hold space for others to do the same.

Students:

Rose Barnes
Ruby Bienen
Alex Cohen
Charlotte Fisher
Chester Griffiths
Brian Harris
Cole Shwabacher
Kris Smith
Jackson Stephens
Jose Varela Castillo
Shanelle Brown
Jonathan Hall
Katehrine Schwab
Riley Siltler

Overhead power lines and a constant hum contrast
The warm interactions I experienced while exploring the neighborhoods adjacent to the Broad Street corridor.

A family sitting and playing out on the street
They immediately took interest in me as I walked past with my camera and when I explained what I was doing they both wanted a picture taken and agreed that the relationship between people and cars in an area dominated by the automobile was worth exploring.

Smoking weed and reflecting on the changing city
This toking porch sitter flagged me down and asked what I was doing. As I explained he told me how just a few years ago, smoking weed on his porch would've landed him in jail, now, he said, no one seemed to care. He said the whole neighborhood was changing, but wouldn't elaborate. He offered me a hit and I continued on my way.

Modified shopping carts, I assume for parades
are parked along the street, waiting to be used. In other situations they may be interpreted as junk or trash, but here they fit right in.

A man and his dog
Saw me taking photos and asked what was up, I explained what I was doing and he immediately wanted to be a part of the project.

TuSABE Design Showcase. Images by Catherine Restrepo

5

CREATIVITY

AS COMMON GOOD

CULTIVATING CURIOSITY AND EMPATHY IN A COMPLEX WORLD

How Design Education Prepares Students to Navigate Uncertainty and Embrace Human-Centered Problem Solving

By Tiffany Lin
Favrot V Associate Professor of Architecture and Design Design Program Director
Tulane School of Architecture and Built Environment

"

Design education's greatest contribution to the common good might be honing human discernment in the age of automation.

"Intro to Design & Creative Thinking students explore the foundational concept of figure/ground reversal by crafting digital vessels from their profiles. This classic exercise encourages students to abstract figural information and creatively manipulate negative space."

An education in Design urges students to steep in the creative process to cultivate curiosity and a flexibility of mind. Studying design builds both intellectual awareness and agility that encourage humility–a sense that the student may not have the answer right away, and empathy–the ability to embody the feelings and perspectives of others. These skills push students to engage with multiple sides of a problem, to understand nuance and process rather than jumping to conclusions or fixating on quantitative metrics.

Our design pedagogy emerges, organically, from the theoretical and practical underpinnings of our architecture curriculum. I sometimes refer to the Design program as architecture without the buildings. For most, the word architecture conjures the built form. "I loved building with Legos as a kid" is an all-too-common refrain on the admissions essays of eager architecture school applicants. This well-meaning mischaracterization of the discipline overlooks the orchestration of complexity that Design brings to the fore: observation, analysis, exploration, translation, and symbiosis. These foundational principles form the tenets of an architecture education, much more so than bricks and windows.

I remember learning this in my own coursework as a 5-year Bachelor of Architecture student at Cornell, when the studio prompt asked us to examine a natural specimen. The first assignment was to observe, analyze and diagram the organizational structure of a piece of fruit. Our studios reeked of wilted peppers, pineapples, artichokes and garlic bulbs, an experience I had not anticipated as an architecture school applicant. After years of practice and teaching, the crucial role of that assignment is undeniably clear: the attention to detail required to hone the eye, the patience necessary to slow down the mind, rather than speed it up, in order to notice the contribution of parts to the whole. We needed to understand a system of nature based on utility, growth, and evolution—key concepts for making a network of components work together. In fact, this process is fundamental to the very meaning of the word "Architecture"—a term that other fields regularly use to describe complex systems: information architecture; software architecture; molecular architecture, etc.

Yet, when my parents asked me, their architect-in-training, to make drawings for a building renovation project, I could not. Our own collective misunderstanding became evident: they thought they were sending their kid to learn how to make buildings, not to draw pineapples. They weren't wrong, but the buildings came much later. As in design, architecture requires the author to have a keen ability to see and understand. Design pedagogy seeks to extend these processes beyond the realm of architecture to all facets of everyday life.

We live in an exhilarating and frightening era. Never before has technology been so advanced as to help solve some of the world's greatest problems. Yet technology has also evolved to such a level of cognizance and animation that we may be deceived into thinking we need not notice; the computer will do that for us. The ethos of our Design pedagogy pushes back on this belief that technology can remove the need to stew in detail; artificial intelligence can't detect some of the fundamental truths of being human. But, our students can.

Our initial projections when launching the Bachelor of Arts in Design program at Tulane in the Fall of 2020 was for 36 majors and 12 minors. No one would have guessed that just 4 years later, we are teaching nearly 300 students. Over half of our students are double majoring in another subject area ranging from mathematics to political economy, from business management to neuroscience. The application of Design principles to these other areas of study helps students synthesize information and deduce what is essential. Design contributes to "the common good" by equipping these students, across all disciplines, to apply the design mindset in their work: to notice, to investigate, to question, to experiment, and to have the intellectual humility to collaborate with experts in other fields.

Sometimes, on the most uplifting teaching days, I feel like we are helping young adults become better humans, citizens and stewards of this earth who know how to slow down and ask questions before making hasty assumptions or succumbing to apathy. There are no finite answers in the design process. Through this work, Design education's greatest contribution to the common good may not necessarily be about the work our students produce, or even anything we can easily see or measure. Its greatest contribution might be honing human discernment in the age of automation and mentoring the flexible mindsets of young adults as they progress through college. ■

CAMINO

ART

2024. Acrylic, oil, chinagraph on canvas. 34" x 62"

"The drawings and paintings of architect Tiffany Lin hover at the intersection of intuition and analysis—combining a crisp architectonic rigor with lyrical lines of expressive representation. For Lin, architectural form and painting composition are reciprocal components of her design process. This work may be read as depictions derived from architectural observation, or as generative fields of spatial investigation." - Scott Bernhard, AIA

This site-specific painting was created for the residence of an architect couple, inspired by photographic images of their journey through agrarian fields Spain. Familiar associations with form, color and opacity evoke the illusion of a landscape while a network of lines frenetically snaps atmospheric depth back to the surface of the picture plane. Within the boundary of the canvas, foreground and background elements give way to one another, compelling viewers to see the picture and the frame as equal partners. This abstraction invites an engagement with the visual tension between datum lines and the perspectival spaces they measure and compose.

CONSUMER CLOTH

ART
2022-2024

Architect /Artist: Jill Stoll

We are consumers. Everything we acquire, whether through home deliveries or by shopping at local stores, arrives in a cardboard box. These boxes accumulate in neighborhoods globally, representing an overwhelming volume of cardboard in our modern world. The complexity of this scenario has been heightened by the challenges of Covid, with lockdown prompting an increased dependence on home delivery services. Our purchasing power often correlates with privilege, leading to a fixation on the convenience and seemingly limitless inventory of online platforms. Our pursuit of instant gratification and unchecked greed has resulted in overflowing landfills and the emergence of plastic islands in our oceans.

This project aims to explore the question of how we can reconcile our addiction to consumerism while becoming responsible stewards of our planet?

Drawing inspiration from indigenous weavers, I harvest materials readily available, as cardboard boxes are ubiquitous. Engaging in scavenger hunts around local businesses and dumpsters, I collect discarded boxes for recycling, including the ones delivered to my own house. The collected boxes are flattened, cut into strips, with corrugated insides removed. This meticulous process yields two weavable strips of kraft paper, serving as both warp and weft. The result is a type of textile I call Consumer Cloth.

TACTILE DESIGN

Omar Ali
Hannah Kenyon
Hannah Berryhill

Career Explorations In Architecture

At the root of the architecture discipline is the study of design. In this two-week course, students focus on techniques of design utilizing hand drawing, mixed media exploration, and physical model making. The course will allow students to embrace the tactile facets of the creative process as a foundation of Architecture and its allied fields. Students will explore the city of New Orleans with their sketchbook, experiencing the spatial, environmental, and cultural context of New Orleans, while creating beautiful work that will be digitally archived for their professional portfolio.

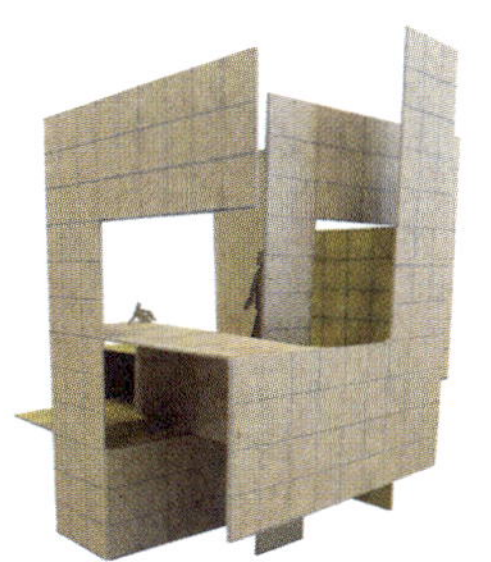

3D DIGITAL DESIGN

Career Explorations In Architecture

Omar Ali
Hannah Kenyon

This course introduces high school level students to the tools, techniques, and workflows of digital design in architecture. Through a sequence of assignments, students gain a working knowledge of design and visualization software while learning the basics of architectural representation. From 2D orthographic projection drawings (plan, section, elevation) to 3D modeling and fabrication, students will be exposed to a myriad of techniques and processes that will help them visualize and communicate form and space.

The studio is a safe space to explore creativity, critical thinking, and camaraderie—students do not only learn from lectures and exercises but also from each other through pin-ups and reviews.

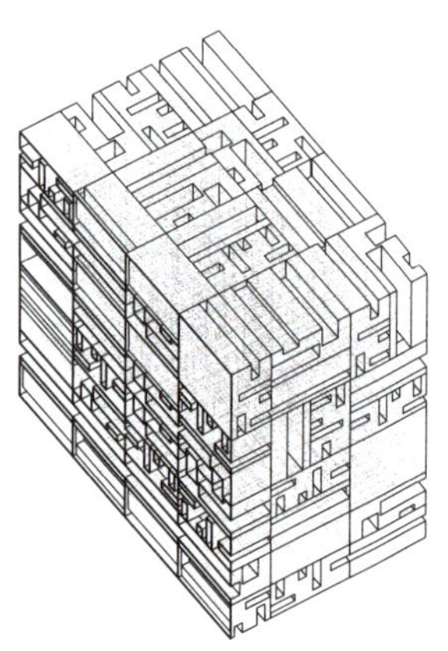

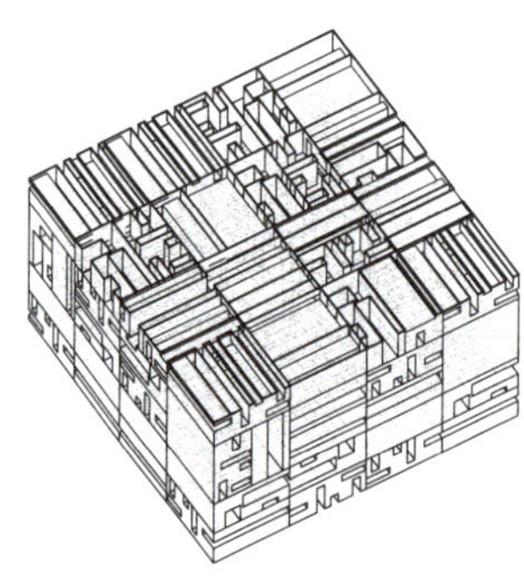

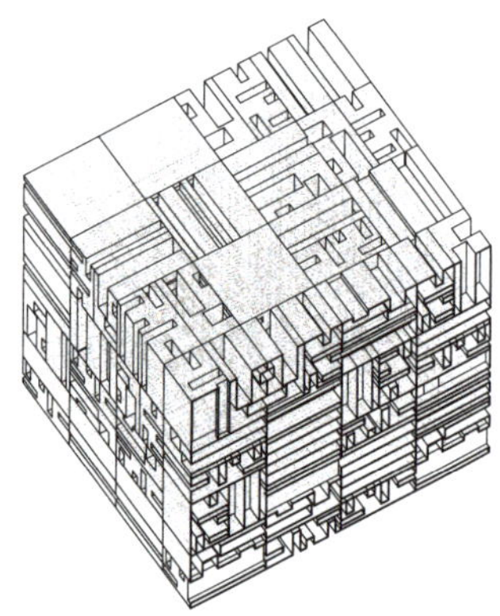

VISUAL COMMUNICATION & ADVOCACY

Meghan Saas [C]
Adam Newman
Thomas Wimberly

Graphic design has the power to act as a megaphone, amplifying messages to reach and resonate with a wider audience. To make a meaningful impact, designers must carefully analyze their audience, refine their message, and skillfully apply a compelling visual tone. By leveraging this power for advocacy, we can steer it towards the greater good.

This 9-week project is an immersive journey through the design process—from thorough research and ideation to development, iteration, production, and reflection. Your mission: select a cause close to your heart, conceive a hypothetical organization championing that cause, and craft captivating promotional materials for its campaign, along with curated branding guidelines.

Multiple deadlines and deliverables, with substantive feedback along the way, challenge students to refine and elevate their concept and design craftsmanship. Informal desk crits, semi-formal pin-ups, and a final formal review all play essential roles in the students' creative growth.

s> Jordie Block **i>** Adam Newman

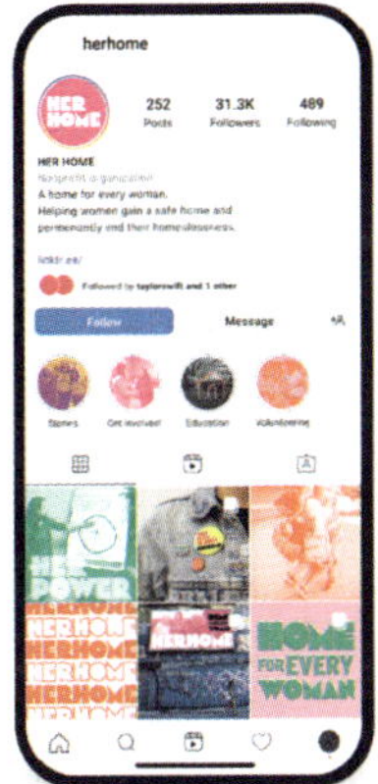

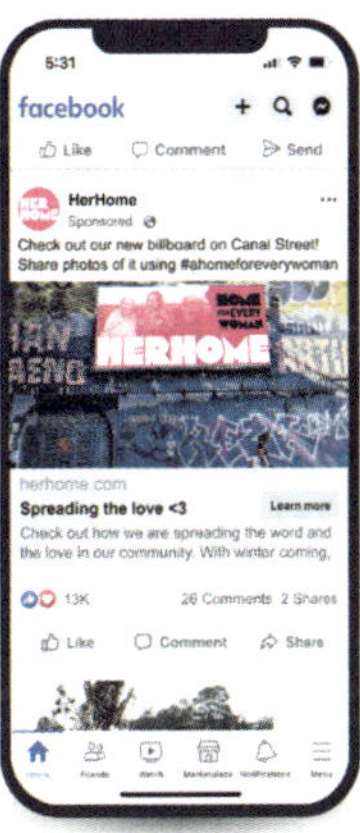

Jordie Block

HER HOME

When walking through the streets of New Orleans, we were struck by the amount of women experiencing homelessness. Hearing their stories, we were struck by the fact that many lost their homes due to domestic violence, poverty, and other traumas. We saw that being a woman made them more vulnerable to violence and harassment on the streets and knew we had to do something to help protect these women and provide them with the resources to rebuild their lives. We started with limited volunteers making care packages and meals to give out to women. As our organization grew, we were able to create a shelter where women could come to feel safe and create a community. We continue working to provide women with the resources to help them get back on their feet, with the goal to aid as many women as possible find a permanent home.

Nely Boycher

OPEN ARMS

Open Arms stemmed from my own experience as a LGBTQ+ teen. Although not as severe of a situation as those who Open Arms helps, I was in a situation where I was unable to come out due to fear of being treated differently by my family. I knew that if I had this issue, there must be many others like myself. After finding out the numbers of queer teens who were homeless with no where to go, starting a company that could support those people seemed like the only option. With support from local allies and members of the LGBTQ+ community, we were able to begin providing teens with everything needed for a successful, loving upbringing into adult life when no one else would.

Sophia Badame

ZEAL

Often, areas and schools that generally receive fewer opportunities or less arts funding are the ones with more at-risk youth. Disproportionate arts access negatively affects racial, ethnic, and socio-economic minority children. The funding for arts education has been declining worldwide. A 2019 study found that schools with large populations of minority students received $23 billion less in annual funding than schools with lower minority populations. Zeal is recognizing children have strengths and weaknesses in different subject categories. We strive to encourage creativity in all children. Every child deserves the opportunity to discover their intellectual strengths which includes the arts. It is important that underprivileged communities have the opportunity to educate their children beyond STEM. We want to give every child the opportunity to discover their passion.

ENVIRONMENTAL GRAPHIC DESIGN

Adam Newman[C]

Environmental Graphic Design (EGD) operates at the intersection of Communications and the built environment. While it is a field that involves conventional graphic design considerations including typography, color, hierarchy, legibility, readability, illustration, photography, etc., it adds factors of physical dimensionality, materiality, and context with surroundings—at scales ranging from discrete objects to individual rooms to whole buildings and even entire cities.

Pushing beyond the physical proportions of a book or handheld device, environmental graphics function in both more immersive and context-aware ways. EGD combines design, communication, and environmental psychology to create visually engaging and functional spaces.

Environmental Graphic Design can involve and intersect with brand design, architectural design, interior design, landscape design, industrial design, and digital design as well as photography, illustration, and—importantly—writing. It can be utilized to create exhibits, systems for way-finding, retail spaces, and branded or themed environments. It is found in transportation centers, schools, hospitals, museums, shopping centers, office buildings, and on any street.

Want to see pictures of the final review?

s> Charlotte Ertmann **i>** Adam Newman

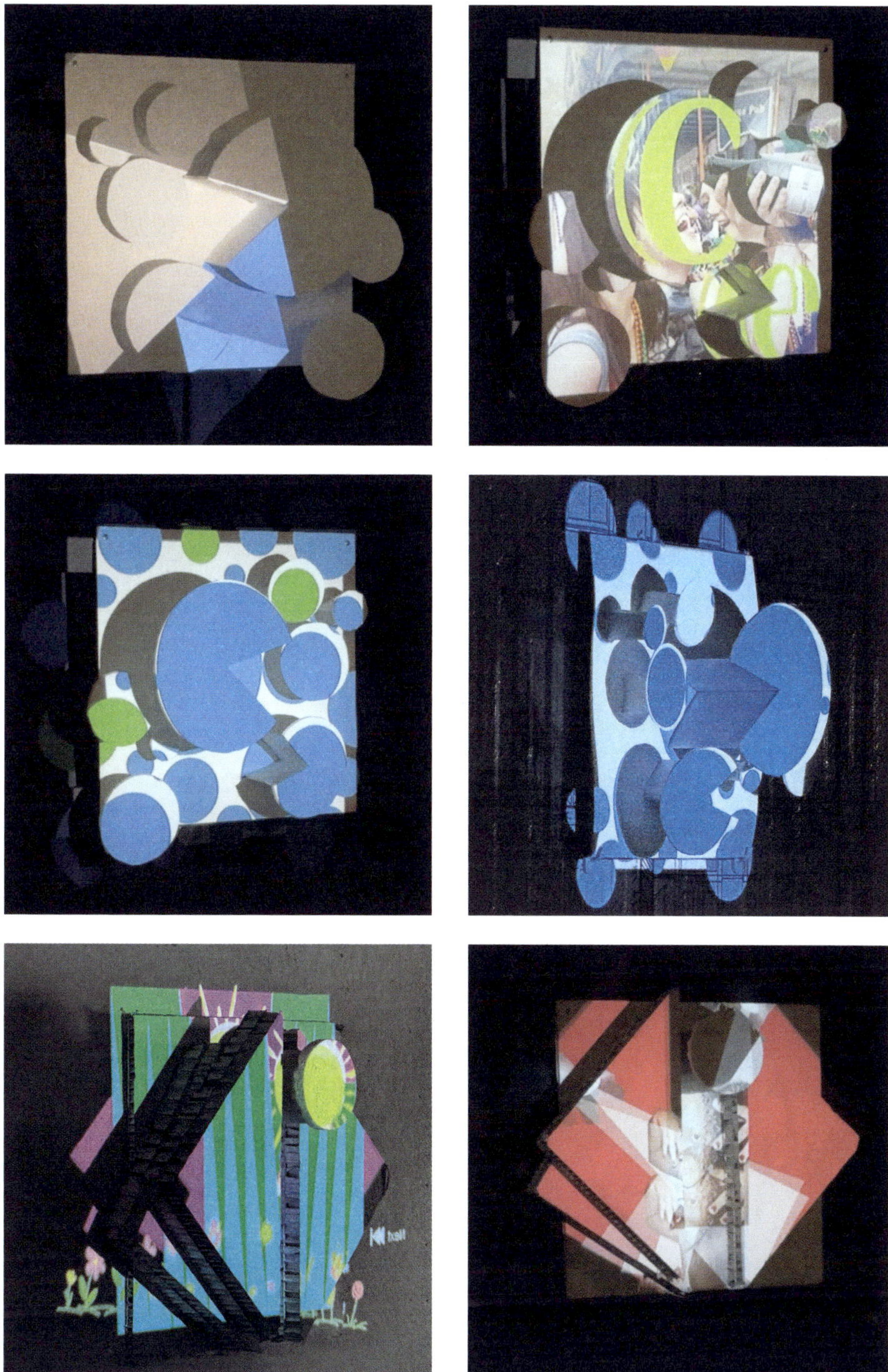

TYPOGRAPHIC SPECIMENS

Meghan Saas [C]

2D, 3D, Motion

Typography is a fundamental aspect of graphic design, and this advanced studio will challenge students to push the boundaries of type beyond convention. The course will examine visual language in historical and contemporary social context, to analyze critical and conceptual meaning and impact. Through workshops and demos, formal and informal critique, and a rigorous iterative process, each student will develop an original font design for functional use. Students will then apply their custom letter forms in 2D, 3D, virtual 3D, and time-based media.

Want to see pictures of the final review?

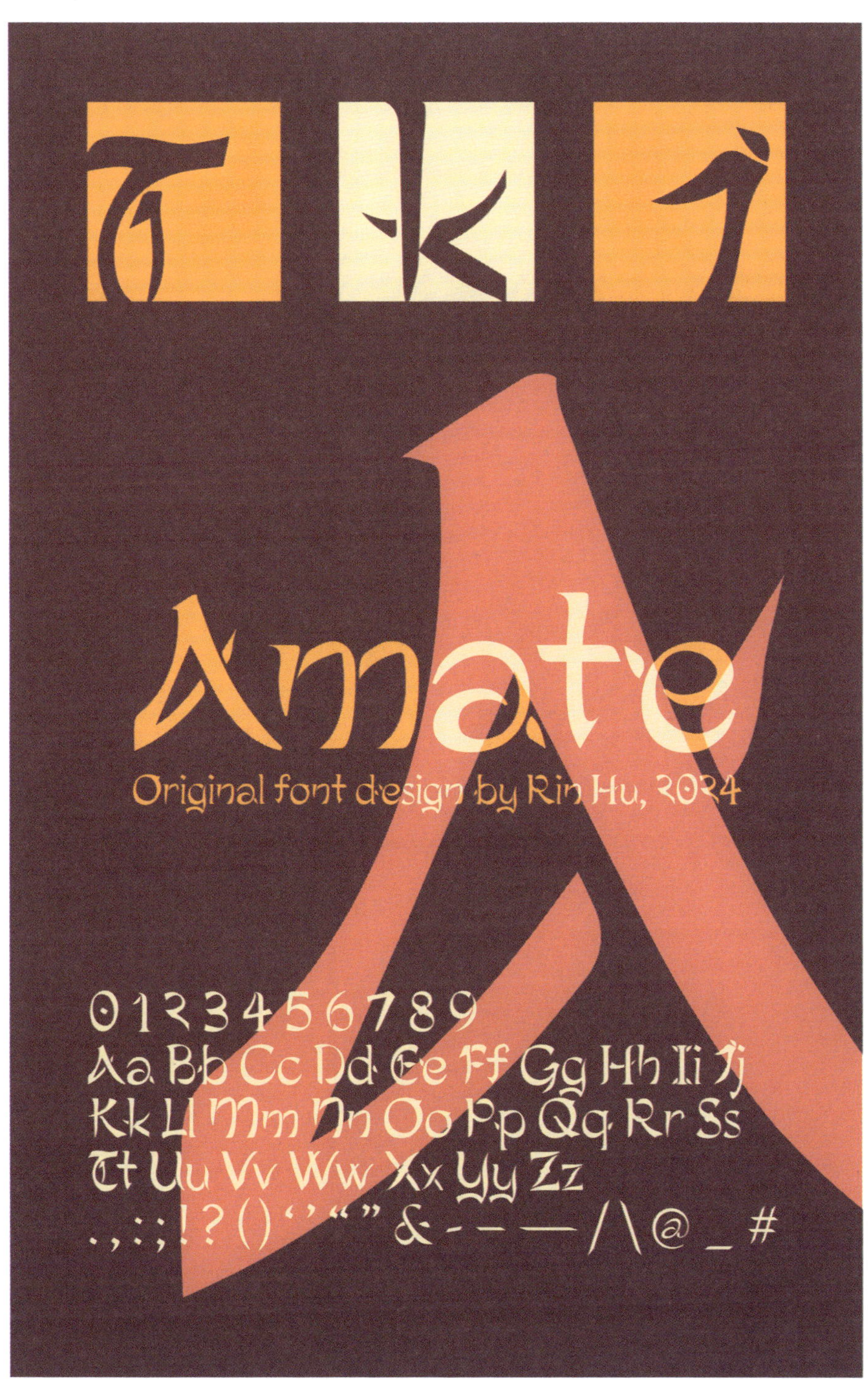
Amate
Original font design by Rin Hu, 2024
0 1 2 3 4 5 6 7 8 9
Aa Bb Cc Dd Ee Ff Gg Hh Ii Jj
Kk Ll Mm Nn Oo Pp Qq Rr Ss
Tt Uu Vv Ww Xx Yy Zz
. , : ; ! ? ( ) ‘ ’ “ ” & - – — / \ @ _ #

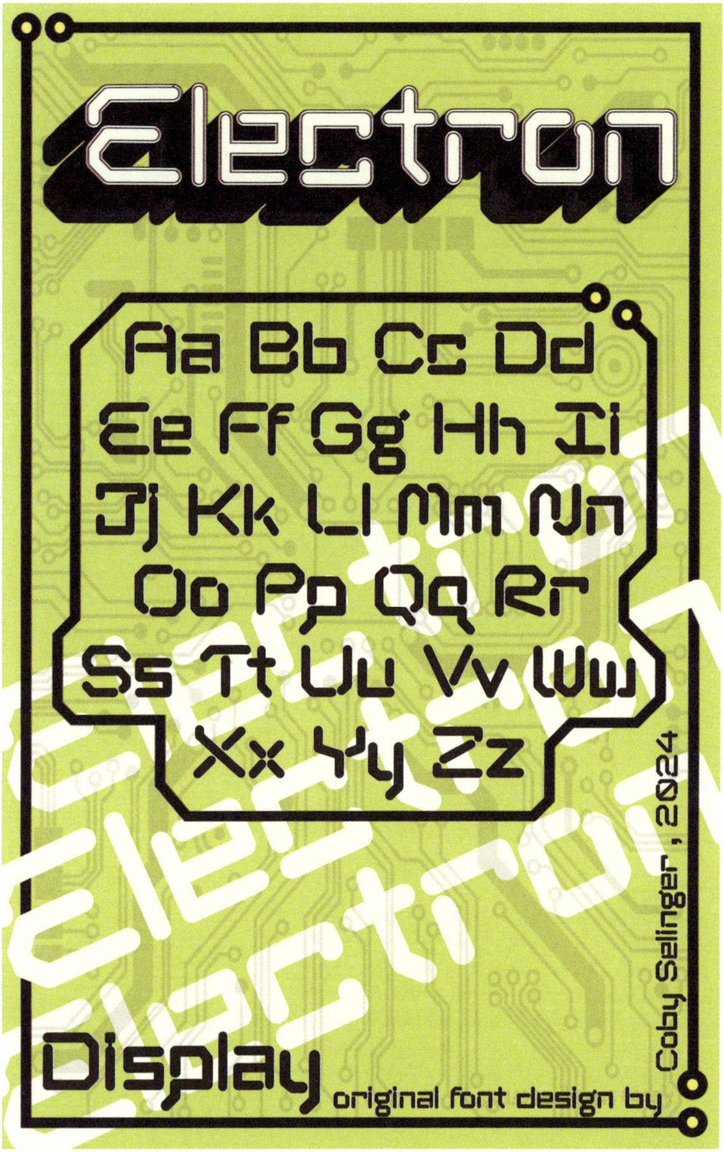
Electron
Aa Bb Cc Dd
Ee Ff Gg Hh Ii
Jj Kk Ll Mm Nn
Oo Pp Qq Rr
Ss Tt Uu Vv Ww
Xx Yy Zz
Display
original font design by
Coby Selinger, 2024

Aa Bb
Gg Hh
Mm Nn
Rr Ss
Xx

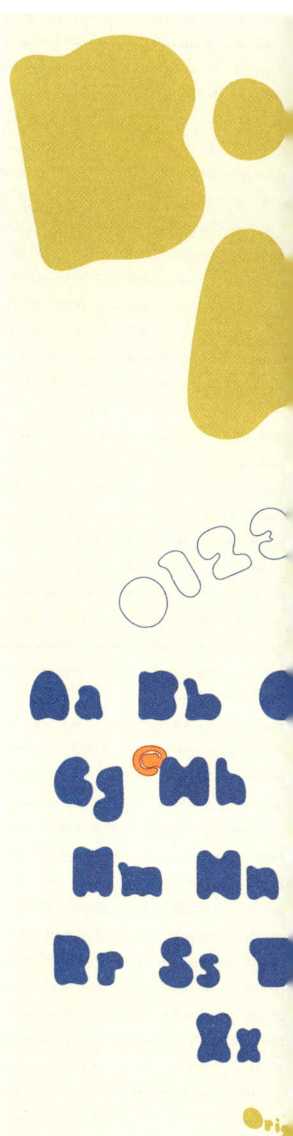

Aa Bb Cc Dd Ee Ff Gg Hh Ii
Jj Kk Ll Mm Nn Oo Pp Qq Rr
Ss Tt Uu Vv Ww Xx Yy Zz
1 2 3 4 5 6 7 8 9 0 # #
. , : ; ! ? ÷ / \ @ &
' ' " " - – — [ ] _
Magneto aZ

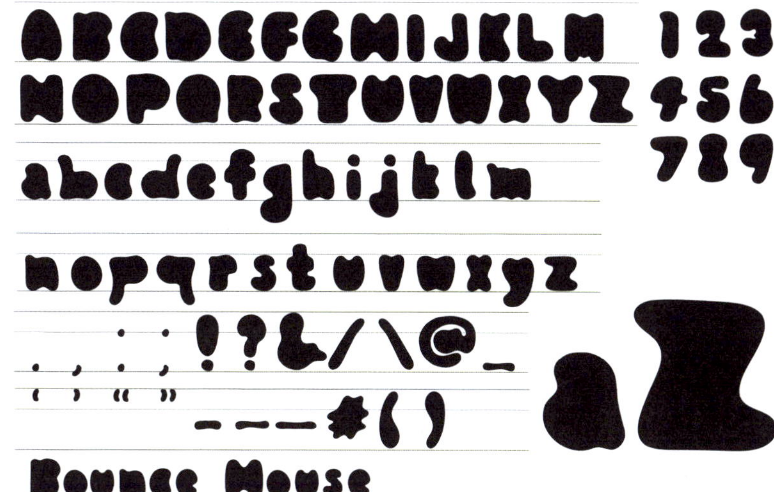

Light Sculpture Exhibition

Curated by Nick Perrin

This semester, Design students studied insect specimens donated by the Tulane Ecology department as inspiration for their light sculptures. Each student chose an insect to analyze, carefully studying its anatomy and behavior and translating those observations into three-dimensional sculpture, light, and shadow. In addition to the conceptual inspiration derived from nature, each project is crafted entirely from biodegradable materials.

DISCOVER

A Pavilion in a Walled Garden

Andrew Liles [C]
Ira Concepcion
Elizabeth Chen
Mitchell Hubbell
Hannah Kenyon
Jonathan House
MC Matucheski

In this introductory design course, the students focused on foundational concepts and methods that were explored through drawing and making. To introduce the shaping of place in an architectural sense, the students were invited to carefully study the world around them, to document what they found there, and through their work create experiences for others. We are all from different places and this perspective helped each student develop projects in relationship to the human body and to the natural and constructed environments. The inherent diversity that students bring to this class will be a resource in our work to respect diversity in culture, background, and perspective. Together students introduced and employed a specific vocabulary to describe the nuances of the physical world. They used this lexicon to link qualities of space to design operations.

Drawing comprises an architect's primary mode of seeing, thinking, and creating as the cornerstone for a studio-based process of critical thinking. The goal as we learn each technique will be to utilize this expertise as a springboard from which to develop new approaches and as yet unknown solutions. The students studied composition, the nature of something determined by its elements, through observing the way in which a whole is made up of interrelated parts. Building an awareness of the relationships between parts will propel the design process by generating the ideas and defining physical properties with which to work.

The learning strategies included lectures and workshops that described free-hand drawing, drafting, constructed perspectives, and manual | analog 3D modeling. The faculty provided lessons in each technique that the students needed in the sequence of assignments so that they had the skills and understanding they needed to be successful in the course. These diverse methods will provide tools to work with both the empirical (what is found through observation and the careful recording of those findings) and the experiential (that described by your senses and emotional connection) to participate in the speculative, or the creative formation of change, as we proceed from recorded information to generative inspiration.

Want to see pictures of the exhibition?

s> Bryn Mortenson

i> Andrew Liles

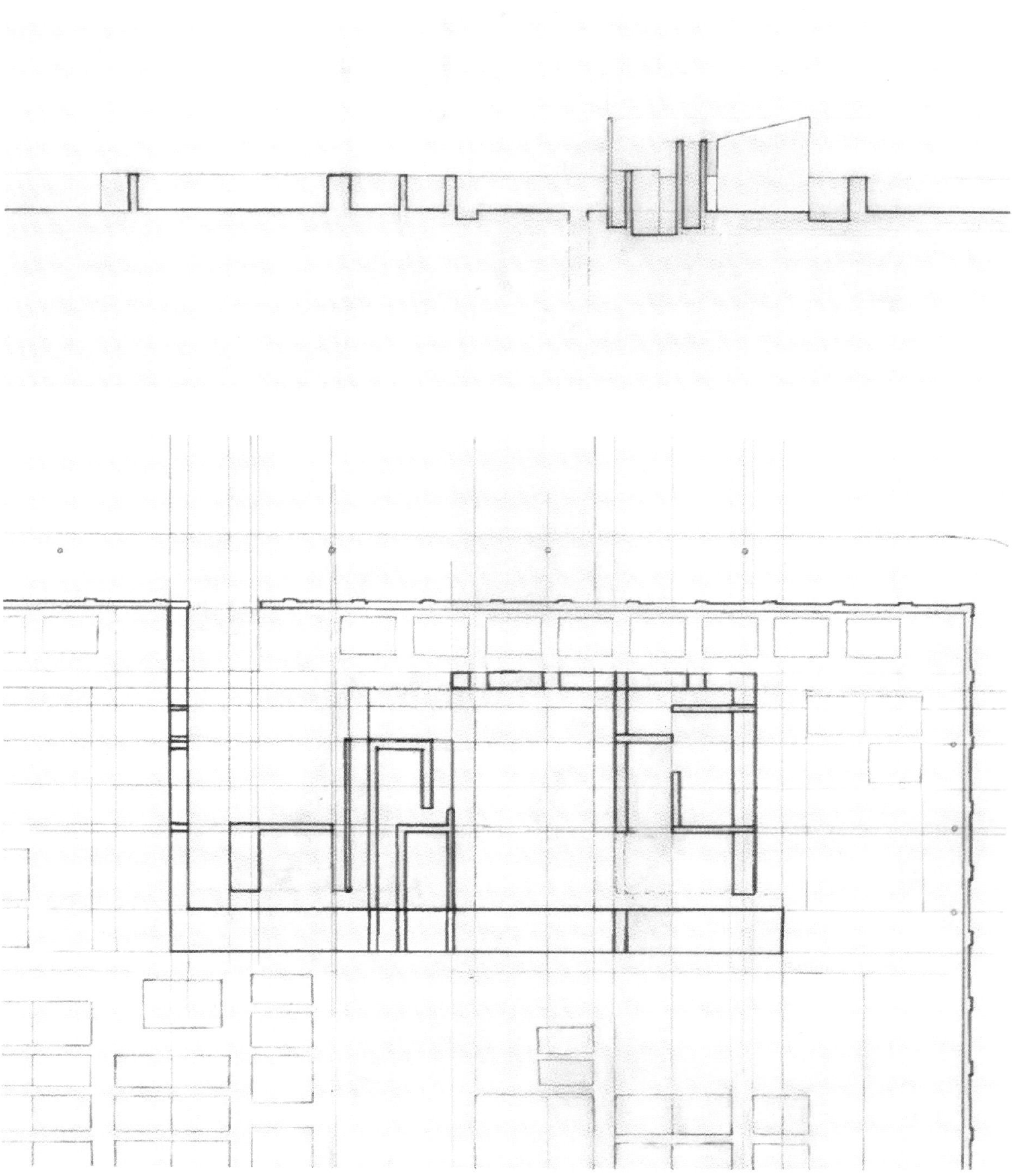

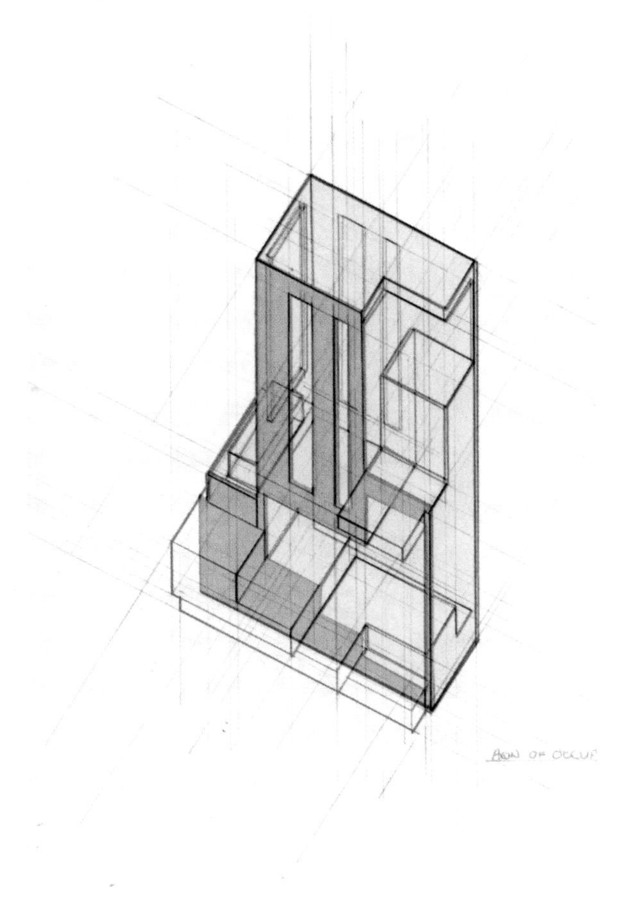

s> Lorelei Schmitzer-Torbert, Bryn Creager, Sofia Farto, Sammy Wolf-Valdes

i> Elizabeth Chen, Hannah Kenyon

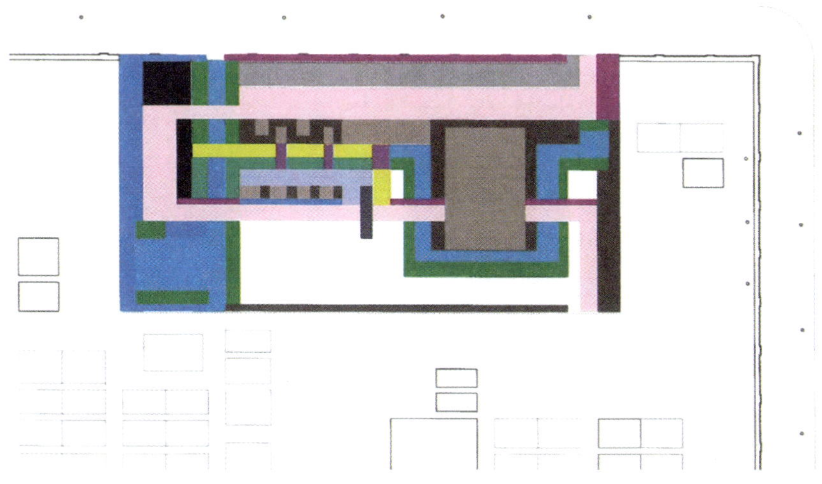

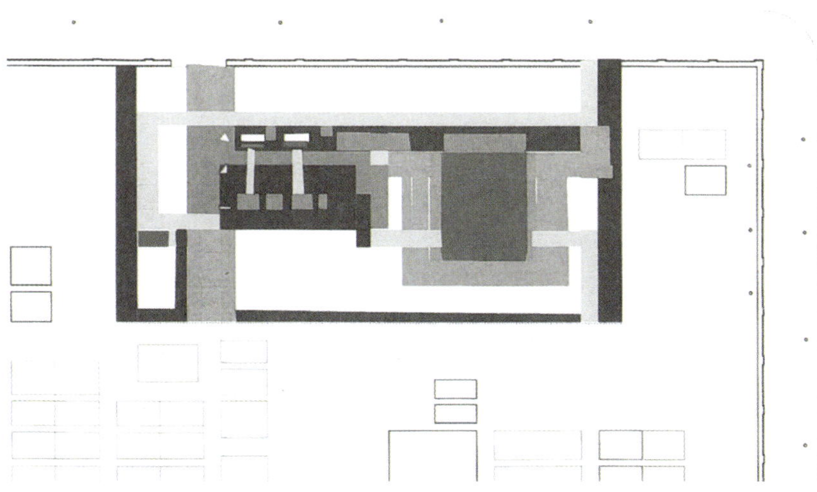

s> Gabriel Smith, Sofia Farto, Kay Tober Hubbell, Marcus Flory

i> Hannah Kenyon, Mitchel Hubbell, Ira Concepcion

DIGITAL MEDIA

Jesse Toohey[C]
Liz Camuti[C]

Tulane School of Architecture and Built Environment's introductory digital media course introduces digital tools and techniques for their application in architectural production. The primary objective is the cultivation of a drawing practice that facilitates critical thinking, the testing of design ideas, and effective communication. Each week explores fundamental concepts in architectural representation that include a range of two and three-dimensional media and workflows. Students will work through orthographic (plan, section, elevation), axonometric, and perspective projection drawings of mixed media with an overall emphasis on the integration of digital drawing techniques.

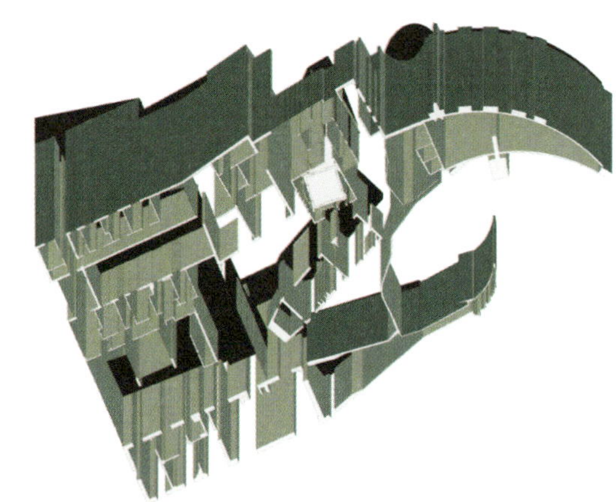

The course uses lecture and workshop formats to foster critical perspectives and technique development, respectively. Classes will consist of lectures, demonstrations, workshops, and pin-ups. During lectures, the teaching team will discuss topics from assigned readings, situate the content in historical and professional domains, articulate lesson objectives, and demo software tools and techniques. During pin-ups, the teaching team will evaluate outcomes from students' drawing lessons of the previous week's assignment. In addition, we will utilize the studio setting for an ongoing workshop format to aid content development, assist with questions regarding the week's assignment, and actively work through lesson goals, tool comprehension, and any other roadblocks or details that materialize. Upon successful completion of the course, students will be proficient in skills and concepts underlying the representational strategies to produce architecture.

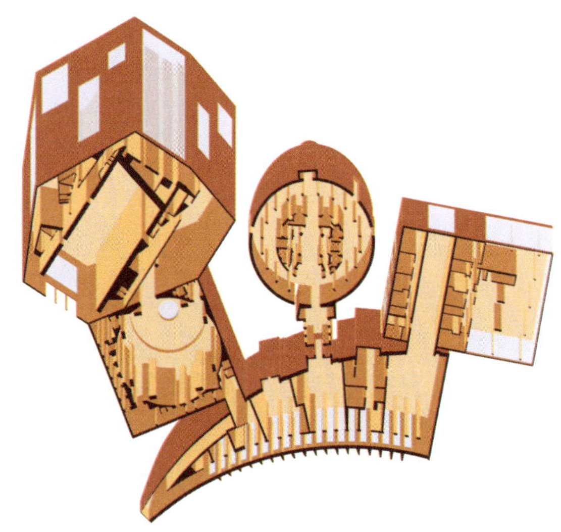

s> Allie Johnson, Nathan Rich, Bernardo Urquieta

i> Jesse Toohey, Liz Camuti

ARCH
2311
+ 6311

Digital Media

UG
+ GR

FA23

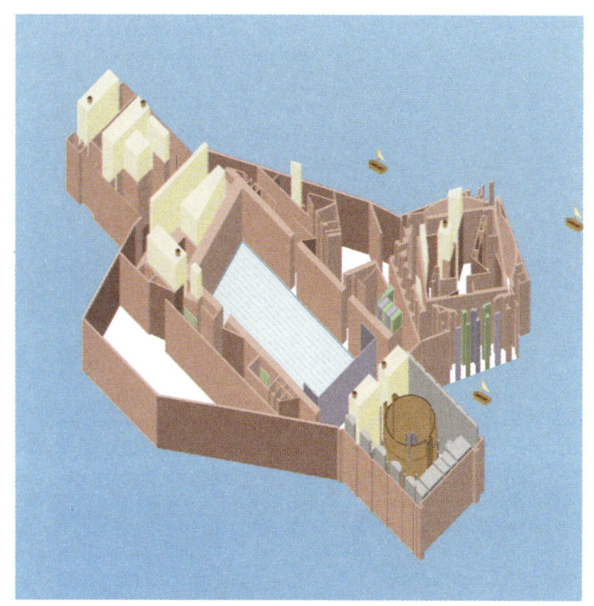

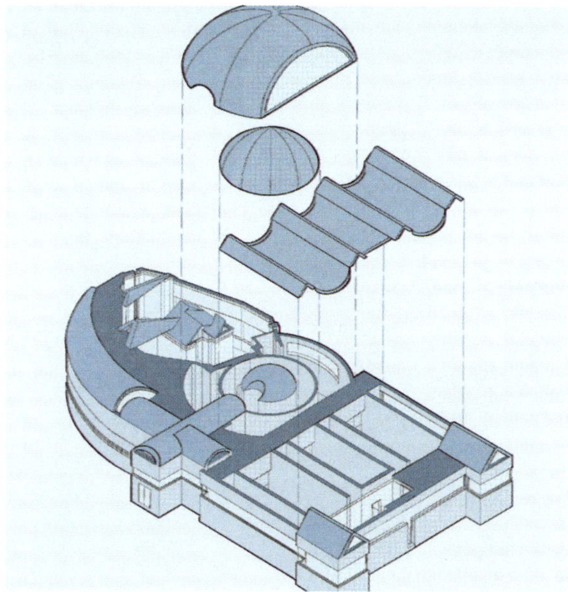

s> Miguel Alvarez Gamez, Javier Castillo, Alyssa Bojenkova, Laura Campbell, Nathanial Maddelene

i> Jesse Toohey

event

Design Showcase

Curated by Megan Saas, Hannah Berryhill, and Luz Briceño

The Design Showcase + Fashion Show is an annual pop-up exhibition at the end of the school year. The inaugural event took place in Fall 2023 in Kendall Cram Hall at Tulane's Lavin Bernick Center. The event features the work of over 100 students enrolled in 8 Design studio courses at Tulane School of Architecture and Built Environment. The Showcase highlights the work of our undergraduate students as they learn to use the power of Design to change the world for the better. The event is free and open to the public with food, drinks, and music. Featured projects include topics such as sustainable textile innovation, non-profit organization branding, innovative multipurpose furniture, nature-inspired light sculptures, and streetcar shelter designs that foster community engagement.

Want to see more pictures?

Image by Professor Mostafa Akbari

6

CLIMATE ADAPTATION

FOR THE COMMON GOOD

CLIMATE CHANGE AND THE REPAIR OF THE BUILT ENVIRONMENT

Adapting the Built Environment

By Jesse M. Keenan
Favrot II Associate Professor of Sustainable Real Estate and Urban Planning and Director of the Center on Climate Change and Urbanism.
Tulane School of Architecture and Built Environment

What if repair meant transforming how we use buildings over time, preserving culture while reducing carbon?

At Tulane School of Architecture and Built Environment, a multitude of faculty are driven by the normative demands and methods of design to advance the material production of the built environment. As the world seeks to decarbonize the built environment, closing the loop of circularity in material extraction may be driven by a variety of approaches. Innovation is not just about the novelty of design and the application of material technologies; it may also be shaped by the practices of preservation and repair. Repair is an increasingly important motivating frame because there is also a critical recognition of the shortcomings of a history of isolation, segregation, and carbonization that have shaped city-making in America.

Very often repair is conceptualized as a replacement of degraded materials and systems. But what if repair was a deeper recognition of the transformation of program and a challenge to the very nature of how we use buildings over time? What if repair and programmatic transformation drove both cultural preservation and the extended amortization of embodied carbon? These questions raise a more fundamental ethical dialogue about whether one can even rationalize some forms of new construction in light of the bounty that already exists in some places.

This might resonate as a clear enough challenge, but many buildings are not designed to transformatively adapt over time. Indeed, light, brittle buildings with a short useful life have their time and place. Beyond this narrow class of buildings, the world is burdened by the inherent conflicts of durability and transformation native to contemporary design and construction.

The material degradation and obsolescence of climate change is well known in buildings, and lifecycle analysis in everything from carbon equivalent to eutrophic emissions is increasingly well-integrated in design. But, what happens when climate renders a building's program obsolete? This obsolescence may be driven by both physical and transition risks. The physical risks may arise in everything from sea level rise inundation to mold saturation that limit residential occupancy, and transition risks may manifest in the obsolescence of everything from gas stations to the office buildings that house the oil and gas services industry. How does one repair a program?

The vernacular and science of adaptive reuse has matured over the course of millennia, but contemporary practice is centered on cost-effective structural conversions that comply with life safety codes. Conversions of commercial buildings to housing tend to populate the popular discourse for programmatic adaptation. The metric of success is not material efficiency or aggregate measures of environmental impact. Rather, success is defined almost entirely by project-level economic savings and population loads. In many cases, a per capita amortization of lifecycle costs that includes the capital expenses of the retrofit far exceed (removing land costs) the costs of new construction when viewed over comparable periods of the useful life of the building. In addition, conversions are locked into perpetuating existing MEP systems that are often obsolete in their own right. This technological path dependency undermines the reality that operational carbon is the true field of play over and above embodied carbon.

In this sense, many are just trying to save face by perpetuating an obsolete building. They are not repairing a program. While there are often unrecognized benefits of avoided transportation, land use, source, and embodied emissions from the same measure of programmatic development at an alternative site, the calculus is often unsatisfying in both its limited utility and its ad hoc design composition. One answer to these challenges comes from the proposition that buildings should be designed to repair their programs.

Designers and developers are tasked with designing the adaptive capacity of a building in year zero. This requires the full parametrization of structural and mechanical configurations that could accommodate a range of different programs in the future (e.g., hotels to senior housing). This often requires redundancy at the cost of existing economic efficiencies and that may in turn drive marginal increases in embodied carbon and operational energy.

However, tools exist to support economic and environmental optimization that nets out the lifecycle implications that include intervening stages of capital investment, operational costs, and future emissions, including a tax on those emissions. Developers have historically balked at the end of investing in designed adaptive capacity because the market did not impose any forward-looking beneficial value on future post-climate programs. However, those days are changing. Forward-looking values discounted by climate change are shaping the entire economy of buildings. Climate adaptive buildings are the best way to repair a program.

At Tulane School of Architecture and Built Environment, our programs in real estate, historic preservation, and architecture are well positioned to define and design this adaptive frontier. ■

ARCH 4042 + 6052 | **Research Studio** | UG + GR | **SP24**

ECOLOGICAL TECTONICS

Architectural Ceramic Assemblies for Climate Adaptation

Adam Marcus [C]

This research studio explores ceramic material assemblies as a locus for expanding architecture's ecological agency. The studio operates across several domains—the material, the communal, and the contextual—to explicitly meld technical knowledge with ecological and social agendas. Projects engage in the tectonic scale of material prototypes, the building scale of domestic architecture, and the ecosystemic scale to synthesize pragmatic questions of fabrication and assembly with social and ecological questions about how architecture can adapt to a changing climate.

Research at the material scale focuses on the production of 3D printed ceramic components and how these systems might open up new forms of ecological performance at an architectural scale. Working in teams, students have deployed this work in a design of a small residential building for a site in New Orleans. They focused on alternative approaches to domesticity and on the building's envelope capacities to modulate climate control, assist with water management, and provide habitat for more-than-human species of plants and animals. This work seeks to reposition the building envelope, traditionally thought of as an impermeable barrier between inside and outside, between humans and "nature," as a deeper, thicker, and more porous assemblage, actively negotiating the sometimes competing and conflicting demands of structure, enclosure, privacy, and habitat. It is in this negotiation that architecture's most elemental purpose—as a boundary, a device of separation—transforms into one of connection, kinship, and ecological stewardship as the envelope becomes recast as a scaffold for multiple forms of life. Full-scale prototypes for this research have been produced in the Digital Ceramics Lab, a new partnership launched in spring 2024 between Tulane School of Architecture and Built Environment and the Newcomb Art Department.

Want to see pictures of the final review?

Students:
Emily Brandt
Ben Cornett
Zaynab Eltiab
Charlotte Kelley
Sophia Lindhal
Kayleigh Macumber
Natalie Miller
Kris Smith
Sofia Vladimir
Daphne Vorel

s> Emily Brandt + Zaynab Eltiab

i> Adam Marcus

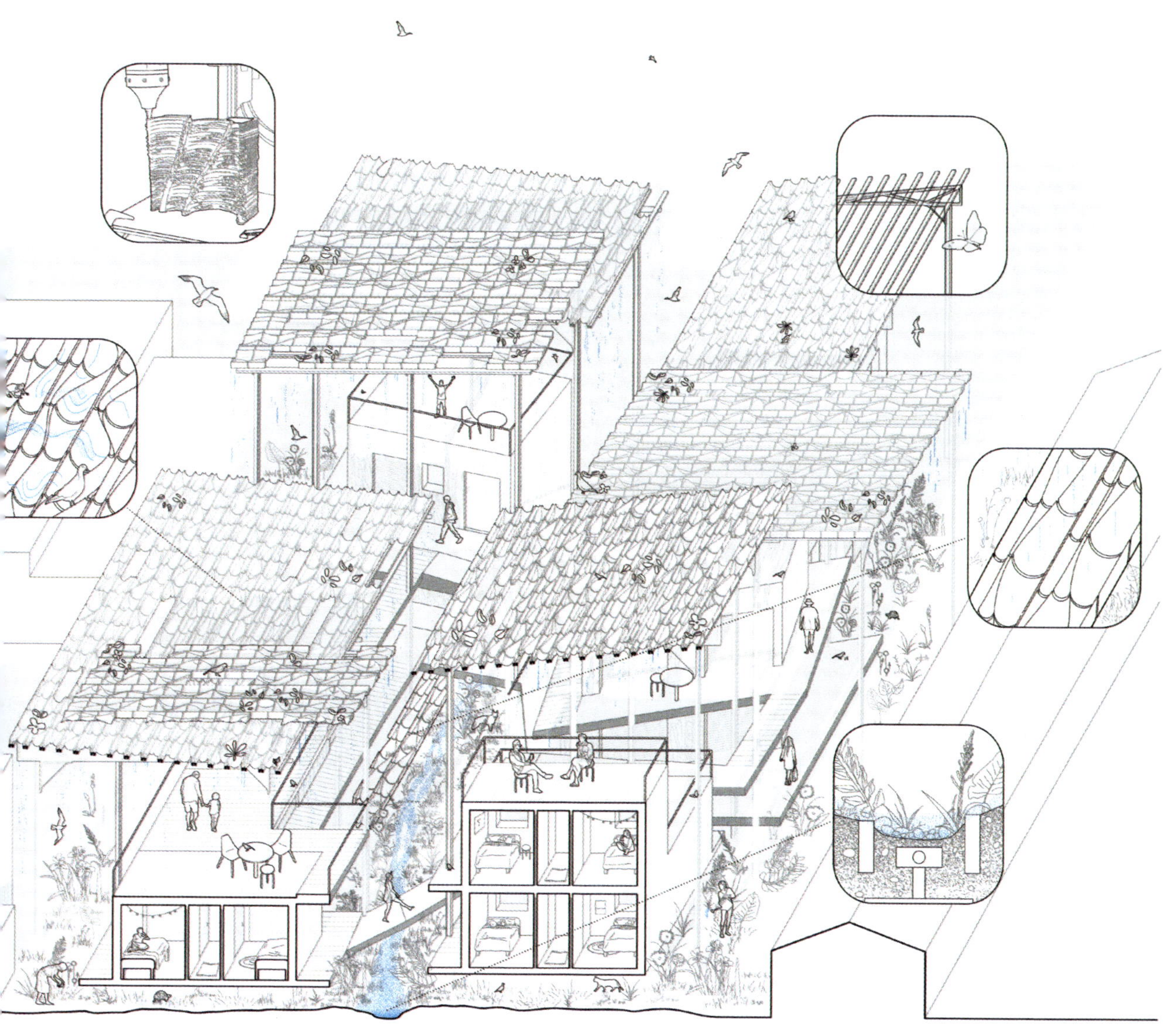

ARCH 4042 + 6052

Research Studio

UG + GR

SP24

Kayleigh Macumber + Ben Cornett

VERTICAL UNDERSTORY

Inspired by the vernacular conditions of New Orleans, this project explores material strategies to promote cohabitation and ecological performance in both passive cooling through evapotranspiration and habitat creation. This project looks to the inherent climatic responsiveness of the traditional shotgun house typology as a starting point for challenging existing paradigms of indoor comfort that rely entirely on mechanical ventilation.

The project incorporates an existing one-story shotgun house and an adjacent lot in the Bywater neighborhood as a testing ground for these ideas. The accidental understory of the shotgun house (due to the required 3-foot elevation above grade for all new construction in New Orleans) becomes an opportunity for considering how deeply familiar contexts might become habitats for fungi and other more-than-human organisms. An elevated first floor permits human access, which is then punctured by vertical columns, composed of 3D printed, ceramic, brick-like modules, that extend the understory conditions vertically, allowing for different types of vegetation to grow according to light access. These columns expand in size to become inhabitable conic volumes, allowing for human occupation as they rise above the understory. The cones introduce multiple scales of space. The micro-scale of the individual brick's textured ceramic exterior loops, sags, and scoops to create niches that promote internal bioreceptivity through unfired clay for fungal growth, and external bioreceptivity through fired clay for leafy plant growth. A gradient of different-sized openings in the textured ceramic façade offers multiple scales for plant habitats, from small-rooted White Clover to climbing Carolina Jessamine, as well as apertures that promote cross ventilation and work with the plants to promote evapotranspiration. At the meso-scale, the ceramic bricks vary and tile across the facade to provide a range of different wall types, from solid walls to more porous conditions, and to promote various scales of plant and fungal growth according to light access. At the macro-scale of the building, the bricks vary based on program to allow for cross-ventilation and plant habitats in specific zones. Spaces for collective living, ecological research, community gathering, and education emerge from the relationship between ecological performance and program, occupying the site corresponding to their climatic and enclosure needs.

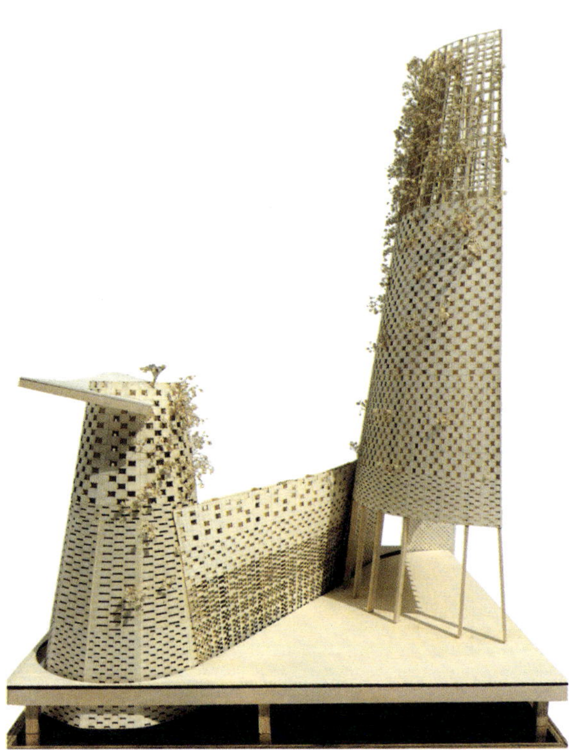

s> Kayleigh Macumber + Ben Cornett **i>** Adam Marcus

ARCH 4042 + 6052

Research Studio

UG + GR

SP24

Daphne Vorel + Sophia Lindahl

COLLECTIVE MEANDER

This project engages with the natural environment and explores new means of integrated domesticity through the connection of collective space with both human and nonhuman inhabitants. This project speculates on how new technologies of design and fabrication might allow us to build greater ecological capacities into conventional building components by reimagining traditional terracotta products.

The facade's variable shingle system integrates typical elements such as the roof gutter, the cistern and the facade cladding. These tectonic parts slow, direct, and store stormwater, while also providing an environment for microbes that can engage in bioremediation. The utilization of 3D printed clay ceramics allows for careful variation of these components through geometry, texture, and aperture, as well as their integration into the domestic space.

 Sophia Lindhal + Daphne Vorel

i> Adam Marcus

ARCH 4042 + 6052 | **Research Studio** | UG + GR | **SP24**

Natalie Miller + Kris Smith

ECO-CERAMIC POROSITY

This project, a multi-family dwelling for the Bywater neighborhood of New Orleans, explores the ecological performance of ceramics in two ways: passive ventilation and bio-receptivity. Passive ventilation is produced by designing sectional geometries according to Bernoulli's principle, which states that air flow is accelerated under volumetric compression. Bio-receptivity is promoted by creating habitat conditions for lichen, moss, and fungi. Traditionally regarded as a nuisance on architectural ceramic surfaces like roofs and gutters, these species offer significant benefits, including oxygen production, pollution absorption, nitrogen fixation, and support of more biodiverse habitats within the broader ecosystem. These species grow best on rough, porous, nutrient-rich substrates and thrive best in indirect sunlight, minimal wind flow, and dampness.

The building surrounds a central courtyard space and has different levels of communal living. The building envelope consists of 3D printed ceramic modules that vary in texture, glaze, and aperture based on promoting these ecological conditions. The cross-ventilation modules are glazed and have small apertures with no texture, while the bio-receptive habitat modules are unglazed and have larger apertures with more texture. The placement of the different ceramic module types depends on site conditions, such as wind flow, visibility or privacy, and sun exposure. Various levels of exterior spaces, like the central courtyard and communal and private balconies, present different conditions to which the parametrically variable facade system can respond.

s> Natalie Miller + Kris Smith

i> Adam Marcus

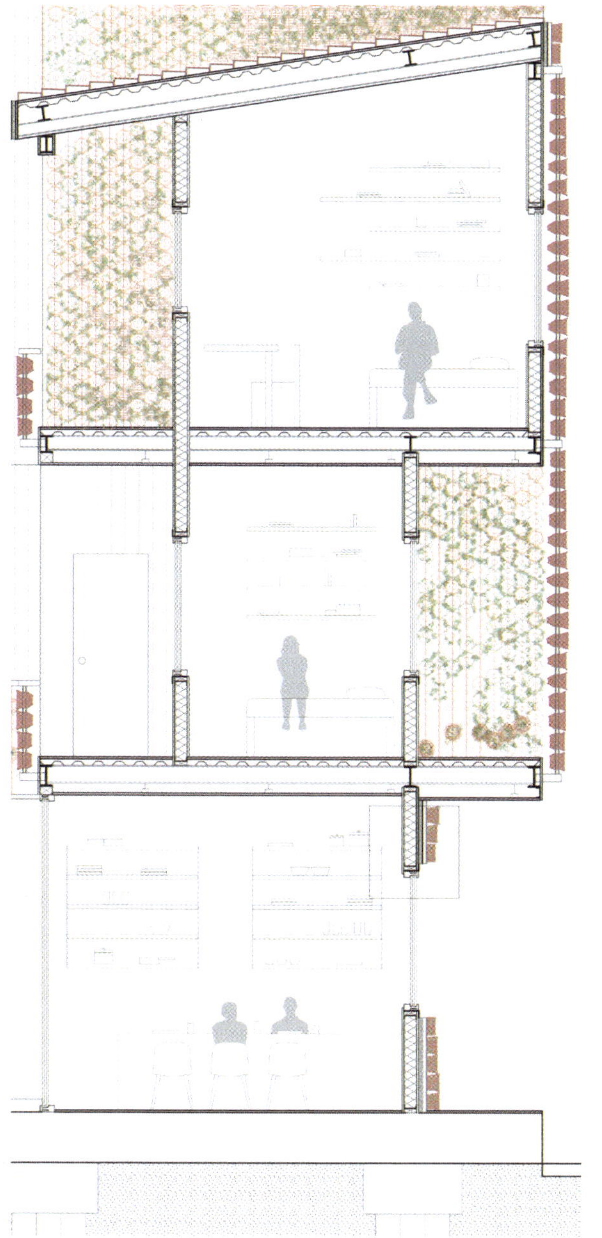

ARCH 4042 + 6052

Research Studio

UG + GR

SP24

Charlotte Kelley + Sofia Vladimir

CERAMIC WETLANDS

The long history of extraction and unequal displacement in New Orleans has left a vulnerable gap inenergy efficient building strategies and thoughtful affordable housing on land that has been stripped ofmuch of its natural resilience. As a response to this predicament, this project proposes a constructedextension of pre-existing wetland systems in the Gulf South by wrapping both an existing and newstructure with a ceramic envelope that directs and slows rainwater before gently releasing it into a naturalrain garden. This happens on the plane of the roof, the wall, and the ground. Fabricating three facademodule types with 3D printed clay ceramics allows for controlled porosity at various scales. Whether it befrom the controlled failure of the printer to create water gaps or the material property of clay itself, thismethod is integral to the rainwater strategy of the project. Additionally, using ceramics for the buildingskin and timber for the building frame minimizes the carbon footprint of the materials because of theirlocal abundance in the Southeast U.S.The spatial organization of this project reinterprets an existing historic shotgun with a side gallery andlarge side yard for multiple inhabitants, adding a new structure that mirrors the original and containsprimarily communal spaces as well as several living units. The project builds upon the vernacularorganization of the linear New Orleans shotgun but maximizes the number of living units on the site,offering a model for denser and more communal inhabitation. The larger communal spaces are a hybrid ofinterior and exterior, allowing for comfort and open social space in a way that does not depend onmechanical systems and allows the living units to be more minimal. The circulation of inhabitants isdriven by cross ventilation, and the circulation of water is driven by passive cooling opportunities andproximity to porous ground. As a prototype, the project speculates how architecture and constructionmight rethink its traditions to be more in alignment with their local contexts and approaching futures ofclimate change.

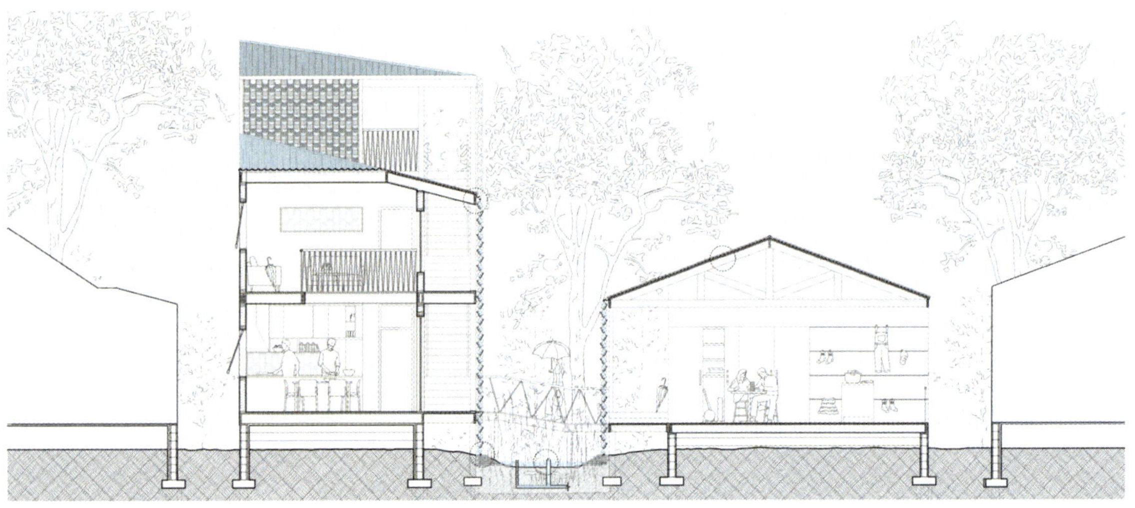

WALL TILE
Speed +Flow

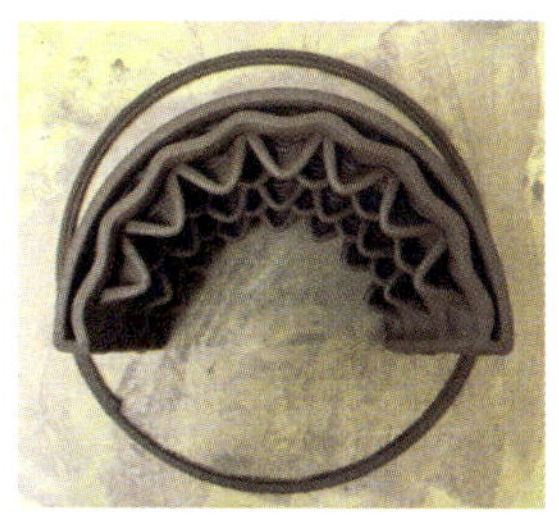

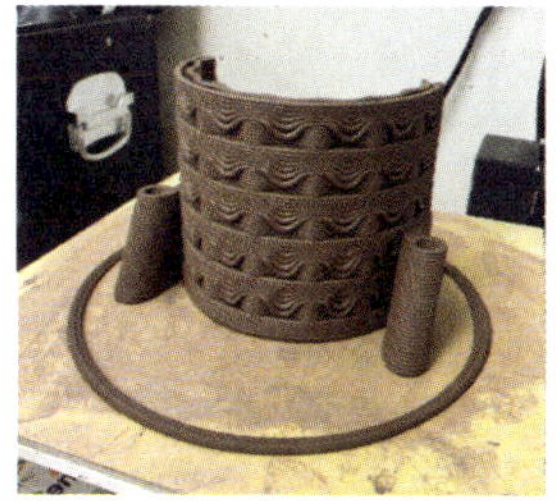

Printing

Module (Printing Orientation)

Water Flow

Aggregation

PERCOLATION PAVER
Soil Erosion + Plant Growth

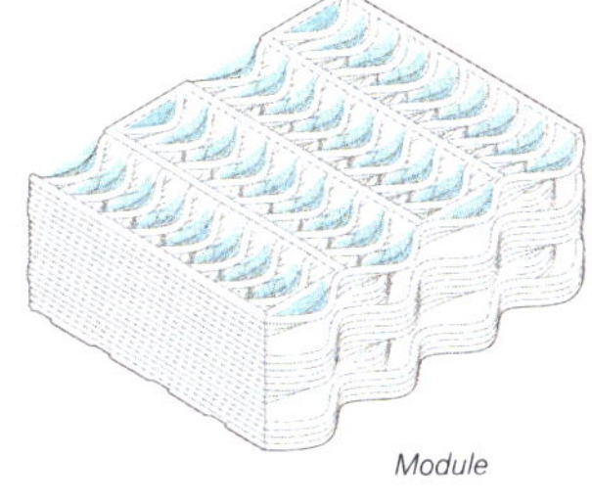

Module

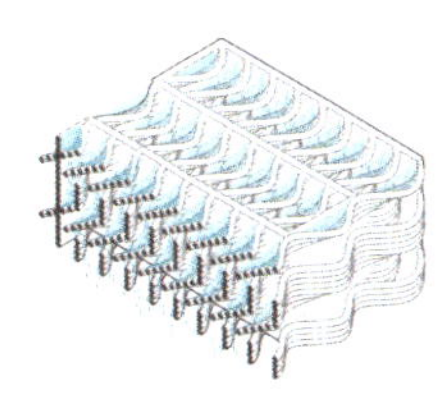

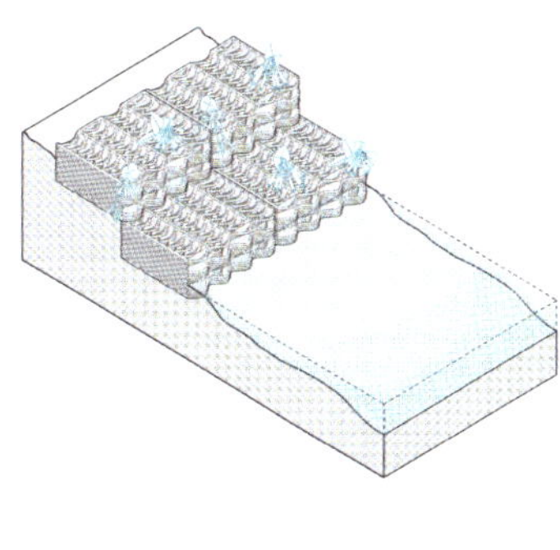

Emily Brandt + Zaynab Eltiab

STORM/WATER/SHED

This project explores stormwater management as a mechanism for forging critical links between humans, the environment, and time. Comprised of a kit of parts with varying material lifespans, the project anticipates varying roles, inhabitants, and degrees of construction and deconstruction as it ages, aspiring to eventually reintegrate into its environment. Several large roof planes reach across site boundaries before guiding rainwater down. Ceramic modules slowly splinter the water's path across, utilizing texture to variably manage flow speed. Solid elements of architecture and collective human habitation are stilted above ground to liberate the earth below, so that rain eventually disperses to meet soil and a bioswale that continues to filter and retain water before it reaches the municipal stormwater system.

These small interventions accumulate to marginally relieve New Orleans' pumping system as well as accelerate ecological processes on site. Aging and deterioration is imperative to this project's function. Time and circumstance influence which inhabitants are hosted, as well as what resources, liberties, and matter are offered to the immediate environment.

s> Emily Brandt + Zaynab Eltiab

i> Adam Marcus

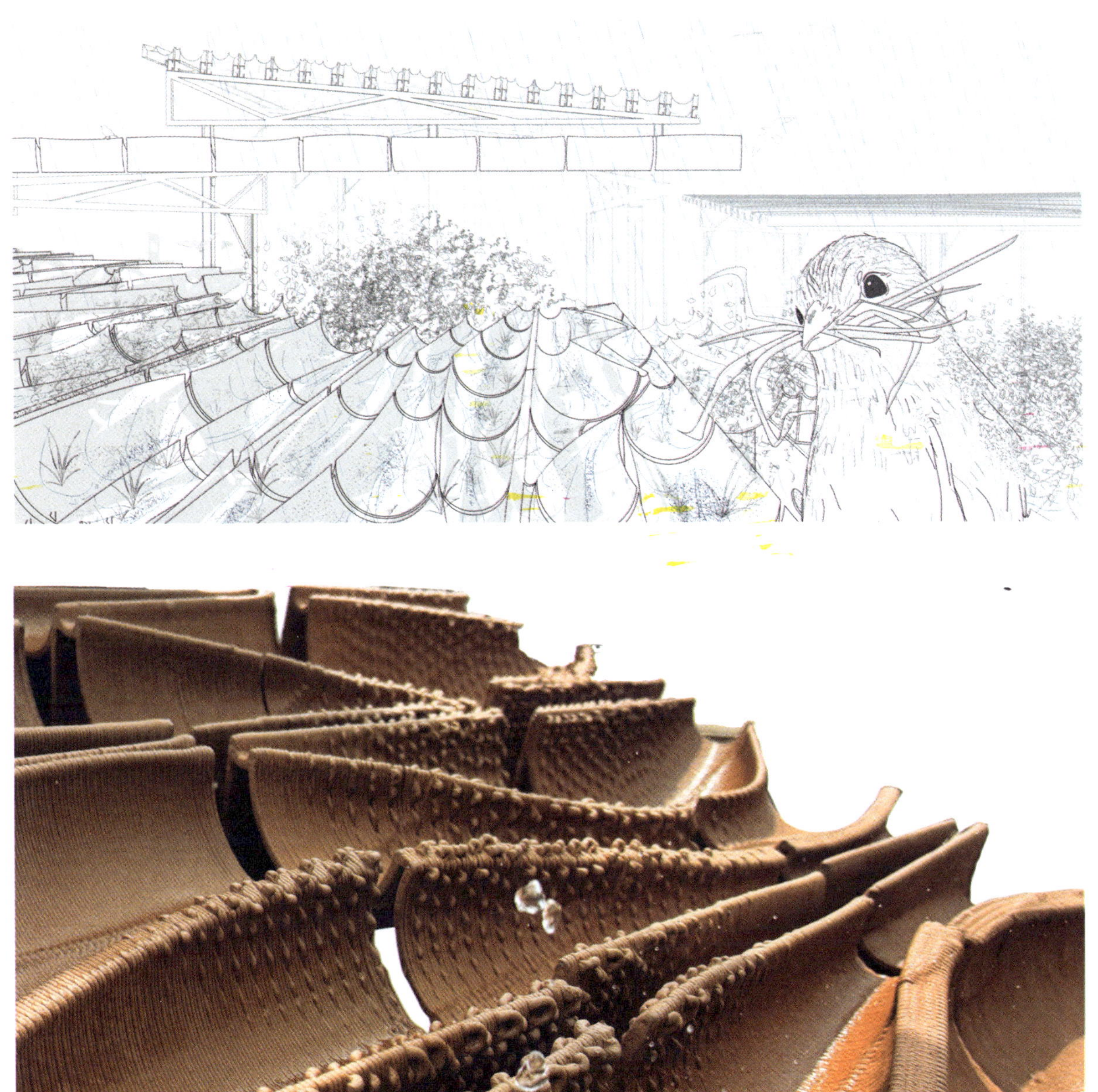

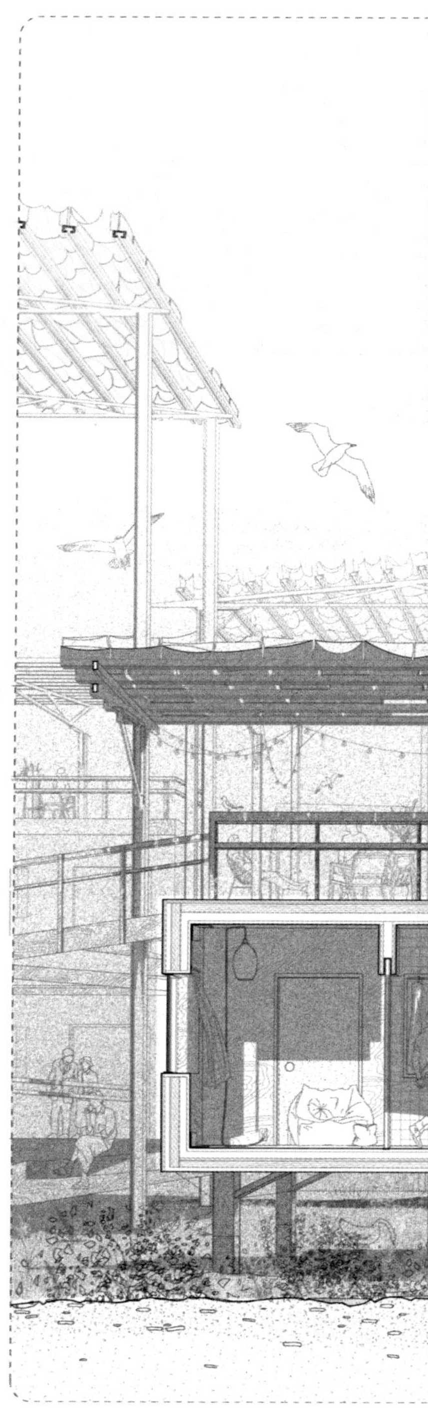

s> Emily Brandt + Zaynab Eltiab

i> Adam Marcus

ARCH 4041/5051 + 6041/6051 | **Research Studio** | UG + GR | **FA23**

DOMESTICATING BIGNESS

Data-Driven Environmental Conditioners

Zaid Kashef Alghata[C]

During the 20th century, metaphorical and literal shifting terrains compelled architects to adapt built environments to the evolving political, socio-economic, and environmental contexts. Architectural designs gradually transitioned from mere aesthetic symbols to reflect the nuanced interplay of ecological dynamics, embracing the microcosmic nuances within infrastructures and the macrocosmic expanses that tie them together.

Fast forward to the contemporary era, where global paradigms such as the pandemic's onslaught and technological breakthroughs have further complicated the urban matrix. The discourse has now evolved beyond simply interiorizing nature, as seen in the endeavors of 19th-century estate owners. The discipline grapples with domesticating these vast spatial and temporal phenomena in an era punctuated by the emergence of artificial landforms, expansive water supply infrastructures, and other 'hyperobject' scales of intervention. Today's challenge lies in navigating this intricate lattice of data, design, and machinery—a nexus reminiscent of weather stations which, in their duality as both inputs and outputs, echo the ongoing tension between nature and the built environment.

Focusing on the intricate situation in New Orleans, the existing flood protection infrastructure, developed post-Katrina, is deteriorating more rapidly than anticipated and needs to be equipped to address the fast-rising Gulf waters and other climatic challenges. These infrastructural shortcomings and projections of impending extreme weather events necessitate an urgent reevaluation of urban planning and resilience strategies. Given the latest data, which includes novel storm-surge predictions and insights into regional sea level rise rates, we must recognize the immediate need to ideate sustainable architectural solutions. Under constant threat, the current infrastructure demands innovations that can withstand the rapid effects of climate change.

Drawing from real-world examples like Hong Kong's exterior systems, infrastructure is explored as not only functional but performative, extending beyond walls into the urban environment. Parameters are determined by innovative approaches to sensing the environment and subsequent actions, inviting participants to conceive unique environmental conditioners balancing function and performance. Critical analysis of multi-use infrastructure considers aesthetic and spatial attributes and addresses environmental injustices. Exploration of new land use functions involves pondering questions about defining, aestheticizing, and addressing environmental issues. Ultimately, the course aims to envision, present, and execute environmental tasks, navigating the evolving dynamics between the visible and invisible and the active and passive aspects of built environments.

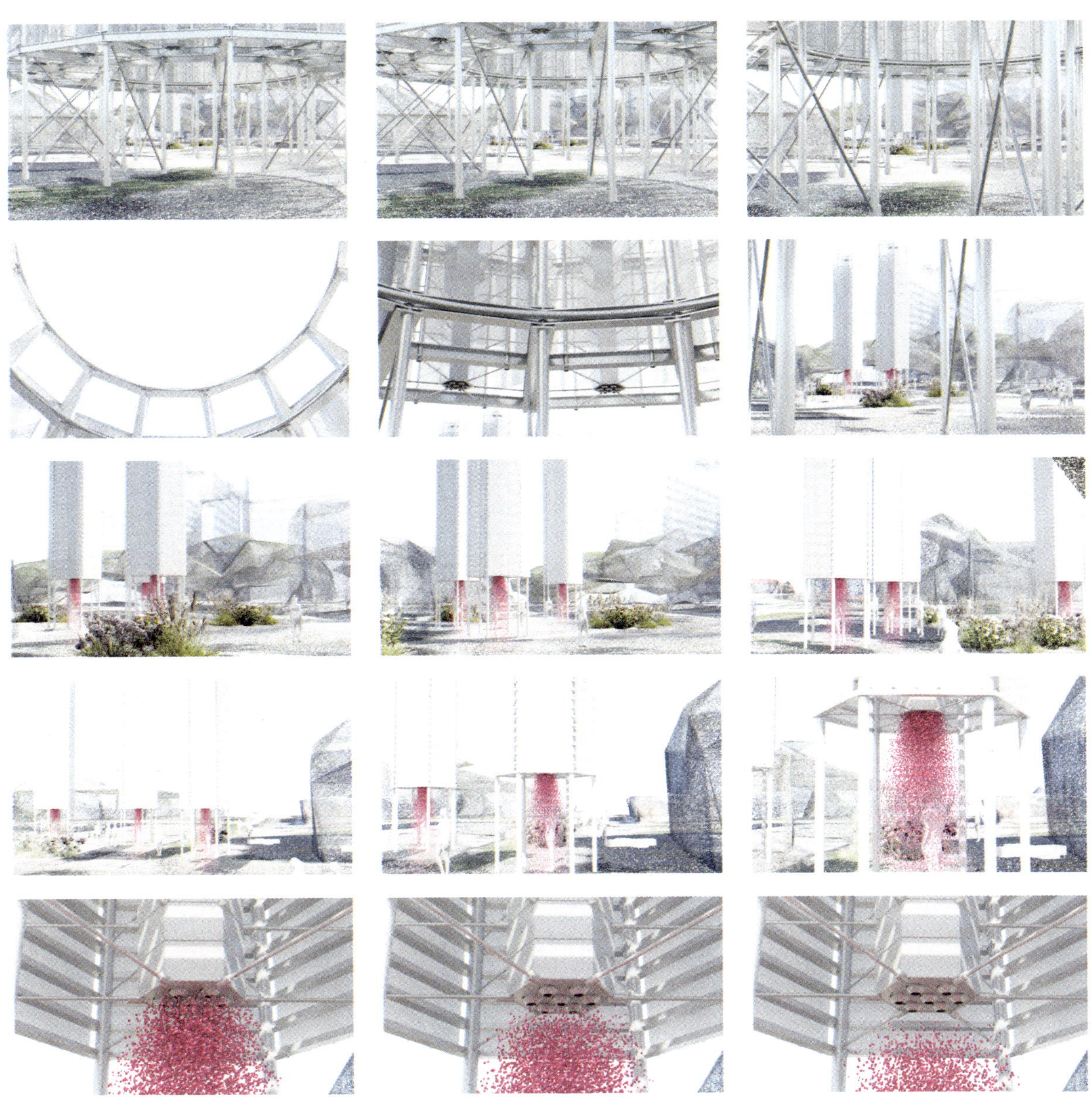

ARCH 4041/5051 + 6041/6051

Research Studio

UG + GR

FA23

Chelsea Kilgore

ENVIRONMENTAL CONDITIONERS AND EXTREME HEAT

ADAPTION, MITIGATION, AND IMPLICATIONS ON THE BUILT ENVIRONMENT

This project seeks to revolutionize responses to extreme urban heat by harnessing environmental conditioners as transformative catalysts. The project seeks to shift from energy-intensive and individualistic cooling practices toward a civic collective infrastructure known as the "cooling commons." Critically evaluating existing mechanical cooling solutions, the project identifies them as contributors to negative feedback loops that prioritize human activities, positioning the climatic condition as an adversary to be conquered, and creating divisions between interior and exterior space.

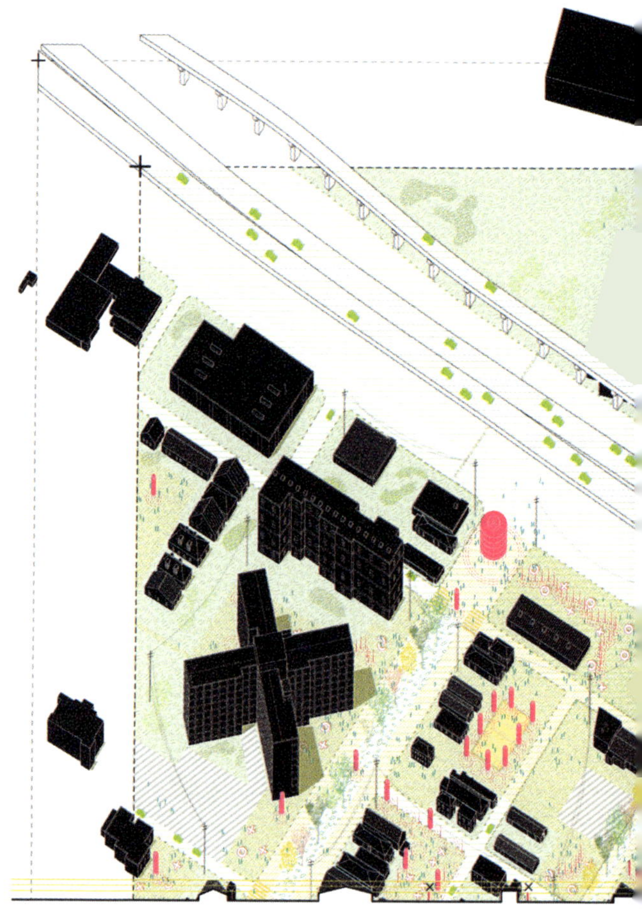

Beginning with a comprehensive conceptual framework, the research addresses the urban heat island effect attributed to anthropogenic factors, particularly increased pavements. Categorizing adaptations and mitigations, the project distinguishes between passive and mechanical solutions. Existing mechanical cooling methods are scrutinized for their tendencies to over-control the natural in favor of the human, ultimately exacerbating climate extremes.

To disrupt these cycles, the project explores mechanical environmental conditioners inspired by natural cooling phenomena—evaporative cooling, ventilation, and convection. These conditioners are strategically designed for operation within public spaces, utilizing processes like evaporation, ventilation, and convection to optimize existing climatic conditions.

s> Chelsea Kilgore

i> Zaid Kashef Alghata

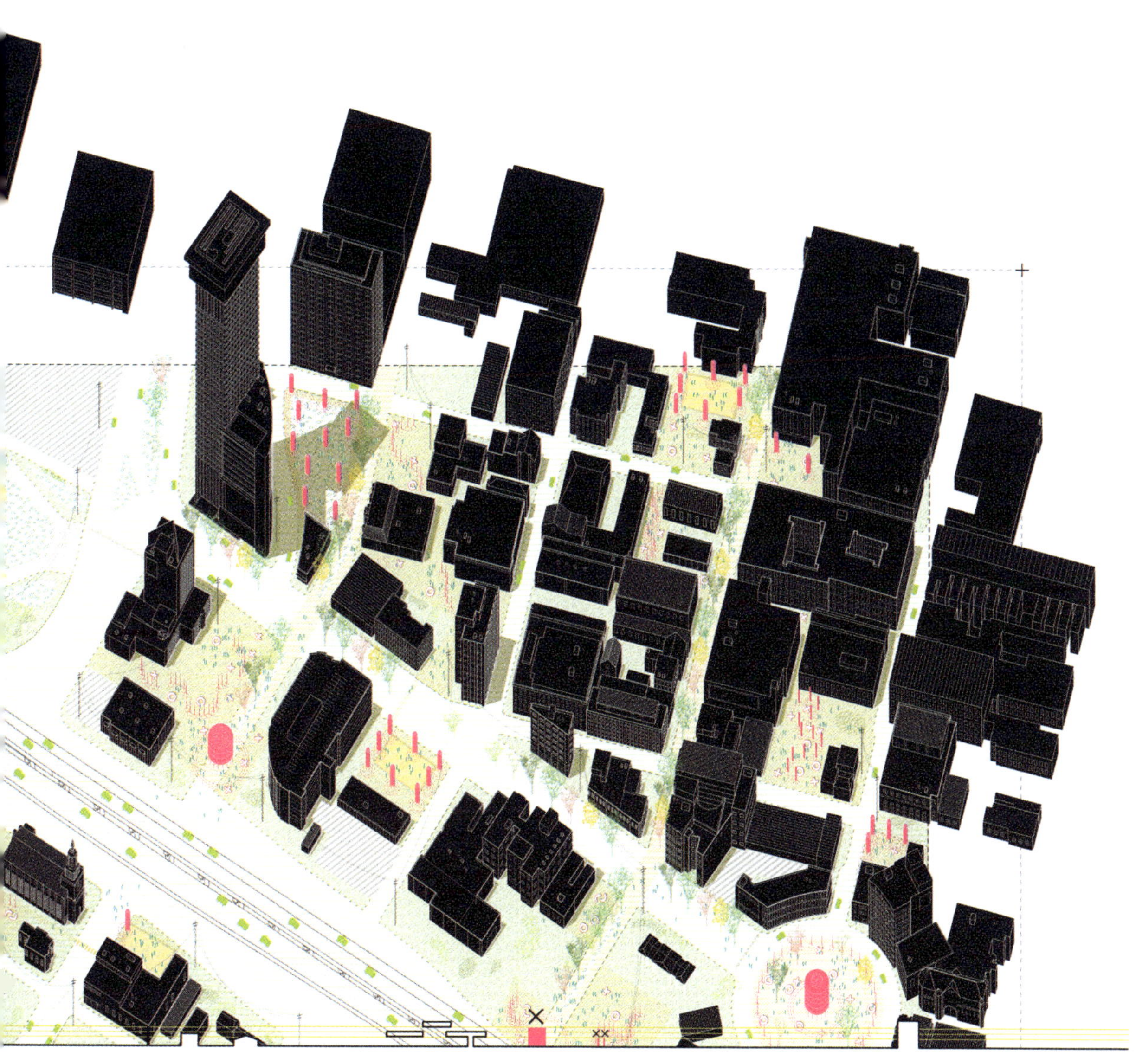

ARCH
4041/5051
+ 6041/6051

Research Studio

UG
+ GR

FA23

The project focuses on the Greater New Orleans area, where the urban heat island effect intensifies due to impervious surfaces and transit corridors. The objects' implementation within public space facilitates the creation of a "cooling commons," activating space in new ways during extreme heat events. These work to combat individualistic cooling mechanisms, decrease energy consumption, and establishes thermal comfort as a public right. The proposed shift from individualized cooling infrastructure to a cooling commons influences both the plan and section of the urban space, aiming to disrupt spatial interdependencies between impervious surfaces, transit infrastructure, heat severity, and health risks.

Implementation of environmental conditioners within the public realm is envisioned as a catalyst for broader urban investments, such as increased tree planting and the creation of new recreational spaces. The conditioners act as both active adaptations to the urban heat extremes, maintaining human comfort and health through new strategies that disrupt the energy intensive existing methods, as well as passive mitigators that catalyze larger urban changes whose goal is to diminish the urban heat island effect through dismantling impervious landscapes and fostering a more sustainable and collective approach to urban cooling.

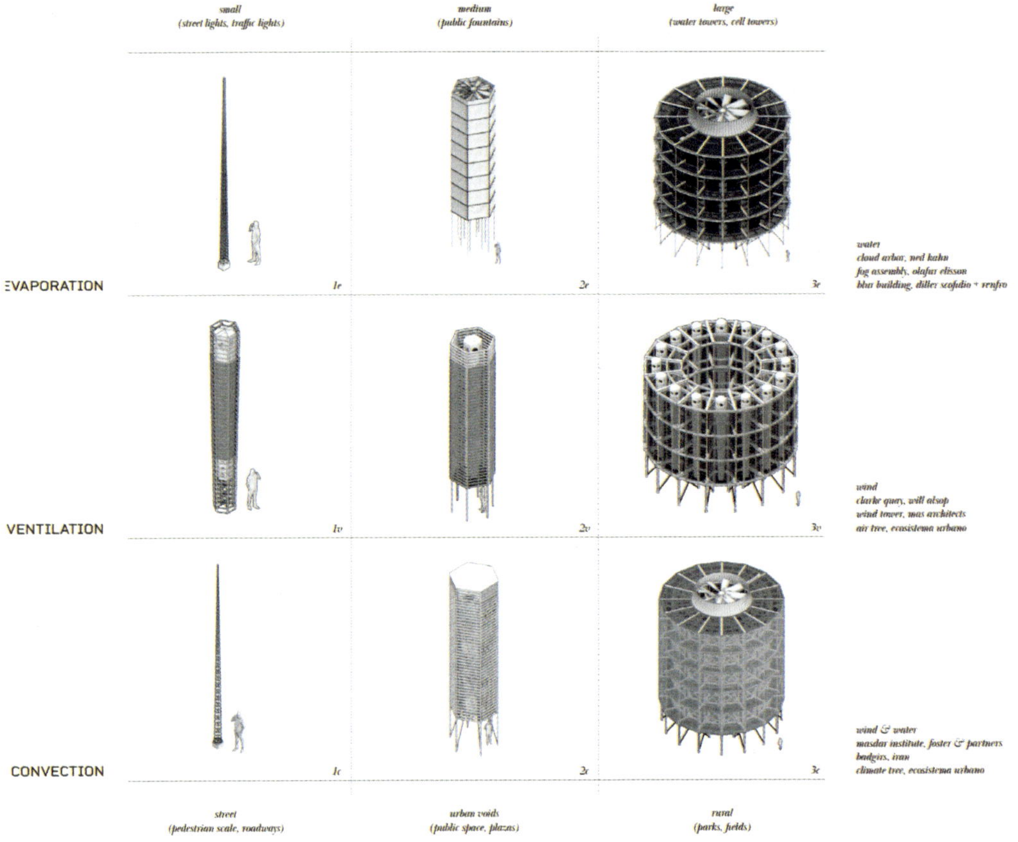

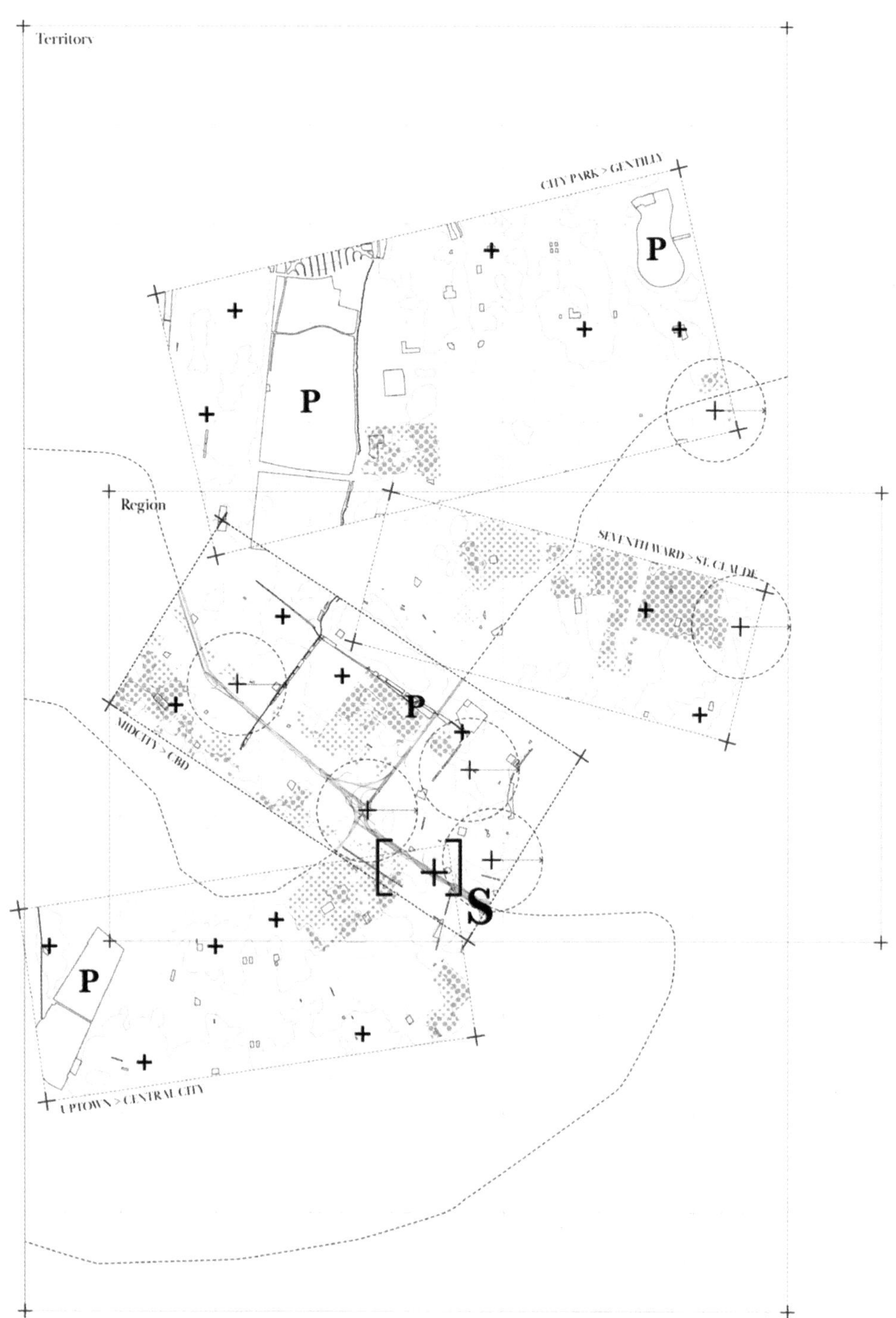
Territory
CITY PARK > GENTILLY
Region
SEVENTH WARD > ST. CLAUDE
MIDCITY > CBD
UPTOWN > CENTRAL CITY
P
P
P
P
S

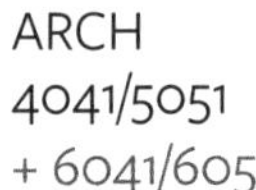

ARCH 4041/5051 + 6041/6051 **Research Studio** UG + GR **FA23**

Max Kronengold

BREATH OF FRESH AIR

MITIGATING AIR POLLUTANTS WITH PHOTOBIOREACTORS

This project investigates the use of environmental cooling machines to create spots of thermal comfort in historically red-lined communities. Historically red-lined communities were preyed on for the development of manufacturing facilities, waste plants, and highways resulting in more impervious surface thus much hotter temperature due to the Urban Heat Island Effect. The nine machines use different passive and active cooling strategies such as evaporative cooling to create areas of thermal comfort during these times of extreme heat. The cool areas can be used for a variety of programs including playgrounds, farmers markets, and religious congregations.

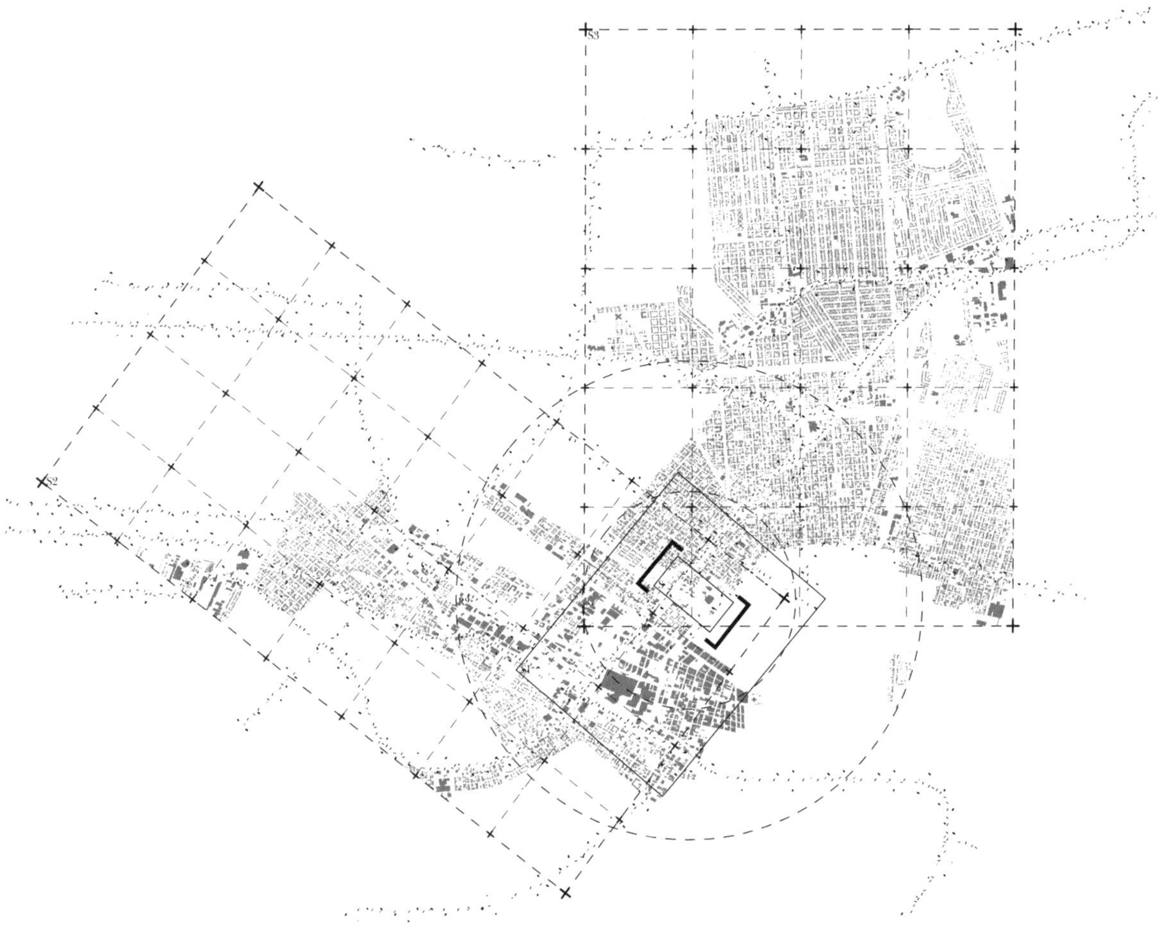

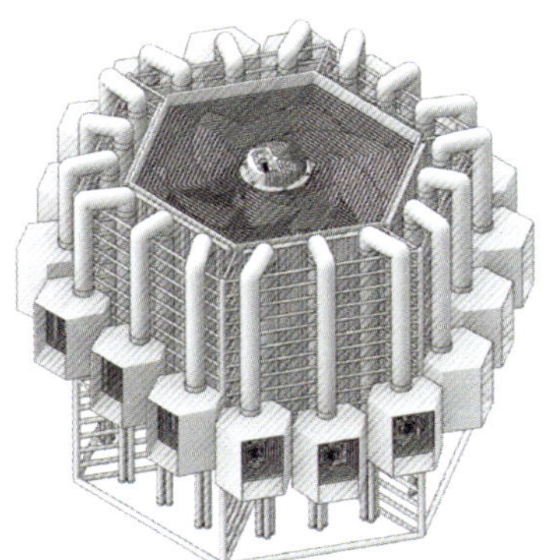

Air Fountain 3.0

An apparatus and method for directly providing clean air to a person's respiratory system.

Shower 3.0

An apparatus and method for showering clean air from above.

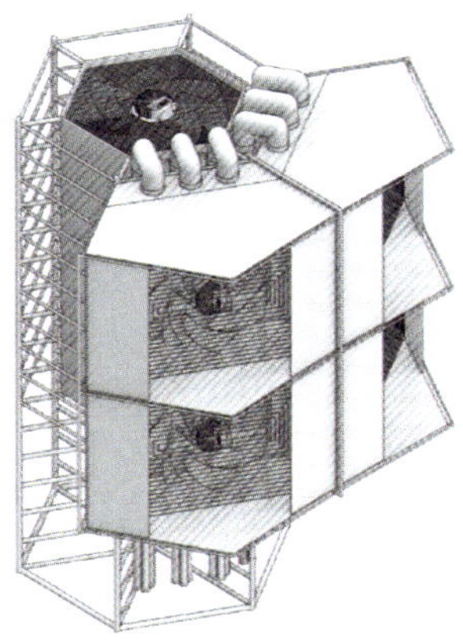

Hydrant 1.0

An apparatus and method for dispensing clean air at high speeds.

ARCH 4041/5051 + 6041/6051 | **Research Studio** | UG + GR | **FA23**

Livi Bowers

CREATING SPOTS OF PLAY

EQUITABLE COMMERCIAL AND SOCIAL GROWTH

This project investigates the use of environmental cooling machines to create spots of thermal comfort in historically red-lined communities. These communities were preyed on for the development of manufacturing facilities, waste plants, and highways resulting in more impervious surface thus much hotter temperature due to the Urban Heat Island Effect. The nine machines use different passive and active cooling strategies such as evaporative cooling to create areas of thermal comfort during these times of extreme heat. The cool areas can be used for a variety of programs including playgrounds, farmers markets, and religious congregations.

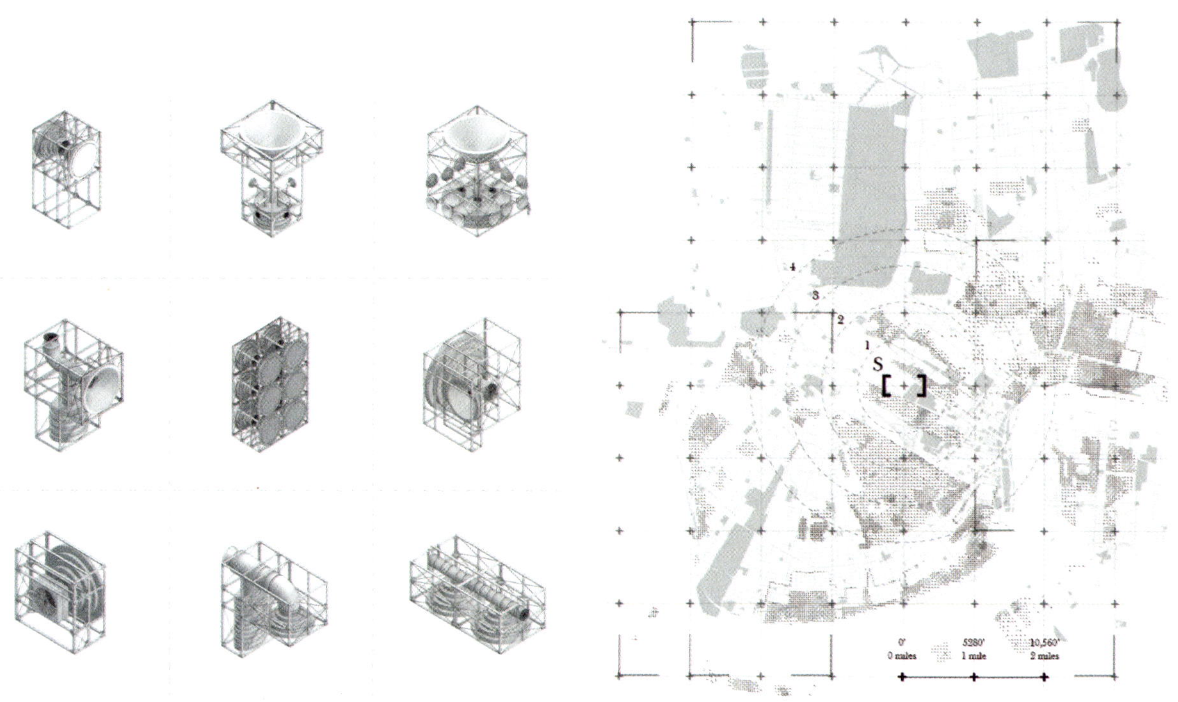

s> Livi Bowers, Leo Dumonteil **i>** Zaid Kashef Alghata

Leo Dumonteil

CITY LIGHTS

URBAN MITIGATION STRATEGY FOR SEASONAL AFFECTIVE DISORDERS

The following project aims to address the issue of Seasonal Affective Disorder (SAD), commonly known as Seasonal Depression. This issue was approached through the lens of infrastructure development as well as machine design and technology. Nonetheless, the project still required extensive research to understand what solutions already exist and what can be done to improve them. This research pointed at existing technologies such as Ultra-violet therapy lights, aromatic diffusers, and light filtering materials. These elements would become the building blocks for the machines to be developed. As a result, 9 machines were developed to address UV exposure and protection and employ aromatherapy as an additional mitigation tool.

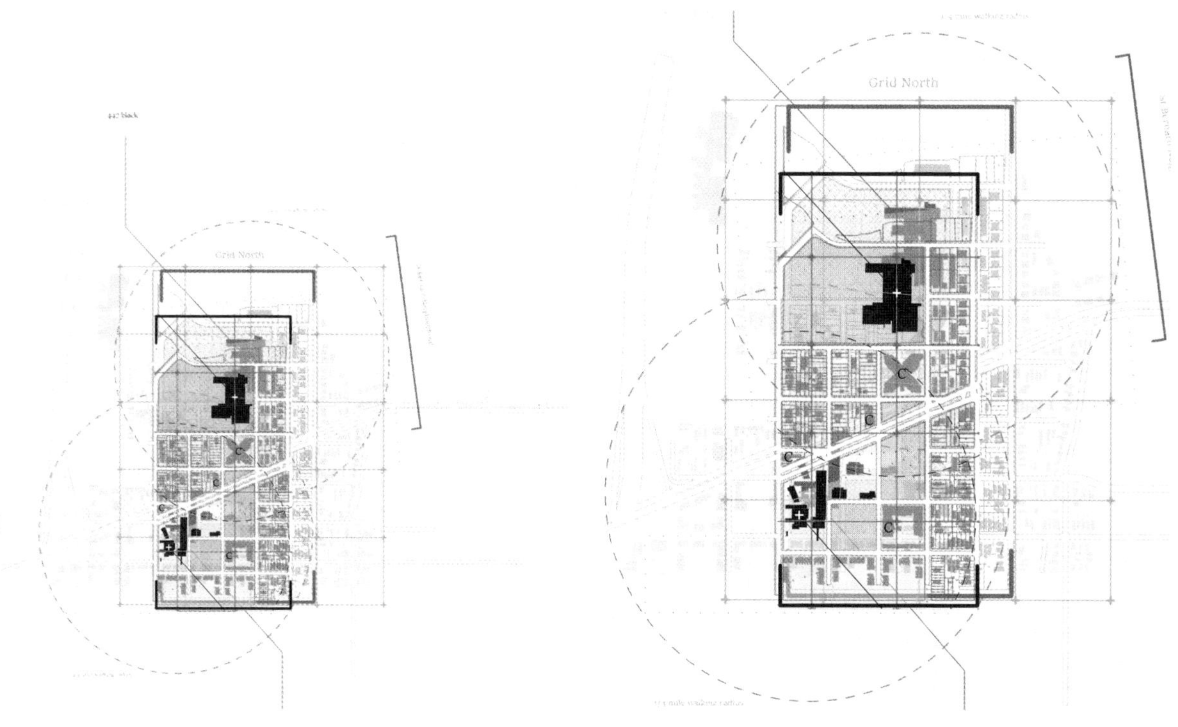

BUILDING, CLIMATE & COMFORT

Sonsoles Vela Navarro [C]

Creating energy-efficient homes is becoming increasingly crucial for our environment, for the wellbeing of individuals and communities and also for our wallets. The key to obtaining maximum efficiency is the strategic implementation of both passive and active systems working together. Architects are in a prime position firstly to encourage clients to choose sustainable options and secondly to ensure the strategic integration of environmental systems into their designs.

Active Systems are required for maintaining the desired environmental conditions within a space. The architect of a building should have sufficient basic knowledge of HVAC (Heating, Ventilating, and Cooling/Air-Conditioning) systems, and can on an equal level with the installation designer, develop ideas and concepts that are worked out in detail by the specialist.

It is not always necessary to install a complex active system to realize an acceptable thermal condition indoors. In this, the building design is an essential factor. Good thermal insulation, high-performance glazing, outdoor solar shading, the use of thermal mass, and night ventilation can sometimes jointly make a cooling system redundant. These forms of passive climate control need less energy for cooling as well as heating and make the indoor environment more stable. Even in combination with an active climate control system, good passive design can make environmental conditions more comfortable.

The architect's basic understanding and ability to design and manipulate their buildings will be especially important as we move into a future where climate change has become a reality and the environmental regulations on the building environment will tighten. Therefore, architects must adapt and respond to every project, whether related to new construction or not.

To address the course, the instructor will present core technical principles in the content lectures and then lead the students on how to apply that lecture content to the real world through H.W. problems and integrated lab sessions to use them in their professional career interests.

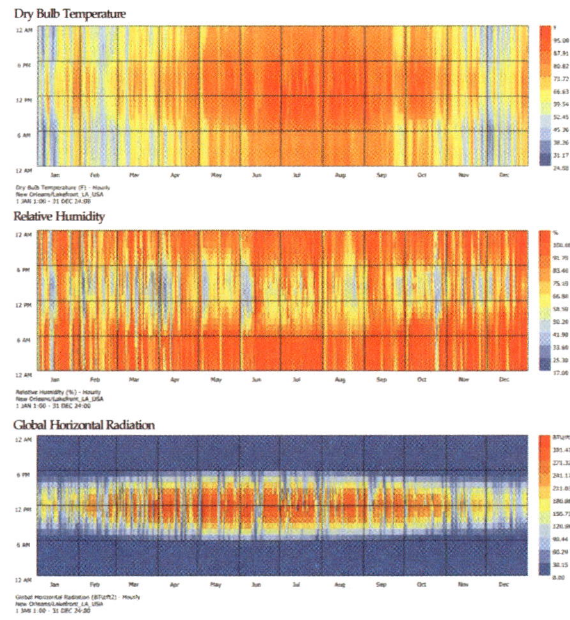

Dry Bulb Temperature

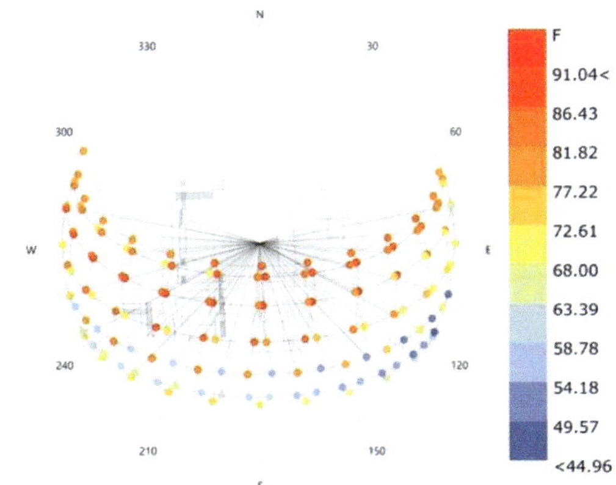

Relative Humidity

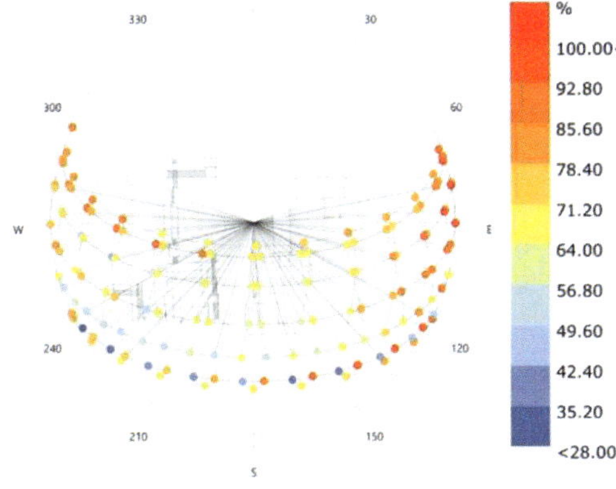

Global Horizontal Radiation

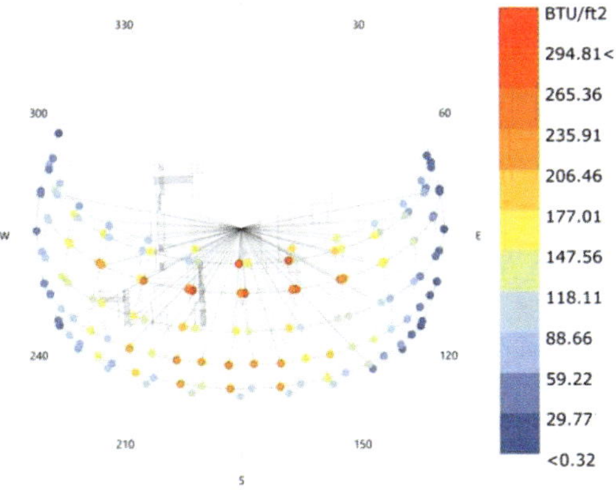

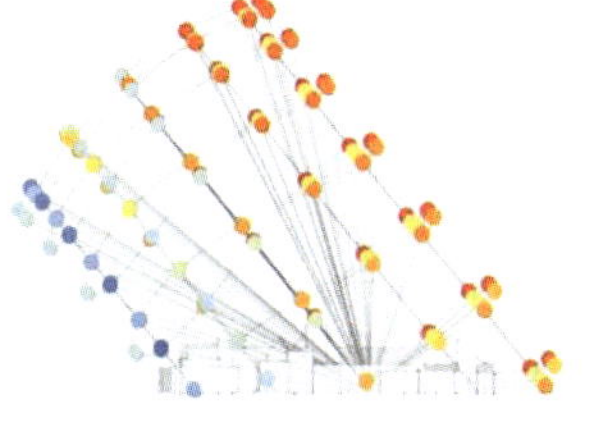

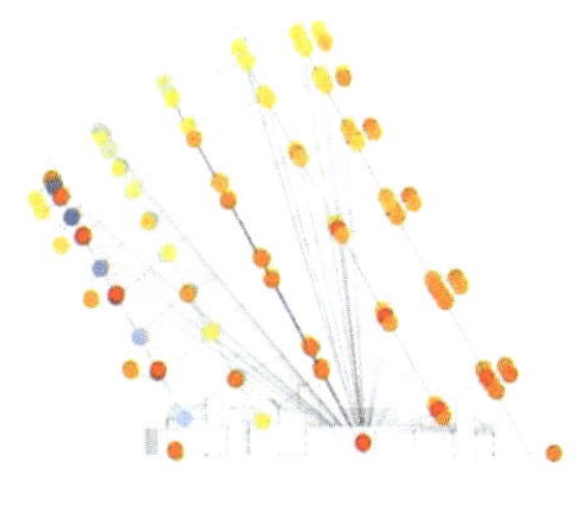

New Orleans is located at 30 Degrees N where it has relatively high radiation and sun position. By minimizing radiation heat gain in the Summer and maximizing in the Winter, the hours of comfort can be increased.

In order to determine the scope of work, an understanding of climate characteristics needs to be defined. The Sun Path Diagram illustrates the critical areas where solar heat gain and sun position would be a factor while combining the data from cloud coverage and radiation level diagrams.

ARCH 2213 + 6213

Required Course

UG + GR

SP24

Illuminance Lux

Leed Credits

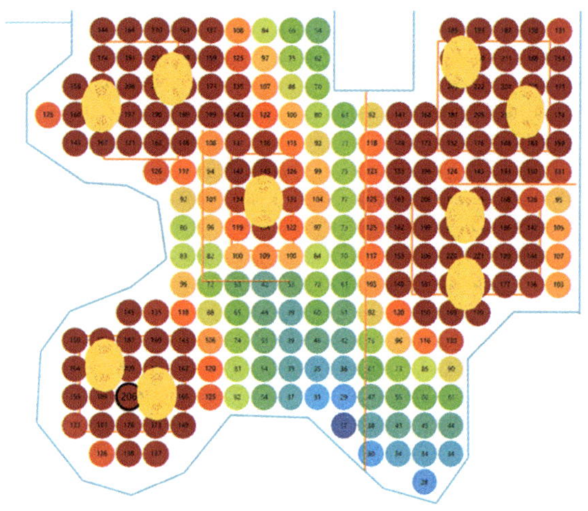

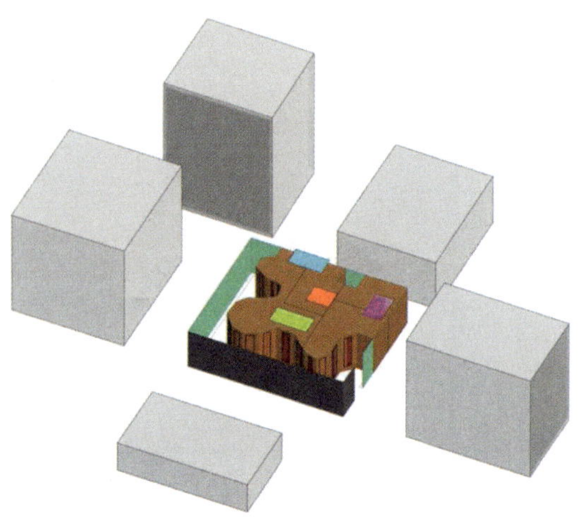

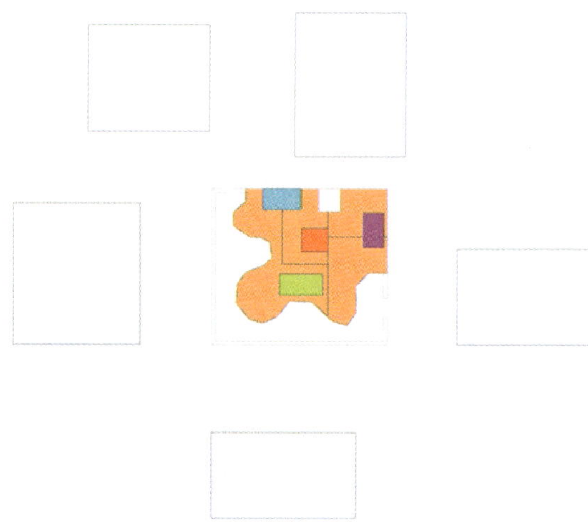

s> Brooks Barrios, Kierston Wilson

Redmond, Oregon

Illuminance
Winter Solstice Summer Solstice

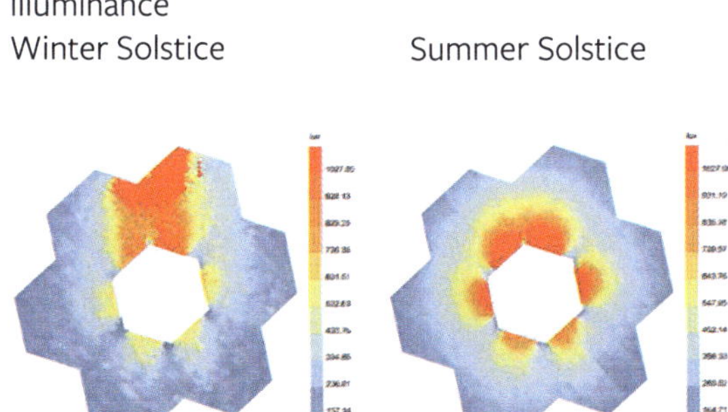

The daylight analysis of the Hexagonal Home in Redmond, Oregon revealed a lot about the luminance. In the bedrooms, the lux is between 164.71 near the outer walls and up to 643.76 along the window walls-the required lux in bedrooms is 100-300 so the rooms meet that requirement. The kitchen ranges in lux from 643.76-1027 in both the Summer and Winter. This meets the 750 lux minimum requirement on the counter top. In the living room the lux ranges from 164.71-931.19 throughout the Summer and Winter. This meets the minimum requirement of 300-500 lux. Overall, the entire home meets the minimum lux requirements for a family home.

Redmond, Oregon

Spatial Daylight Autonomy Summer Solstice
Winter Solstice

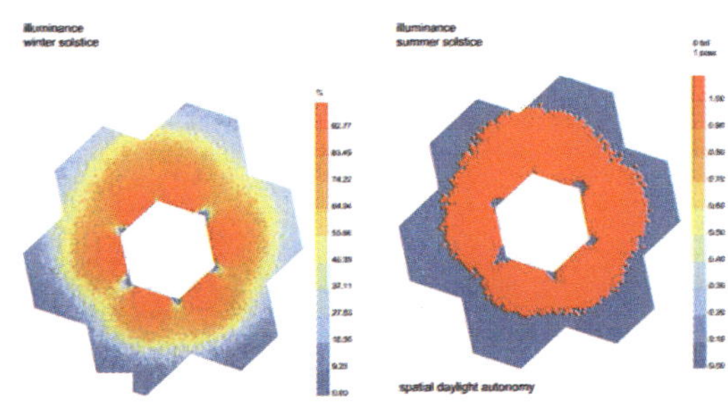

i> Sonsoles Vela Navarro

Miami, Florida

Illuminance
Winter Solstice Summer Solstice

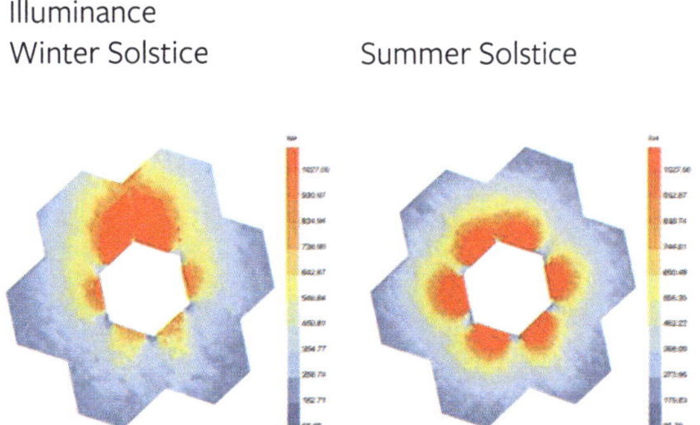

The daylight analysis of the Hexagonal Home in Miami, Florida revealed a lot about the luminance. In the bedrooms, the lux is between 179.83 near the outer walls and up to 1027 along the window walls-the required lux in bedrooms is 100-300 so the rooms meet that requirement. The kitchen ranges in lux from 744.61-1027 in both the Summer and Winter. This meets the 750 lux minimum requirement on the counter top. In the living room the lux ranges from 273.96-1027 throughout the Summer and Winter. This meets the minimum requirement of 300-500 lux. Overall, the entire home meets the minimum lux requirements for a family home.

Miami, Florida

Spatial Daylight Autonomy Summer Solstice
Winter Solstice

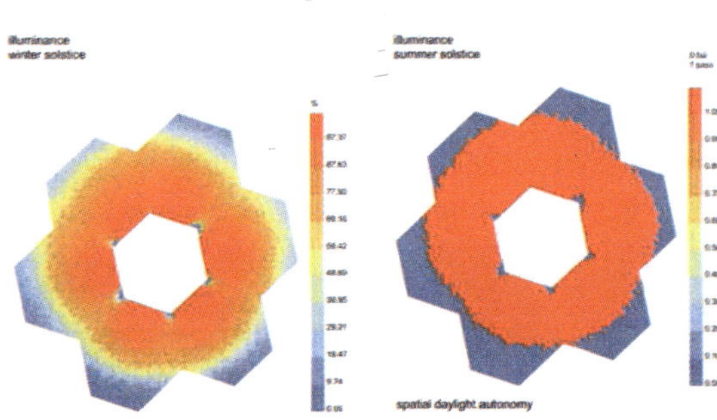

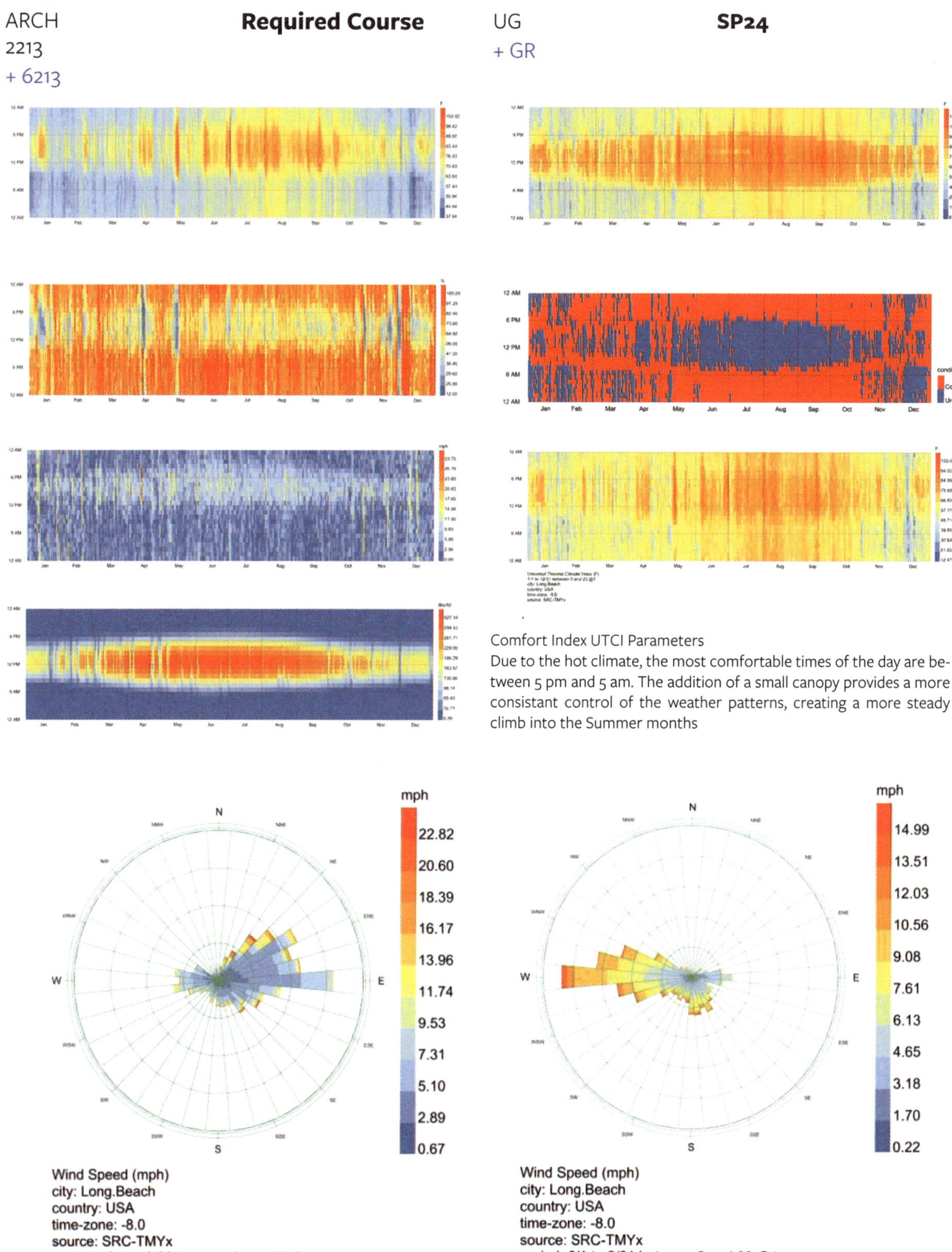

Comfort Index UTCI Parameters

Due to the hot climate, the most comfortable times of the day are between 5 pm and 5 am. The addition of a small canopy provides a more consistant control of the weather patterns, creating a more steady climb into the Summer months

s> Ryanna Henson, Sofia Falls

i> Sonsoles Vela Navarro

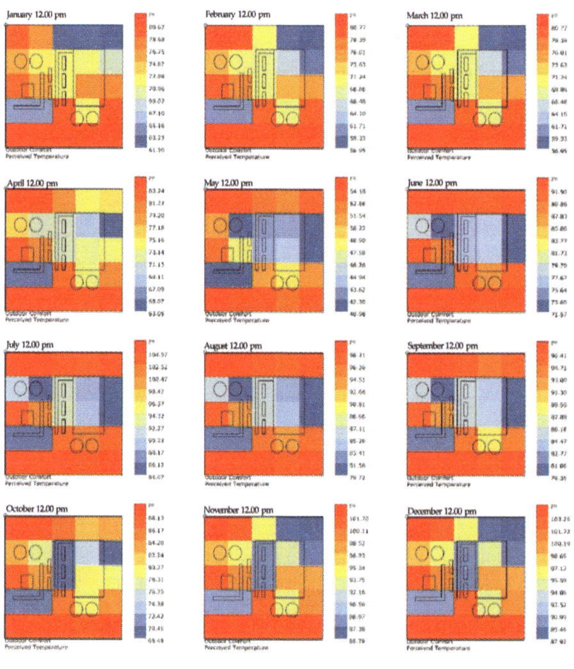

In this seating area, which has two L-shaped partition walls, and one partial sunroof, there is a consistent temperature fluctuation in the gap of the east-most partition. During the Spring months, due to the lower angle of the sun, the pavilion accepts sunlight, reaching up to 100 degrees F on a hot, April day. This fluctuates completely in the Summer, where this same space sips to 90 degrees, even though the average temperature is considerably hotter. This diagram reveals that the placement of partitions that are open facing north does not block out sun effectively. It also informs a decision to place plants in the southern quadrant, where the walls do not compromise the access to sunlight.

The heavy insulation of the walls makes sure indoor temps are very well managed and seem to be comfortable all on their own in both Winter and Summer. The accordion door on the hallway is leaking a lot of heat. While it ends up separated from the rest of the house by the doors on either side of the hallway, it might be worth searching for a solution or removing it entirely.

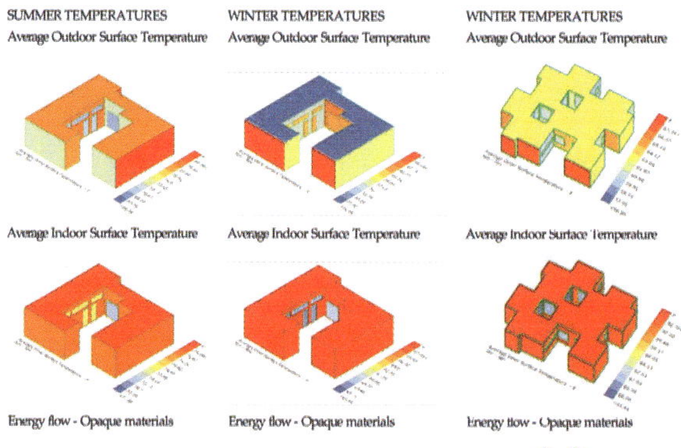

Outdoor Surface Temperature

The southern facade is the warmest at around 68 degrees F, while the north is coolest around 60 degrees F. This whole range is within liveable and comfortable conditions.

Indoor Surface Temperature

All indoor surfaces are around the 70 degrees F mark, which is within acceptable liveable ranges. The windows are lower, in the mid-60 degree F range.

Surface Energy Flow

Energy loss through all walls and the roof is uniformly low on an annual basis. The primary energy loss through surfaces comes via the windows, which are all quite high.

Glazing Energy Flow

The primary energy gain is through the northern windows, as they allow southern light in, and the southern windows which face north are actually losing energy.

Image by Charlotte Kelley + Sofia Vladimir

7

TECHNOLOGY & MAKING

AS COMMON GOOD

CODE, CARBON, AND CONTEXT

Leveraging Technology Towards Ecological Engagement

By Adam Marcus
Associate Professor of Architecture and Research Director,
Center on Climate Change and Urbanism
Tulane School of Architecture and Built Environment

Technology—in all its forms—becomes pivotal as architects grapple with the growing impacts of climate change and the need to develop compelling and viable strategies for mitigation and adaptation.

Buoyant Ecologies Float Lab, by Adam Marcus, Margaret Ikeda, and Evan Jones (CCA Architectural Ecologies Lab with Moss Landing Marine Laboratories and Kreysler & Associates)

Technology is a fraught word within architecture. Across professional and academic domains, it can mean many different things: design technology (tools to help architects design buildings), fabrication technology (tools for making components of a building), construction technology (tools for assembling those parts into a building), and building technology (the systems of assembly, mechanical conditioning, and operation that contribute to a building's structural and thermal performance).

As architects grapple with the growing impacts of climate change and the need to develop compelling and viable strategies for mitigation and adaptation, technology—in all these forms—becomes pivotal. However, as evident from the definitional ambiguity, there remains a tendency in architecture to isolate technology as a singular, discrete pursuit, divorced from and sometimes at odds with its capacities for social engagement and ecological impact. We see this in architectural practice, where design technology and building technology constitute niches within an increasingly balkanized hierarchy of specialized expertise profiles. We also see this in curricula, where technology is often relegated to digital skill-building courses or "building technology" coursework that can artificially isolate questions of technique and performance from broader concerns of design and context.

A siloed approach to technology seems especially curious given that computational and digital processes have never been more ubiquitous—in society and culture at large, but also within architecture. Computation now infuses and informs all aspects of designing and making the built environment, from ideation and representation to fabrication and, increasingly, assembly and construction. If we shift our understanding of technology to reflect this reality, might we leverage computational technologies to forge new possibilities for broader engagement and impact across social and ecological domains? The following are some initial provocations for a more expansive, integrated, and critical understanding of how technology can enhance architecture's capacity to address the pressing issues of our time.

How might computational technology help architects reduce embodied carbon within the built environment?
Given that buildings contribute to nearly 40% of global carbon emissions, it is imperative that architects develop more effective strategies for mitigating this impact. Computational tools are now widely accessible to optimize structural systems, minimizing material weight and volume, and thereby lowering the carbon footprint. Machine vision and machine learning workflows can help inventory and organize recycled building components, reducing the reliance on virgin materials. Advancements in material science technology to synthesize new biomaterials and geomaterials offer potential substitutes for conventional materials that are heavily dependent on extractive industries.

How might computational technology support decarbonization and climate mitigation in a building's operational phase?
Even more significant than the embodied energy of building materials is the energy consumed by buildings as they operate over time. To reduce this operational carbon, ever more sophisticated energy modeling technologies allow architects to better simulate and calculate the energy implications of design decisions related to siting, massing, building envelope, and material specification. New onsite, renewable technologies of energy production, such as high-performance photovoltaics, distributed wind power, and advanced geothermal systems, promise to create buildings that are self-sustaining, reducing dependence on non-renewable energy sources and shifting from a net-zero target to a net-positive outcome.

How might the notion of "building performance" expand beyond the singular building to engage broader environments and ecosystems?
Building technology is typically concerned with conditioning the interior environment for human occupation. However, many techniques of performance-driven design—such as energy modeling, simulation, and emerging techniques of artificial intelligence—can be leveraged beyond the scale of the building by encoding environmental and ecological parameters into their algorithmic logics. By expanding the purview of building technology beyond the interior to include the exterior context and environment, architecture embraces its entanglements with larger ecosystems, engaging other species of plants, animals, and fungi as active constituents in its making. Such a paradigm shift would enable architects to design not only for human comfort but also for expanded ecosystems, reinforcing both human capacities to adapt to climate change and the resilience and biodiversity of the broader environment. ■

THE CONSCIOUS COLLECTION

DESIGN
New Orleans, 2019

Credits
Tchoup Industries (Patti Dunn) x Habeas Corpus

The Conscious Collection is a collaboration between Tchoup Industries and New Orleans design studio Habeas Corpus. Together, designers Patti Dunn and Fawn developed a capsule collection that married Tchoup Industries' bag making expertise with the highly considered material sourcing of Habeas Corpus. The resulting products maximized compostability and minimized use of oil-based materials and chemical dyes.

Initially launched in the Spring of 2019, each item was crafted locally with high quality, durable materials. At the end of their long life, these products are either compostable or will leave a minimal lasting impact on our environment. During the launch, Patti Dunn shared that "Tchoup Industries uses a lot of recycled synthetic materials that are re-used but won't necessarily break down quickly once the user is done with them. We're targeting a different problem with this collection and thinking of the full life cycle of the product."

The item listings provided customers full transparency into the origin and fiber content of each material.

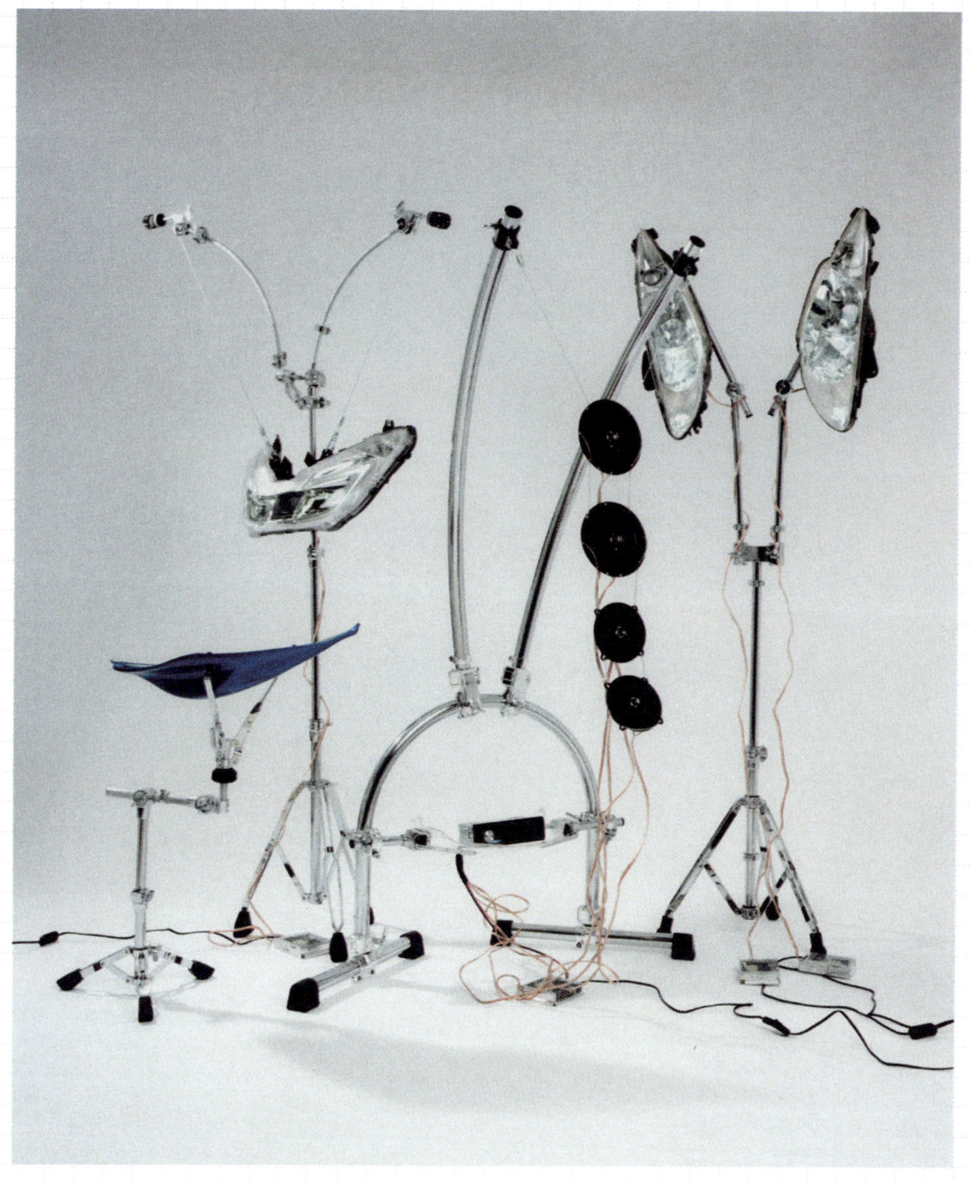

TUNING

ART

Madrid, Spain, 2024

Credits

Architect: Jesús Meseguer

Artists: REPARTO (Margil Peña y Ana Viglione)

REPARTO was born from the premise of linking fashion with day-to-day concepts that connect with its audience. Each collection features a cast of characters created from anecdotes or storylines treated with humour, in a theatrical and caricatured style. TUNING is the home line for these characters. These pieces of furniture have been conceived from the reuse and reassembly of audiovisual structures and auto-scrap. A readymade for the rave subculture. A domestic dissidence formalized in two headlight lamps, an ashtray-motorbike, and a *parkineo*- loudspeaker.

In 2024, REPARTO and the architect Jesús Meseguer collaborated to create 'TUNING'. Tuning means to adjust, a word used to refer to a vehicle's modification for adaptation. With this idea of readjustment, the previously used stage structures were reassembled and detached from their initial function. What were once music stands and tripods were reconfigured into new anatomy, becoming support structures for discarded fragments of car workshops. The second-hand parts from the tuning scene, such as car and motorbike headlights, chassis, speakers, and radios, were obtained from car repair shops in Madrid city. It was in one of these spaces where Javier, a specialist in car tuning, made the circuit electrical connections with transformers and wirings to ensure the correct functioning of all the tuning components. The assembly of all these fragments was a collaborative design process between REPARTO and Jesus Meseguer. Now, the polished stainless-steel sparkle coexists with copper cables, daytime running headlights and Bluetooth speakers. A furniture kit suitable for the home of any tuning enthusiast.

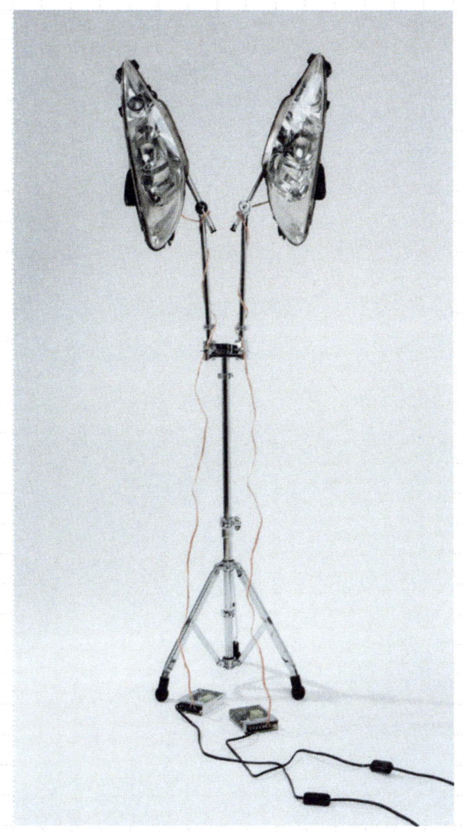

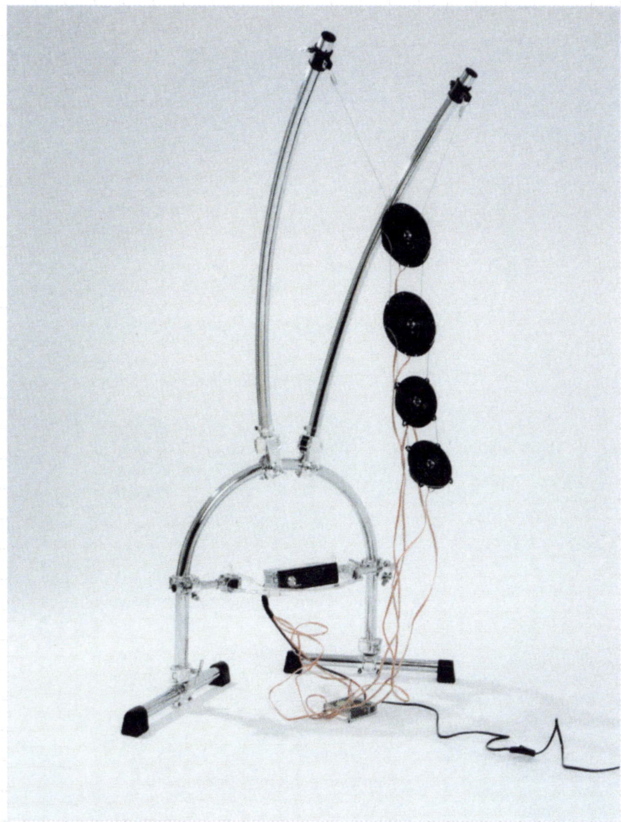

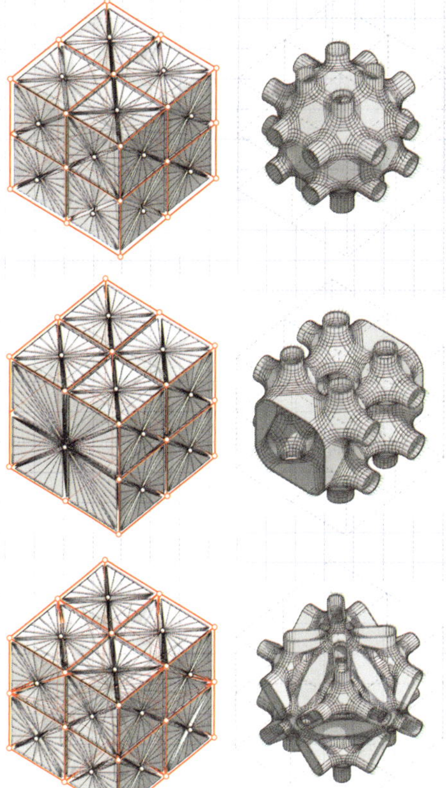

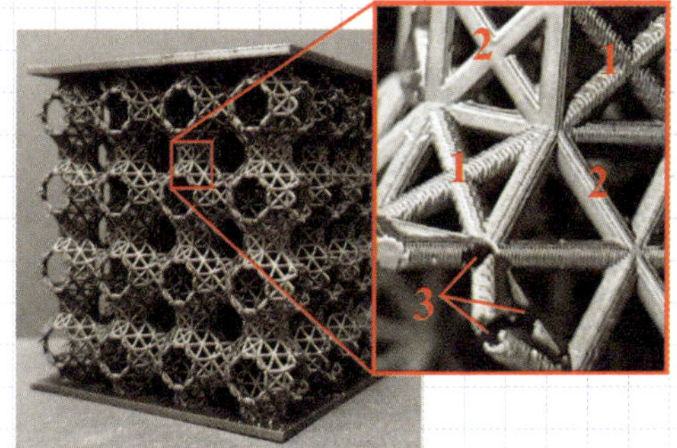

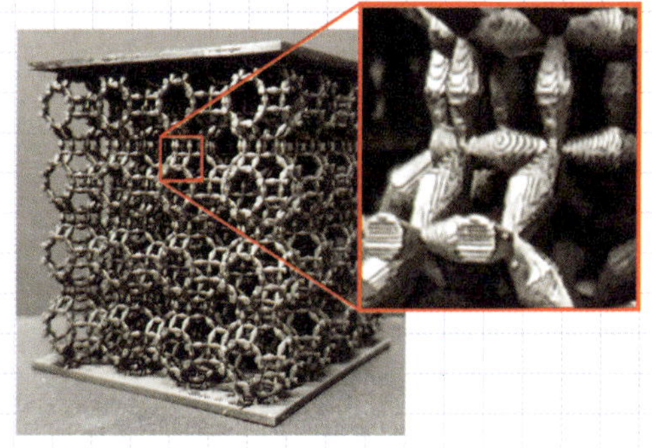

STRUT-BASED CELLULAR TO SHELLULAR FUNICULAR MATERIALS

RESEARCH ARTICLE
Advanced Functional Materials, vol. 32, no. 14, 2022

Credits

Researchers: Mostafa Akbari, Armin Mirabolghasemi, Mohammad Bolhassani, Abdolhamid Akbarzadeh, and Masoud Akbarzadeh

This work presents a novel approach to designing lightweight cellular materials by leveraging 3D graphic statics to establish a correlation between internal force distribution, geometry, and boundary conditions. Unlike traditional methods, which often overlook this relationship, the proposed strategy is based on static equilibrium principles, polyhedral frame equilibrium, and the reciprocity of form and force. This methodology enables the transformation of bending-dominated truss systems into shellular architectures with significantly improved mechanical properties.

By manipulating unit cell topologies, employing alternative strut materialization schemes, and introducing bracing elements, this approach systematically tailors mechanical behavior, achieving a range of properties from soft and flexible to stiff and load-bearing. Multiscale homogenization techniques validate the effective elastic properties of these cellular structures, demonstrating their robustness across various applications. Experimental validation through 3D-printed prototypes confirms the viability of the proposed methodology, highlighting its potential in structural applications, tissue scaffolds, and metamaterials with exotic properties, such as metafluidic behavior.

Furthermore, the study examines how different base solid materials influence mechanical performance, revealing that strut-based architectures exhibit minimal dependency on the Poisson's ratio of the constituent material, while shellular structures demonstrate greater sensitivity due to higher material connectivity. The agreement between numerical simulations and experimental results underscores the manufacturability and real-world applicability of these funicular cellular and shellular materials, paving the way for their integration into advanced engineering and architectural applications.

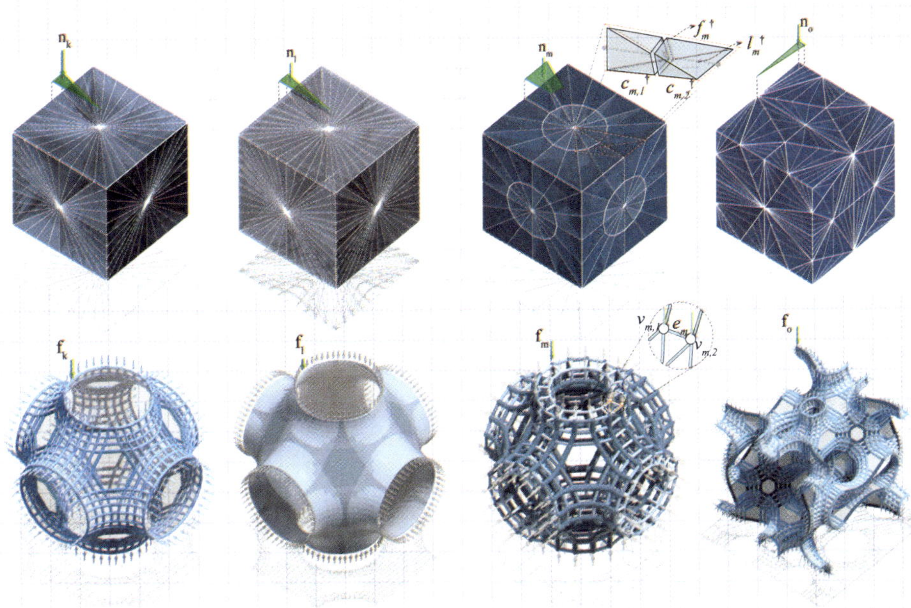

ARCH 4041/5051 + 6041/6051 | **Research Studio** | UG + GR | **FA23**

MATERIALS OF ABOLITION

Design + Build Studio

Project Leads:
Emilie Taylor Welty
Jackie Summel
Jose Cotto

Faculty:
Ann Yochim
Nick Jenisch
Endale Bekele

More than 2 million people in the United States are currently incarcerated—around 90,000 are subjected to indefinite solitary confinement. The devastating and often irreparable effects of systemic isolation— especially in environments devoid of natural materials and connections—include alienation, dehumanization, despair, disorientation, paranoia, and suicidal ideation.

Growing from an acknowledgment of the harms our profession contributes to, and in collaboration with community partners working to abolish systems of oppression, the Materials of Abolition studio focused its research on: 1) understanding the material palettes and practices that shape our built environments, 2) the potential of material compositions and production to reduce our carbon footprint, and 3) how we can seed more equitable design processes and outputs to cultivate sustainable social, economic, and environmental ecosystems.

Students explored hyper-local material and manufacturing, grounding investigations in the work of our partners at Solitary Gardens. Building on the bio-based materials work of firms like Grimshaw, Material Cultures, and academic research projects like the Parsons Healthy Materials Lab, the studio developed new material composites using bio-based byproducts of local industry, concluding in the design and fabrication of two small-scale structures and an exhibit sharing the research outcomes. The pressing environmental and social issues we face are complex, layered, and seem beyond an individual's ability to change. The semester was a case study in small collective acts with impact and interdisciplinary collaborations that raise awareness, build support, and advocate for change.

Collaborators of the studio include Solitary Gardens, Prisoners Apothecary, and the John Thompson Legacy Center.

Students:
Abby Carlton
Naomi Smith
Joey Tomshe
Malia Bavuso
Anna Kathryn Becker
Tracy Jones
Shanelle Brown
An Le
Anthony Gagliano
Tom O'Brien
Ryan Russell
Riley Siltler
Allison Slomski
Yi Wei

s> Small Center Team

i> Small Center Leads + Faculty

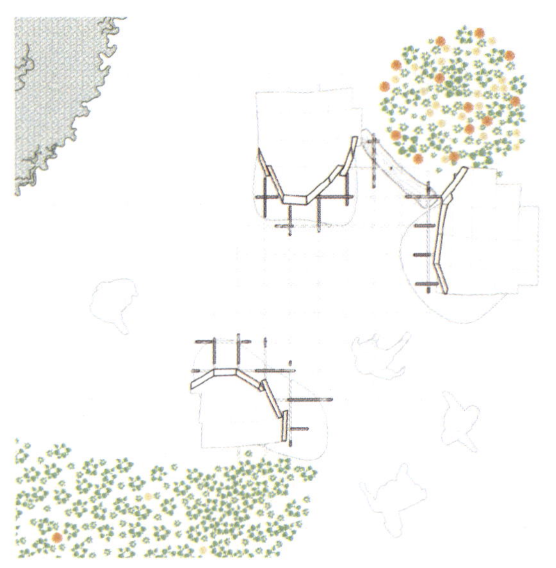

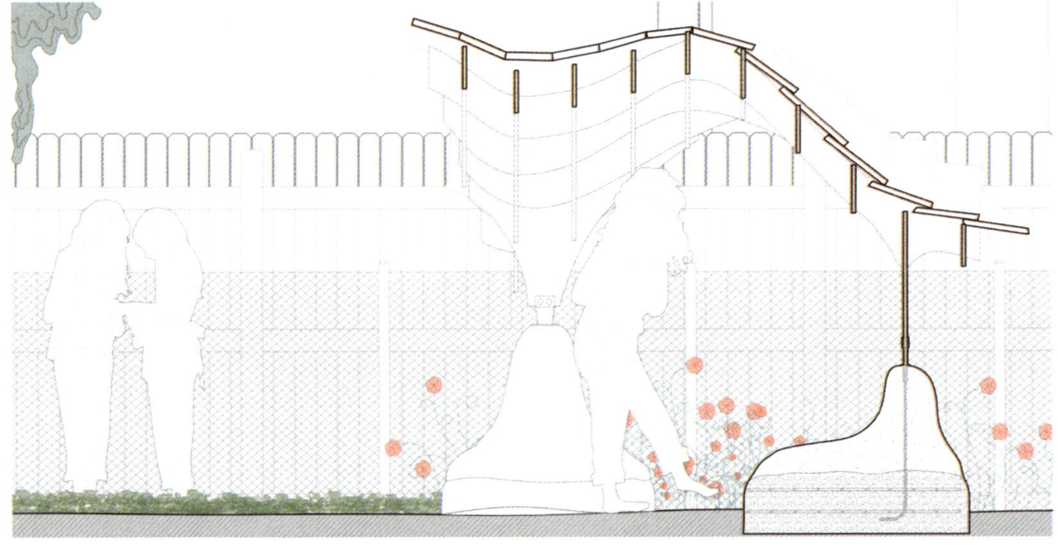

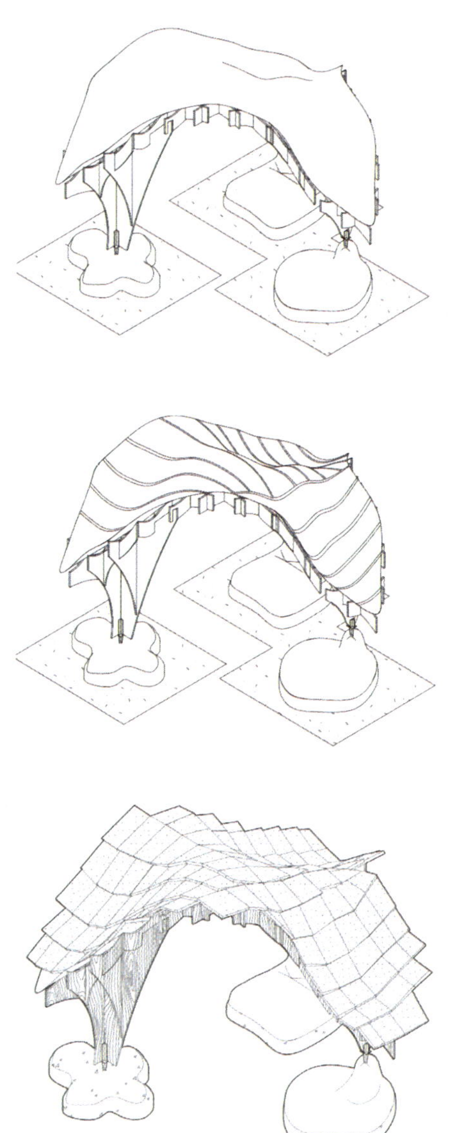

Leaf Sheath (Exteriors)
Leaf Sheath (Fibers)
Semi-Dry Palm Leaves
Test #1
Test #2
Materials

A large portion of the semester's research and design work centered on understanding how systems we have created have failed us—from the prison industrial complex to our modes of construction. Building materials are a key component in how violence and harm are perpetuated onto people and environments. With this understanding, students dove into research and exploration of bio-based materials that could be restorative and generative—challenging the building blocks we as architects use to create space. Materials included bagasse, straw, mycelium, natural clay, oyster shells, and palm. Additionally, three students made the journey to Lumberton, Mississippi, to participate in Sage Stoneman's natural building workshop, where they learned the traditional methods of cob, wattle, and daub construction.

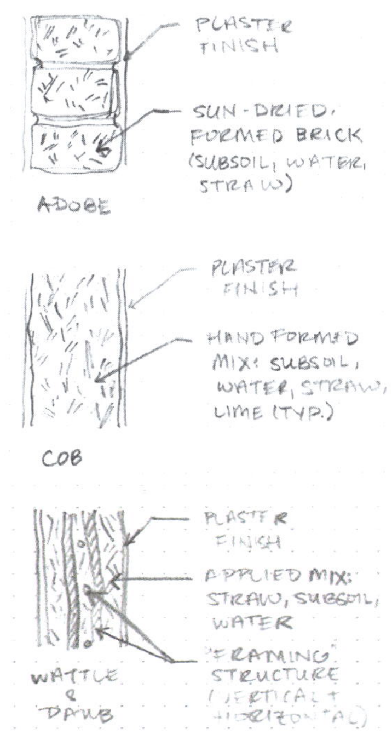

ARCH 4041/5051 + 6041/6051

Research Studio

UG + GR

FA23

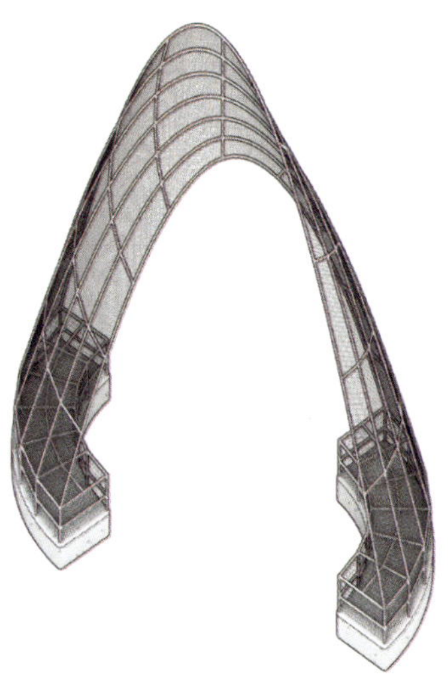

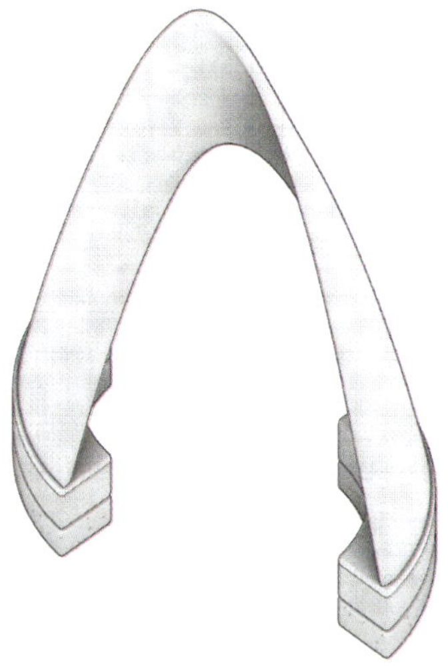

Using the material investigations from the semester, students worked in groups to design structures rooted in the symbolic and physical rewriting of oppressive or harmful systems. The proposals drew from spiritual, medicinal, and metaphorical concepts & ideas to design two structures that subvert the purpose of a solitary cell—transforming a 6' x 9' footprint intended to inflict harm into spaces that meant to gather and foster community.

our state economy improves
& industrial emissions increase
when we lock up more people

To ground the Materials of Abolition studio, students began by exploring the roots—the often unseen origins—that anchor philosophies, practices, and projects that makeway for an architecture of carcerality. Each studio member developed a guidingquestion that directed their research into a topic of their choosing—ranging from theeconomic impacts and abuses of our criminal justice system, the role that the AIA andbuilding codes play in perpetuating or reducing harm, and the ways the materiality ofprisons impacts the well-being of those incarcerated.

ARCH 4041/5051 + 6041/6051 | **Research Studio** | UG + GR | **FA23**

our state economy improves
& industrial emissions increase
when we lock up more people
Mass incarceration sustains three conditions that continually increase industrial emissions:
the construction of new prison facilities
the production of goods that incarcerated people must consume
the use of incarcerated labor to expand state economic growth
CAPTIVE LABOR

JOHN THOMSON LEGACY CENTER

DESIGN VISIONING

As part of the studio, we also engaged in a design visioning project for the John Thomspon Legacy Center (JTLC), a community anchor for organizations and individuals working on restorative justice and abolition efforts. To gather insights on current uses of the space, goals and aspirations, and better understand the impact and legacy of John Thompson, the studio organized two engagement sessions that helped shape and inform a design direction for 1212 St. Bernard Avenue. The final vision addressed issues of accessibility, expanded the multipurpose space into the back courtyard, and re-imagined the second floor to include a greenhouse and artist-in-residence program.

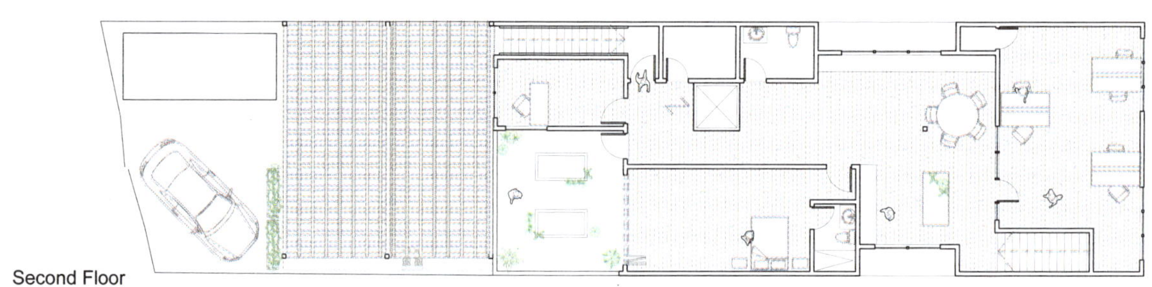

Second Floor

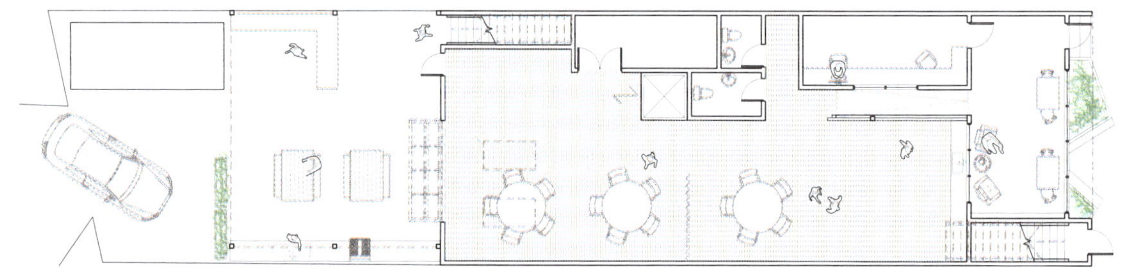

First Floor

ARCH 4042 + 6042 | **Research Studio** | UG + GR | **SP24**

URBANbuild 19

Byron Mouton [C]
Hugh Jackson
Hannah Berryhill

Tulane School of Architecture and Built Environment's award-winning URBANbuild program has had the mission since 2005 to develop responsible housing prototypes in the New Orleans context, focusing on the community's common needs. URBANbuild combines the efforts of students, faculty, and local community partners to design and build housing each year.

This prefabricated "Tiny-House" prototype is the outcome of a collaborative research and development assignment. The strategy can adapt to various site conditions and may also satisfy the needs of various user groups.

This project was initially developed with no defined site or occupant. However, it was always intended to function as a "deployable" model home. The challenge of the assignment was to create a prototypical "Tiny-House" that can adapt to numerous programmatic applications: an accessory dwelling unit, a starter home, or infill housing. The architects were also asked to provide a model home that could easily be deployed and quickly assembled amidst dense urban settings. Therefore, the sizing of components was crucial to the project's success.

In addition to portability, affordability also had to be carefully considered throughout the design/build process. These factors influenced the development of a prefabricated system of panels that could be "flat-packed" and delivered using a common quarter-ton pickup truck and a standard two-axle trailer. In addition, the construction system relies upon common building materials aiming to keep the vision achievable amidst various locations of the region.

Despite a reliance upon the standardized replicable assembly system, the prototype also provides opportunity for customization through variation in window, cladding and screening options. Late in construction of the prototype, a user and site were identified, and the project will be used as transitional housing for occupants escaping homelessness. That program greatly influenced final developments of the scheme's secure covered outdoor porch, its screening, and its security—as it is expected that the user may initially experience comfort in transition by first sleeping on the porch.

Students:
Isabel Baum
Ben Brimer
Brendon Cook
Sarah Fisher
Clair Fisher
Sabrina Lafaye
Noah Lion
Ryan Russell
Elliot Slovis
Yi Wei
Kuangi Zhang

Want to see pictures of the final review?

Building Area(sqft): 350 (enclosed space), 250 (covered porch)
Cost Per Square Foot: $225
Construction Cost: $90,000
Date of Completion: May 2024

 URBANbuild team

i> Mouton, Jackson, Berryhill

Unlike other URBANbuild projects, URBANbuild 19 was initially assembled in the Albert and Tina Small Center, dissembled, and then reassembled on site.

Bathroom
1
Porch
4
Bedroom
3
Kitchen/Living
2
ENTRY
PROPERTY LINE
FIRST FLOOR
1/2" = 1'-0"

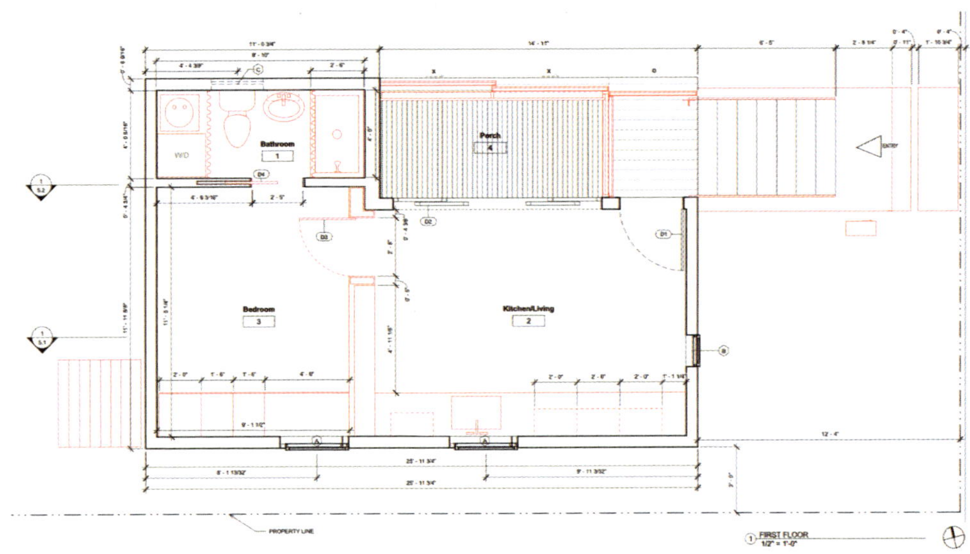

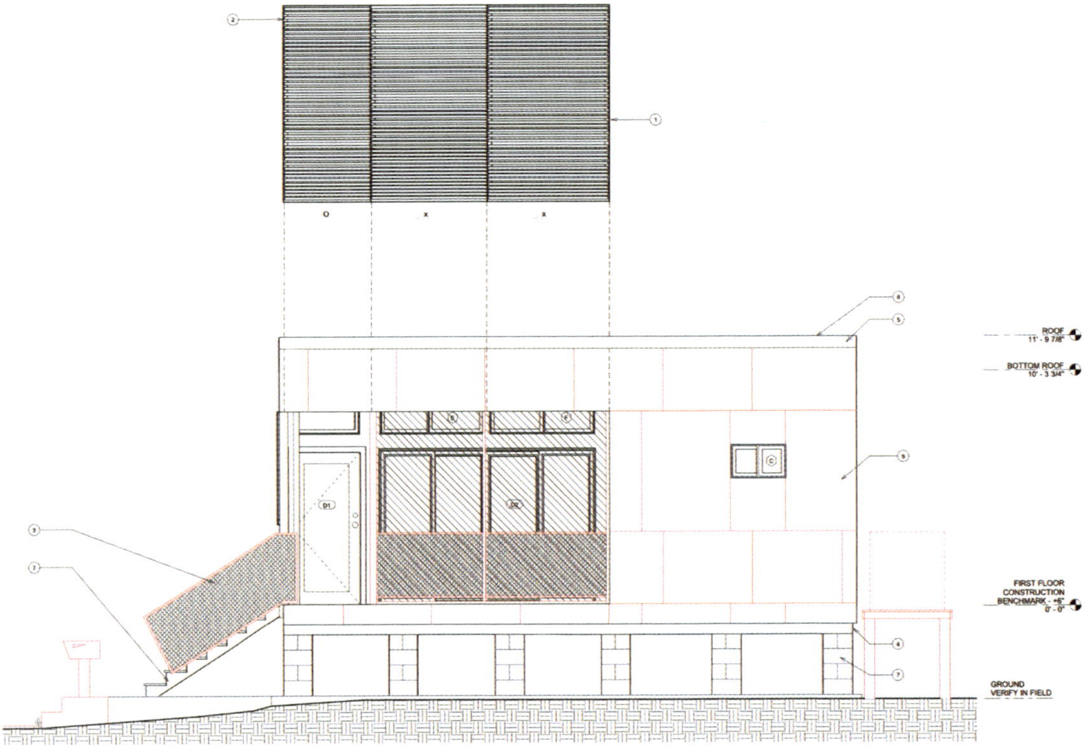

ROOF
11' - 9 7/8"
BOTTOM ROOF
10' - 3 3/4"
FIRST FLOOR
CONSTRUCTION
BENCHMARK - +6"
0' - 0"
GROUND
VERIFY IN FIELD

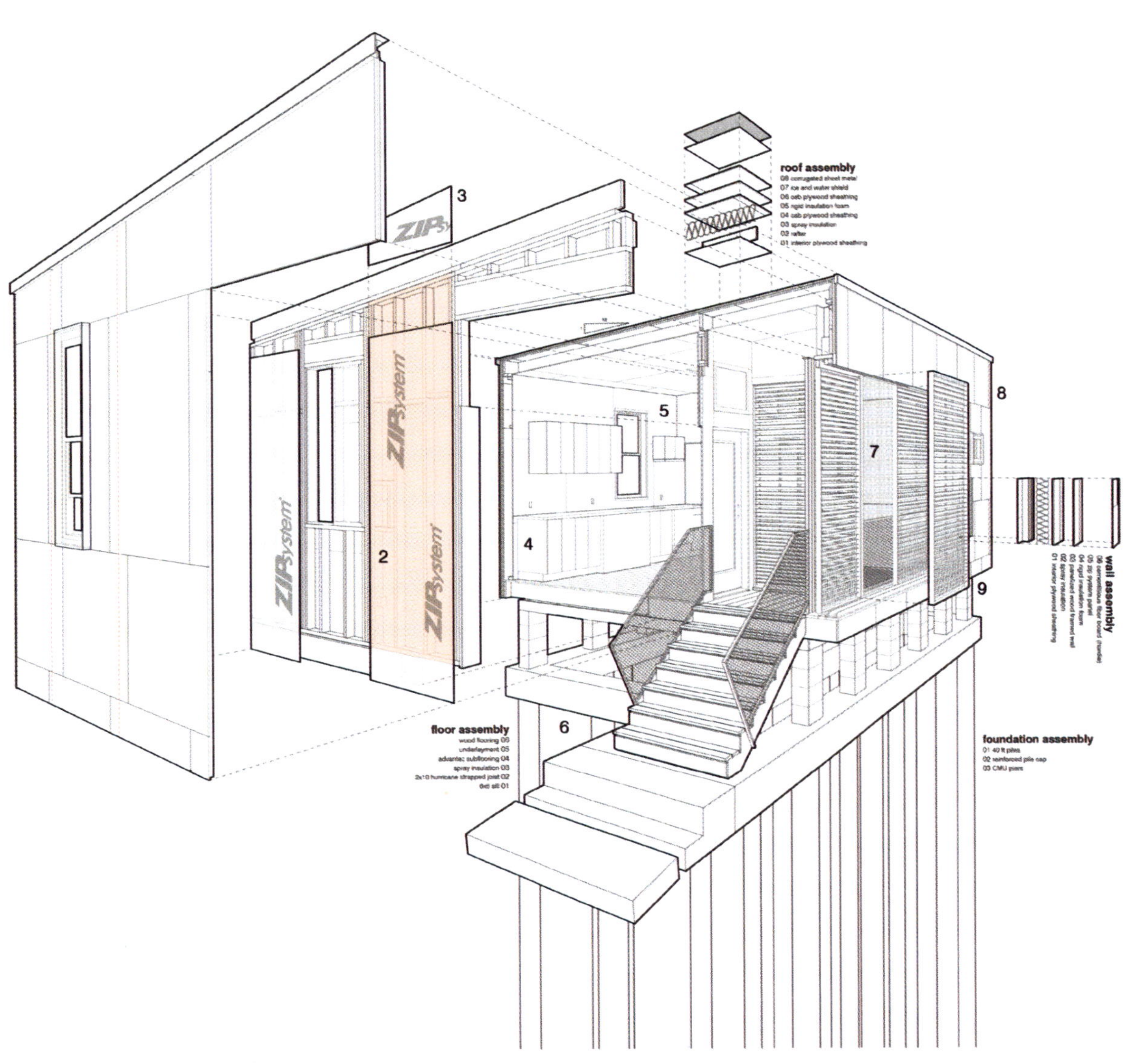
roof assembly
08 corrugated sheet metal
07 ice and water shield
06 osb plywood sheathing
05 rigid insulation foam
04 osb plywood sheathing
03 spray insulation
02 rafter
01 interior plywood sheathing
3
ZIPSystem
2
5
4
7
8
9
6
wall assembly
floor assembly
wood flooring 06
underlayment 05
advantec subflooring 04
spray insulation 03
2x10 hurricane strapped joist 02
6x6 sill 01
foundation assembly
01 40 ft piles
02 reinforced pile cap
03 CMU piers

ADVANCED DIGITAL MEDIA

Adam Marcus [C]

Over the past three decades, computation and automation have transformed and become central to the practice of architecture. In the design and construction of buildings and cities, computational workflows now inform and augment processes of design, representation, communication, fabrication, and assembly. And yet, as is often the case with computational paradigms in our broader society and culture, we tend to engage these technologies uncritically, easily accepting predefined processes as given without questioning or customizing them. This course challenges such "blackboxing" of computational workflows in architectural media, cultivating a foundational understanding of algorithmic processes and a critical sensibility with regard to deploying them in architectural practice.

This course emphasizes computational methods of design, fabrication, and representation as integral aspects of the architectural design process. The agenda is framed by a general introduction to computation as it relates to architecture, and the course incorporates technical skill-building, historical/theoretical context, and understanding how such tools can be integrated into broader design processes in productive ways. Students are introduced to 2D and 3D techniques of parametric design, digital fabrication workflows, and digital methods of visualization—with the emphasis on critical understandings of these tools and how all three elements can synthetically strengthen the architectural design process.

Want to see pictures of the exhibition?

s> Brian Harris, Grace DeLaune

i> Adam Marcus

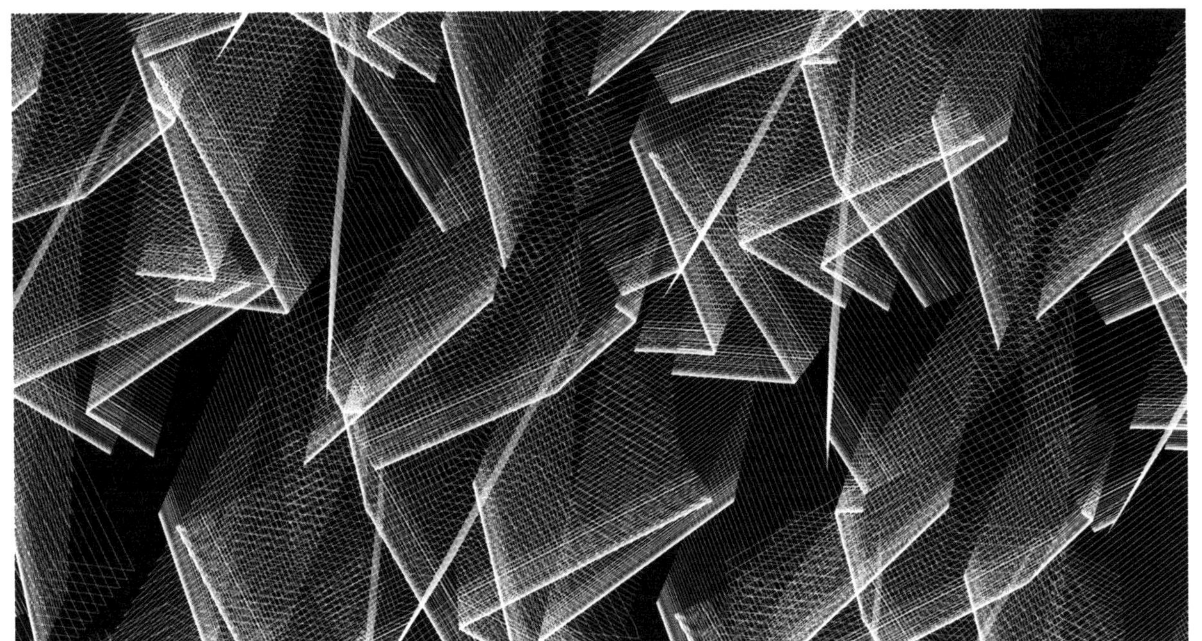

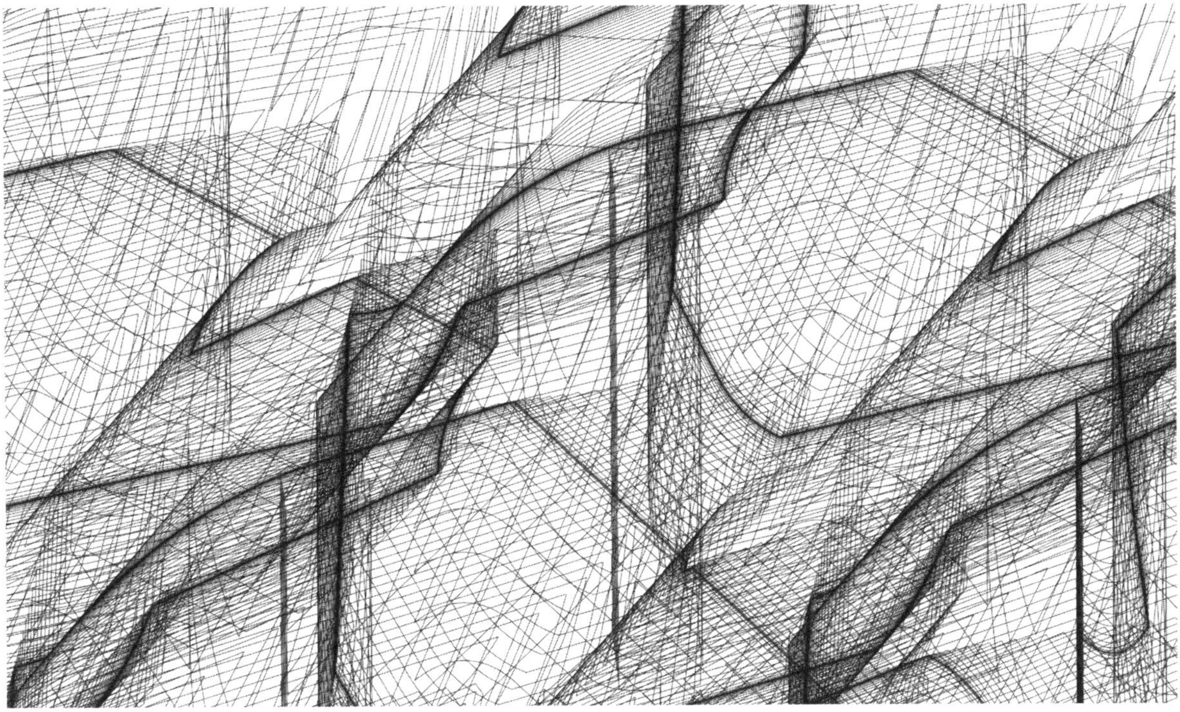

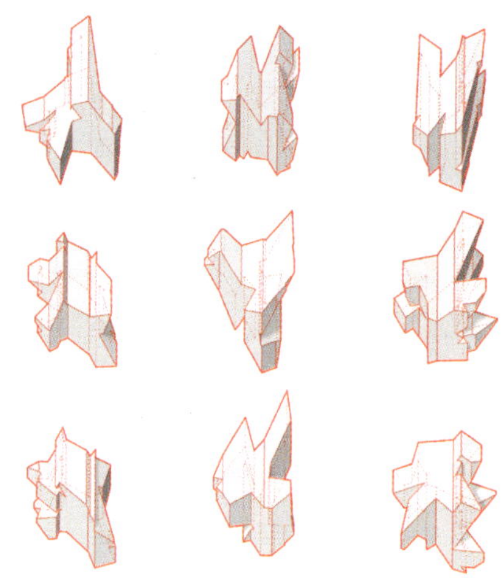

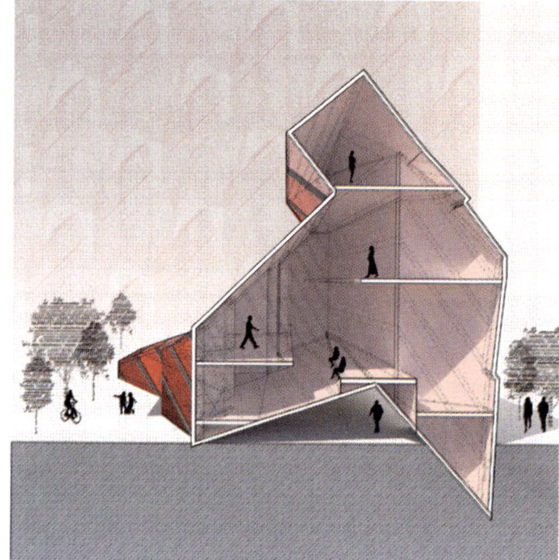

s> Anjali Anand, Jackie Hemman

i> Adam Marcus

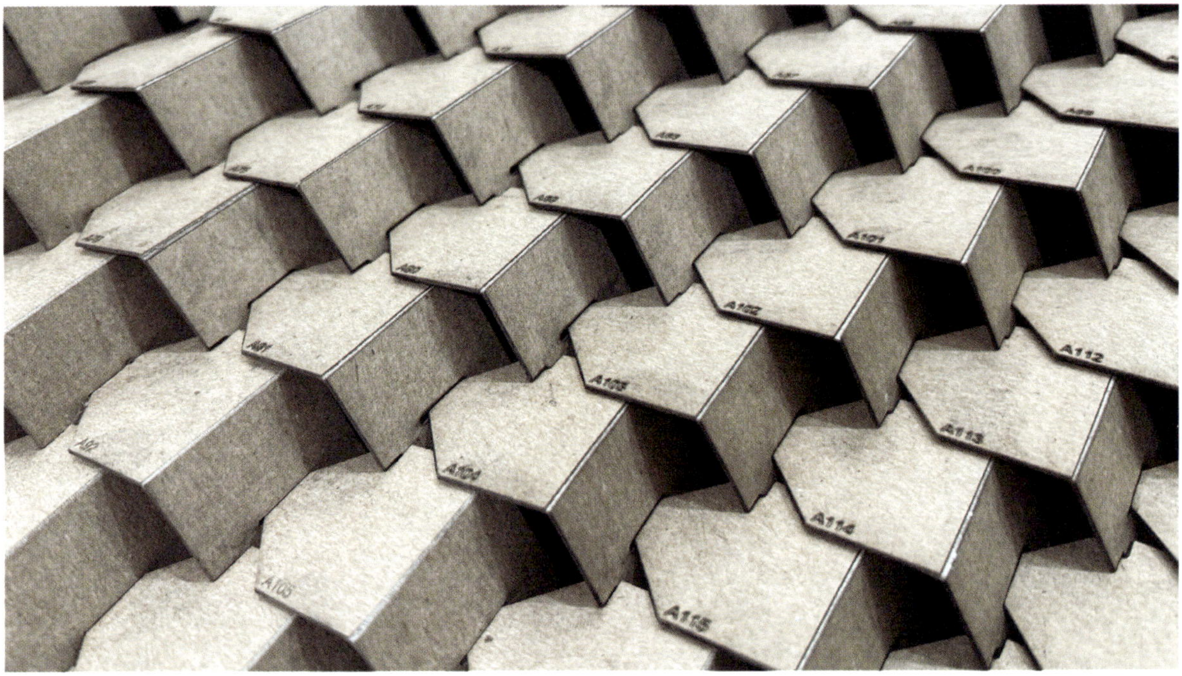
A112
A113
A114
A115

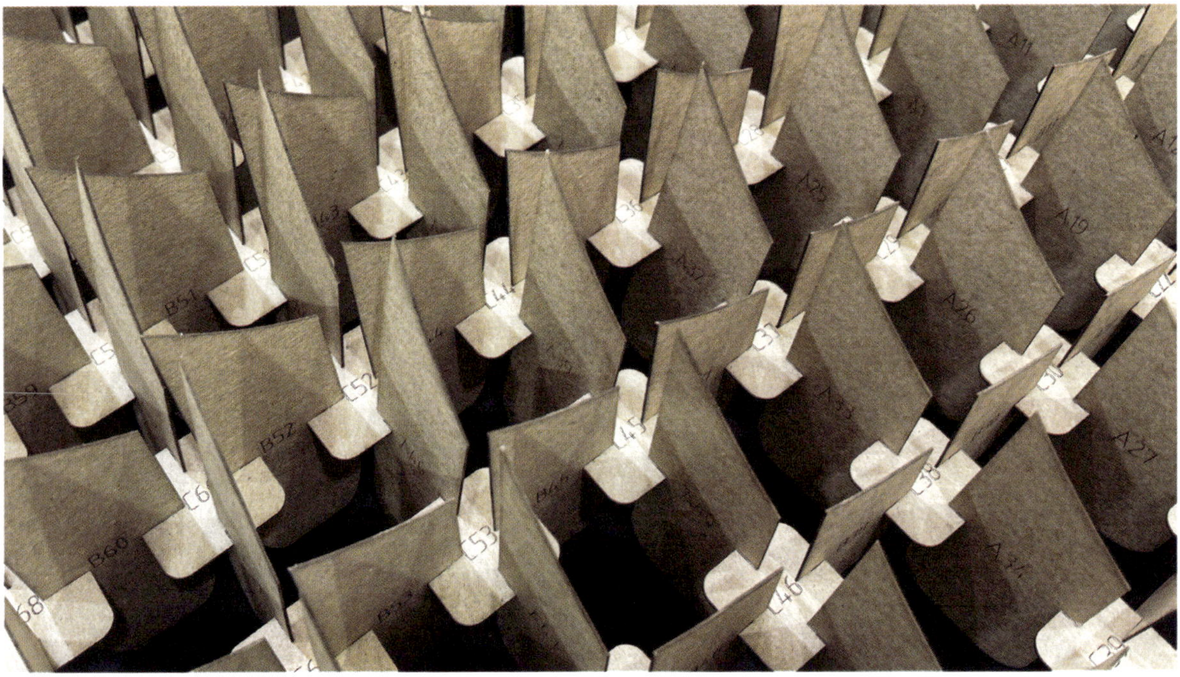
B51
B52
B60
C52
A19
A26
A27

s> Caleb Schroeder, Asha Hokanson, Alexa Trapani, Alex Cohen

i> Adam Marcus

FUNDAMENTALS OF DESIGN & MAKING

Hannah Kenyon [C]
Jesse Toohey
Marion Forbes
Kelly Tierney

"Design" refers to a work process of creating objects (product) and activities (service) with an intention to improve human experience through negotiating complex problems. The ability to cut through multiple issues (function, aesthetic, economic, social, political, environmental, etc.) laterally and simultaneously through the use of visual means is paramount. This course focuses on cultivating the visualization and communication skills necessary to analyze design problems and to synthesize creative solutions through the iterative process. This studio will explore architectural form as a language that conveys cultural meaning. Our goal is for you to assemble a rich and agile repertoire of strategies for exploring and communicating your architectural ideas and the ability to know which ones to use when.

The goals of DESG1005 Fundamentals of Design and Making are to challenge what our students know about the visual world and to evolve beyond roles as rote consumers of culture; we encourage them to participate in the production of it.

To achieve this, the class will engage the act of making to introduce the fundamentals of the iterative design process. Students will analyze design problems and synthesize creative solutions through two and three-dimensional media. The course culminates in a digital portfolio to highlight their strongest projects, providing a framework to build on beyond the classroom/course.

The foundation of design-thinking is based on what we refer to as the Five C's: Concept, Craft, Commitment, Contribution and Creative Bravery.

Want to see pictures of the final review?

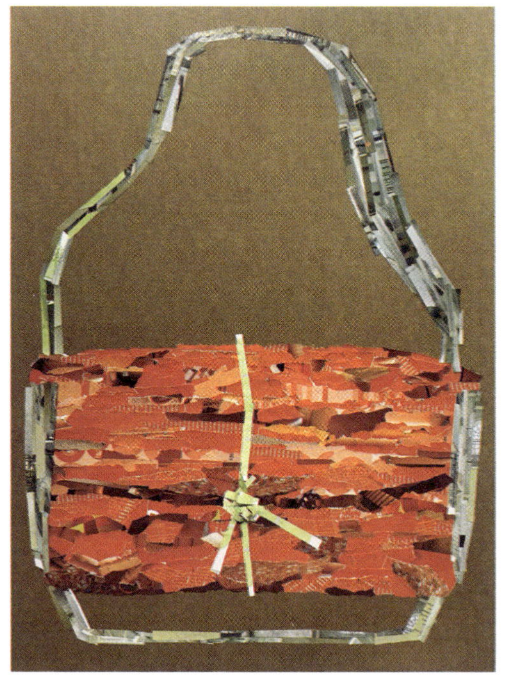

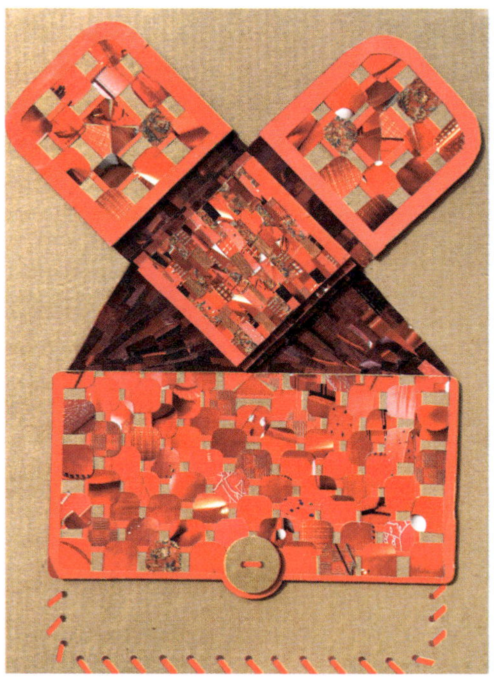

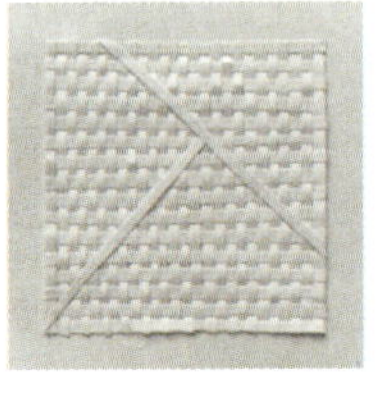
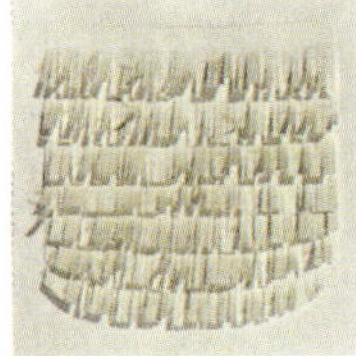

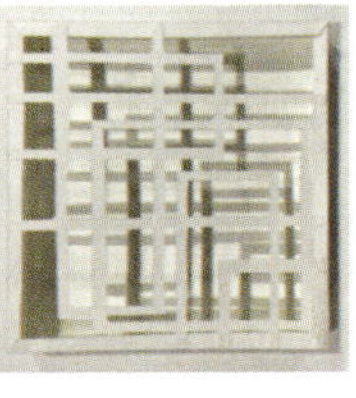

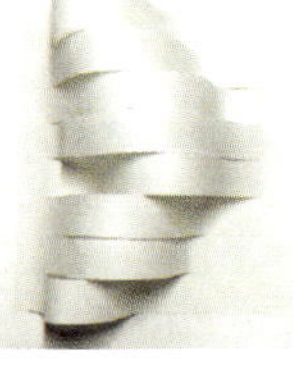

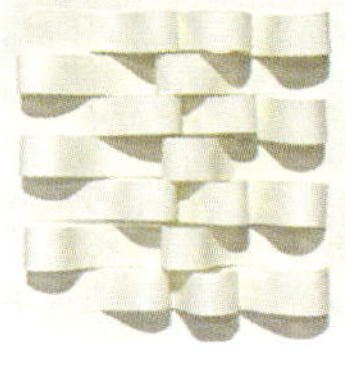
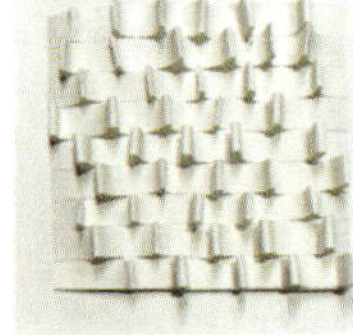

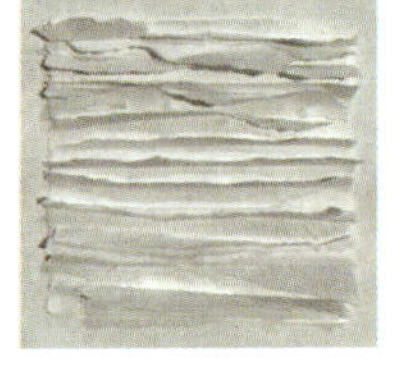

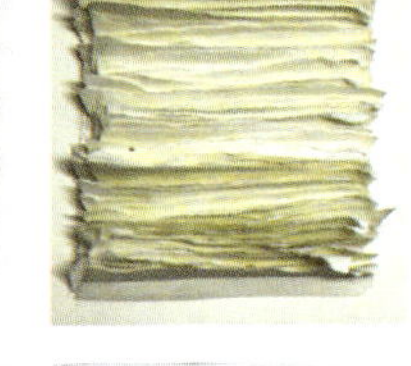

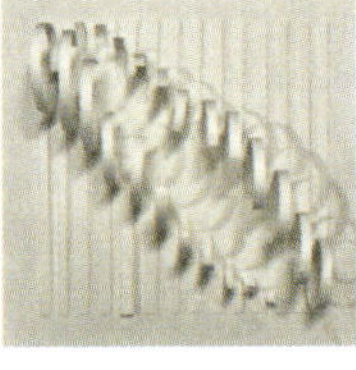
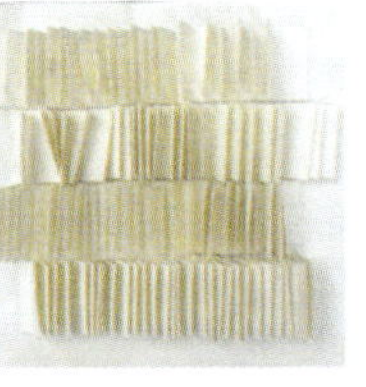
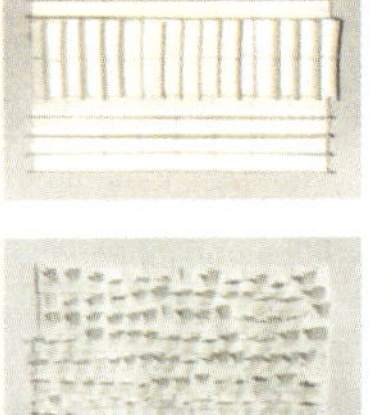
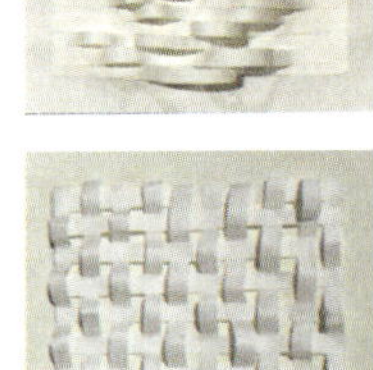

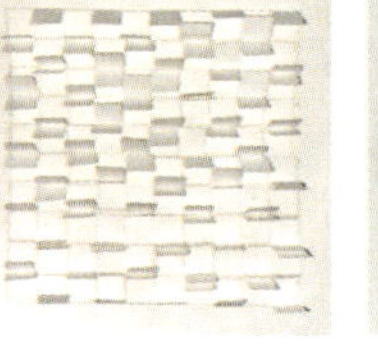

DESIGN STUDIO I

Nick Perrin [C]
Andrew Liles
Jonathan House
Hannah Berryhill

In Design Studio I, students fine-tune skills of rigorous observation, analysis, and creative problem solving through the iterative design process. The studio begins with an analysis of organizational structures that occur in nature. Each student diagrams a plant specimen to understand its underlying geometry, symmetry, structure, and integral patterns. These diagrams are later translated into two-dimensional wallpapers and three-dimensional shadow models, exploring rules of symmetry, color theory, light, and shadow.

These explorations in rigorous analysis, tessellations, iteration, well-crafted details, 2D and 3D representational drawing techniques, and light and shadow culminate with the students' main project of the semester: a hand-crafted light sculpture. Students work through multiple iterations of their light sculptures (either in the form of a pendant or table lamp) and embrace new technologies such as laser-cutting and three-dimensional digital modeling to create and represent their designs. Additionally, students learn about the wellness and spatial implications that light has upon the human body and the built environment and integrate human-centered considerations into their designs.

Want to see pictures of the exhibition?

The work of the studio is developed in four projects:

Diagrammed Specimens:
After a visit to the New Orleans Botanical Garden, students choose one natural specimen to diagram at a micro, mezzo, and macro scale. The concept of a "diagram" is introduced through the students' analysis of elements such as structure, growth, symmetry, motif, depth, flow of nutrients, and geometry found in their chosen plant.

Nature-Inspired Wallpaper:
Students reconsider their drafted diagrams of natural specimens as motifs in a pattern. There is an emphasis on scale: how do these motifs reveal themselves at various scales throughout the wallpaper? The rigorous, digital study of their specimens is synthesized with handmade reactions: each design should incorporate both digital and analog media.

Kirigami Shadow Models:
Having thoroughly studied and represented the specimen's organizational structures in two dimensions, these concepts are then translated into formal and spatial relationships via paper models folded using the kirigami technique.

Light Sculptures:
In the longest project of the semester, students design a "light sculpture," either pendant or table lamp. Using their diagrams and paper models as a point of departure, this analysis becomes a three-dimensional, functional object that must translate important elements of their chosen plant while also integrating considerations of utility, fabrication, and user experience.

s> Caroline Sosler i> Nick Perrin

s> Cole Hildebrandt, Hannah Gagliano, Taylor Fisherman

i> Nick Perrin, Andrew Liles

Specimen Study

Drafted Diagrams

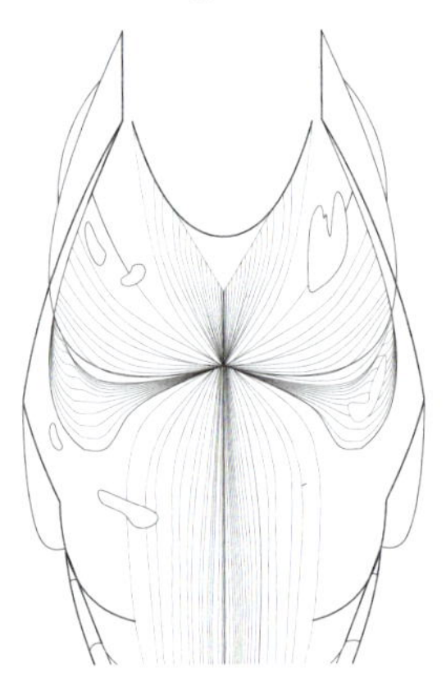

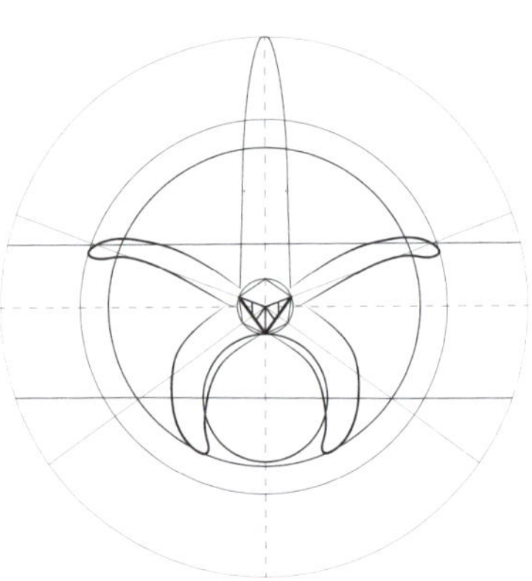

Shadow Models

Structure

Expansion

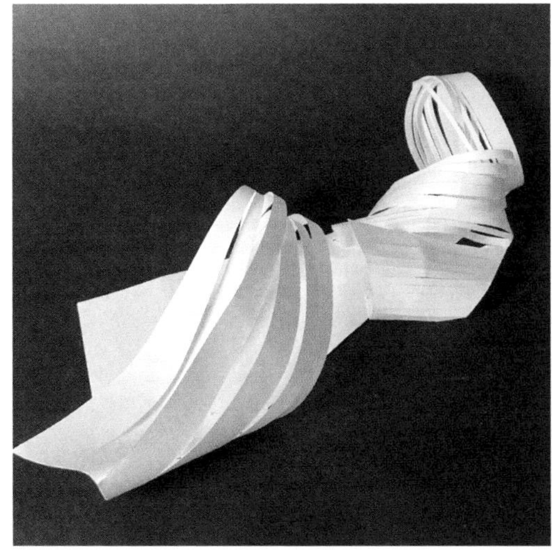

Hierarchy

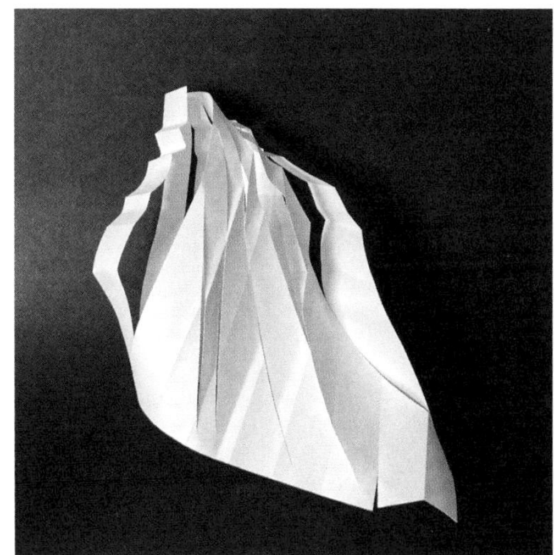

Growth

Specimen Study

Drafted Diagrams

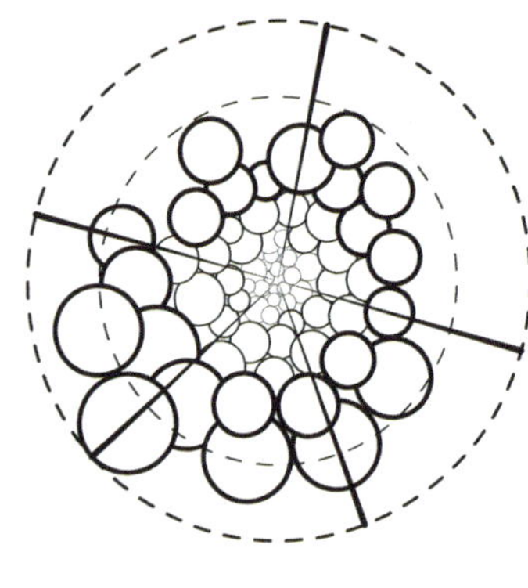

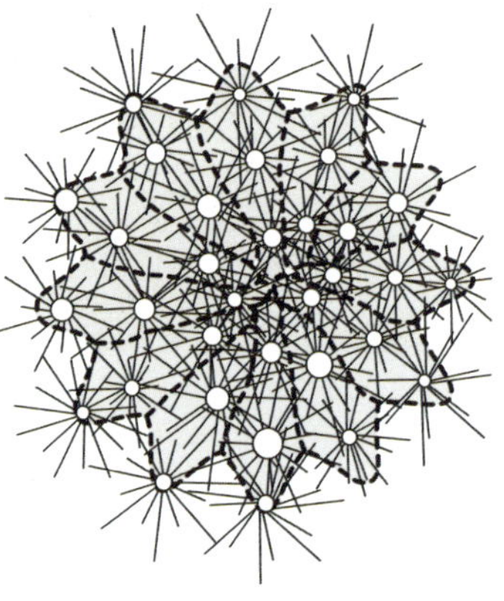

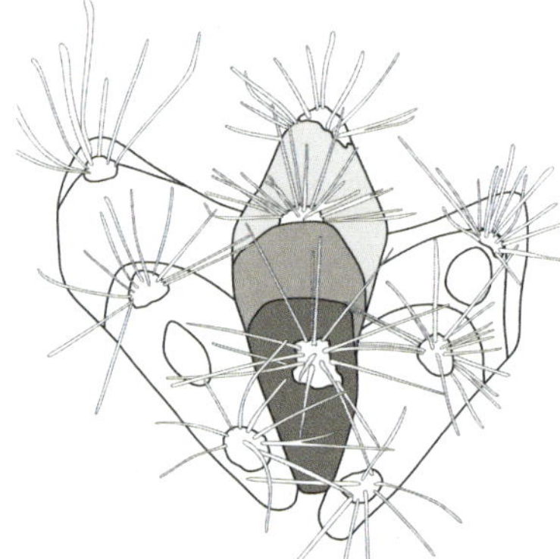

Shadow Models

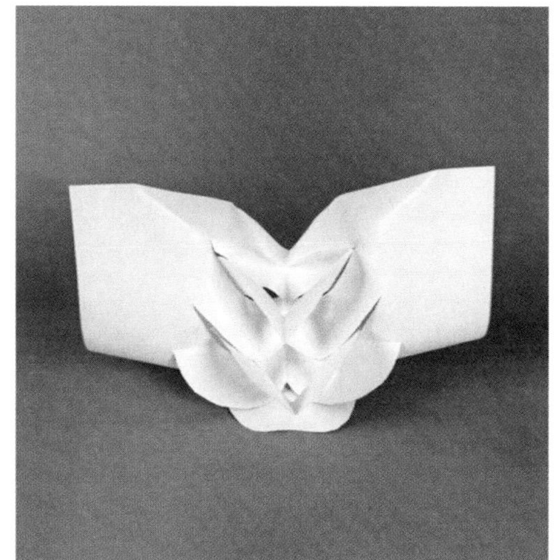

Symmetry/Motif

Motif/Part of Whole

Depth

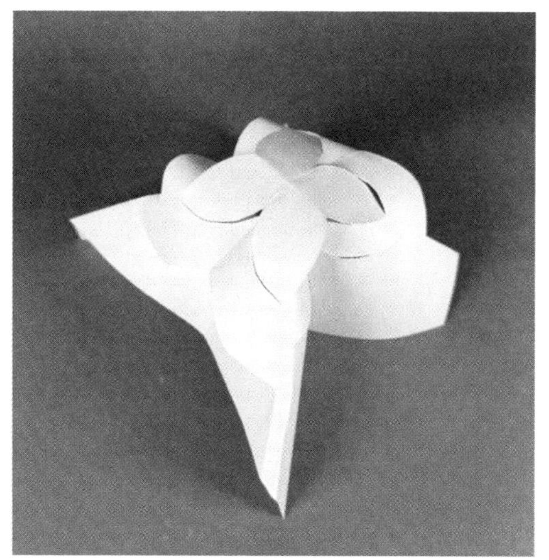

Structure/Hierarchy

PROTOTYPING SOLUTIONS

Nick Perrin [C]
Bryan Bradshaw
Jesse Toohey

This upper-level course draws upon foundational design skills from studio prerequisites to explore form-making through physical prototypes. Students will first analyze archetypes (e.g, stool, table, sawhorse), then will work to develop concepts, uses, and formal qualities to be tested on their own design. The iterative process will include material studies, physical and digital model making, and constructed fabrication drawings that inform individual projects at full scale. Understanding design as inseparable from making is central to this course. The final prototypes are simultaneously a studied work and an object that can be refined.

Prototyping Solutions is an introduction to various topics in design and instruction in navigating from ideation through execution. The class discusses terms and examines a range of approaches and production. 3 Phases anchor the class and divide the semester accordingly. Working with material is a critical component of this course and students pursue an agenda that views design as making. A "Portmanteau" serves as a prompt before becoming an object that students consider and interpret through iterative making.

Want to see more furniture?

s> Claire Callahan, Hannah Gagliano, Audra Marcus, MJ Lauland, Charlotte Ertmann, Zoe Hill

i> Bradshaw + Toohey, Perrin

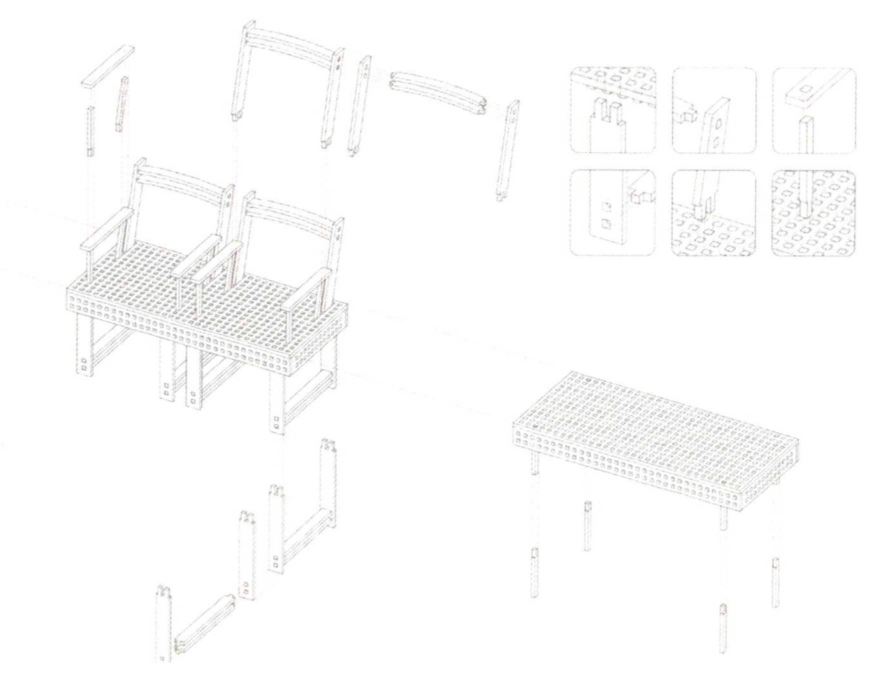

s> Olivia Roginson, Ella Galaty **i>** Nick Perrin

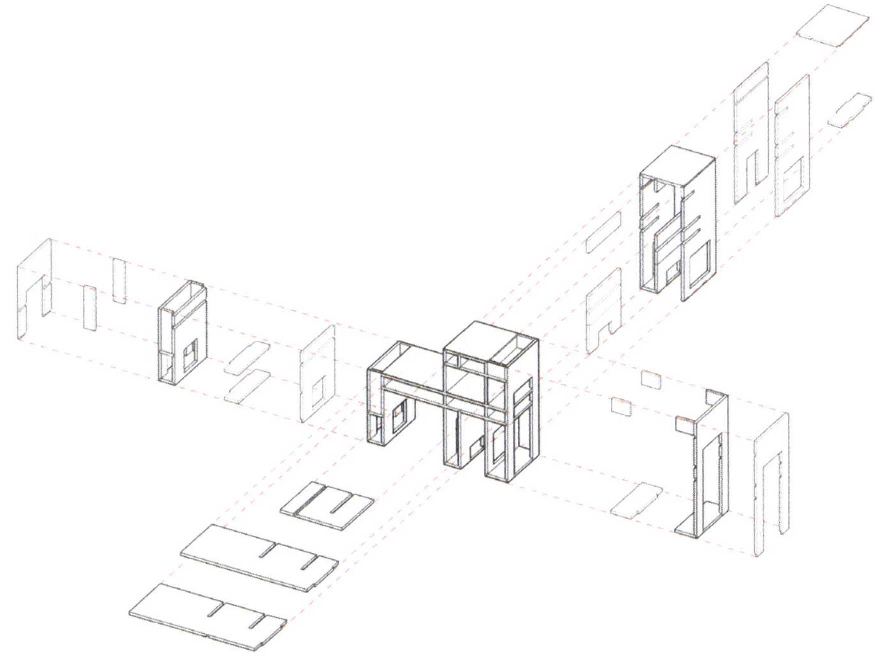

s> Colby Francis, Jacob Starr

i> Nick Perrin

INTEGRATED BUILDING SYSTEMS

Kentaro Tsubaki
Javier Marcano

The primary objective of Integrated Building Systems is to equip students with the knowledge and skills to seamlessly incorporate major building systems into their architectural designs. This course, taught in tandem with Integrated Studio (ARCH 6032), focuses on the technical requirements and integration of systems such as illumination, acoustics, structures, mechanical, electrical, and plumbing (MEP) systems, fire suppression systems, codes and regulations, water management systems, envelope systems, and ADA accessibility.

Students engage in a series of assignments that challenge them to though fully integrate these systems into their studio projects. The course is designed to provide both theoretical knowledge and practical application. In lecture sessions, students learn about the technical aspects and requirements of each system. They then apply this knowledge in their studio work, ensuring that their designs are not only aesthetically pleasing but also technically sound and compliant with relevant codes and regulations.

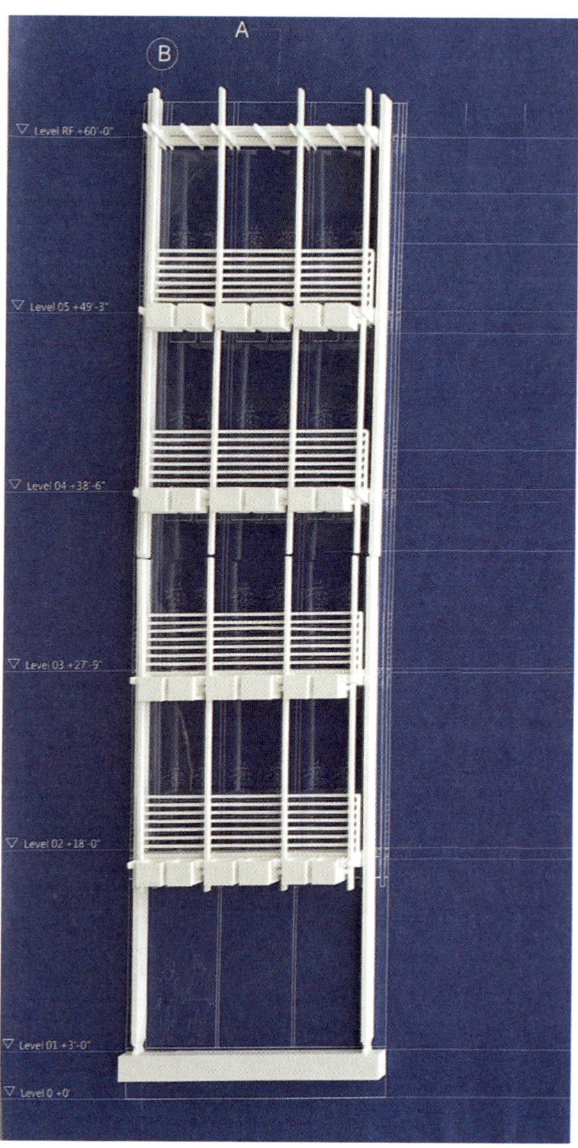

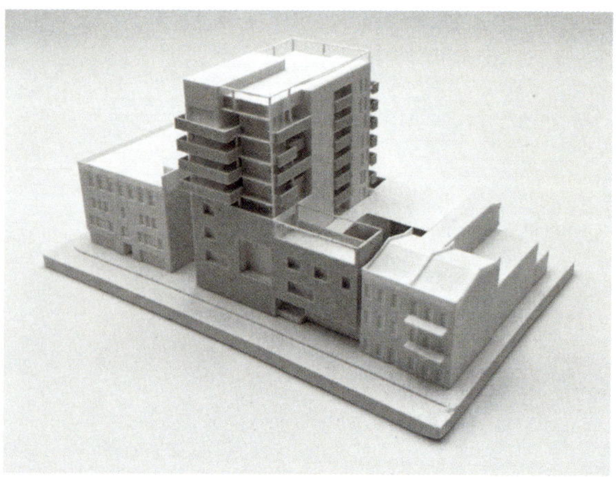

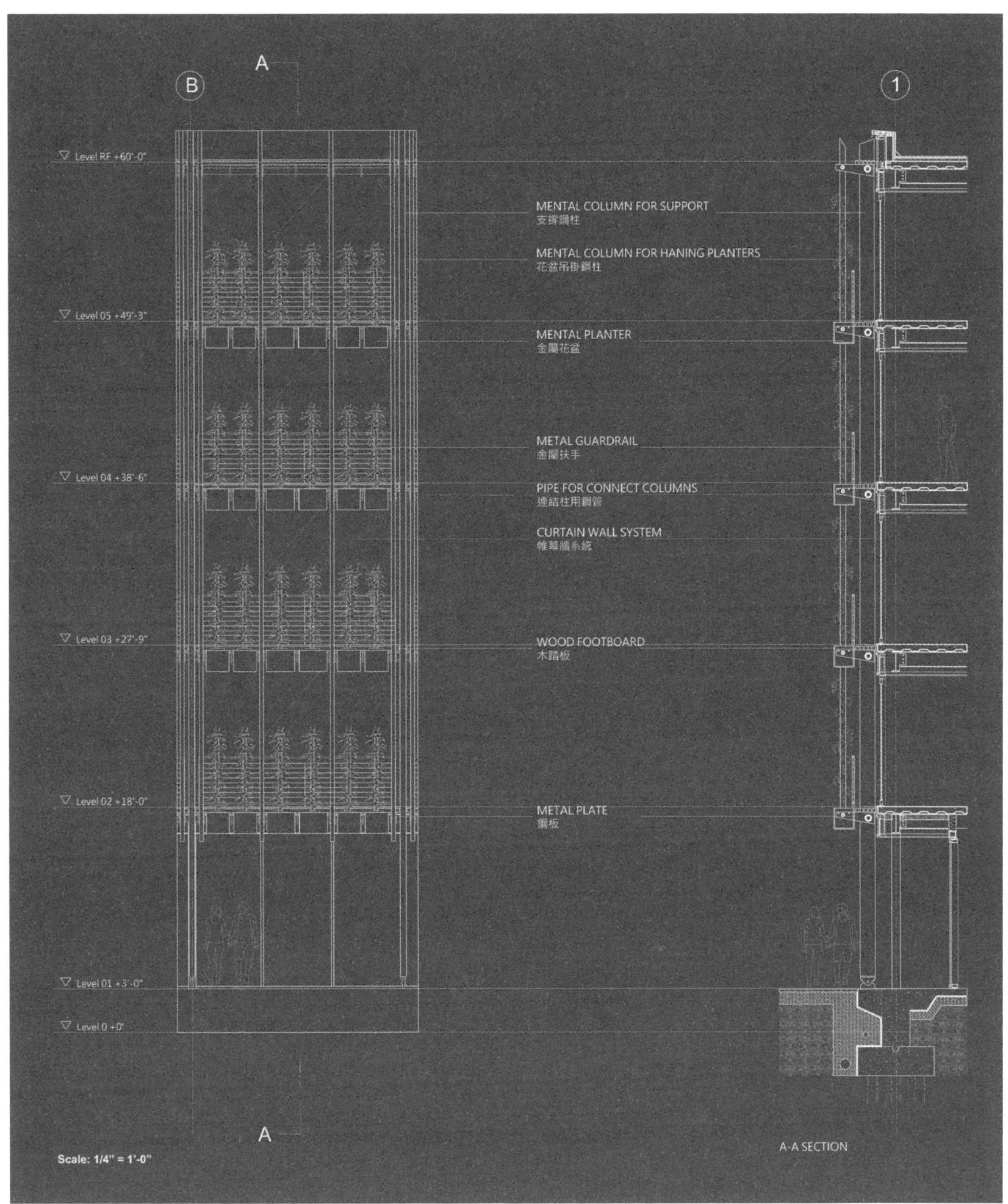
A
B
1
Level RF +60'-0"
Level 05 +49'-3"
Level 04 +38'-6"
Level 03 +27'-9"
Level 02 +18'-0"
Level 01 +3'-0"
Level 0 +0"
MENTAL COLUMN FOR SUPPORT
支撐鋼柱
MENTAL COLUMN FOR HANING PLANTERS
花盆吊掛鋼柱
MENTAL PLANTER
金屬花盆
METAL GUARDRAIL
金屬扶手
PIPE FOR CONNECT COLUMNS
連結柱用鋼管
CURTAIN WALL SYSTEM
帷幕牆系統
WOOD FOOTBOARD
木踏板
METAL PLATE
鋼板
A
Scale: 1/4" = 1'-0"
A-A SECTION

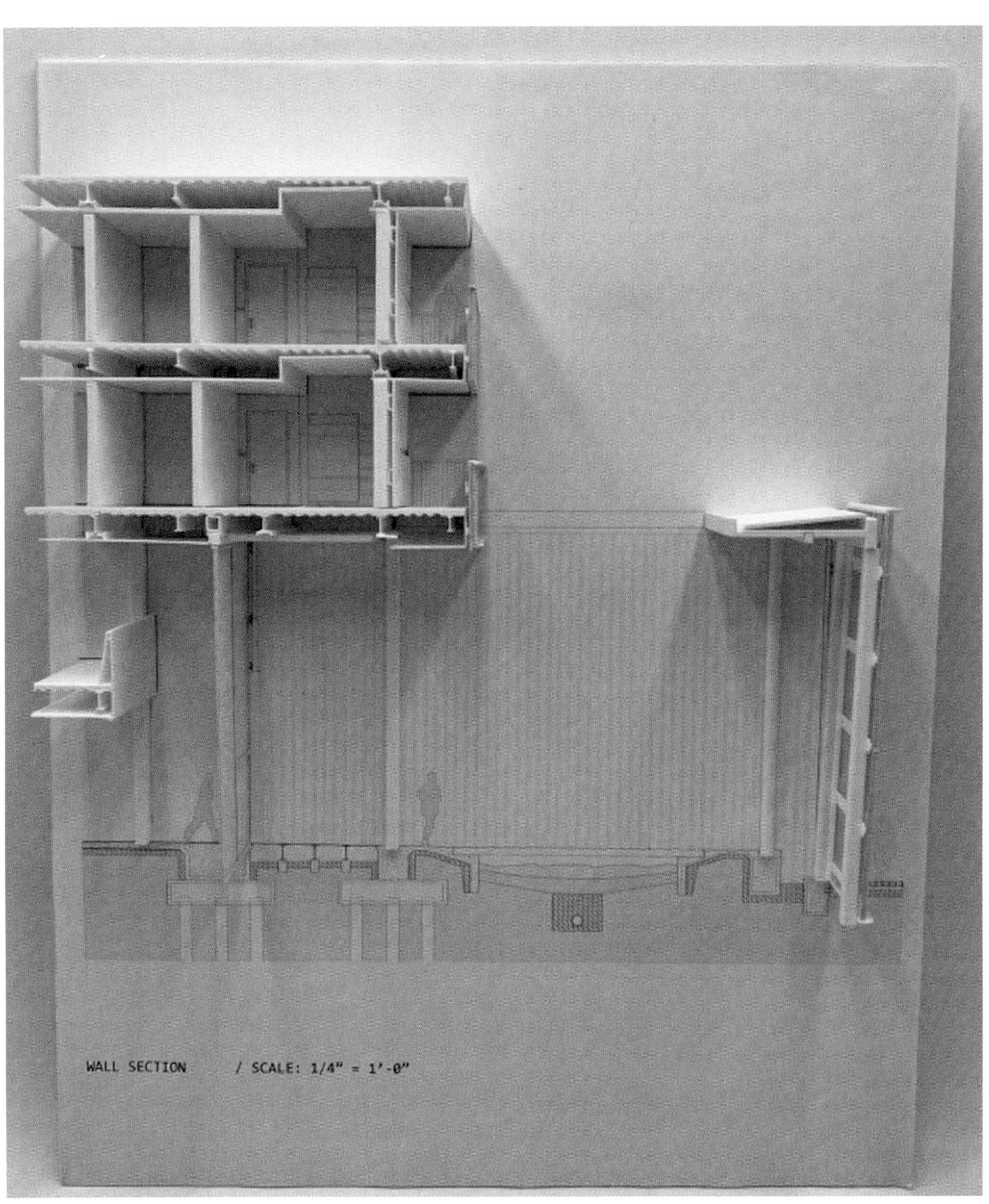
WALL SECTION / SCALE: 1/4" = 1'-0"

s> Hunter Darby, Laura Neises

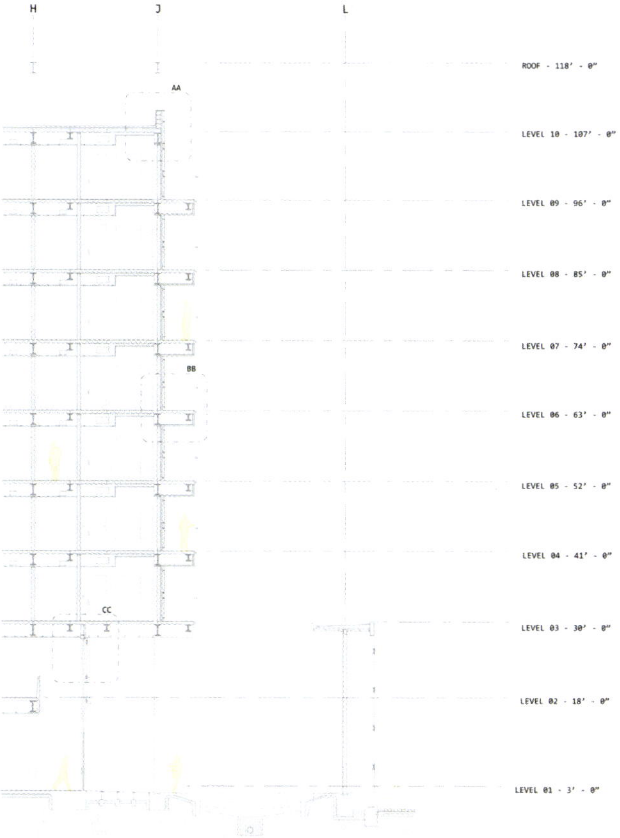
H
J
L
ROOF - 118' - 0"
AA
LEVEL 10 - 107' - 0"
LEVEL 09 - 96' - 0"
LEVEL 08 - 85' - 0"
LEVEL 07 - 74' - 0"
BB
LEVEL 06 - 63' - 0"
LEVEL 05 - 52' - 0"
LEVEL 04 - 41' - 0"
CC
LEVEL 03 - 30' - 0"
LEVEL 02 - 18' - 0"
LEVEL 01 - 3' - 0"

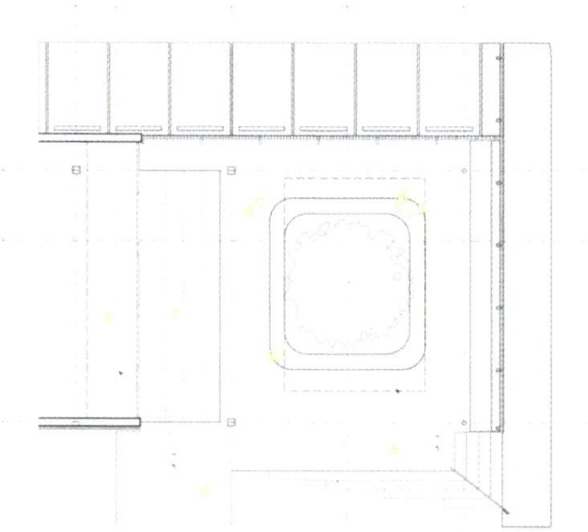

i> Javier Marcano, Kentaro Tsubaki

WALL DETAIL
1 Terracotta panels
2 Terracotta clips and air gap
3 Sheathing
4 Rigid insulation board
5 Vapor barrier
6 Sheathing
7 6" steel stud with batt insulation
8 Gypsum board

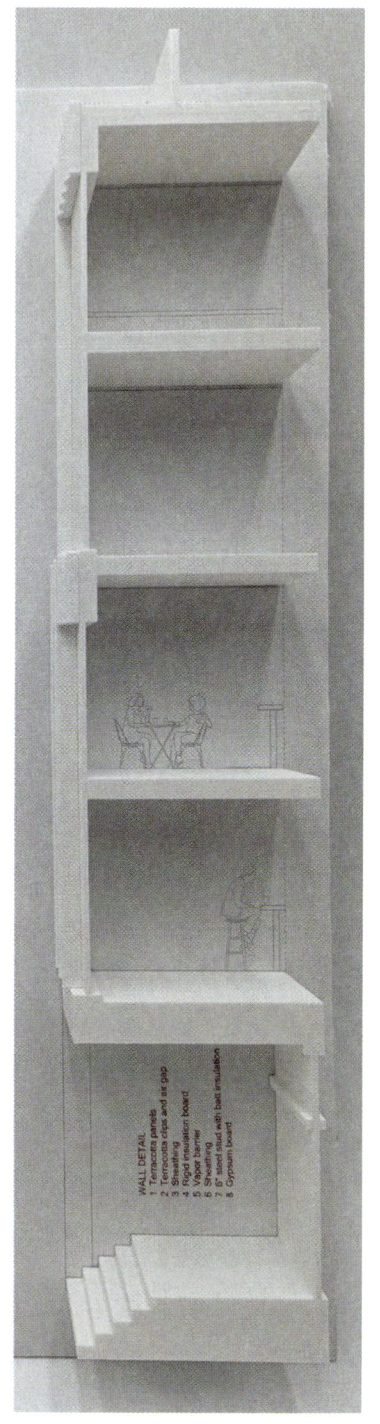

By The Albert and Tina Small Center

8

DIALOGUE

AS COMMON GOOD

ARCHITECTURE AS DIALOGUE FOR THE COMMON GOOD

Empathy, Compassion, and Care as Foundations for a More Inclusive Built Environment

By Edson Cabalfin
Associate Dean for Equity, Diversity, and Inclusion
Tulane School of Architecture and Built Environment

Achieving the common good through dialogue means that a diversity of perspectives must be considered and reconciled.

Architecture and the built environment do not exist in a vacuum but are inextricably enmeshed within the socio-cultural context. Architecture cannot just be treated as an inert and neutral object divorced from society. Social, technological, ecological, economic, and political dynamics are embedded within and acting upon architecture.

People matter in the built environment. We cannot simply dismiss the importance of considering who creates, uses, and engages with architecture. What makes architecture work is how it should consider the myriad dimensions that people inevitably imagine, employ, and participate in its formation. People are important stakeholders in architecture, whether as users, clients, designers, critics, bystanders, or observers.

People, however, are not just one type. The idea of an "average person" is a myth. People come in many different forms and sizes with various lived experiences and backgrounds. Despite the differences, people share similar dreams and aspirations for a comfortable, healthy, and safe life filled with love and kindness. The built environment should contend with the diversity of people while at the same time celebrating our common humanity.

But how might we acknowledge diversity and celebrate our shared humanity? Dialogue is key in practicing the common good. Dialogue can be understood here as the process of engaging in a conversation between individuals, conditions, communities, and even worlds. Part of the goal of participating in a conversation could be how to negotiate or mediate between differing positions or opinions. Dialogue might also mean establishing a common ground to achieve a collective understanding. Achieving the common good through dialogue means that a diversity of perspectives must be considered and reconciled. Furthermore, the common good means that we share a life and a world that is beneficial for everyone.

But creating dialogue is also not easy. It requires us to go beyond what we are comfortable with. Sometimes, it demands that we contradict what we have been accustomed to. But by stretching ourselves beyond our comfort zone and moving towards growing and learning, the process of dialogue becomes essential in ensuring that a more equitable built environment is created in the future.

So, how might we achieve dialogue for the common good? In the built environment, this means that we practice empathy, demonstrate kindness, and open our minds and hearts.

Practicing empathy compels us to not only put ourselves in somebody else's position but also understand where people are coming from. As people embody their specific lived experiences, we need to consider how their contexts, conditions, and histories all shape their present and future lives. Given that we all have different experiences, empathy then expands our awareness of the differences we have and then amplifies the shared hopes and fears that people hold. Empathy opens the possibilities for a better connection between people.

Being kind is also crucial in any kind of work that endeavors to achieve the common good because compassion is fundamental in any type of human and non-human relations. Empathy is connected to an ethos of compassion and care. We must be kind to people who might be different from us. We must also be kind to ourselves. We must be kind to plants, animals, and the earth we live in. We must also extend kindness to the future generations.

The act of opening your mind and heart is necessary in the practice of empathy and compassion. Sometimes, we are so stuck with our old ways of doing and thinking that we end up becoming complacent. Fear takes over and we refuse to accept things that we are not familiar with. This same fear of the unfamiliar prevents us from opening a dialogue, thereby hindering us from truly embracing change. We need to open up our hearts and minds so that kindness flows through us and onto the world.

The challenge now is how to transform the practice of architecture and the built environment into a praxis of compassion and care towards humans and non-humans. Dialogue must happen at all times. It is incumbent upon us to create this dialogue for the common good. Through empathy, compassion, and care, we can create a more inclusive, sustainable, and equitable built environment for the present and the future. ■

PARTICIPATION AND THE COMMON GOOD

By Patricia Fraile
Editor, The ReView
Tulane School of Architecture and Built Environment

To design for the common good is to recognize that architecture is inherently political—shaped by power, identity, and access—and that reclaiming participation is not just about design, but about restoring civic agency, collective authorship, and the right to shape the spaces we inhabit.

In past centuries, cities have been defined by centralized planning, expert-driven design, and a hierarchical approach to architecture, where architects and policymakers dictated form and function. Yet, architecture has always been an act of collective making —from vernacular traditions to self-built settlements. It was only with the rise of professionalization and industrialized urban planning that the power to shape space became concentrated in the hands of a few. But a shift is underway—one that reclaims architecture as a participatory, community-driven process. The growing movement of civic engagement in architecture and urbanism reflects a larger societal demand for agency, equity, and shared authorship over the spaces we inhabit. This shift is not merely a reaction to systemic inequalities but a reimagining of how we design, educate, and build for the common good.

Reclaiming participation in architecture is not just about design processes—it is inherently a political act. The built environment, like any shared resource, is a commons that should be democratically designed rather than dictated by capital or institutional power. The collaborative nature of community engagement's approaches stems from a recognition of the challenges facing modern cities. The loss of community identity and social ties, the absence of a dominant culture, and a growing disillusionment with traditional models of governance, among other factors, are driving the move toward more inclusive and locally driven decision-making processes.

At the same time, the production of architecture and urban space has increasingly shifted away from public power and into the hands of private corporations. The great civic projects once led by governments or religious institutions have been replaced by the corporate urbanism of Apple and Walmart campuses, or the rapid, speculative expansions of Gulf cities driven by oligarchic interests. In this accelerating neoliberal landscape, architecture and urban development are no longer expected to serve the common good, but rather private capital, often with little regard for public interest or social equity. While professionalization may have distanced architecture from communal agency, it is the dominance of private capital over the built environment that has truly severed its ties to the public good. In this context, participatory practices are not only an act of resistance but a crucial attempt to restore architecture's civic responsibility.

Projects involving self-built, informal, and post-disaster settlements further underscore the urgency of this approach. While 98% of the built environment remains unrecognized within formal architectural discourse, informal architecture plays a crucial role in housing millions of people worldwide. Recognizing these spaces as legitimate forms of urbanism forces architects to switch their focus from imposing solutions to supporting self-determined processes.

Community engagement challenges the conventional role of the architect as the all-knowing expert and instead embraces facilitation, education, and advocacy as integral to their practice. It is not about relinquishing expertise, but rather about acknowledging that design is most powerful when it is collaborative. By fostering dialogue between professionals and communities, architects can transition from designing *for* citizens, to designing *with* them (or even designed *by* them!). Likewise, in a landscape increasingly defined by corporate interests, without citizen input and sometimes even against their well-being, this approach recenters civic life in the design process, ensuring that the built environment better reflects the collective needs, identities, and aspirations of its inhabitants.

This is evident in the rise of Design/Build programs and Community Design Centers across academic institutions across the U.S. These initiatives immerse students in real-world projects, reinforcing the idea that learning is inseparable from doing. Programs like Urban Build and The Albert and Tina Small Center for Collaborative Design at Tulane School of Architecture and Built Environment bridge the gap between education and practice, empowering students to create tangible social impacts while redefining architectural pedagogy, an architectural pedagogy that must be radically reimagined if it is to truly serve the public good. The dominance of reductive pedagogies that oversimplify social and urban complexities, formalistic and endogamic in nature— focused on the object while disregarding its context—has long marginalized alternative approaches to design, reinforced hierarchical structures within the profession, and perpetuated cultural norms. A critical pedagogy must address these blind spots by: questioning this system; challenging the existing canon to include diverse voices, traditions, and methodologies; promoting democratic knowledge production; ensuring that students learn from community stakeholders, activists, and local builders; bridging academia and practice through hands-on methodologies that prioritize social responsibility over mere formal experimentation; and decentering the master-apprentice model in favor of collaborative learning environments where students and communities co-create knowledge. Their work serves as a reminder that education must not only reflect the realities of the world, but actively participate in building a more just and inclusive future.

But even as participation becomes more widespread, challenges remain. The increasing privatization of public space, the commodification of digital participation tools, and the rise of technocratic governance models risk reducing engagement to aestheticized data points rather than genuine civic empowerment. Architects and urbanists must actively resist these trends by advocating for public agency in shaping urban futures.

To design for the common good is to recognize that architecture is not a neutral discipline—it is deeply embedded in issues of power, identity, and access. Whether in the form of participatory design studios or radical pedagogies, the key challenge is the same: how do we create environments that serve and empower all, rather than the privileged few? This is not a utopian ideal; it is a return to how cities and communities have always been built—through collective labor, negotiation, and shared vision. Reclaiming this tradition is not just as an aesthetic or technical exercise, but as a profound act of social justice and collective care. ■

EMILIE TAYLOR WELTY
& SETH WELTY

BAXDEL RESIDENCE

RESIDENTIAL
New Orleans

Credits
Colectivo Design Team: Seth Welty, Elliott Petterson, Emilie Taylor Welty
Nick Licausi (drone shots)
Developer: Patronat Municipal de l'Habitatge

How do you design new in a city full of histories, typologies, and expectations of what a house should be? For a family with two young children their hope was to upend the local expectations of a long narrow double occupancy shotgun home. This house, affectionately called the Iceberg, splits the two residences into a front and back with an entry courtyard between. The two units combined are 3,200 s.f.

The home and its details are designed not to mimic their context, but to embrace the funkiness of New Orleans culture and community and dance to its own beat. The rooflines, materiality, and window boxes are a call out to local precedents but unique in this configuration.

The street face of the residence welcomes visitors in and under a generous covered porch space and through a central entry courtyard. The Iceberg's corrugated metal is pieced by deep window boxes which frame views from the interior and provide deeper shadowlines on the exterior facade.

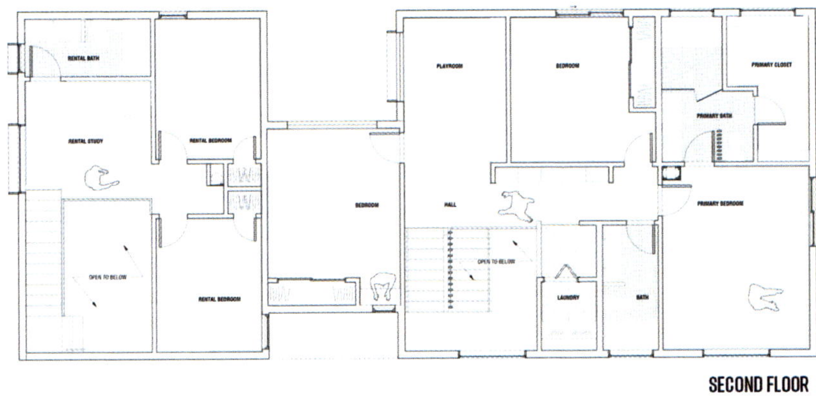

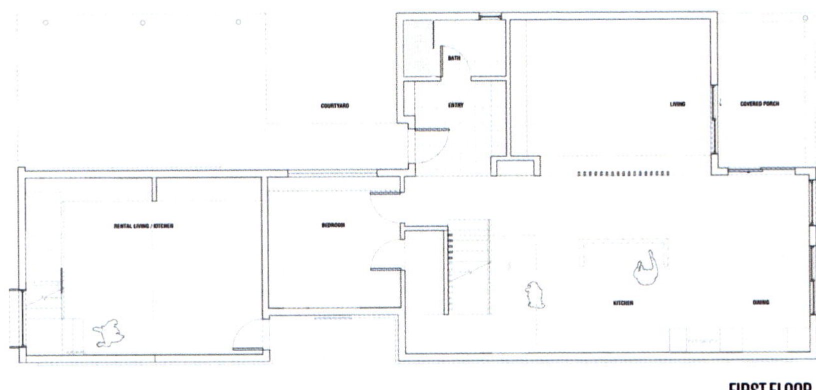

Fig. 1 Floor plans

Fig. 2
Interior image from the kitchen

Figs. 3, 4
Exterior views and entrance

event

Gradschool Nights

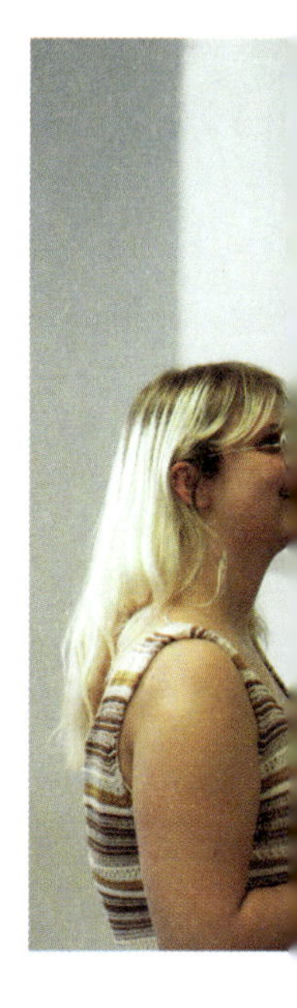

411
412

event

Career Days 2024

TuSA
CAREER
DAYS
2024
JANUARY 31 - FEBRUARY 2

Career Days 2024

PERMANENT INTERACTION

Besthoff Foundation, Magazine Street

Ammar Eloueini [C]
Sean Fowler

This Studio focuses on a contemporary architecture intervention in a historic context. New Orleans is the oldest, most preserved city in the United States. It is the perfect laboratory to investigate and test possible contemporary architectural interventions. The studio will focus on a collection of lots and buildings at the intersection of Magazine and St. Joseph Streets. A number of historic buildings, some dating from the late 1800s, two warehouses from the 1950s and more recent buildings constitute an interesting site to host an art foundation. In recent years and around the world, art foundations are becoming a common program. In most cases art foundations are new buildings (Cartier Foundation, Louis Vuitton Foundation...), and in some other cases they take on existing buildings and transform them (Pinault Foundation, Prada Foundation...).

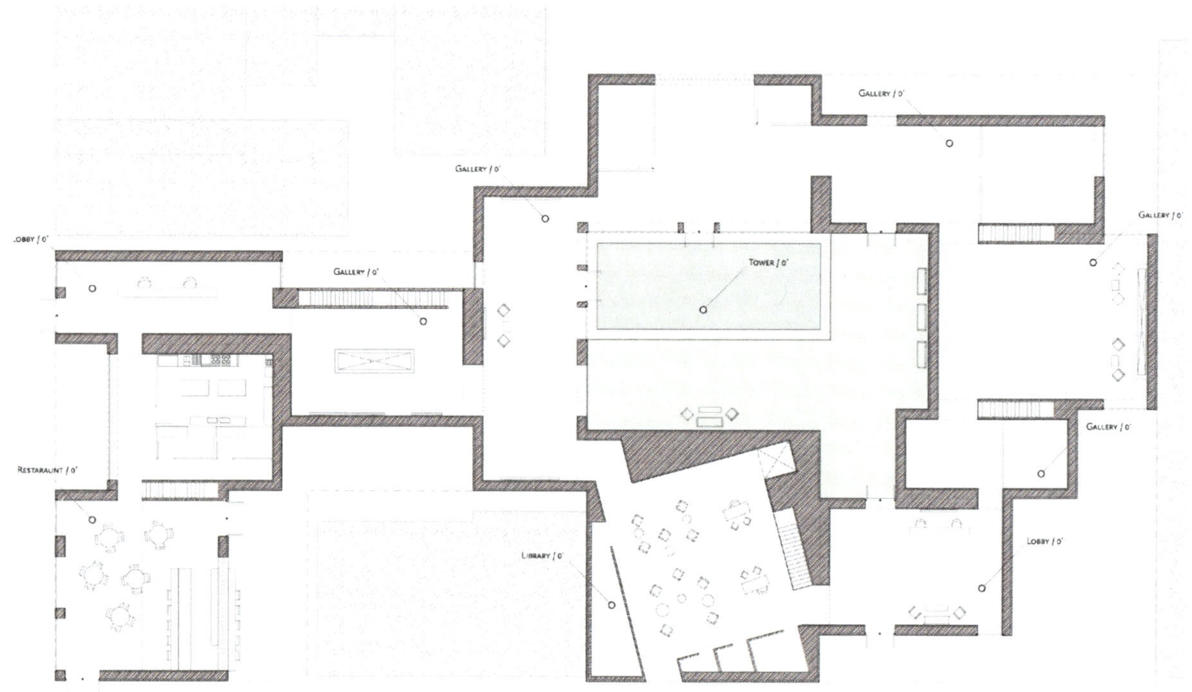

s> Alec Rosen + Akhil Singh

i> Ammar Eloueini, Sean Fowler

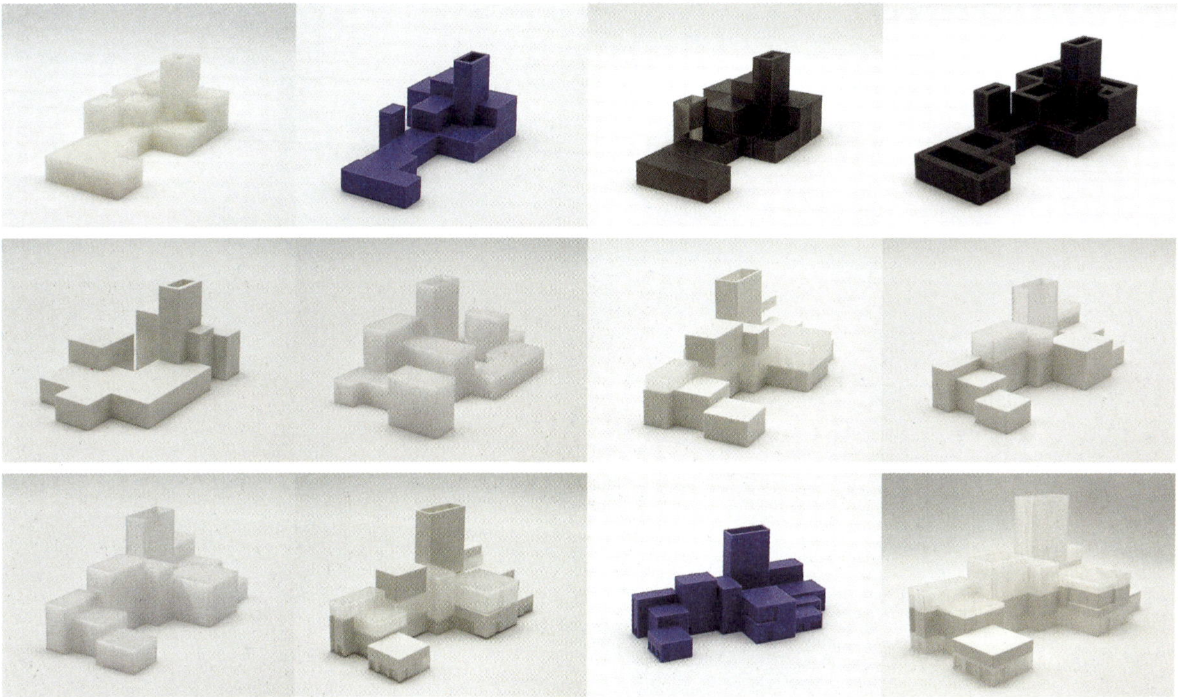

s> Alec Rosen + Akhil Singh

i> Ammar Eloueini, Sean Fowler

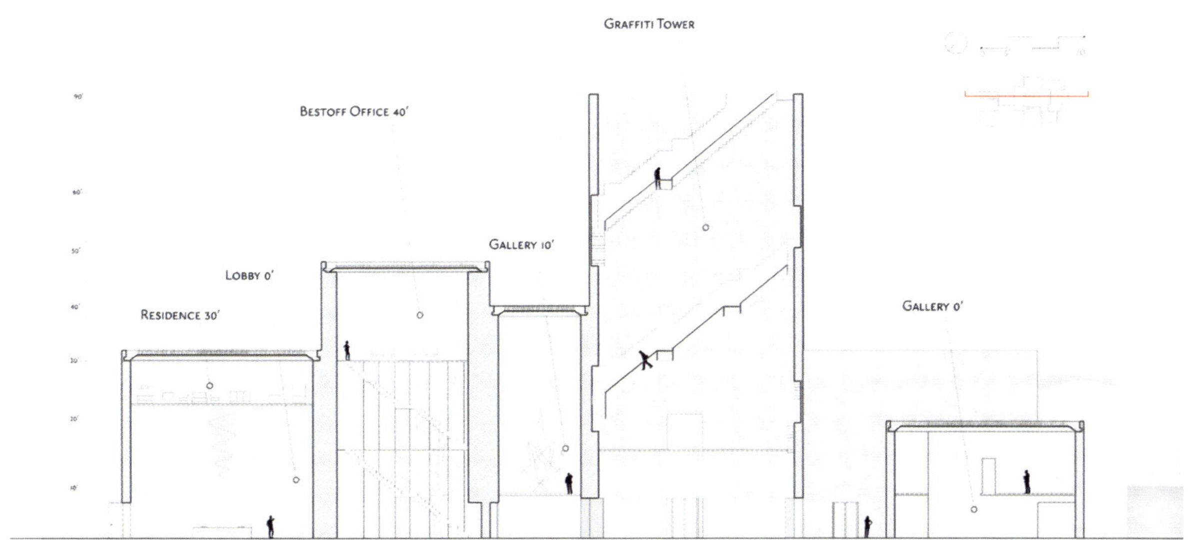

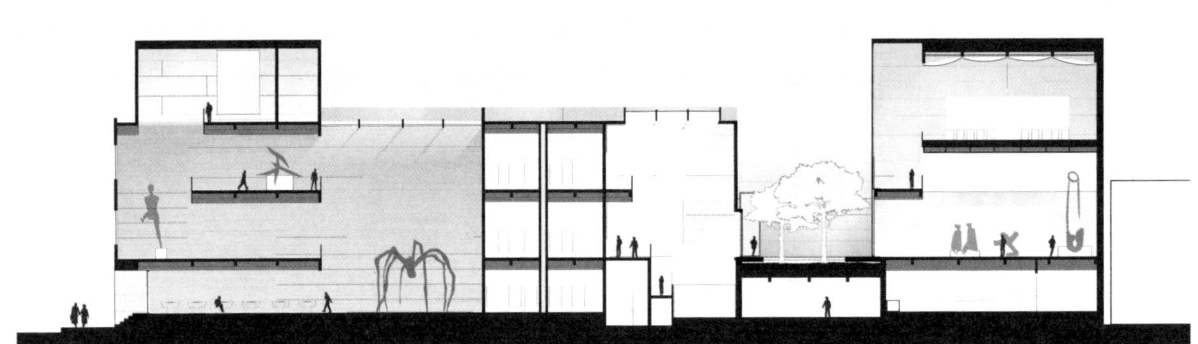

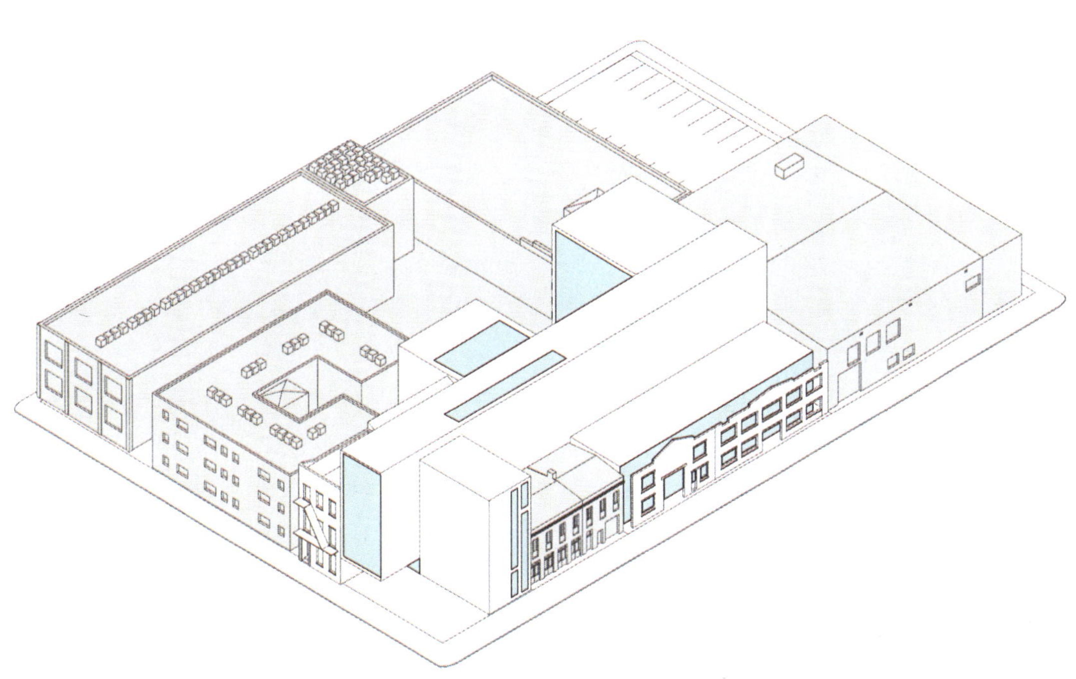

Play It Louder

The Albert and Tina Small Center for Collaborative Design
Curated by Jose Cotto

Too often, data dehumanizes, is incomprehensible, and manipulates the truth. Play It Louder counters these realities by creating space for students, artists, and community partners to collaboratively explore the architectures of carcerality and abolition.

Through design investigations, interactive works, and installations grounded in data and research, the exhibit aims to amplify the impacts of carceral systems and the potential of abolitionist principles to restore.

Play It Louder isn't just a collection of artifacts; it's a symposium of ideas, a dialogue between numbers and narratives, and an invitation to engage, empathize, and reflect. The exhibit builds on past partnerships with Jackie Sumell of Solitary Gardens, the John Thompson Legacy Center, and also features work by RENEE ROYALE, Langston Allston, and students at Tulane's School of Architecture and Built Environment.

This project is supported in part by the National Endowment for the Arts. To find out more about how National Endowment for the Arts grants impact individuals and communities, visit www.arts.gov.

Paintings by Langston Allston

Louisiana
centers. There
the custody
State juvenile

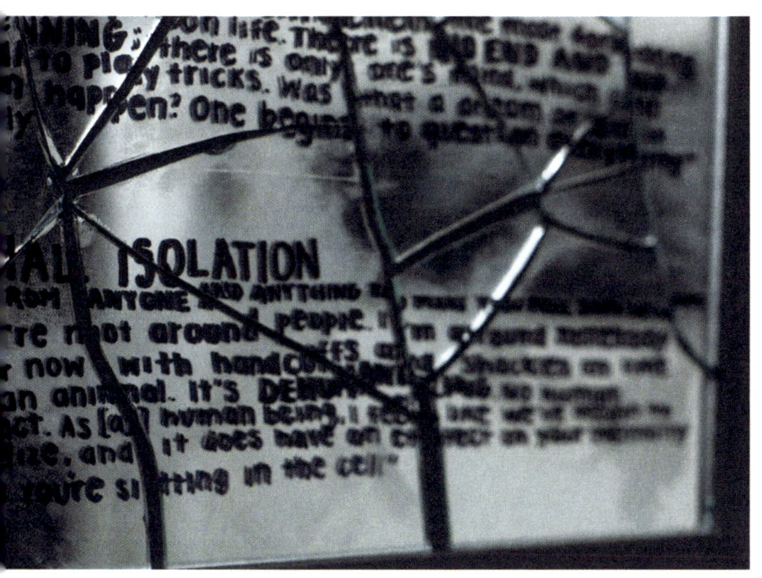

state pr
tionwide
been first
y age 18. While
women are 3 times
n to be victimized by
ff. There was a 750%
nber of incarcerated
1980 and 2017. More
omen in jails have no
crime and are a

event

AER Symposium

Led by Zaid Kashef Alghata

The Architecture's Ecological Restructuring Symposium was a workshop-style event at Tulane, following the inaugural session in 2023. The symposium featured academics from around the country, including Debbie Chen (*Rhode Island School of Design*), Rebecca Choi (*TuSABE*), Liz Galvez (*Berkley College of Environmental Design*), Mae-Ling Lokko (*Yale School of Architecture*), Antoine Picon (*Harvard Graduate School of Design*), and Meredith TenHoor (*Pratt Institute School of Architecture*).

Image by Professor Wes Michaels

9

MISSISSIPPI

AS COMMON GOOD

ON COMMONS, COMMISSIONS, AND COMPROMISE

The Case of the St. Mary Batture

By Richard Campanella
Associate Dean for Research, Senior Professor of Practice in Architecture and Geography, and Mintz Professor in Architecture
Tulane School of Architecture and Built Environment

The tension between common goods and individual rights—between 'Welcome' signs and 'Keep Out' signs—is exactly that, a tension... existing in dynamic equilibrium without easy answers.

Next time you're downtown, take a stroll along Tchoupitoulas Street, specifically the 800 block between Julia and St. Joseph. Once home to light industry and maritime services, this neighborhood is now something of a boutique district, with art galleries, bistros, condominiums, and hotels. But 220 years ago, the space where Emeril's Restaurant now stands became a flashpoint for a discourse—and a discord—ongoing to this day, and it touches upon the *ReView's* theme of the common good.

First, some background on river dynamics. The Mississippi at that time flowed much farther inland, skirting Tchoupitoulas Street, which formed the crest of the natural levee. This being the point-bar side of a great channel meander, the current velocity tended to slow along this bank, which reduced kinetic energy and allowed suspended sediment to fall out. A recent shift in the channel exacerbated this trend, and in 1803, a sandy beach began to form off the Tchoupitoulas Street land owned by Jean Gravier in the *Faubourg Ste. Marie* (Suburb St. Mary), today's Central Business District.

Delighted by the gratuitous accretion to his property, Gravier sent workers to build a levee around the beach, protecting it from the vagaries of the Mississippi and preparing it to be put to money-making use. With the Louisiana Purchase recently signed, the incoming American regime would bring English common law to Louisiana, a legal philosophy that viewed such riparian formations as belonging to the rightful owner of the adjacent land—in this case, Jean Gravier.

But French Creoles viewed things differently—and they had seen these bankside beaches before. They described them as *terre d'alluvion* and called them *battures*, from the past participle of the French verb *battre* (to beat), as in "beaten down by the river," submerged during high stage and strewn with sandbars and driftwood when the water dropped. According to the Roman civil law statutes that had guided Louisiana jurisprudence during the French and Spanish colonial regimes, the batture was public space—a commons open to all, for people to extract renewable resources such as freshwater, sand, firewood, and fish, or simply to promenade and enjoy the breezes rolling off the river, a favorite evening activity in this steamy subtropical city.

And now, suddenly, with these brash new Americans moving in and taking over, someone was barricading off the batture and claiming it *for himself*? A *French Creole*,

This 1798 map, annoted in 1875, shows the alluvial ground known as the St Mary Batture_courtesy of Library of Congress

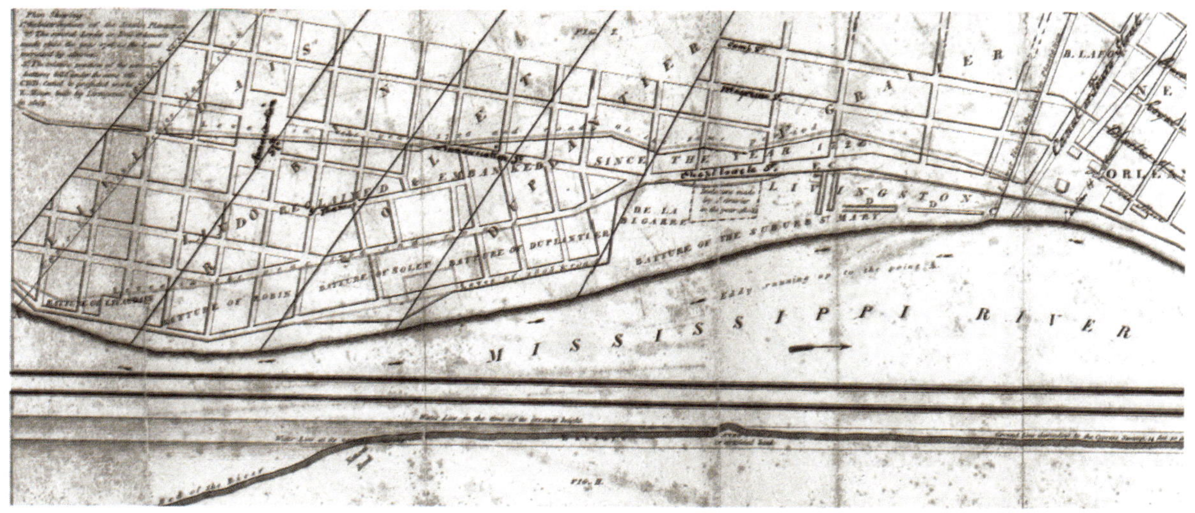

1810 map showing St Mary Batture and Gravier claim_courtesy of The Historic New Orleans Collection

On this block in 1803, Jean Gravier built a levee around the batture--and started a legal battle that would last for years_photo by Richard Campanella.

no less? The very notion outraged local citizens, and they responded in kind, demanding in 1804 that the *Conseil de Ville* (City Council) declare explicitly that the batture was public property.

But the private-property camp had firepower too, in the form of New York lawyers who foresaw the value of new riverfront land in the booming Port of New Orleans, and wanted in on the action. Lawsuits were filed in what became known as the St. Mary Batture Case, and in 1807, rather unsurprisingly, the American-dominated Justices of the Territorial Court ruled in favor of privatization.

That's when New Orleanians themselves engaged. Cognizant they were about to lose a cherished right, they marched to Gravier's batture—or rather, *their* batture—nightly through the summer of 1807, demanding that the fence come down, the levee be removed, and the batture be returned to the people. They protested with enough rigor for opposing lawyers to describe them as a "mob" in a nearly riotous mood.

Lengthy court cases ensued for years, each with complex legal arguments and counterarguments, and all with national implications. President Thomas Jefferson became personally involved in the case because his vision for an agrarian nation rested squarely on free and open access to the Mississippi River and its tributaries. Ironically, that put Jefferson on the Creole side of the argument, despite that he was of British ancestry and acculturated to English common law. There were also Creoles on the American side of the argument, among them Jean Gravier.

The St. Mary Batture Case came to something of a compromised resolution, at least at first. As John Adems Paxton explained in 1822, Gravier's batture claim, "which has made so great a figure in the history of litigation, is now divided among a great number of proprietors...and a liberal arrangement with the...city has put it in a situation in which it may be improved and made useful to the public, as well as a source of profit to the owners." This compromise explains why we have the Warehouse District today, and why you're able to walk around freely on Commerce Street, South Peters, Fulton, and Convention Center Boulevard—all of which occupy the former batture, and remain in the public domain. But it also explains why you cannot enter any of the private spaces on those blocks, unless you're an owner, visitor, or customer—at Emeril's, for example.

In the two centuries since the initial compromise, batture law in Louisiana has become perfectly convoluted. Various judicial rulings have allowed for private ownership and leasing of battures, while other judgements have sided with public access. Today, one may find battures that constitute private space in the private domain (such as that fenced-off riverfront at the foot of Walnut Street); private space in the public domain (such as the heavily secured Port of New Orleans, a state agency); public space in the private domain (such as the Riverwalk Mall); and public space in the public domain (such as Woldenberg Park or Audubon Riverfront Park, a.k.a. The Fly).

Perhaps this convolution should be of no surprise, given modern Louisiana's mixed legal jurisdiction of both Roman civil and English common law. But it should not be a surprise on a broader American level either. The tension between common goods and individual rights—between "Welcome" signs and "Keep Out" signs—is exactly that, a *tension*. It exists in dynamic equilibrium, I believe, and has no easy answers or irrefutable ideologies.

Readers of this *ReView* might find themselves sympathetic to the argument of the common good, like those protestors at the St. Mary Batture two centuries ago. But the field of architecture tells a different story, as this client-driven profession depends largely on the commissions of private landowners devising for-profit developments, as Jean Gravier did two centuries ago. Moral support for the common good will have to reconcile with the astonishing wealth-creation capacity of privatization, and some sort of compromise may well be the eventual outcome—just as it was on the St. Mary Batture.

John Adems Paxton sensed as much in 1822. "All this commerce centers on the Batture," he marveled while watching the nonstop maritime traffic at the Port of New Orleans. "It would be difficult to select in any city in the world a spot in which more extensive business is done in the same space. *The property then must soon become invaluable*." ■

ARCH 4052 + 6052 | **Research Studio** | UG + GR | **SP24**

NEW ORLEANS PUBLIC SPACE PROJECT

Sean Fowler [C]
Iñaki Alday

The New Orleans Public Space Project proposes to examine the transformations needed in the city's public space in order to address its long-term sustainability through the street network's capacity to address water management, mobility changes, connectivity across neighborhoods, urban ecology, heritage revitalization, and relation with its main geographical features. The project is structured in four parts: Streets, mobility and water management; Barriers, disruptions and reconnections; Heritage streetscape recover; and City and river stitching.

The studio is organized as a lab, with two research directors (faculty) and twelve team members working in different group configurations and individually, exerting individual agency while pushing a collective endeavor. Individual creativity, interests and abilities are focused in identifying the critical issues and propose the best comprehensive answers. Each student is challenged to face the entire complexity and produce unique responses, responsible and adventurous at the same time. The current team builds on the knowledge produced by the previous generations of the Yamuna River Project Studio.

The methodology is organized in 3 main steps: Search, Research (multi-scale Design Research) and Evaluation. It is critical to note that this series of steps are not cleanly delimited and there are overlaps and a process of going back and forth. The design process is not linear when searching for information, speculating, proposing, testing and evaluating. From each of these moments, the design process moves to the next and, almost always, to the previous at the same time. Similarly, the scales of design are multiple and the process includes the movement from each one to the more detailed and the more general alternatively, if not simultaneously.

The outcome is a collective design research that produces a coherent proposition of multiple coordinated pieces, a common strategic plan and individual/small team-specific propositions for specific sites/situations. Each of the last ones is a test of the critical interventions necessary to implement the strategic vision and a detailed design response.

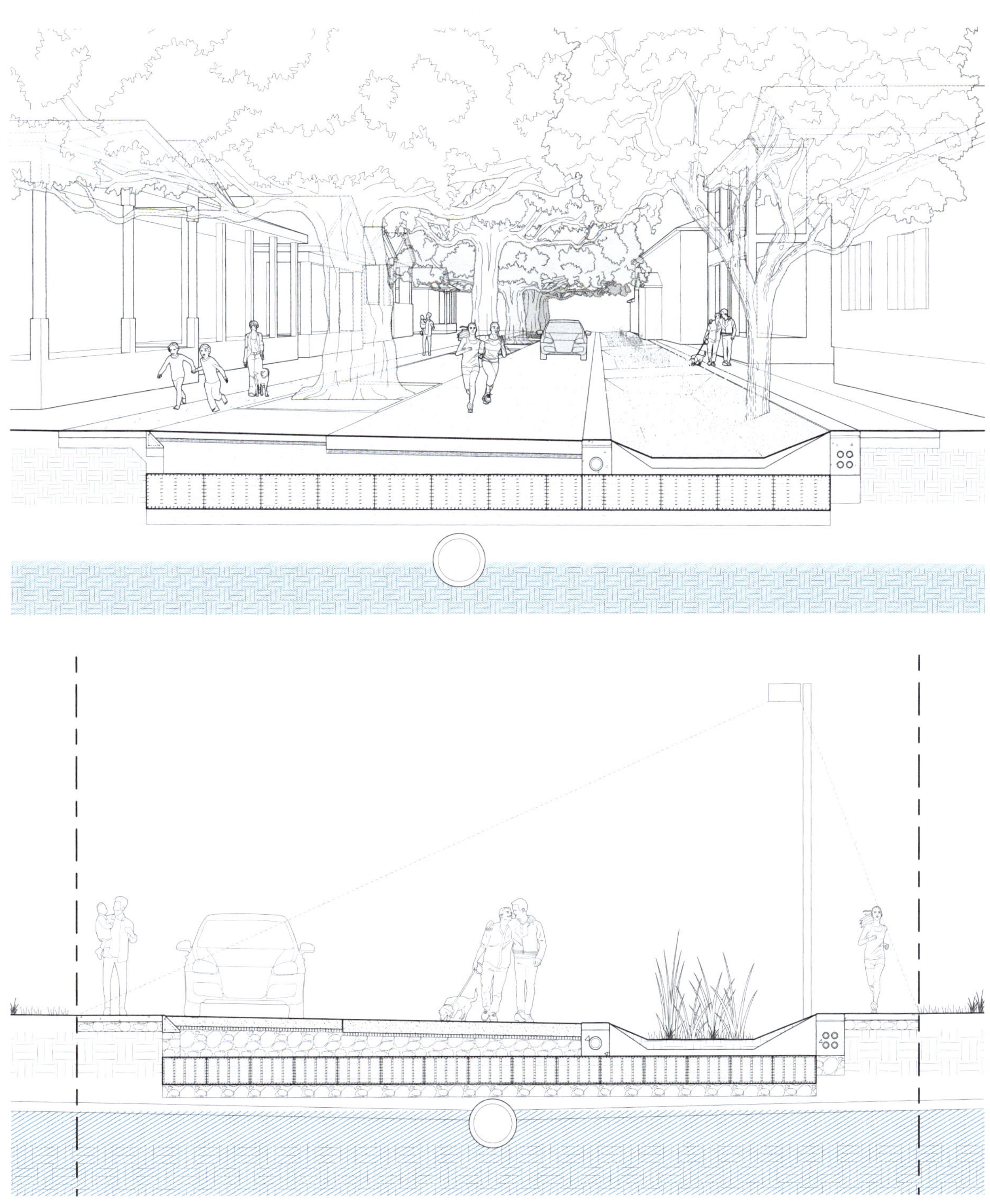

ARCH 4052 + 6052 | **Research Studio** | UG + GR | **SP24**

"A Vision for Vibrancy on South Claiborne Avenue"

South Claiborne Avenue is an underutilized commercial corridor and artery for the city of New Orleans and can be to the 21st century what St. Charles Avenue was for the 19th and 20th centuries. This corridor connects Tulane University's Uptown campus with the University Medical Center, Charity Hospital redevelopment and Tulane University's Downtown campus, giving access to some of the largest employers in the city.

However, South Claiborne does not adequately support this connection and could be rethought as a thriving commercial corridor focused into distinct zones along its length.

This project proposes rethinking the development of this corridor through a case study along its length. First, the neutral ground is considered as a public amenity and a space to manage stormwater in a way where it can be treated as a resource. Then, the vital traffic along the road is considered, replacing parallel parking with dedicated bus stops and lanes to prioritize function. Finally, the highest and best use for the developable land along the corridor is considered, proposing densification to better serve existing community needs and also the greater connections fostered by this redesign.

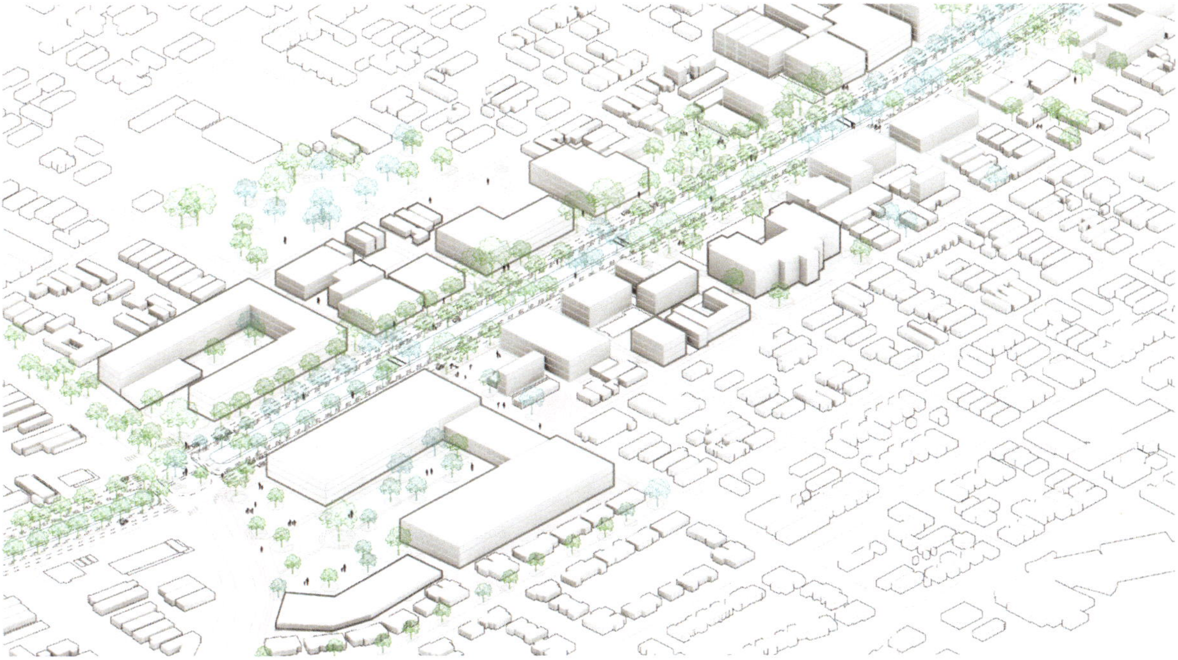

ARCH 4052 + 6052 | **Research Studio** | UG + GR | **SP24**

“A People’s Promenade”

Napoleon Avenue may be reimagined as a space both to manage water and for the public to engage with water as a resource and for recreation. This includes rethinking the Napoleon corridor with transit-priority infrastructure and adjusting the right-of-way for public and pedestrian use.

Magazine Street may be reimagined as a pedestrian-first promenade with limited automotive access to better serve as a walkable pedestrian commercial corridor. Reclaiming space dedicated to storing cars allows for more street-front eateries, outdoor shopping and circulator transit. This space also becomes performant as water-management infrastructure is in alignment with surrounding blocks.

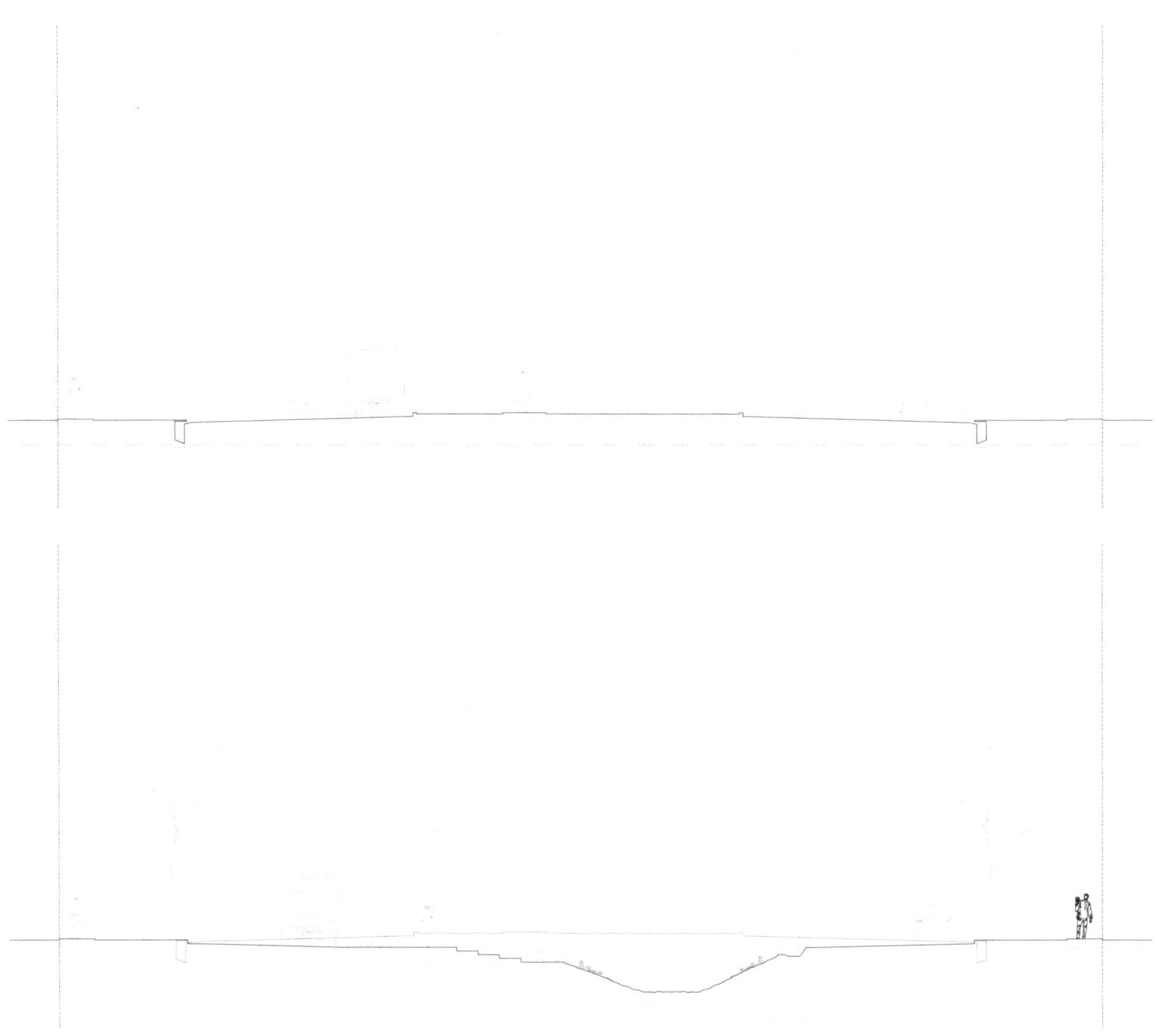

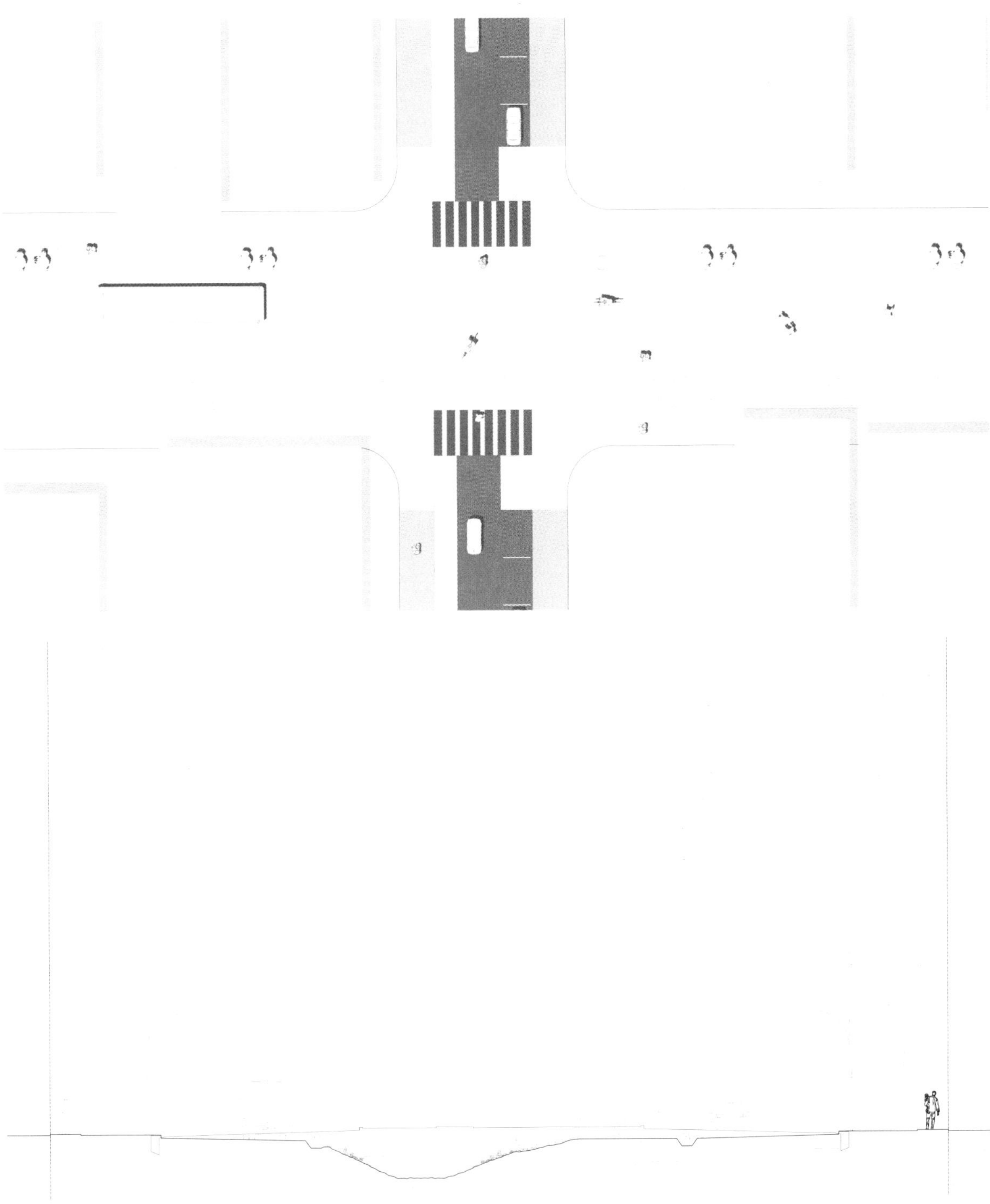

The Water Park, Zaragoza 2008, Spain. Floods on January 22, 2013. Photo by Envuelo SL

10

WATER

AS COMMON GOOD

WATER AS COMMON GOOD

A Call to Sustainable Stewardship

By Iñaki Alday
Dean, Richard Koch Chair in Architecture
Tulane School of Architecture and Built Environment

Water is the ultimate common good, vital for life, equity, and resilience, demanding sustainable stewardship in the face of global challenges.

Water and air to breathe are probably the most acute physical needs of a human being. Water sources are deities, or at least mythological elements, in every culture, from the Indian river goddesses to the Greek Naiads, the Native American sacredness of water or the Maori personhood of the rivers. As the basis of life on planet Earth, and thus the ultimate common good for humans and non-humans, water has innumerable aspects that affect well-being, both physical and emotional, and equally numerous challenges, exacerbated by climate change, rapid urbanization, and acute inequalities.

Access to safe drinking water is considered a basic human right, with all the complexities of price and cost of providing it. Drinking water infrastructure has the greatest impact on the pursuit of equity, health and basic quality of life. Surface water is most often the source for human consumption, for irrigation and food production, and for sustaining the ecosystems that support life. Seas are sources of food, complex ecosystems, and the most important planetary element for climate stability. Pollution, overexploitation, or privatization challenge the condition of rivers, lakes, and water bodies as essential public goods. Underground water suffers from invisibility in the eyes of society. Aquifers are planetary resources, most often privately exploited with short-term profits in mind, facing similar challenges of exhaustion, pollution or saline intrusion in many latitudes. Their overexploitation or mere over-pumping affects the stability of the ground on which millions of people live, in large capitals like Mexico DF and Singapore, in historic cities like our New Orleans, or in small communities surrounded by rising seas.

But water is also essential to the common good in many other ways. Floods, although sometimes catastrophic, are the natural behavior of rivers and natural drainage systems that people need to reconnect with in order to become part of larger ecological systems. There is little doubt that new generations of architects, landscape architects, engineers, urbanists, and many other professionals need to design a new relationship between themselves and human settlements. New Orleans and Louisiana, in the Mississippi River Delta, have no choice. River floods have literally built this area and are still the best way to inhabit it in the face of sea level rise and tropical storms by depositing sediments and building marshes. There is so much work to be done under a ticking clock, as it happens in many other vulnerable coasts in the planet at every scale: from the roof, the façade and the building's metabolism, to the territory and its urbanization.

Much like flooding and stormwater runoff, wastewater is in urgent need of a paradigm shift. Until now, sewage has been a problem to get rid of as soon as possible. Dilution has worked for millennia, until the world's population growth and high concentrations required its management. Today, we are starting to go beyond a certain level of cleansing and are discussing recycling and even regeneration of wastewater. Some municipalities see wastewater as a commodity to be sold to industry or agriculture. The real paradigm shift, however, is to consider wastewater as a public good and a guarantee for the survival of our territories. Reconceptualizing our cities from consumers to producers of water has the capacity to insert back human inhabitation into healthy ecological systems. Cities are to become tributaries of the rivers they sit in, switching from ecological hazards to assets in the reconstruction of the riparian ecosystems. A few of us have started working on how this will happen, reconceptualizing sewage treatment plants and stormwater systems as springs and sources of life.

There are so many more declinations of water as a public good, beginning with the geography of water and the human need for access to river, lake, and ocean shores. The spiritual or mental health implications of water open infinite lines of inquiry. Architecture and the built environment are technical endeavors with profound cultural and social implications. The spaces of water, all of the above, are probably the most critical to focus on in addressing our climate change crises, with all their environmental, health, and social equity implications. ■

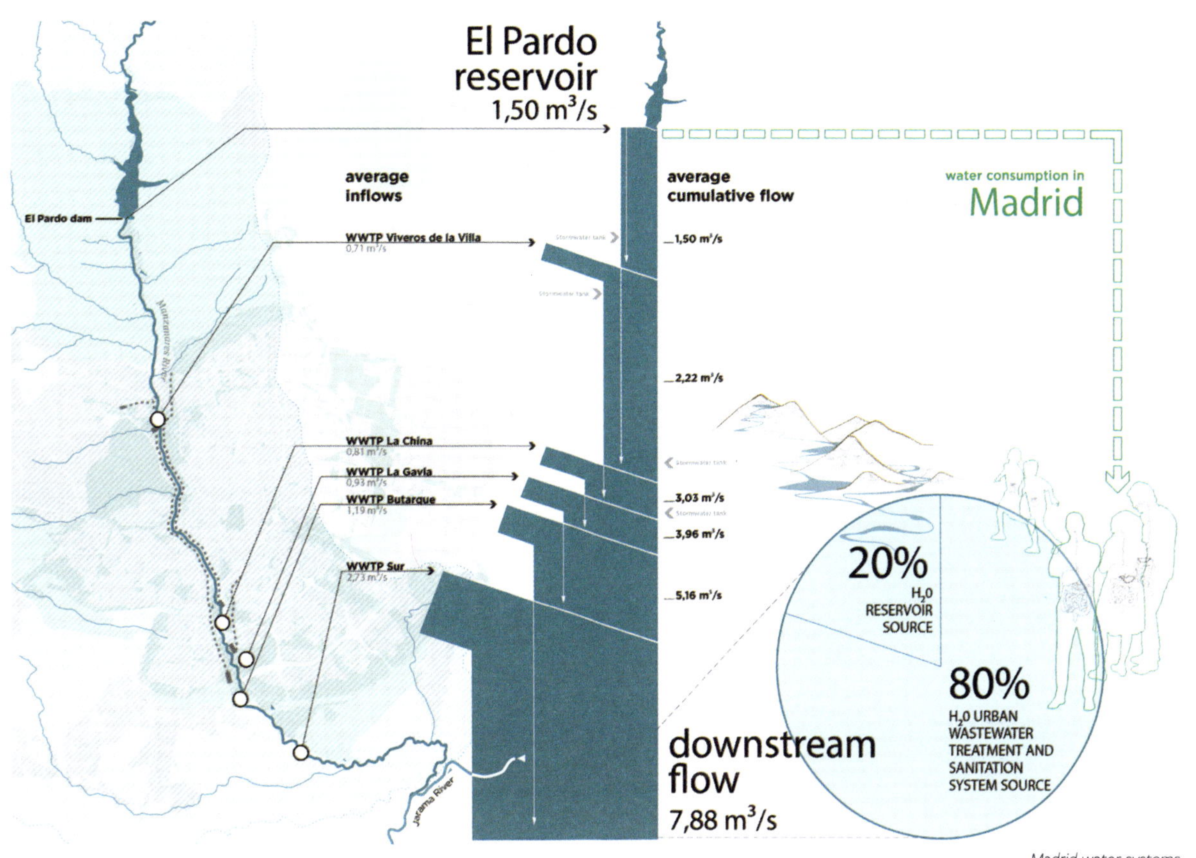

Madrid water systems.
aldayjover architecture and landscape

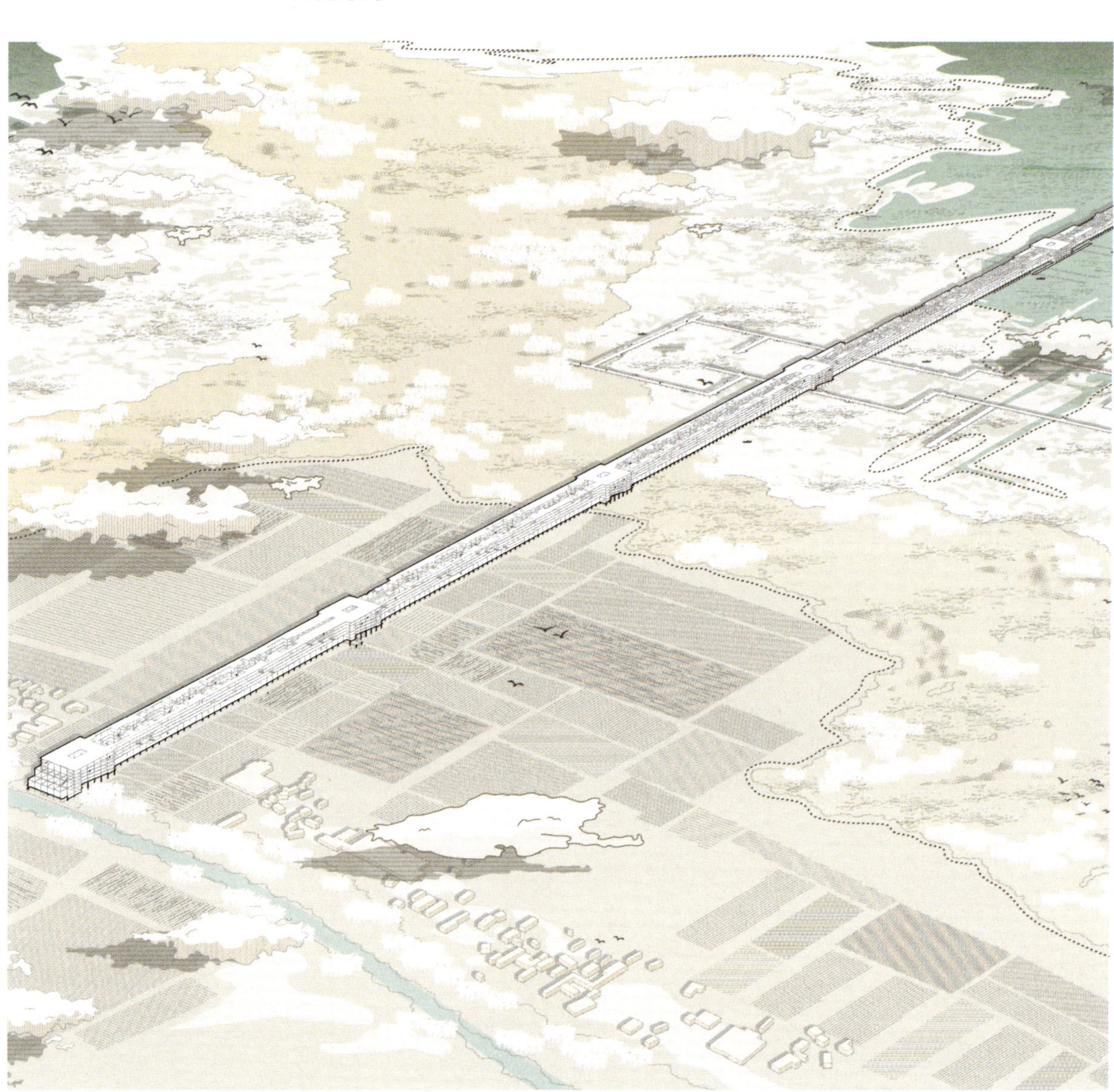

Amanda Bond + Chelsea Kilgore

TIDAL SHIFT:

Toward Post-Anthropocentric Futures for Coastal Louisiana

ARCH 5990 Instructors:
Cordula Roser Gray + Todd Erlandson

Climate change and sea level rise are impacting coastal communities around the globe, creating increased risk of storm surge and flood inundation—threatening human safety, economic development, and infrastructure. Louisiana has lost 2,000 square miles of coastal land since the 1930s, and up to 3,000 square miles are projected to be lost within the next 50 years, impacting the rural and urban developments along the coast and causing billions of dollars in damages to the built environment.

Existing adaptations within the built environment respond to these threats through "risk reduction projects," which work to manage increased natural disasters through infrastructure, presuming an ability for humans to control, dominate, and domesticate nature's forces. These types of projects are often reactive rather than proactive, and work to maintain existing human development in perpetuity, fighting in a metaphorical war for stability within a dynamic landscape.

In this way, the human resists true adaptation to the changing climate, which manifests into a binary reaction of fortification or retreat, a result of occupational models that seek control of the natural for the sake of long-term human settlement.

As the response to climate change in the built environment continues to be resistant adaptations, a feedback loop is perpetuated that preserves urban models that are unsustainable in the long term. These existing occupational modes pose the "enemy" to be fortified against as the forces of nature, missing the opportunity and the urgency to attack the anthropogenic causes at the root of the climate crisis.

"Tidal Shift" aims to critique the processes of colonization, industrialization, and globalization that have irreparably impacted Louisiana's coastal landscape in favor of human benefit. Land degradation has occurred along the coast as a result of these processes, and we aim to question what it would take, as a human species and design profession, to re-imagine the ways we live with our new nature, so that we can then change our collective human impact on the planet.

Our medium is a design proposal that manifests these criticisms into an occupational model that accommodates more than human interests, in order to make clear that in response to and to pivot from climate change, we must modify our approach to designing built environments.

In summary, we believe that there is space for the design of a speculative and imaginative new urban model typology, that imagines these what-if scenarios of the future, in order to provoke thought about the consequences of our collective human action, what we can do to change it, and how it impacts our approach to built environments.

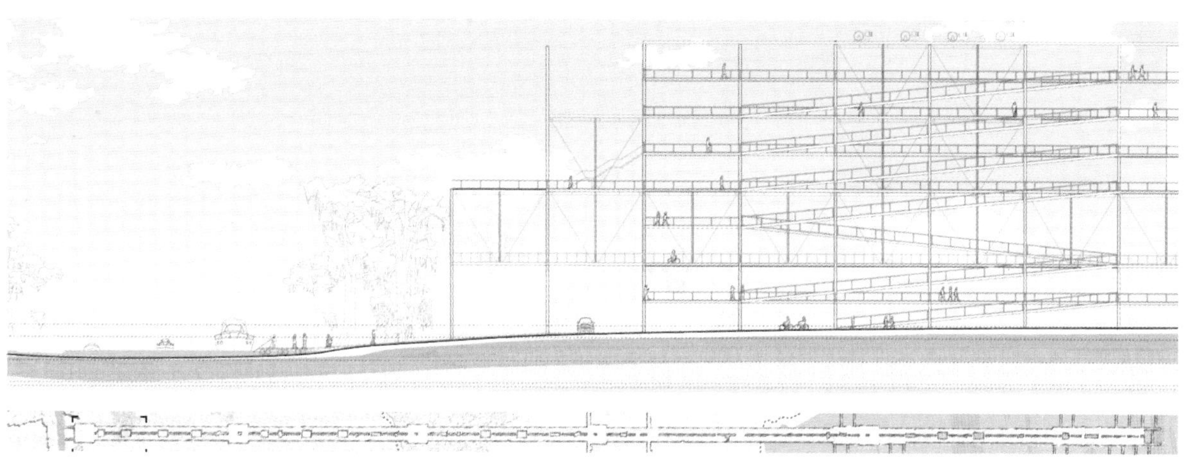

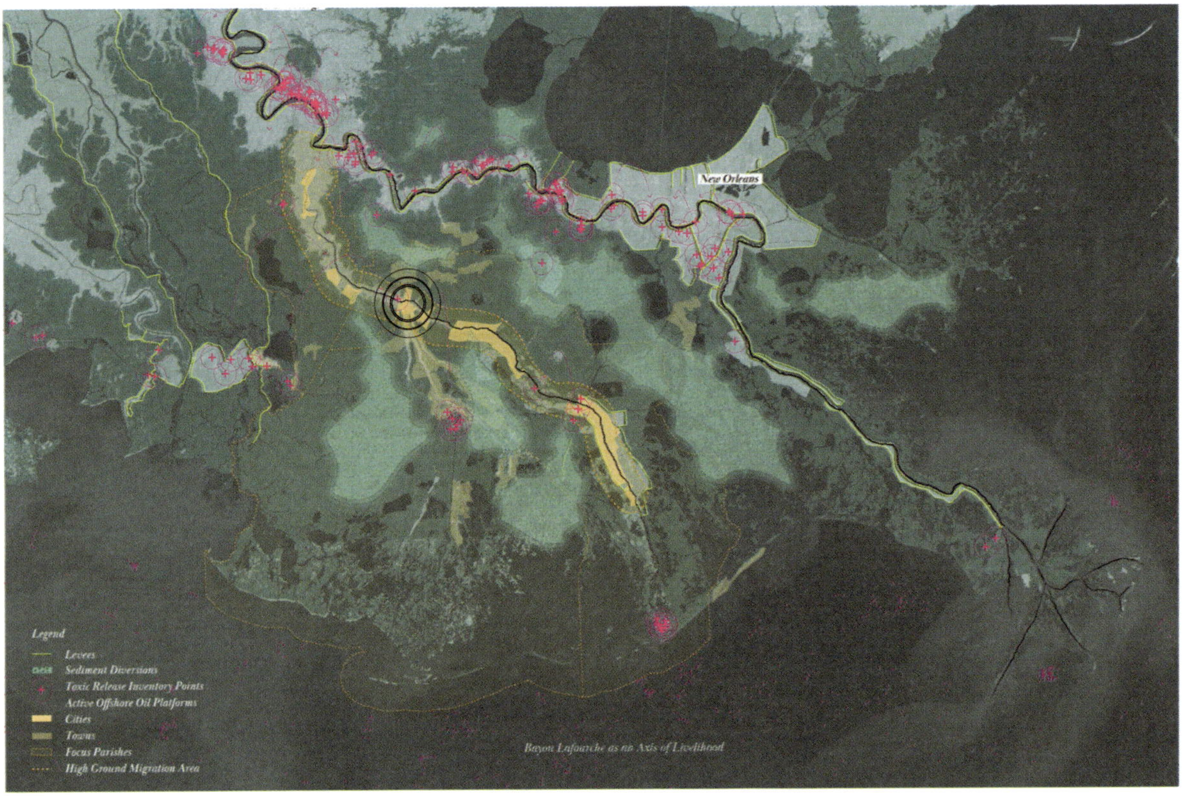

New Orleans

Legend
Levees
Sediment Diversions
Toxic Release Inventory Points
Active Offshore Oil Platforms
Cities
Towns
Focus Parishes
High Ground Migration Area

Bayou Lafourche as an Axis of Livelihood

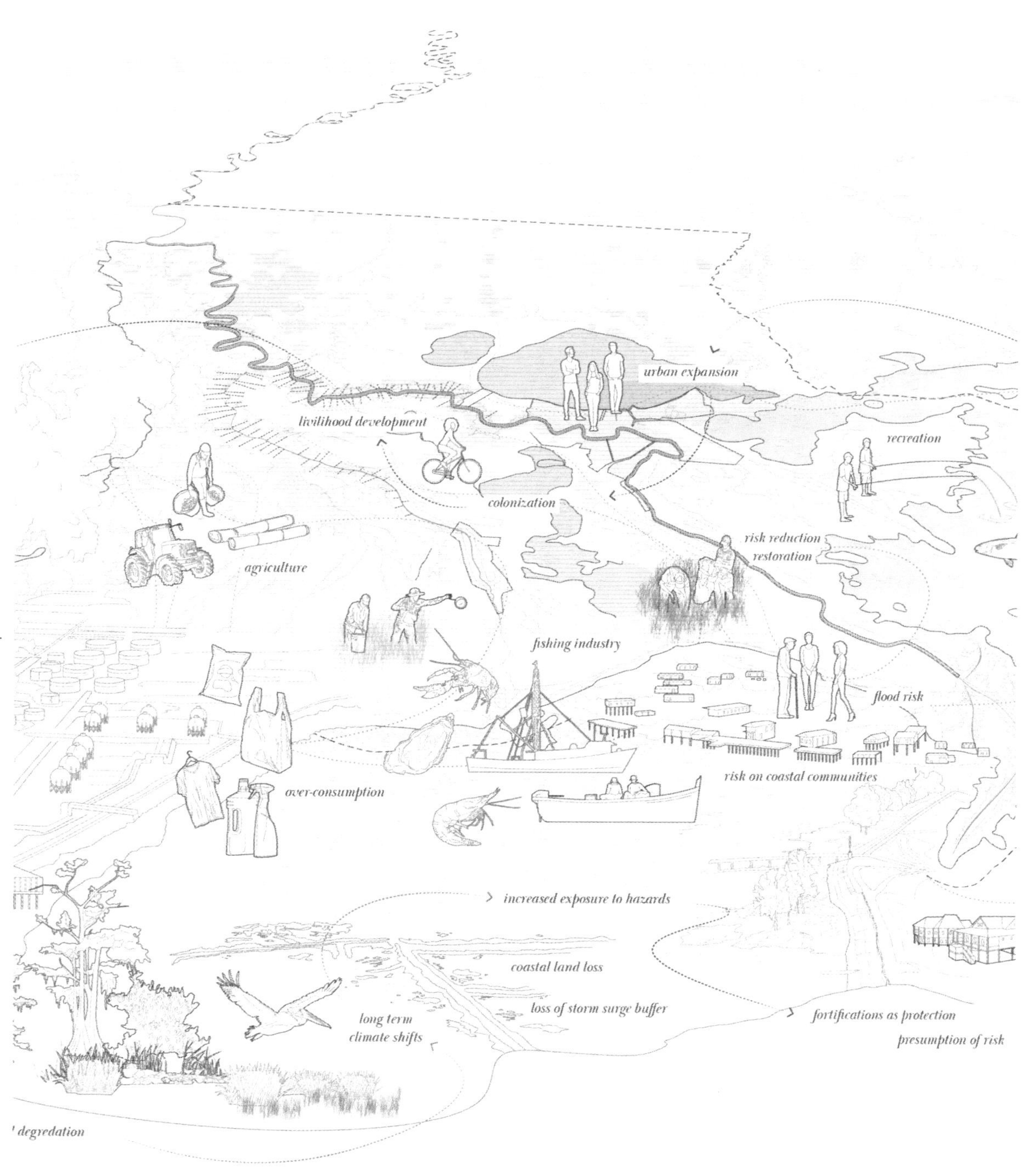
urban expansion
livilihood development
recreation
colonization
risk reduction
restoration
agriculture
fishing industry
flood risk
risk on coastal communities
over-consumption
> increased exposure to hazards
coastal land loss
loss of storm surge buffer
long term
climate shifts
> fortifications as protection
presumption of risk
degredation

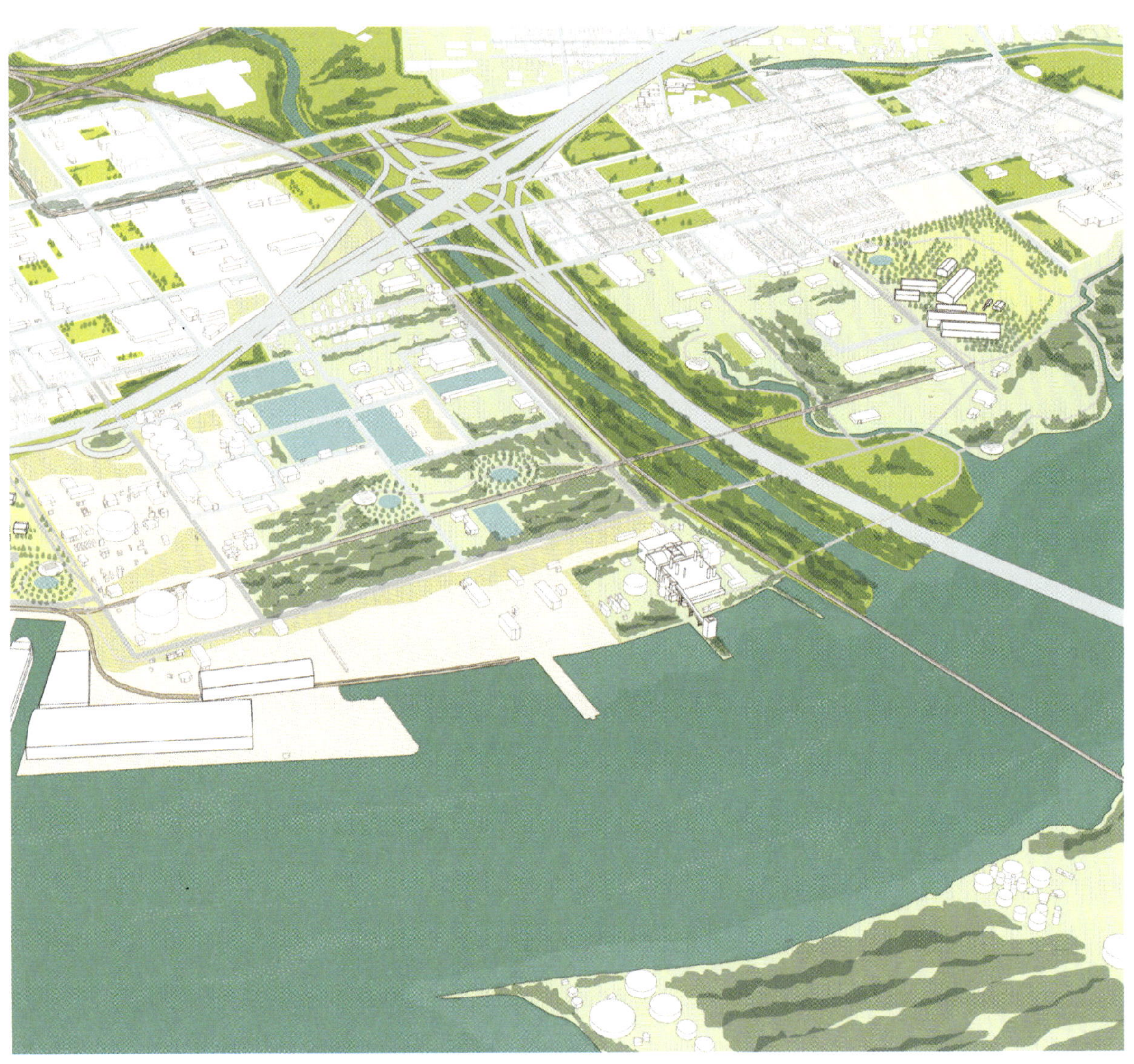

Allison Slomski

INSISTENT PROCESSES:

Strategies for Socio-Ecological Cohabitation on the Working Waterfront

ARCH 6990 Instructors:
Margarita Jover [D] + Liz Camuti [A]

s> Allison Slomski

i> Margarita Jover + Liz Camuti

As cities around the world face the compounded challenges of climate change, the redevelopment of their post-industrial waterfronts has become a straightforward opportunity to implement new climate resilience strategies, particularly through "green infrastructure." The general lack of inclusion of industrial processes in climate resilience planning, compounded by their local-regional economic importance, makes them particularly vulnerable to climate hazards. Like most riverine cities, Philadelphia has begun to experience a significant increase in climate crisis events, including severe weather flooding, hazardous air quality, and heat waves. The city has assigned the mitigation of these climate hazards to individual municipal agencies, without providing a comprehensive vision for a sustainable and responsive urban fabric. Instead, private development initiatives have been ushered in to shape the future of Philadelphia's riverfronts, where flood risk is concentrated.

The thesis, using one of Philadelphia's remaining industrial waterfronts as a case study, proposes the reconceptualization of this area as an "eco-industrial ward." Implemented at the Port of Philadelphia's Tioga Marine Terminal, this new entity is a park-like management system that balances industrial, ecological, and civic needs with green infrastructure strategies. Through adaptive, collaborative monitoring and maintenance processes backed by private-public partnership, the ward is intended to improve public access to the Delaware riverfront, combine environmental remediation and ecological restoration with flood mitigation strategies, and preserve (and potentially enhance) the economic performance of industrial site actors. Ideally, this cohabitative strategy can be applied to Philadelphia's other working waterfronts, and become a replicable design process transferable to other cities.

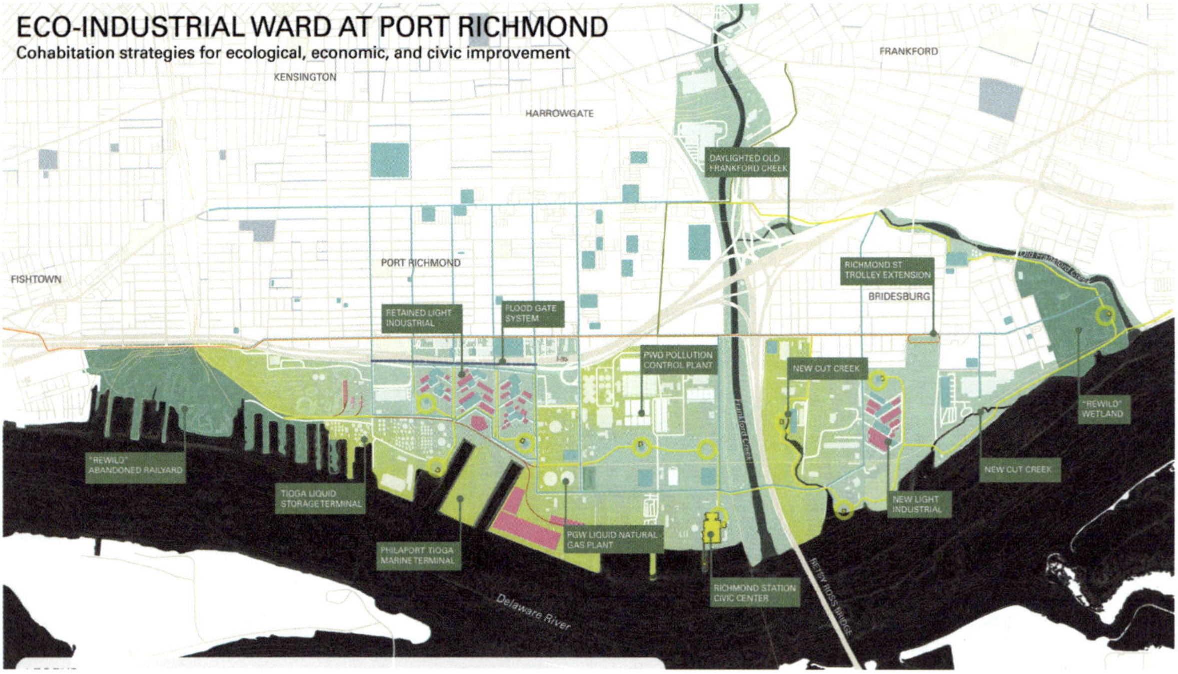

ECO-INDUSTRIAL WARD AT PORT RICHMOND

Cohabitation strategies for ecological, economic, and civic improvement

KENSINGTON
FRANKFORD
HARROWGATE
DAYLIGHTED OLD FRANKFORD CREEK
PORT RICHMOND
FISHTOWN
RICHMOND ST TROLLEY EXTENSION
BRIDESBURG
Old Frankford Creek
RETAINED LIGHT INDUSTRIAL
FLOOD GATE SYSTEM
PWD POLLUTION CONTROL PLANT
NEW CUT CREEK
"REWILD" WETLAND
Frankford Creek
"REWILD" ABANDONED RAILYARD
TIOGA LIQUID STORAGE TERMINAL
NEW CUT CREEK
NEW LIGHT INDUSTRIAL
PHILAPORT TIOGA MARINE TERMINAL
PGW LIQUID NATURAL GAS PLANT
RICHMOND STATION CIVIC CENTER
Delaware River
BETSY ROSS BRIDGE

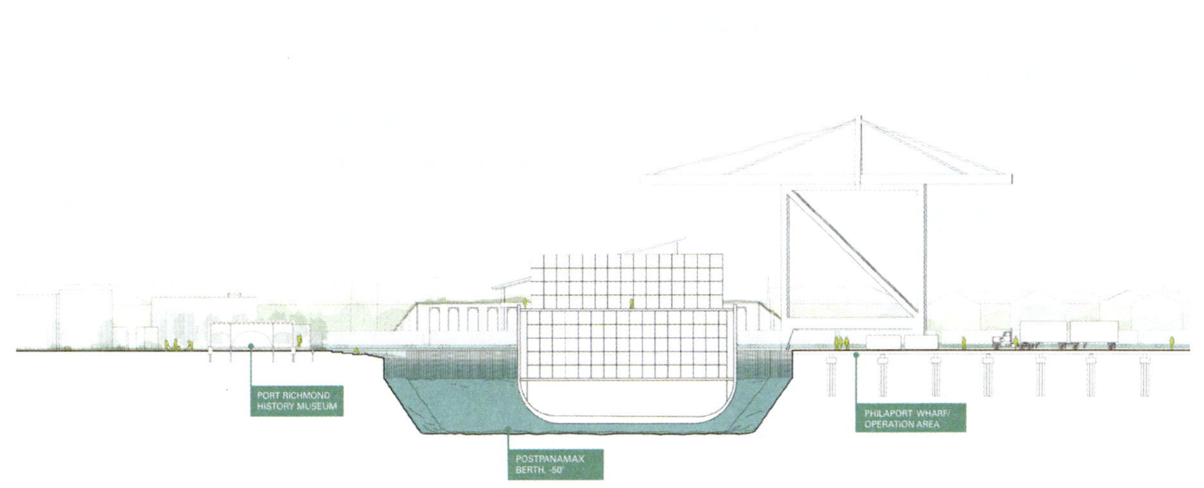
PORT RICHMOND
HISTORY MUSEUM
POSTPANAMAX
BERTH, -50'
PHILAPORT WHARF/
OPERATION AREA

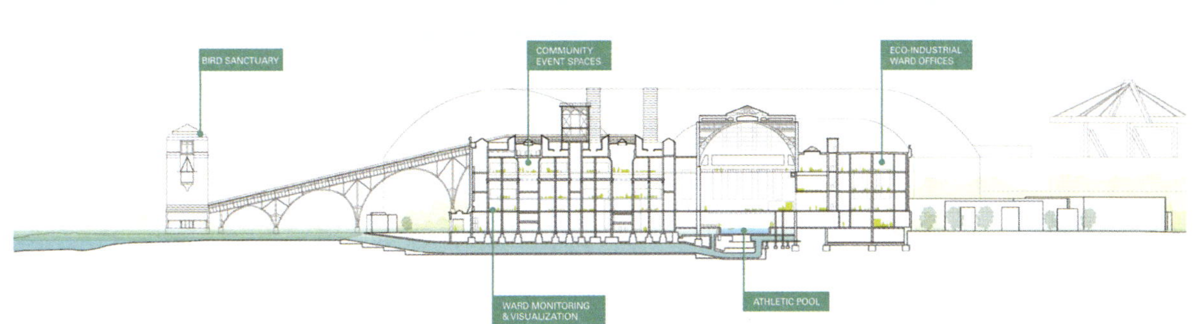
BIRD SANCTUARY
COMMUNITY
EVENT SPACES
ECO-INDUSTRIAL
WARD OFFICES
WARD MONITORING
& VISUALIZATION
ATHLETIC POOL

WATER MANAGEMENT & BUILT ENVIRONMENT

Tyler Antrup [C]

Tulane University requires all undergraduate students to complete community service through Academic Service Learning prior to graduation. Academic Service Learning is an educational experience based upon a collabortive partnership between the university and the community. "Learning by doing" enables students to apply academic knowledge and critical thinking skills to meet genuine community needs. Through reflection and assessment, students gain deeper understanding of course content and the importance of civic engagement.

The Water Management + the Built Environment course will lead students from the history and drivers of urban water management, through policy and practices that have shaped the field of practice and finally into implementation by developing and building urban green stormwater infrastructure projects in partnership with Water Wise Gulf South.

Students will work collaboratively with the community partner and faculty from the School of Architecture and Built Environment to co-design a neighborhood storm water project through a series of community workshops. Once designed, students will work with the community partner to construct the project and work with the responsible party to develop a strategy for long-term operations and maintenance of the project. Students met with the Hollygrove-Dixon Neigborhood Association in March to discuss flooding issues in the neighborhood and identify a site for a potential project. The neighborhood ultimately felt that the Brooks Shaw site was high profile for the community and could generate the most visible benefits. Students met again twice in April with the Brooks Shaw Temple United Methodist church community to select a project type and materials. Church members selected the planter boxes in brown metal for their ease of long term maintenance and durability. Students constructed the project the weekend of April 27, 2024 in two shifts. By the numbers: 160 gallons of stormwater diverted from the drainage system; 2 cubic feet of bioretention soil to soak up the runoff; 1/2 cubic yard of limestone gravel to store runoff before it soaks into the ground; 12 native plantings to absorb runoff, filter pollutants, and provide a beautiful habitat for pollinators.

Scan here to learn more about how you can reduce flooding in our neighborhood

Students:

Patrick Balters
Ethan Barletta
Joe Casey
Bailey Despanie
Fin Gallagher
Ben LaFontan
Timothy Luke
Sam Shemtov
Arielle Weiss
Zues Machado
Femando Soriano
Jeb Wells
Josh Liebman
Arthyr Greenup
Joe Albanese

By Sarie Keller

11

LANDSCAPE & TERRITORY

AS COMMON GOOD

LANDSCAPE AND TERRITORY AS COMMON GOOD

Towards Alimentary Coastal Infrastructure

By Liz Camuti
Assistant Professor in Landscape Architecture
Tulane School of Architecture and Built Environment

The transformation of ecologies into many systems of circulation and accumulation to serve the few is the project of settler colonial infrastructure... We suggest that effective initiatives for justice, decolonization, and planetary survival must center infrastructure in their efforts, and we highlight alimentary infrastructure–infrastructure that is life-giving in its design.

—Winona LaDuke and Deborah Cowan, "Beyond Wiindigo Infrastructure," The South Atlantic Quarterly 119:2, April 2020

In an era of mounting environmental challenges, coastal infrastructure's dual role in both protecting and perpetuating systems of extraction has become increasingly clear—most visible in the ways seawalls and levees simultaneously defend industrial assets while redirecting environmental hazards toward vulnerable communities and ecosystems. The path forward in a changing climate requires a fundamental reimagining of infrastructure's role in society, one that centers justice, ecological restoration, and planetary wellbeing in its conception and design.

This reimagining has become particularly urgent as rising sea levels and increasingly extreme weather events transform coastal regions. While conventional approaches to coastal protection have often prioritized the preservation and protection of the most significant economic assets and highest property values, a paradigm shift is underway that recognizes infrastructure's potential to serve a larger conception of the common good—one that encompasses not just the interests of the people with the most power but strives to center ecosystem wellbeing and environmental justice through innovative, multi-benefit strategies.

This approach increasingly positions landscape architects and engineers as agents working at the forefront of climate justice, seeking to create infrastructure that is fundamentally life-giving in its design. In coastal contexts, this means developing spaces that not only accommodate both human activities and aquatic species but actively work to repair historical inequities. Projects like Seattle's Central Sea Wall and Living Breakwaters demonstrate how infrastructure can create structured habitats while ensuring vulnerable communities have equal access to both protection and amenities. From breakwaters that double as marine habitats and public gathering spaces to reconstructed wetlands that protect against storm surge while providing recreational access, innovative projects led by landscape architects show how infrastructure can serve multiple communities while fostering the kind of encounters across social boundaries that philosopher Michael Sandel identifies as crucial to democratic life.

The abundance of aging industrial infrastructure along our coasts also presents unique opportunities for transformation, particularly in communities that have borne the brunt of environmental injustice. Decommissioned structures from the petrochemical industry—terminals, platforms, and pipeline networks— are increasingly ripe with possibilities for re-imagination. The Gulf Coast Climate Futures research project at the School of Architecture and Built Environment demonstrates this potential, with students exploring how offshore rigs might be converted into artificial reefs and fishing congregation points or reimagining how abandoned pipelines might be repurposed to support climate adaptation and mitigation simultaneously.

These emerging practices embody a crucial principle: the need to reunite human activities with ecological processes. Rather than producing new materials and infrastructure that increase our collective carbon footprint, we must rethink and repurpose the mechanisms that have led to environmental degradation, ensuring that historically marginalized communities lead these processes of transformation. This approach recognizes humans as contributors to ecological damage and potential agents of regeneration.

As we contemplate the future of coastal regions and other vulnerable landscapes, our conception of infrastructure must continue to expand beyond engineered solutions to embrace a more ambitious vision of the common good. This vision requires bringing together technical expertise with community knowledge, understanding that the most effective and enduring projects often arise when local communities take lead. Such leadership is already visible in initiatives near and far: The Pointe-au-Chien tribe in Louisiana developing a living shoreline project that combines coastal protection with oyster restoration, the Swinomish Indian Tribal Community's Kukutali Preserve project integrating traditional ecological knowledge into salmon habitat recovery alongside flood management, and community-led efforts in Puerto Rico transforming the Caño Martín Peña channel into a climate-adaptive waterway that combines flood protection with new public spaces and restored mangrove habitats. These projects demonstrate how community-led infrastructure projects simultaneously protect against climate threats, restore ecological systems, and create new spaces for public life.

The following chapters explore these themes through various lenses and scales, from specific case studies to broader design frameworks. They examine how vulnerable communities are transforming their relationship to infrastructure, how designers are reimagining the interface between land and water, and how policymakers and designers are working together with communities to redefine what infrastructure can and should do. Together, they demonstrate how reimagining our approach to landscape and territory through the lens of the common good can create a future where human prosperity, ecological flourishing, and social equity are mutually reinforcing. ■

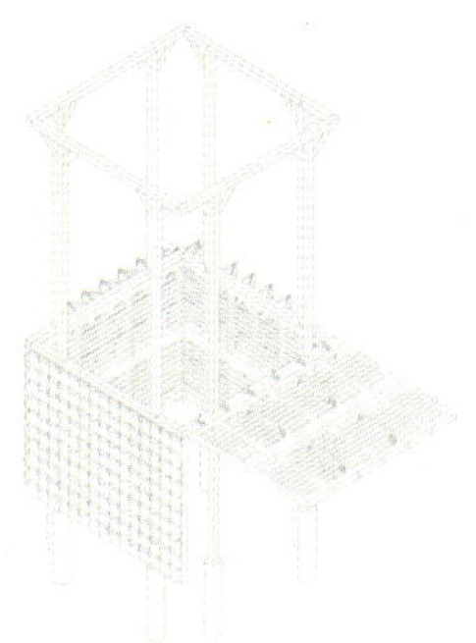

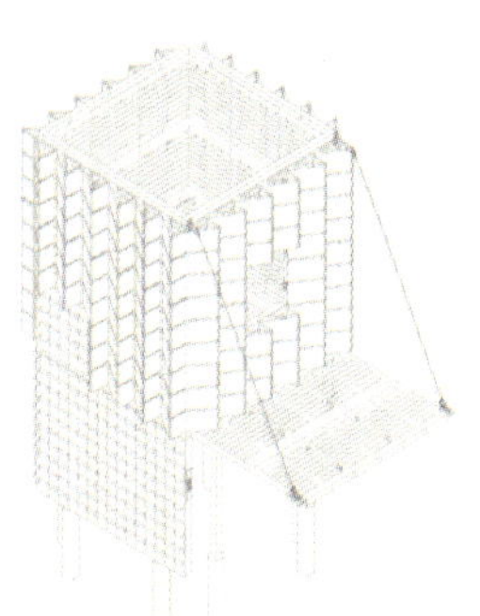

CLOUDBURST FOREST

COMPETITION
Sansusi Forest, Latvia, 2023

Architects: Austin Lightle

Cloudburst Forest uses an inclusive gathering place, the ease of constructibility, and sustainability as guiding principles for the design of the Sansusi Forest Food Court. Three caterer spaces reach into the sky acting as way-finding devices and marking the location of a central, communal gathering space. Curved benches along the main path act as a both eating areas for festival goers and double as informal, in-the-round performance stages.

The caterer spaces are designed so volunteers without previous knowledge can assemble them with only basic scaffolding and tools. Taking inspiration from off-road camp sites, the primary structure can be assembled on the ground then tilted up to create simple frames. Modular facade elements are also constructed on the ground then connected to the frame. Green walls attach to the facade and can be used to grow herbs, vegetables, and fruits.

The exterior design of the pallets was derived from fog catching systems using natural mesh to capture water vapor from the atmosphere and supply the edible green wall providing a sustainable and local food source for the festival. Up-cycled wood pallets are used as secondary structure to help eliminate landfill waste and wall openings are created to keep workers comfortable with passive cooling.

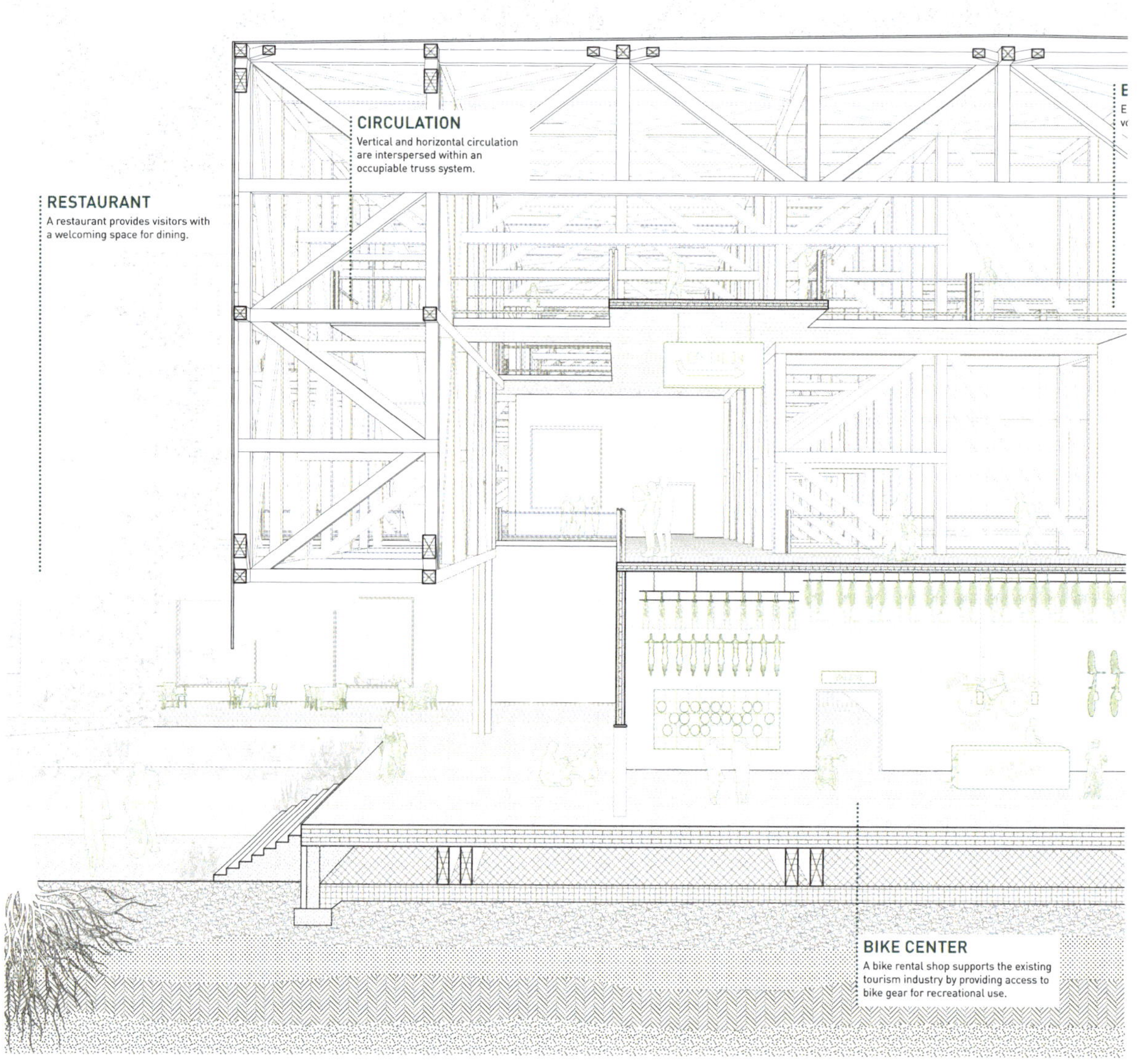

Sarie Keller + Olivia Vercruysse

INDUSTRIAL FUTURES IN TIMBERLAND

ARCH 5990 Instructors:
Cordula Roser Gray + Todd Erlandson

s> Sarie Keller + Olivia Vercruysse

i> Cordula Roser Gray + Todd Erlandson

In envisioning a future for former timber towns, this thesis designs the forest and the built environment as a unified system to support mass timber as a catalyst for economic recovery and environmental healing.

The urban and architectural proposal for an engineered wood plant conceptualizes the building footprint as an extension of the contextual envelope. Situated on former mill sites with existing adjacencies to both river and rail, a series of timber superstructures allow for the integration of both industry and tourism.

Visitors engage with the process of mass timber manufacturing from above by inhabiting the double-layer truss system of the reinvented canopy. The long spans offered by the series of trusses leave the ground floor open for industry while also creating a human-scaled experience among the members themselves.

The investigation of tectonic laminated timber through the lens of the forest and their timber communities is fueled by an ambition to better understand building life cycles—from resource harvesting to occupation and disassembly. To achieve this, we must look beyond our role as designers to incorporate perspectives of the forest, the timber industry, and the public.

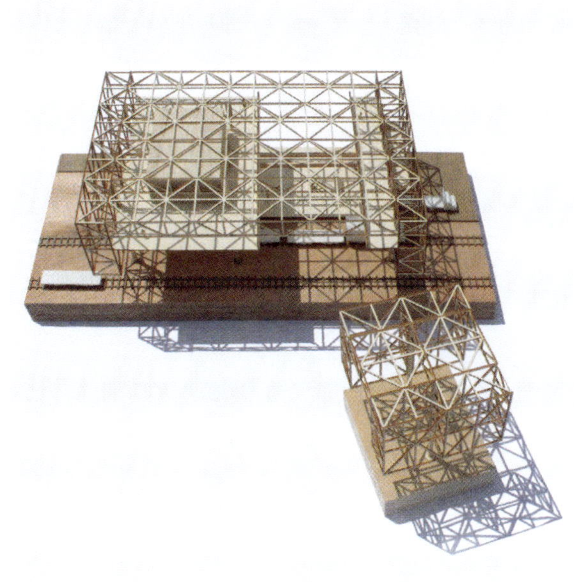

ARCH 4041/5051 + 6041/6051 | **Research Studio** | UG + GR | **FA23**

NASEM GULF STUDIO

Exploring Gulf Coast Climate Futures

Liz Camuti [C]
Margarita Jover

The Gulf Coast Climate Futures Research Studio, funded by the National Academies of Science, Engineering and Medicine's Gulf Research Program (NASEM-GRP), is a multi-year design research initiative that explores strategies for climate adaptation in the Gulf Coast region, spanning from Houston to Mobile. The studio adopts a methodology for territorial analysis, diagnosis, and generating hypotheses for transformation at regional, metropolitan, and architectural scales.

Through interdisciplinary collaborations with specialists from various fields and collective ways of working, students engage in map-based analysis and synthesis of regional systems related to energy, water, ecosystems, and urbanization. Utilizing GIS mapping techniques, students investigate the complex interdependencies between these systems and their impact on the built environment.

The studio aims to imagine equitable and ecologically sustainable futures for the Gulf Coast, grounded in the region's historical and contemporary realities. By examining the legacy of extractive practices and environmental degradation, students develop critical perspectives on the challenges facing the region and propose innovative strategies for climate mitigation and adaptation. Throughout the course, students cultivate skills in regional scale map-based analysis, verbal and visual storytelling, teamwork, and design thinking to address complex challenges at the intersection of climate change, social equity, and the built environment.

The course culminates in multi-scalar design proposals that envision transformative interventions for specific sites within the broader regional context. These proposals serve as a foundation for further research and collaboration, contributing to ongoing efforts to build resilience and promote sustainable development in the Gulf Coast region.

The projects presented here share a common vision for reimagining the future of the Gulf Coast region in the face of climate change and the ongoing energy transition. Each project proposes innovative strategies for adapting existing infrastructure, industries, and practices to promote ecological regeneration, reduce carbon emissions, and build resilience in coastal communities. By re-envisioning the roles of power plants, military installations, shipping routes, oil and gas pipelines, and animal agriculture, these projects challenge the status quo and offer optimistic scenarios for a more sustainable and equitable future. The projects emphasize the importance of learning from historic practices, embracing new technologies, and fostering collaboration between diverse stakeholders to address the complex challenges facing the region. Ultimately, these projects demonstrate the potential for design to catalyze transformative change at multiple scales, from the remediation of individual sites to the restructuring of regional systems, while centering the healing of both people and landscapes.

MISSISSIPPI
LOUISIANA
BATON ROUGE

ARCH 4041/5051 + 6041/6051 | **Research Studio** | UG + GR | **FA23**

Frank Taylor

NAVIGATING CHANGE

ADAPTING GULF COAST SHIPPING INFRASTRUCTURES TO AN EVOLVING GREEN ECONOMY

This project explores the potential benefits of reforming shipping practices, adopting new navigation routes, and designing new port infrastructure to regenerate the Mississippi River's land-building capacity and position the region as a critical player in a changing energy economy. Drawing lessons from the successful sediment deposition south of Morgan City, the project proposes redirecting the central navigation channel from the Port of New Orleans to the Gulf Intracoastal Waterway (GIWW) through the Port of Morgan City.

This new route necessitates a shift from large container ships and oil tankers to smaller electric barges, enabling the Mississippi River downstream of English Turn to transform into a network of diversions. The Port of Morgan City becomes a critical site, adapting its existing functions to become a model for resilient and ecologically vibrant ports along the GIWW, ultimately envisioning a regenerative Intracoastal economic framework that reconnects coastal communities to the dynamics of a river-dominated delta.

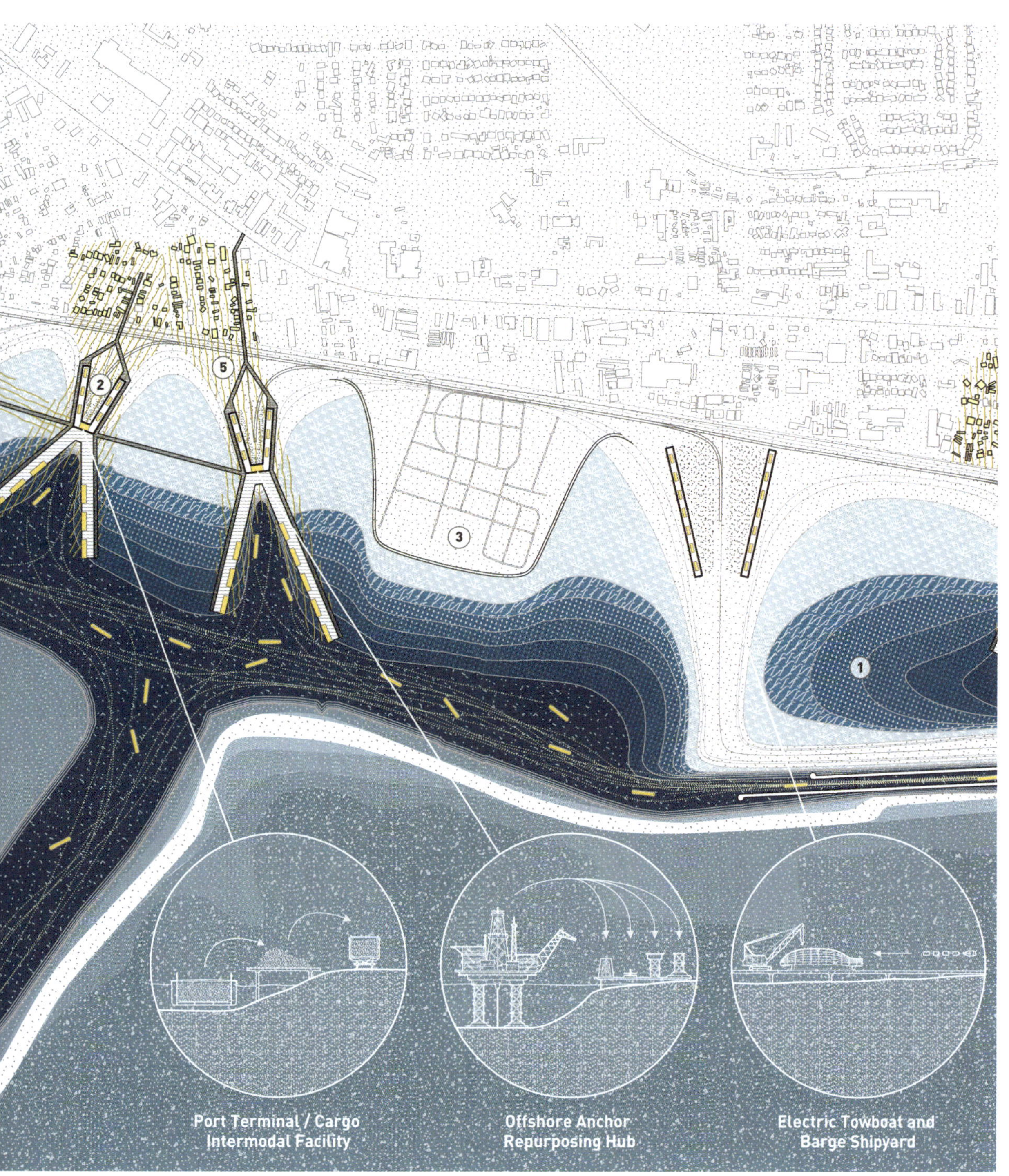
2
5
3
1
Port Terminal / Cargo Intermodal Facility
Offshore Anchor Repurposing Hub
Electric Towboat and Barge Shipyard

ARCH 4041/5051 + 6041/6051 | **Research Studio** | UG + GR | **FA23**

Jose Varela Castillo

FLIPPING THE SWITCH

RE-ENVISIONING POWER PLANTS AS CIVIC ENERGY

This project re-envisions the role of power plants in the Gulf South, transitioning them from fossil fuel reliance to civic energy generators that integrate into neighborhood fabrics while providing the foundation for a renewable energy future. Using TCP Houston's Power and Chemical Plant as a test site, a time-based framework is proposed for transforming existing power plants through strategies focused on land remediation, energy transition, and community empowerment. The adaptive reuse of the plant will meet local demands for commercial programs, housing, a transit hub, and areas of renewable energy production. This design proposal seeks to define a new aesthetic for the adaptive reuse of petrochemical-era infrastructure, emphasizing the seamless integration of critical infrastructure and promoting communal life. By re-imagining how energy is generated and consumed on a regional scale, this project puts forward a future in which cities re-purpose plants as electricity storage facilities to support a decentralized network of renewable energy production.

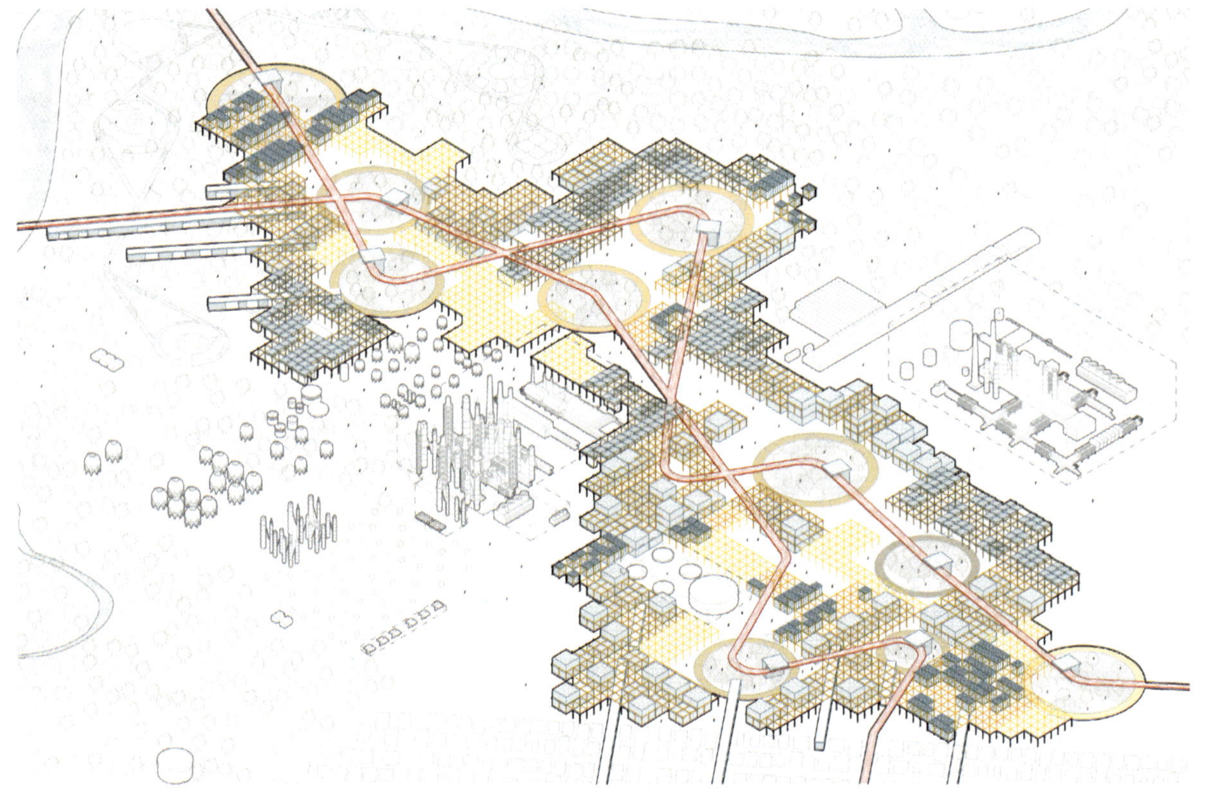

s> Jose Valera Castillo **i>** Liz Camuti, Margarita Jover

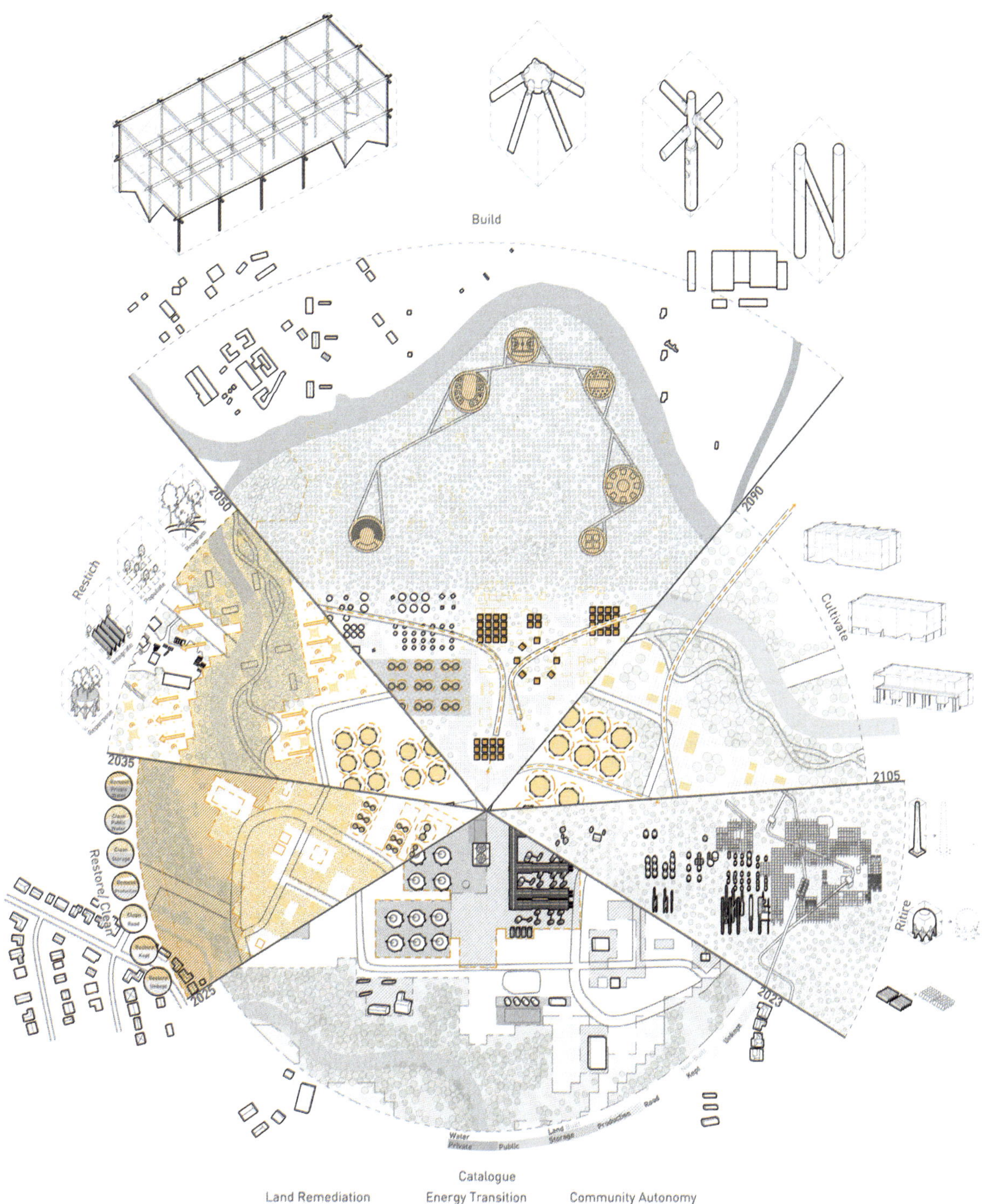

Olivia Vercruysse

THE DEPARTMENT OF CLIMATE DEFENSE

RE-IMAGINING FORTIFIED LANDSCAPES

This proposal envisions a scenario for transitioning military infrastructure and skilled labor in the GulfCoast region to support sediment flows and land-building processes, reducing the need for energy-intensive coastal fortification projects while building resilience along the coast. The project aims to break the cycle of interdependence between military installations and petrochemical industries, which contributes to increased frequency and magnitude of extreme climate events. By adapting military operations and labor toward projects that reduce energy consumption, stimulate local economies, and mitigate climate risk to coastal communities, the proposal focuses on the Mississippi coast from Gulfport to Pascagoula as a representative sample of region-wide military presence. Existing assets, includinginstallation footprints, skilled labor, and physical infrastructure, are considered as inputs for proposed design strategies at each site. The central concept of adapting ships for sediment systems can be deployed at a larger scale across the region to provide critical functions during storm preparation.

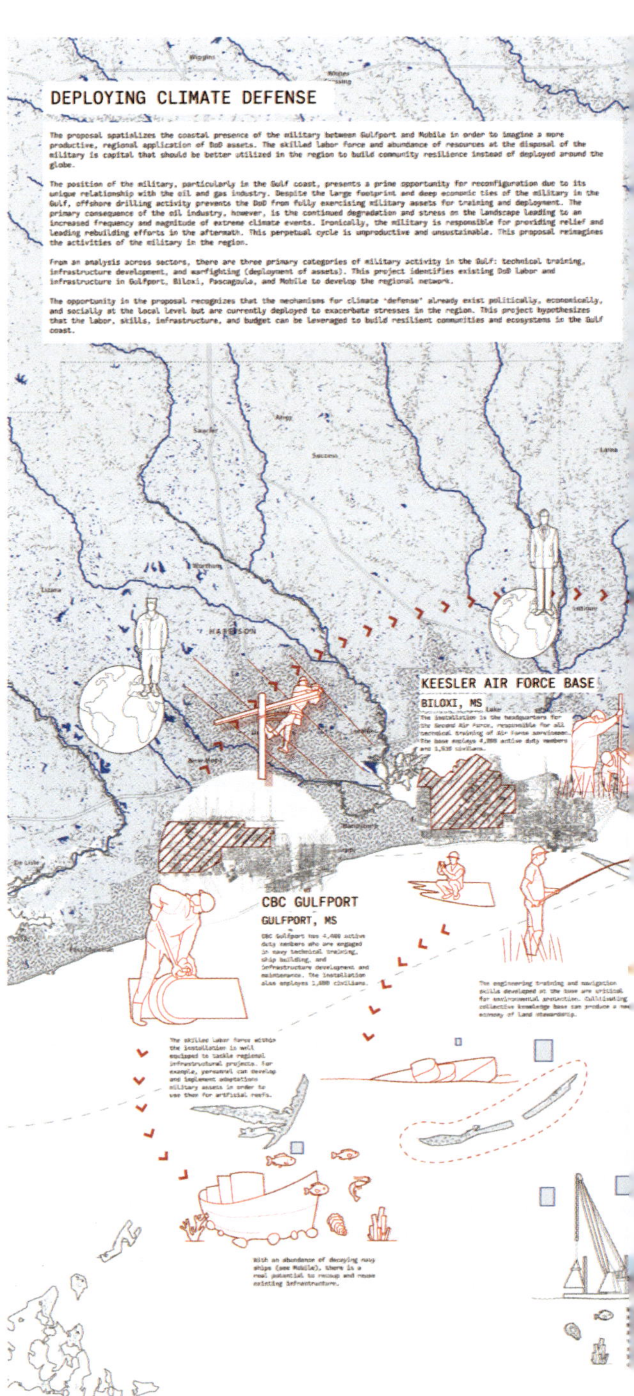

s> Olivia Vercruysse

i> Liz Camuti, Margarita Jover

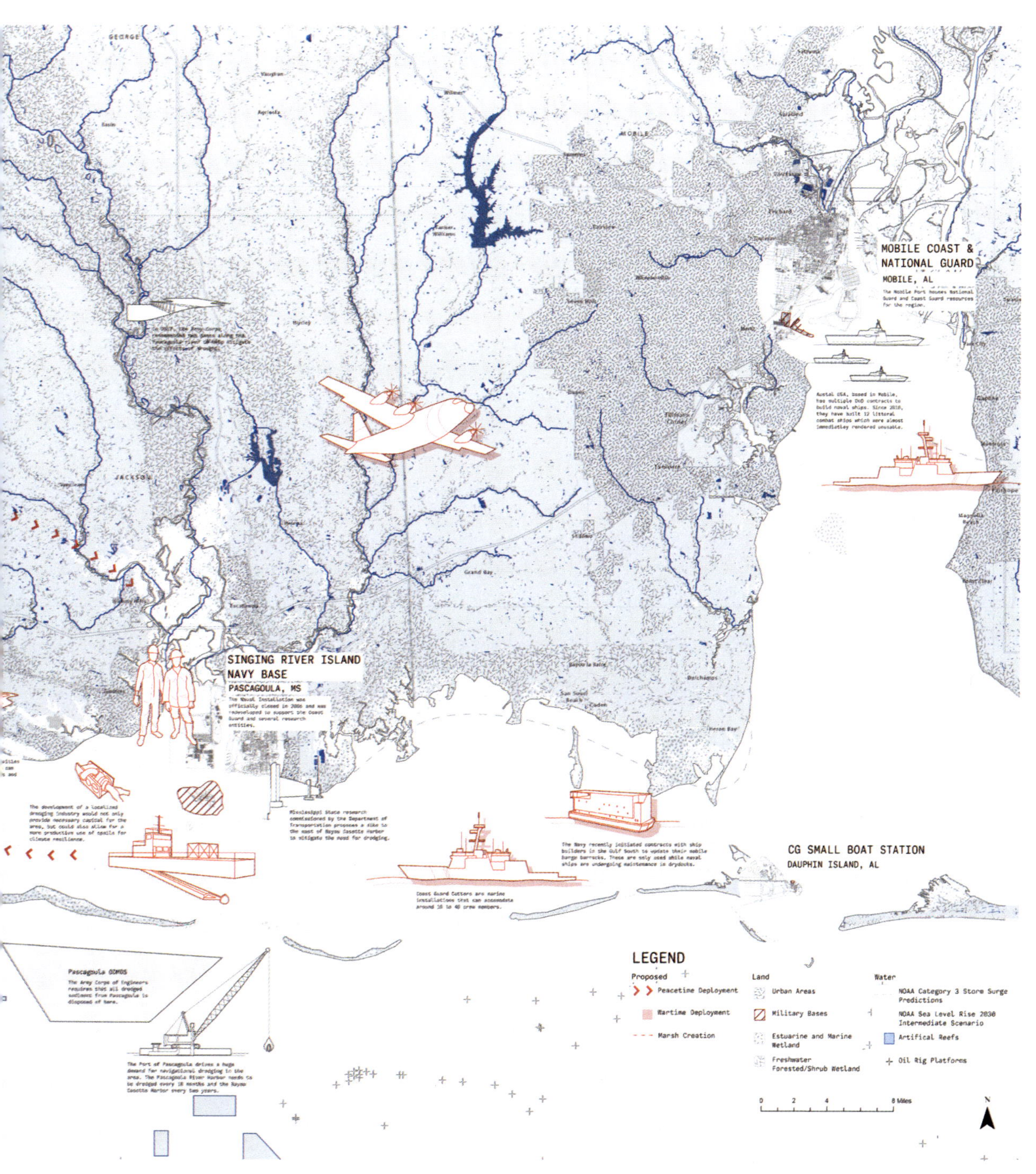

ARCH 4041/5051 + 6041/6051 | **Research Studio** | UG + GR | **FA23**

Brooke Mehney

REGENERATING THE RANGE

FUTURE FRAMEWORK FOR LIVESTOCK MANAGEMENT IN THE GULF SOUTH

This project proposes a design framework for adapting animal agriculture practices in the Gulf South to a changing landscape and economy, focusing on the Chenier Plain region of Southern Louisiana. By reviving ecologically responsive historic practices, utilizing innovations in conservation agriculture technology, and proposing new logics for regional cattle drives, the project aims to reduce carbon emissions, regenerate coastal landscapes, and adapt this regionally significant economy to a changing climate. The project reconceptualizes historic cattle drives within the Chenier Plain, promoting regional grazing rotation and limiting overuse of land through virtual fencing and drones. Three test sites explore strategies for creating artificial chenier ridges, cultivating meat alternatives, designing stilted barns, implementing silvopasture landscapes, promoting shared community ownership of livestock, and adapting existing farms to heal soil and ecosystem degradation. By hybridizing conservation agriculture innovations with ecologically sensitive historic practices, the project envisions a future for animal agriculture that responds to climate change while healing the landscape.

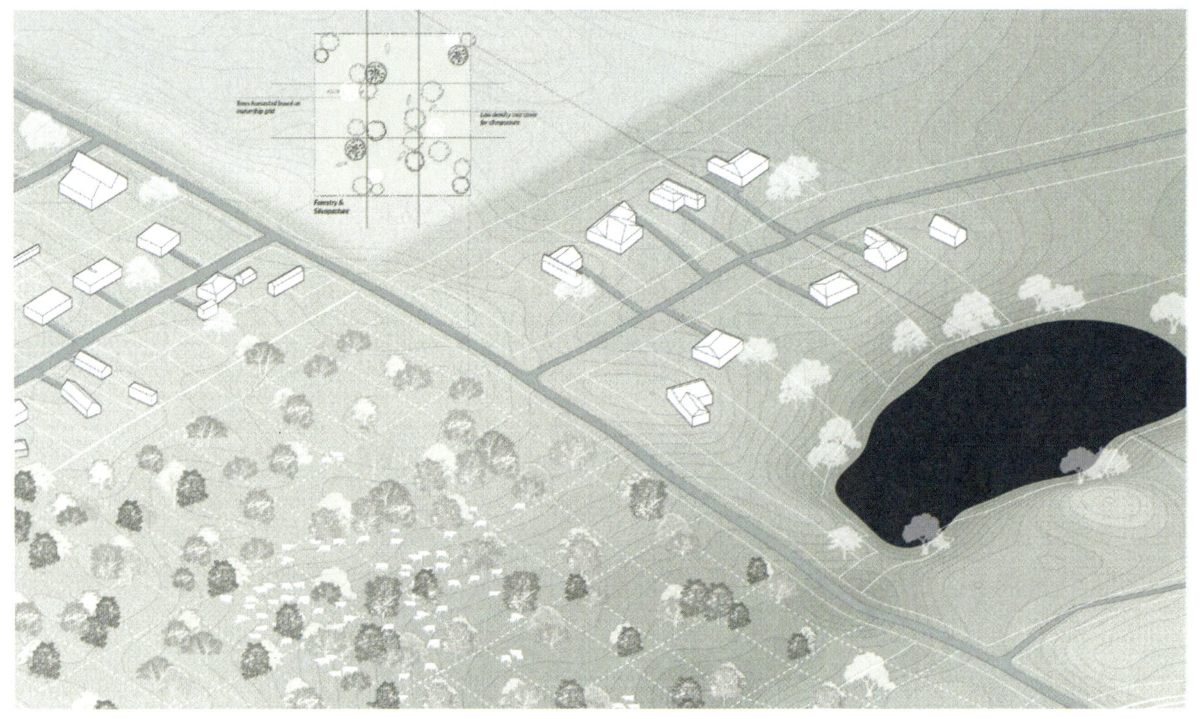

s> Brooke Mehney

i> Liz Camuti, Margarita Jover

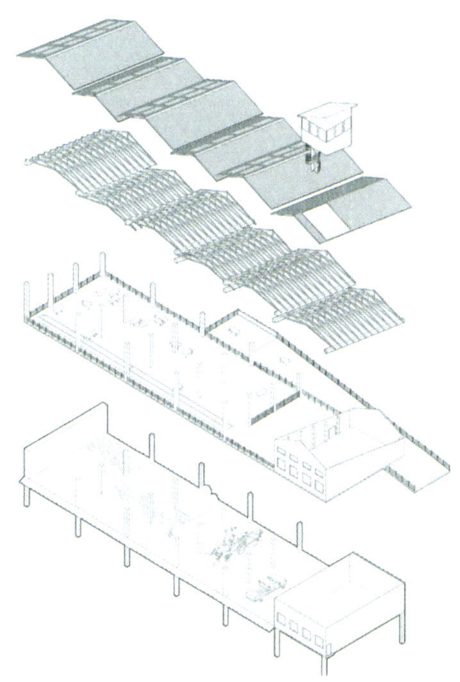

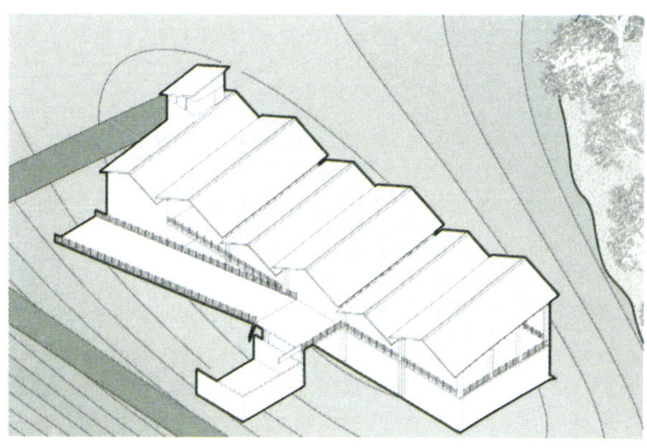

ARCH 4041/5051 + 6041/6051 **Research Studio** UG + GR **FA23**

Sarie Keller

THE STEEL BENEATH OUR FEET

HEALING PETROCHEMICAL LANDSCAPES WITH THE RELICS OF EXTRACTION

This project proposes a suite of strategies for addressing the challenges posed by the 2.6 million miles of abandoned oil and gas pipelines in the United States, particularly focusing on the 12,500 miles of vulnerable pipelines in Texas and Louisiana. As the global energy transition renders these pipelines increasingly obsolete, the project envisions new pipeline removal processes and adaptive reuse design potentials that prioritize landscape regeneration, energy conservation, and reducing carbon emissions.

Through a catalog of retrofit and remediation design strategies, the project offers visions for how these former energy transport systems might be remediated, reconfigured, and deployed to support the renewable energy transition, create ecological scaffolding for various habitats, and reduce emissions from the steel industry. By centering the healing of both people and landscapes, the proposed design strategies inspire creativity and stimulate additional ideas for adapting legacy oil and gas infrastructure across the region.

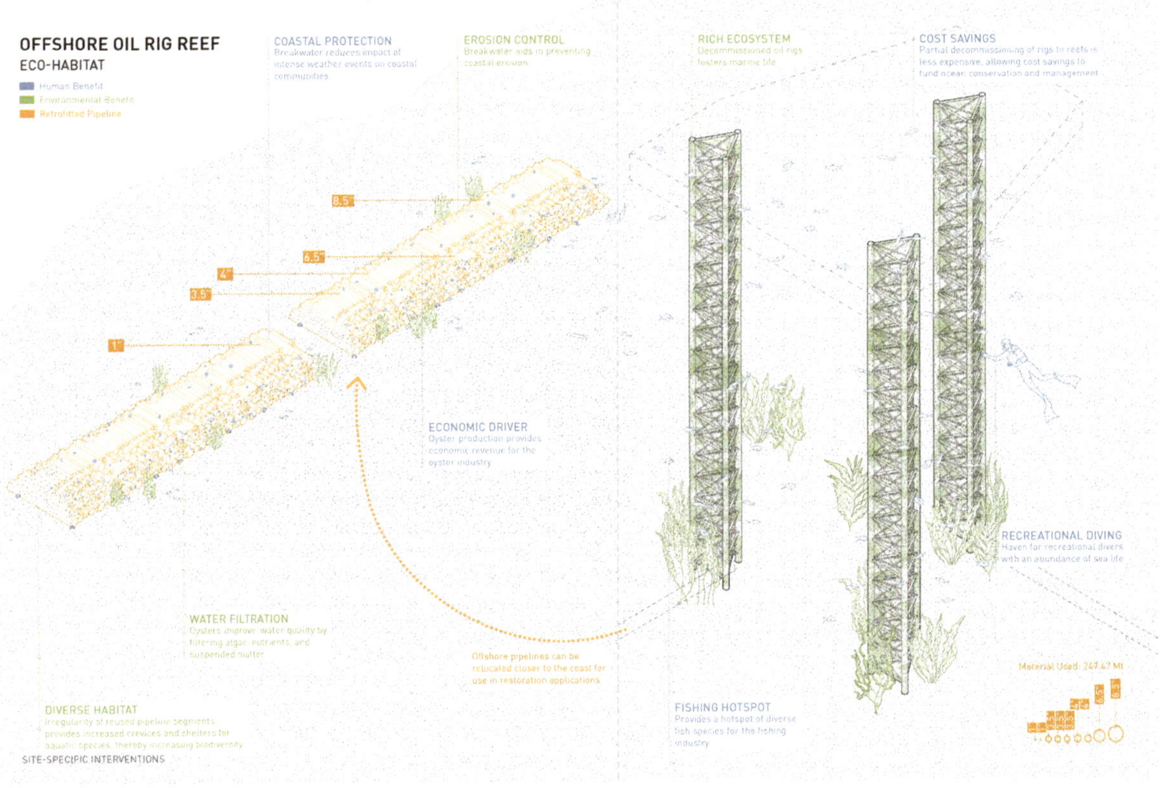

s> Sarie Keller
i> Liz Camuti, Margarita Jover

CROP IRRIGATION
Recycled pipes irrigate local crops, saving water and nutrients by allowing water to drip slowly to the roots of plants
24"
20"
14"
AQUACULTURE
Provides a basin for aquaculture and increases food production
WATER CHANNEL
Excavated pipe trench acts as a water source for local pastures
Material Used: 20.77 Mt
14"
20"
22"
22"
24"
36"

SITE-SPECIFIC INTERVENTIONS

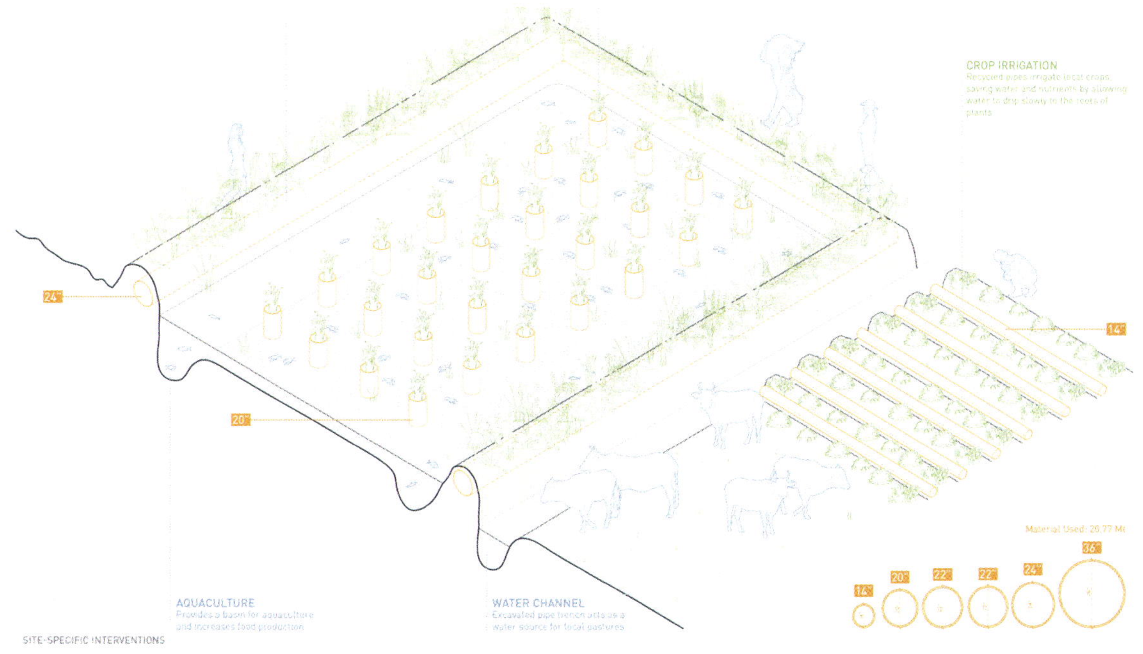

SUBURBAN STORMWATER MANAGEMENT

FLOOD PROTECTION + DRAINAGE + COMMEMORATE

- Human Benefit
- Environmental Benefit
- Retrofitted Pipeline

STORMWATER MANAGEMENT
Retrofitted pipeline is integrated with the bioswale to collect stormwater and redirect it
FLOOD PROTECTION
Protect nearby communities from flooding during storm surges through a levee structure
PUBLIC WALKABILITY
Increase walkability in areas of unstable soil conditions with public promenades
COMMEMORATIVE MARKERS
Plants indicate the former extractive pathways in the landscape
EROSION CONTROL
Pipe acts as a line of defense between suburban plastic and nearby lake and reduces risk of erosion
8"
24"
16"
16"
FLOOD MITIGATION
Perforated pipe transports water out of flooded areas and can supplement the existing water drainage system when overwhelmed by major weather events
UTILITY RESILIENCE
Retrofitted pipeline serves as a conduit for local utilities, further protecting services during major weather events
BIODIVERSITY
Vegetated markers increase pollinators and plant biodiversity
Material Used: 2,677.6 Mt
8"
16"
16"
22"
22"
24"

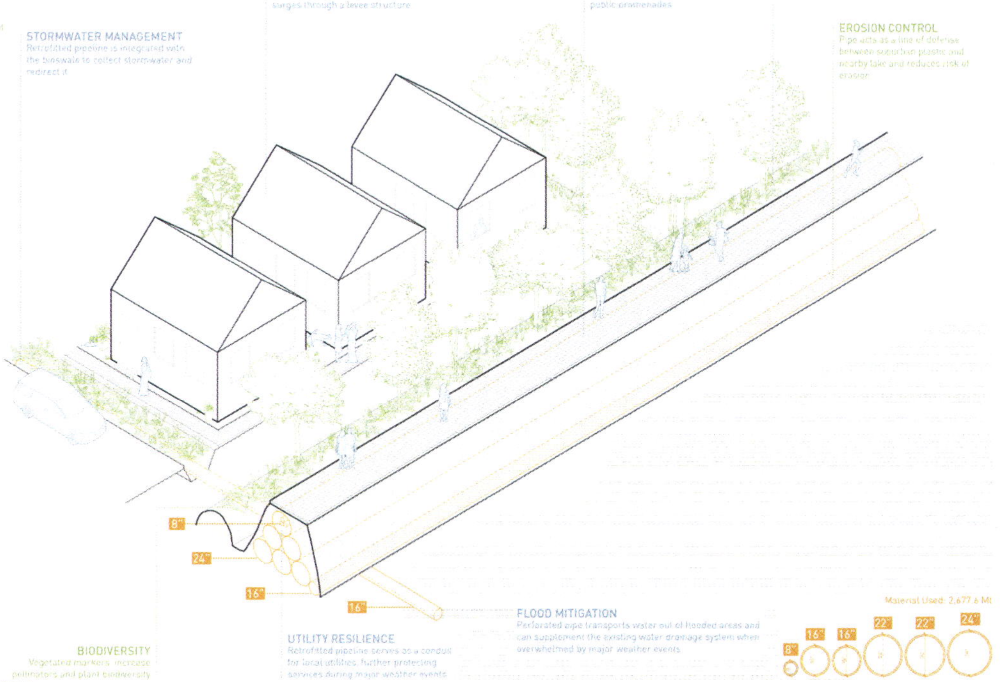

SITE-SPECIFIC INTERVENTIONS

SITE: BONNET CARRE SPILLWAY VISITORS CENTER

Cordula Roser Grey [C]
Judith Kinnard
Megan Slattery
Austin Lightle

This studio will focus on the role of the landscape in architectural design and the development of basic skills in site analysis, site design, and site representation. Site characteristics will be understood as both natural (a result of the actions of nature) and political-cultural (a result of the actions of people). Students will be introduced to a range of conceptual strategies for articulating the relationship between building and site. The course will highlight the designer's ethical obligations to the larger network of social and ecological systems and conditions. Design approaches will be grounded in organizational strategies aligned with their immediate and extended surroundings' vegetation, soils, and water. Building design themes will include spatial organization and hierarchy, circulation, structure, and enclosure. The studio will be integrated with digital media classes to ensure that students gain fluency in computer-aided design processes, drawing, spatial modeling, and digital design techniques.

Design—How the program instills in students the role of the design process in shaping the built environment and conveys the methods by which design processes integrate multiple factors, in different settings and scales of development, from buildings to cities.Ecological Knowledge and Responsibility—How the program instills in students a holistic understanding of the dynamic between built and natural environments, enabling future architects to mitigate climate change responsibly by leveraging ecological, advanced building performance, adaptation, and resilience principles in their work and advocacy activities.

Want to see pictures of the final reviews?

s> Nia Fletcher **i>** Cordula Roser Grey

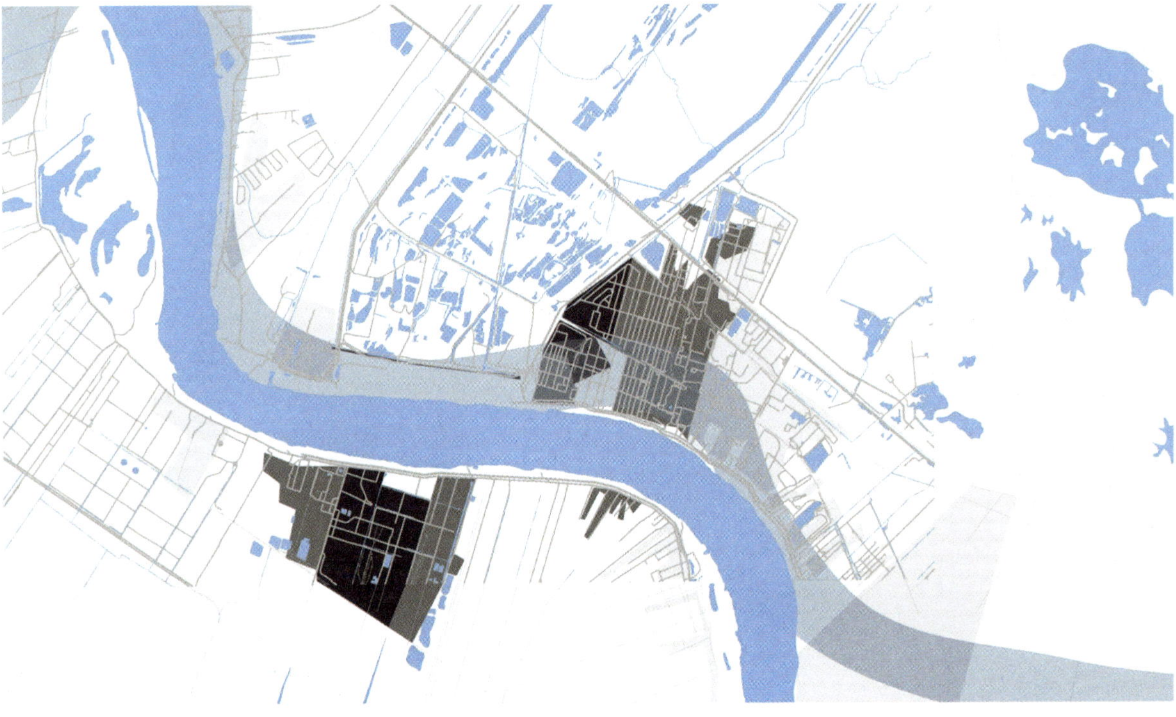

s> Charlie Hazel Pon, Kendra Johnson

i> Judith Kinnard, Megan Slattery

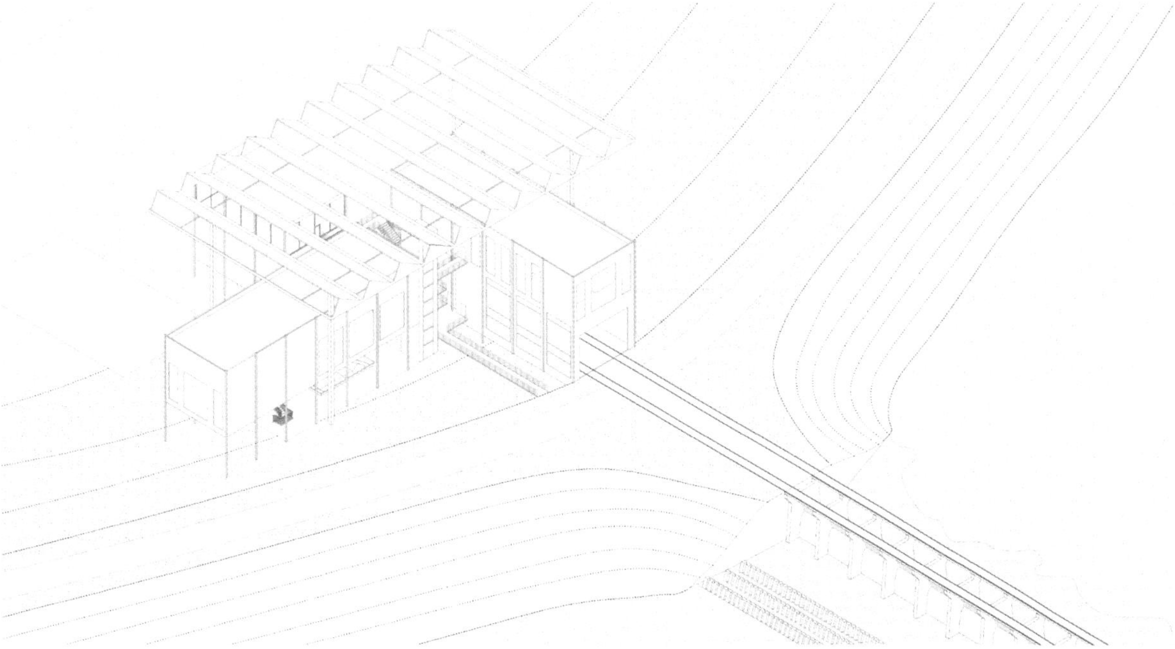

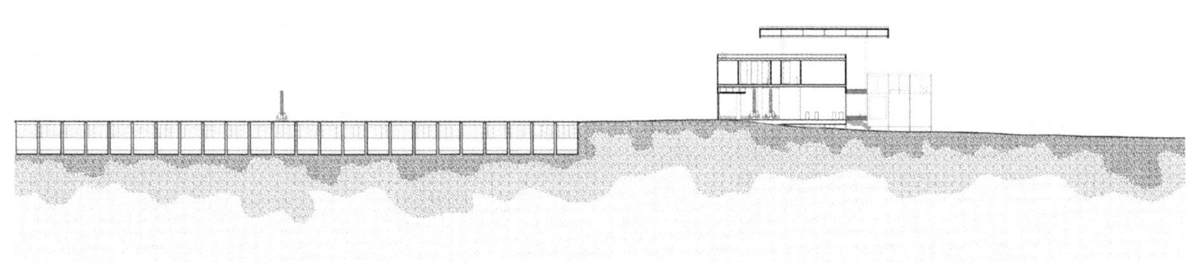

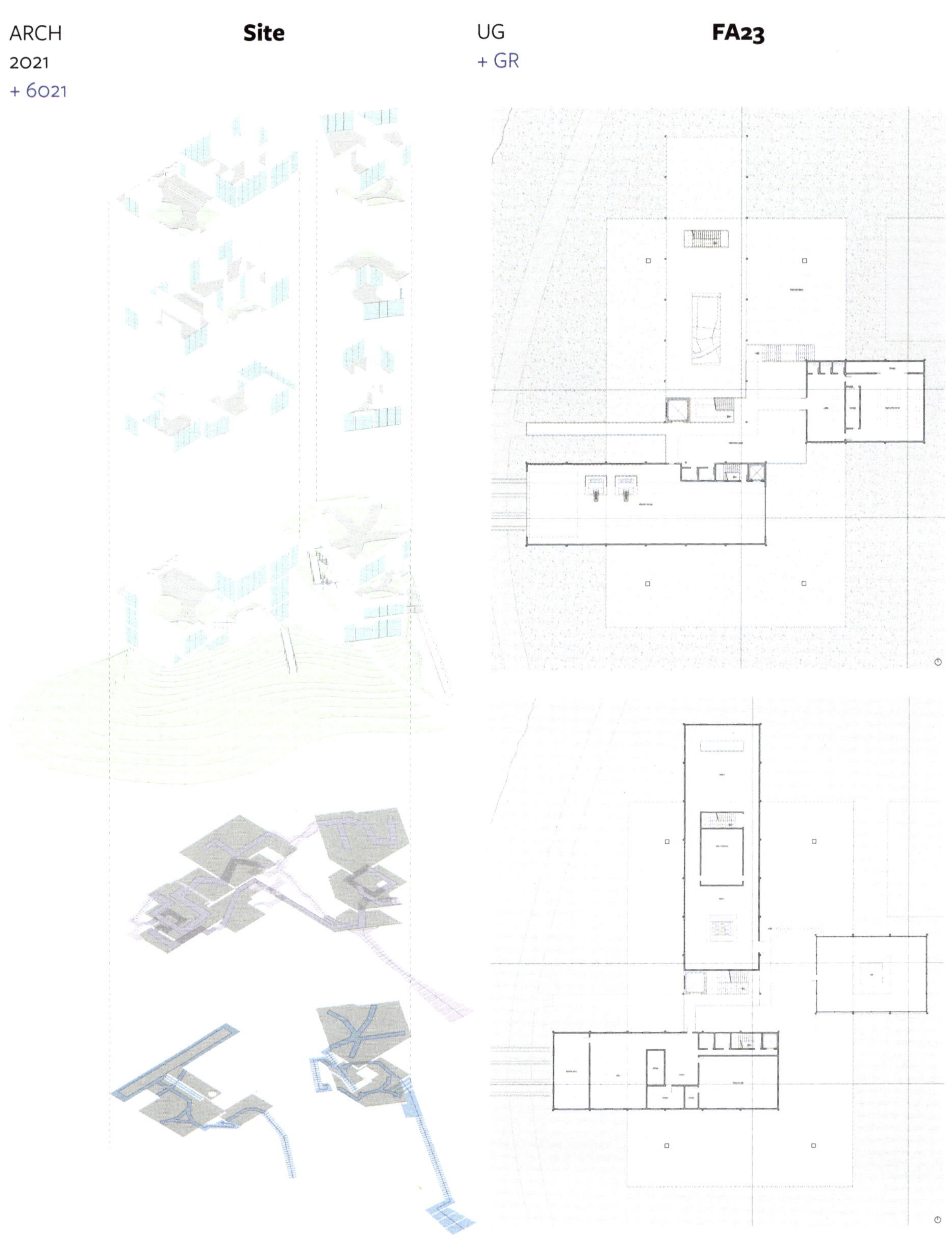

s> Sophia Atkins, Charlie Hazel Pon **i>** Austin Lightle, Judith Kinnard

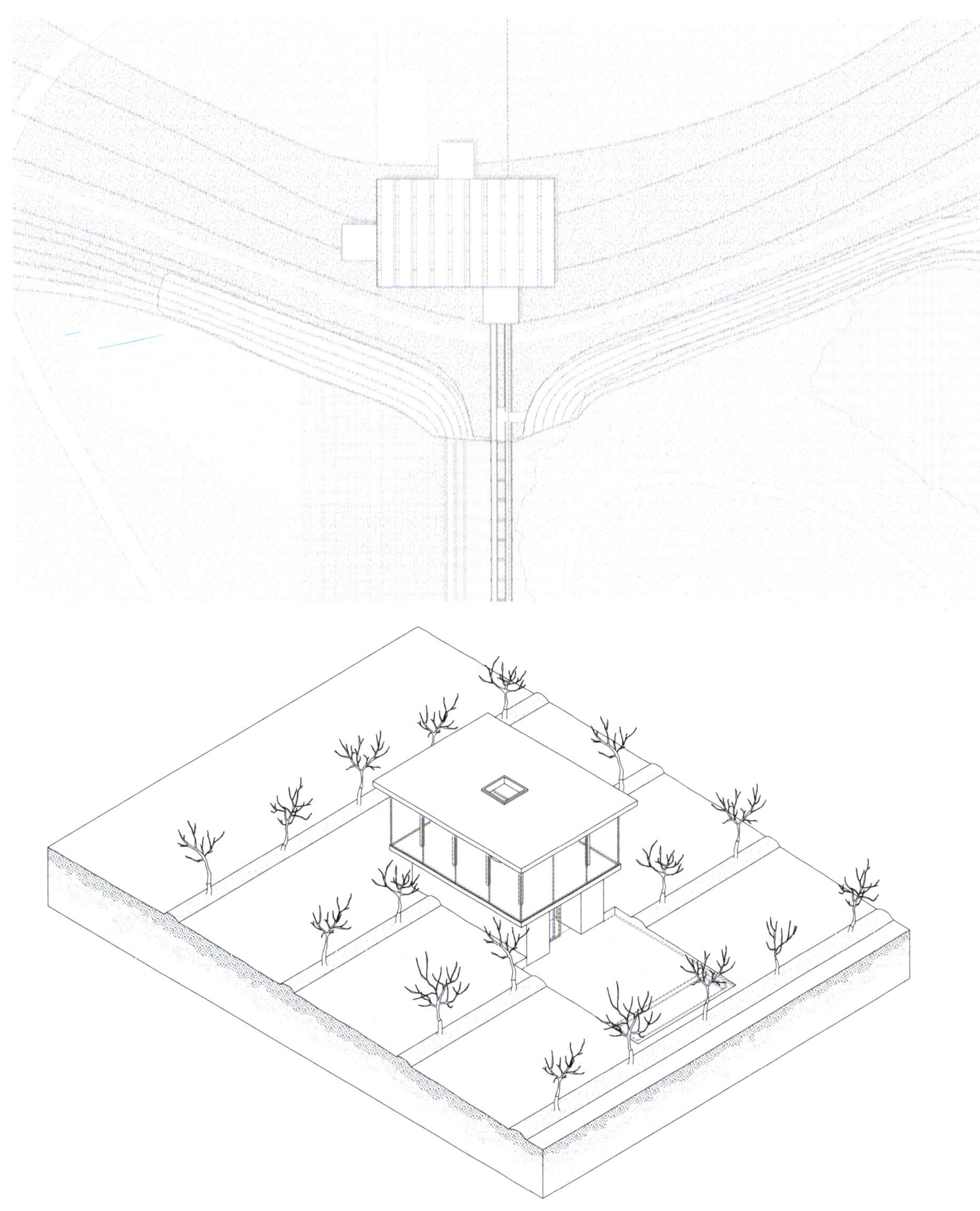

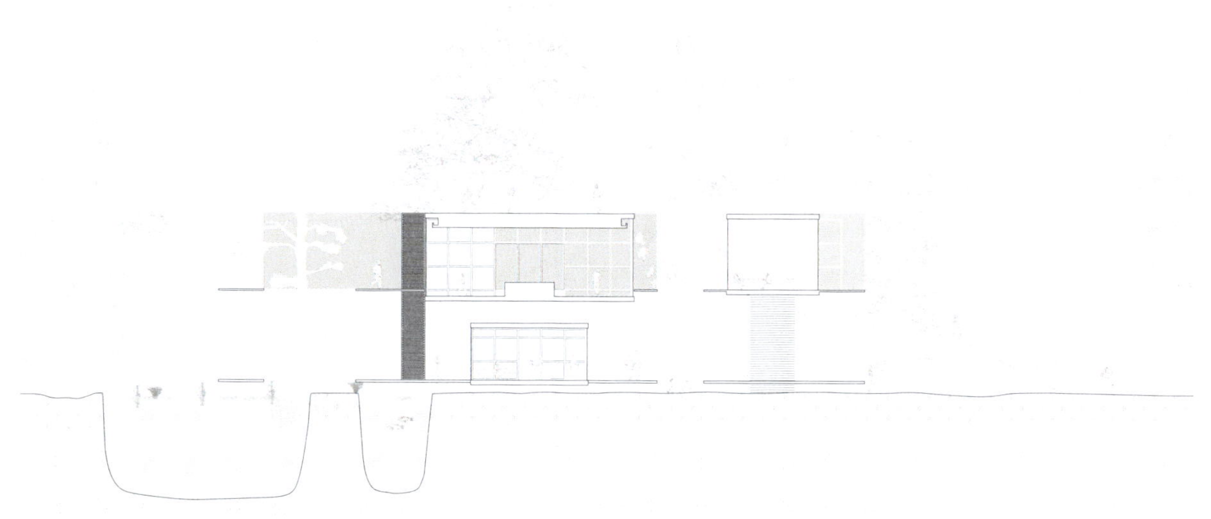

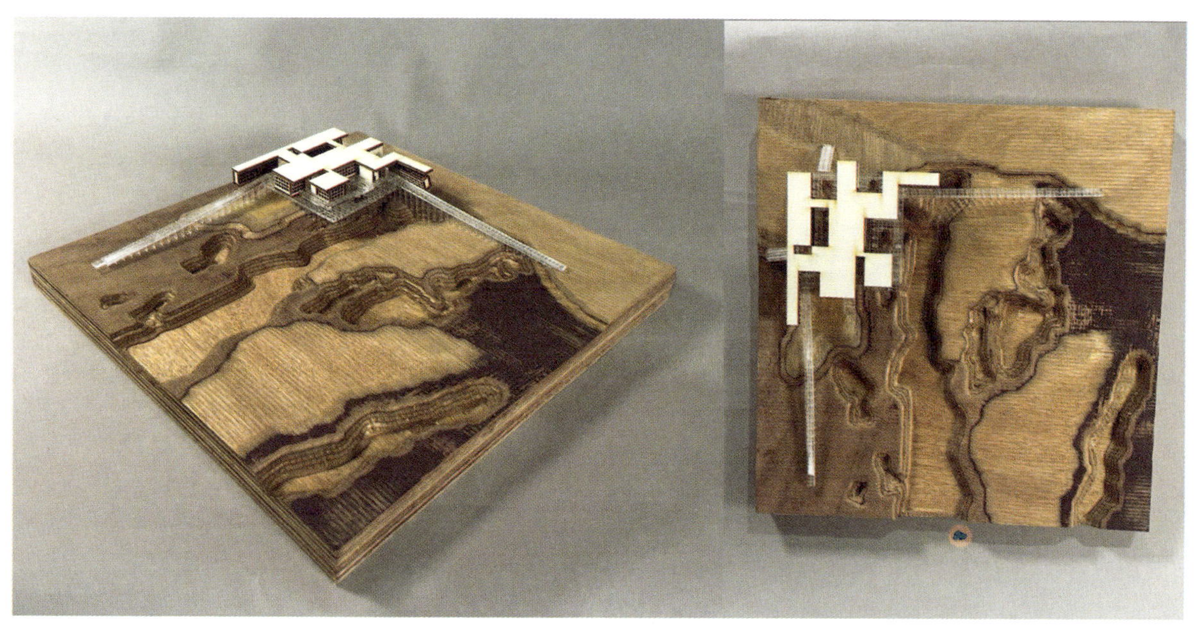

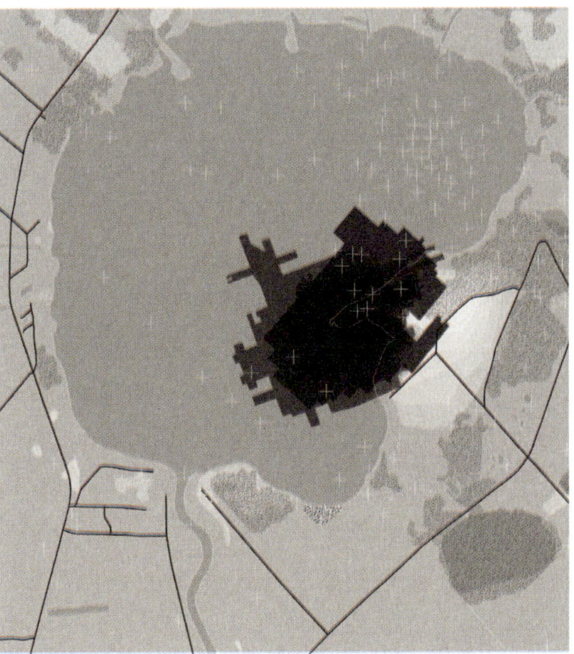

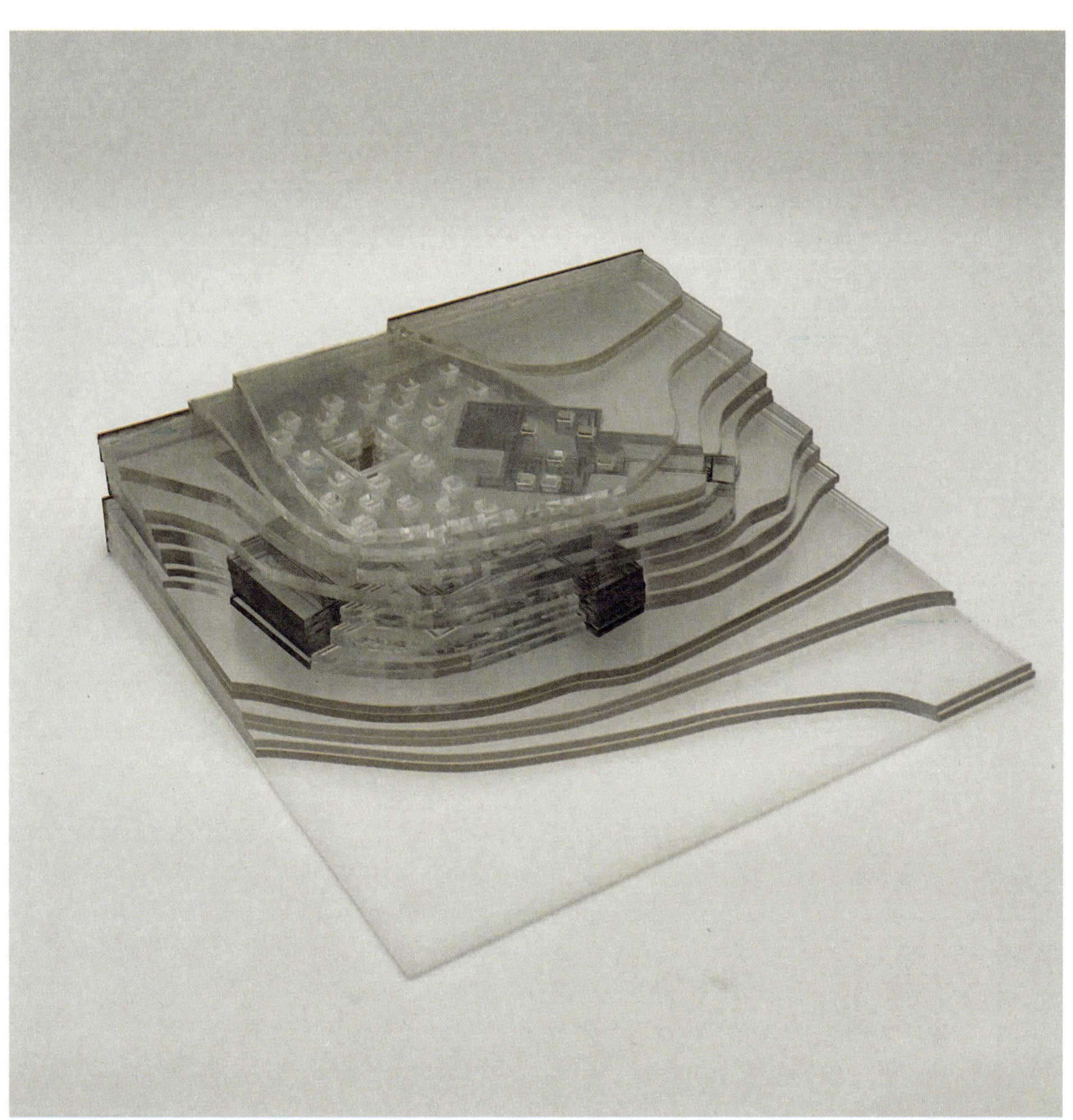

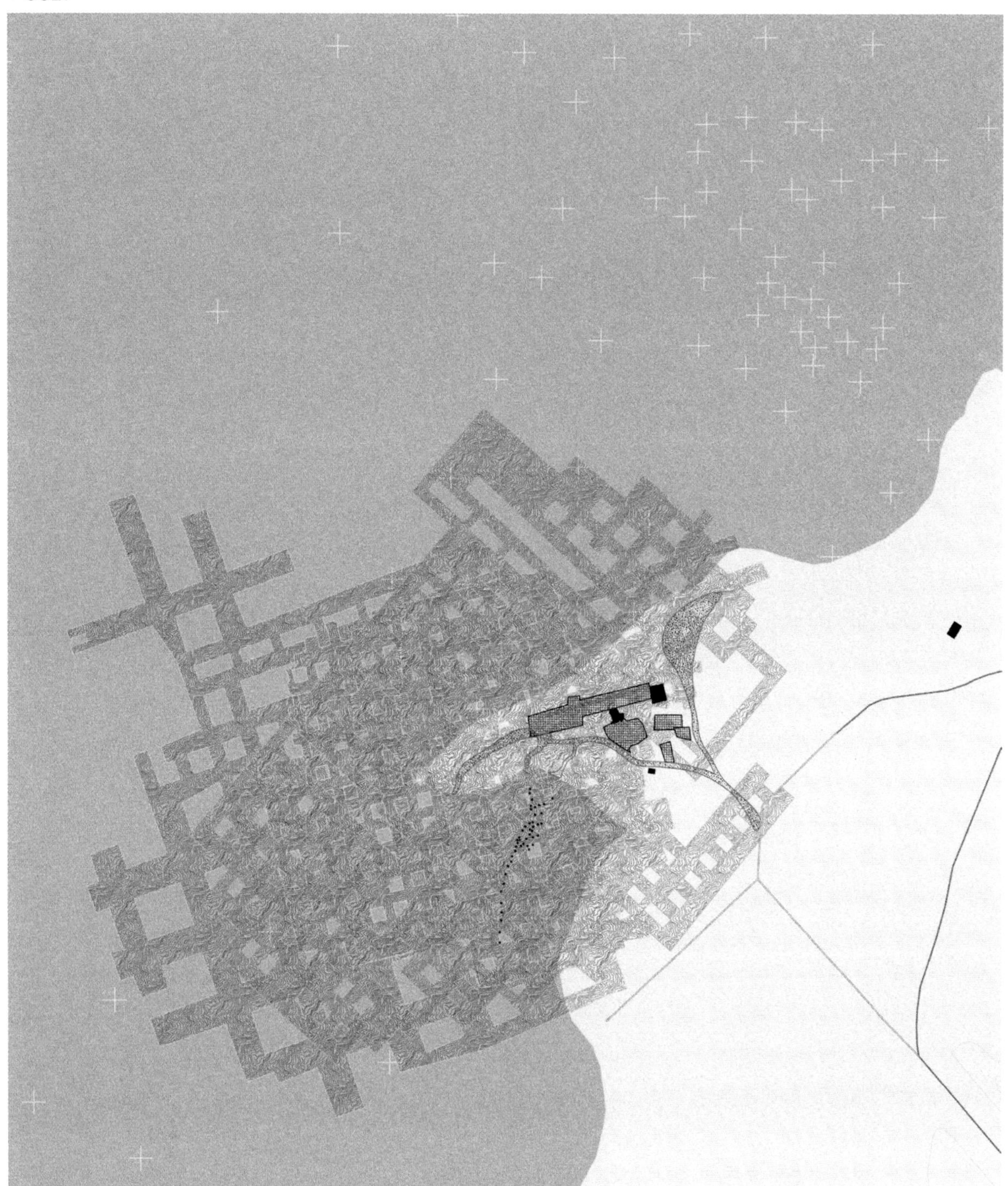

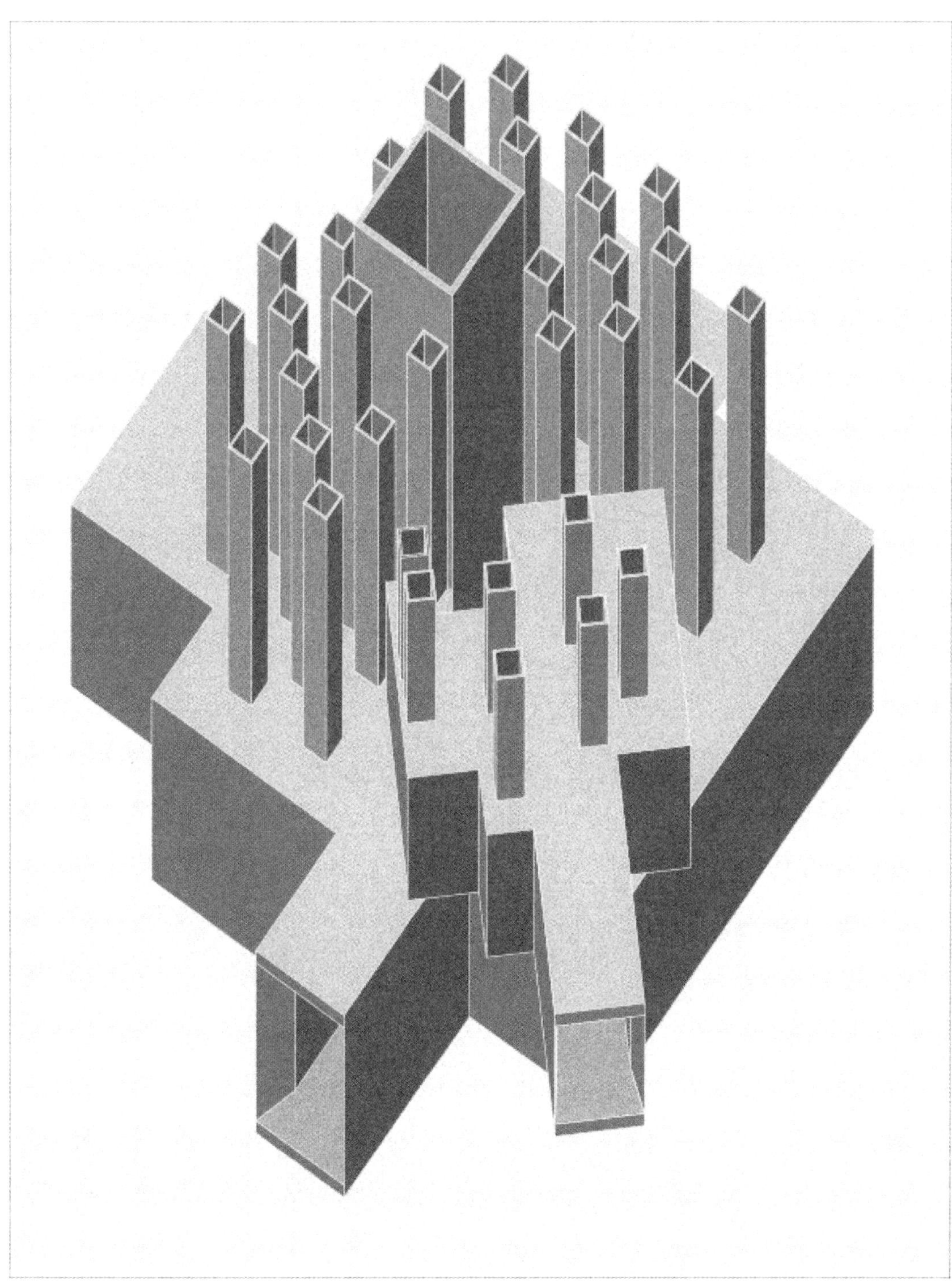

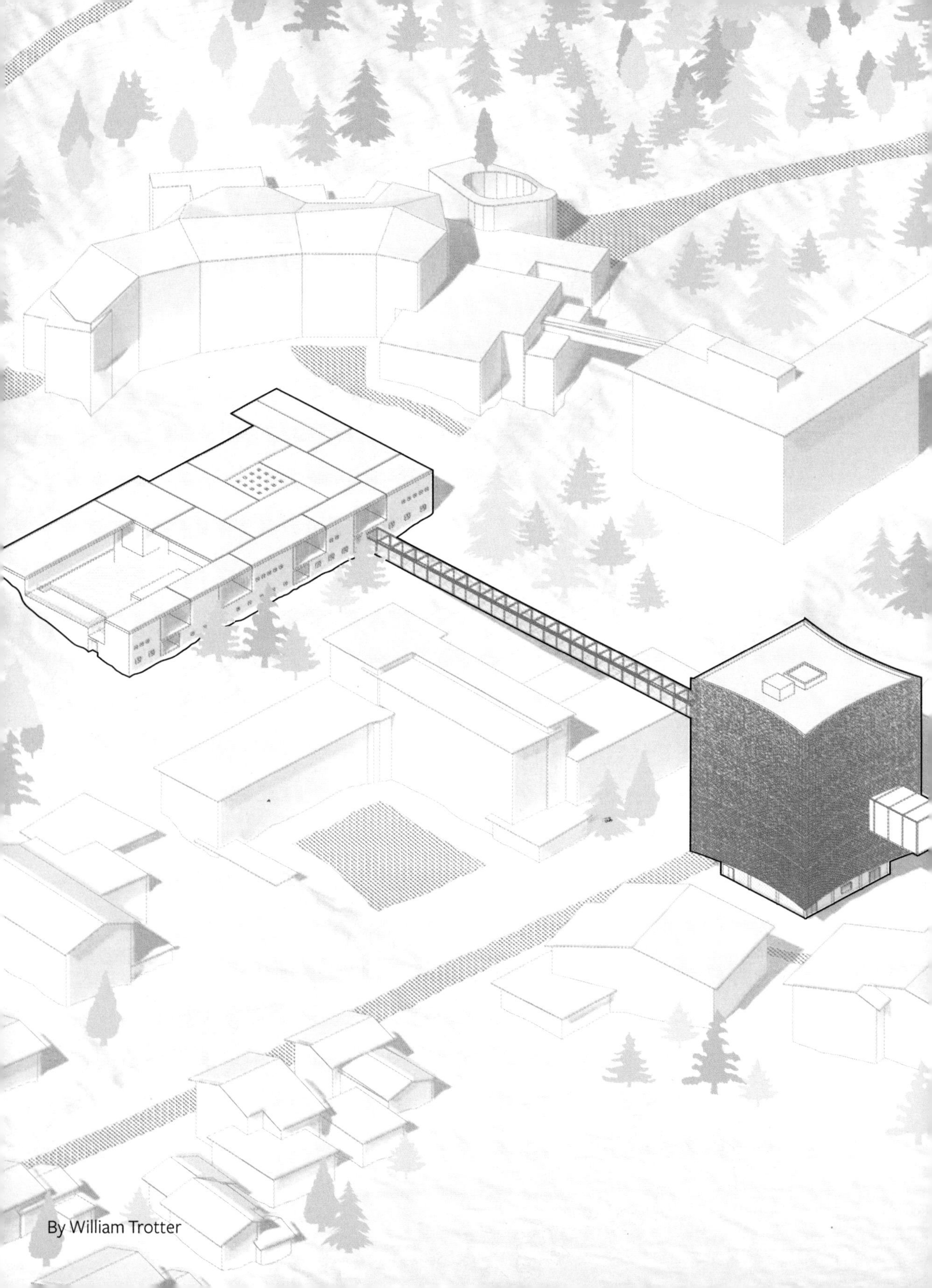

By William Trotter

12

CONTEXT & PLACE

AS COMMON GOOD

PLACE AS COMMON GOOD

Designing Public Spaces for Equity: Balancing Private Interests with the Common Good

By Iñaki Alday
Dean, Richard Koch Chair in Architecture
Tulane School of Architecture and Built Environment

Public space, since the Greek Agora, is the space of democracy and the most powerful urban element to generate equality or, on the contrary, to show or exacerbate inequalities.

Usually, architects work for a private client, with a greater or lesser awareness of the impact of the work on the common good, whether by program, location, contribution to the city, consumption of energy and resources, or impact on an environment that affects the entire community and the planet. On other occasions, the rarer ones, architects work on public projects where the objective of the common good is an explicit mandate, although often conditioned by the personal preferences of the administration's representatives. Sometimes, this has led to conflicts when we (in our firm, aldayjover architecture and landscape) have had to make decisions in favor of the needs of the citizens and against the will of, for example, the mayor.

Public space is probably the best physical embodiment of the idea of the Commons. One of our most significant public space projects, the introduction of the new tramway in Zaragoza, was an urban transformation on a large scale and a major improvement of the commons, but not only because of the extraordinary change in the capacity and efficiency of the public transport system and the changes in the overall mobility of the entire city. Unlike a metro line, which only occasionally affects public space by perforating stations, the tram reconstructs 8 miles of streets, boulevards and squares that cross the city. We know that public transportation is a key tool to balance and generate equity by making all portions of the city accessible to all its inhabitants. We also know that public space, since the Greek Agora, is the space of democracy and the most powerful urban element to generate equality or, on the contrary, to show or exacerbate inequalities.

In Zaragoza, the City Council drafted a "reference project" for a private consortium to develop, build, supply the trains, operate the line, and finance the city's new tramway. With this consortium as our client, we were confronted with multiple conflicting and intertwined interests. A municipal project that transforms the key elements of the common good: public transport and space, at the direct service of the citizen. A private client: two of the largest construction companies in the country, a train manufacturer, two financial institutions and a tram operator. The municipal project had chosen high-quality materials (granite and other natural stones) for the city center and much lower quality materials for the rest (70%) of the spaces along the line. The disparities between the proposal of the City Council as the representative of the citizens, the economic interests of our client (the private consortium), the differentiation between representative central urban spaces and peripheral spaces, and the notion of equity in public space beyond the economic capacity of the neighbors, generated a conflict that was apparently beyond our decision-making capacity.

As architects and landscape architects, we proposed an alternative solution that seemed to respond to all the conflicting interests. We designed a homogeneous system of pavements and urban elements from the beginning to the end of the public spaces along the line, including universal accessibility for all ages and abilities, imperceptible slopes and changes of elevation, pedestrian priority over motorized vehicles, elimination of private cars in the most densely used and narrow pinch points along the way, favoring the least powerful user. But above everything, the new system of pavements and urban elements was to be equal from the furthest and least affluent neighborhood to the wealthiest and to the most representative spaces downtown. The approval for this complete change from the municipal project came from the mayor when he visited the full-scale mockups. It took him less than a minute to give his opinion: "Of course we are not going to treat our voters in the periphery worse than conservative voters in the city center, same for all!"■

Original Project:

Two solutions of the original reference project side by side: natural stone for downtown prefabricated concrete for the peripheric neighborhoods.

Alternative Proposal:

aldayjover proposed and approved alternative: natural stone for curbs, pedestrian accessibility elements and all continuous elements; prefabricated concrete for pavement "fill"

STEVE DUMEZ
& JAVIER MARCANO

THE BRUCE MUSEUM

CULTURAL
Greenwich (CT), 2023

Architects: EskewDumezRipple (Steve Dumez, Noah Marble, Shawn Preau, Javier Marcano & more)
Photos: Tim Hursley

The Bruce Museum is a regionally based, world-class museum located in Greenwich, Connecticut with a multi-disciplinary collection and exhibition program bringing together art, science, and natural history. The project is a complete renovation of the original 32,500 sf structure, and the addition of a 42,000 sf new wing providing permanent and changing gallery space, expanded collection storage, and a new public entrance lobby and lecture hall for the museum.

The design draws inspiration from the site's geology, particularly the rock outcroppings and stone quarries of the Connecticut coast. The façade, made of precast concrete panels mimicking the striated layers of a quarry, interacts dynamically with light and shadow throughout the day. The design also borrows from what is known as "Lace Walls" in the region—the early settlers in the region constructed walls on their property by loosely stacking stones to create what are known as lace walls. These low stone walls create a condition where the built wall is "as much air as it is stone." The design reinterprets both of these two precedents to create a rich interplay of texture and contrast, and an implied relationship of the natural and the crafted.

Comprising four floors, the expansion more than doubles the existing square footage of the facility and creates a welcoming visitor experience with clear circulation, generous galleries, and sufficient exhibition, storage, and archival spaces for the Museum's growing collection.

Fig. 1 Aerial view

Fig. 2
Interior stair

Fig. 3
Entrance

Figs. 4, 5 Exhibition spaces

carPORCH

RESIDENTIAL
Lake Nantachie, Montgomery (LA), 2022

Architects: bildDESIGN, bildCONSTRUCTS: Byron Mouton, Hugh Jackson, John Tyler Young, Jason Blankenship, Joey Aplin

Acknowledging a common vernacular of the rural Central Louisiana region, this lake house was conceived as an occupiable garage, or a "carPORCH." The project blurs the line between indoor and outdoor activities as it facilitates a lifestyle unique to the culture of Louisiana.

While evacuated from New Orleans due to Hurricane Katrina, the owner of this project, a New Orleans native and design/build professional, discovered the often-overlooked region of Central Louisiana and came to appreciate the distinct landscape and rural culture of the region. For eight years following Katrina, he searched for a plot of land to be developed as a combination evacuation destination, satellite studio, and nature retreat. Finally, he settled on a property with ample frontage along Nantachie Lake, just a few hours north of New Orleans.

The project was realized over nine years of weekend visits; the owner constructed the project during those trips with periodic help from staff and local tradesmen. The design concept combines a simple volume with the application of a covered deck; it is an occupiable garage, a "carPORCH," designed to house the owner's RV and support related social outdoor activities. The wall between conditioned indoor space and the adjacent deck is entirely operable—extending interior activities onto a south-facing porch that overlooks and frames a special view to the lake.

The camp's location amidst thousands of acres of pine forests, where logging is the predominant industry, influenced the selection of interior and exterior cladding materials. However, where pine could not withstand direct exposure to the often harsh elements, a common corrugated metal cladding was used in response to severe sun and rain.

As originally intended, the project serves a multitude of purposes. It is sometimes a country office, periodically an evacuation destination, and often a retreat where cooking and entertainment take place both inside and out. Finally, the swampy, freshwater cypress lake not only provides beautiful waterfront views but also makes the shed a perfect fishing camp for the owner's favorite outdoor pursuit.

Fig. 1 West facade

Fig. 2 Northwest facing

Fig. 3 Porch area

Fig. 4 Kitchen area

Fig. 5 Living room from the loft

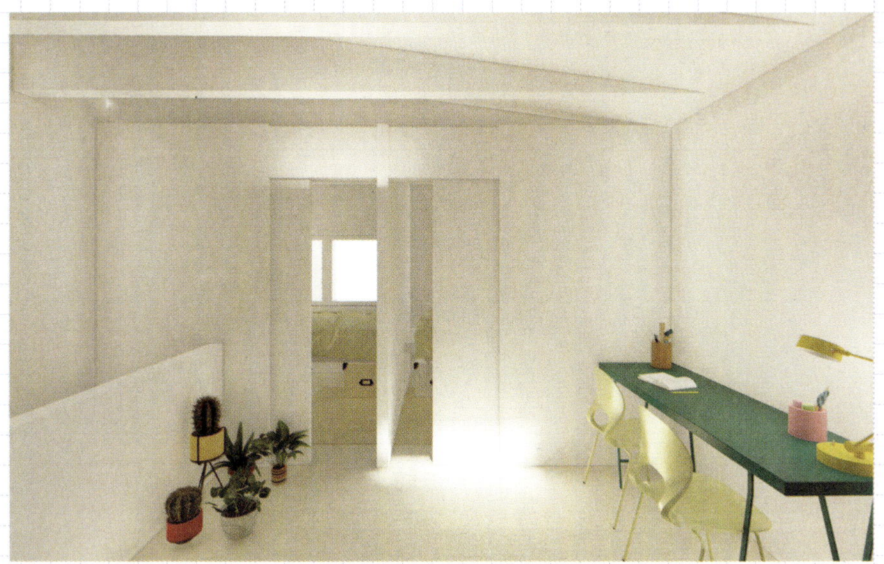

LACAL

RESIDENTIAL
Madrid, Spain, 2024

Architects: Andrea Bardón de Tena and Pía Mendaro Ruiz de Larramendi
Collaborators: Pilar Jiménez Bereilh
Constructor: Over all

LACAL is the renovation of a family house consisting of a couple with two daughters. The current volume must remain intact, but the new inhabitants and their lifestyle force us to rethink the original distribution. This is a project in time: for the present and its near future.

The house's previous overlapping lives have turned it into a peculiar L-shaped construction—in fact, two intertwined L's: a garden and a house [1]. The relationship between the two results in an inner and an outer face to the project [2]. The outer perimeter (party walls) houses all the services: bathrooms, laundry, and a staircase, while the main rooms—bedrooms, living room, dining room, and kitchen—face the garden [3+4].

It is essential for this family to have a place for everyone to work and to share their daily routine. This center is located upstairs, between bedrooms, and enjoys the zenithal light between the palomeros partition screens of the first construction that remain visible. At the same time, the project is carried out considering time as a crucial variable. Small future modifications are foreseen in all the premises—especially a division of their daughters' room into two independent bedrooms in the coming years [5 + 6].

Ultimately, considering the existing is full of opportunities. As often happens to us, in resolving the detail, we find the character of the project. The combination of technical challenges—necessary structural reinforcements—and the choice of honest materials gives us new possibilities: a beam to which we can attach floating objects in the kitchen or the recycling of some trap doors so that we can call out from the shower if dinner is ready.

1

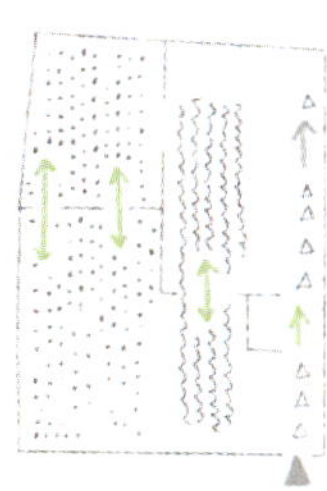

2

3

4

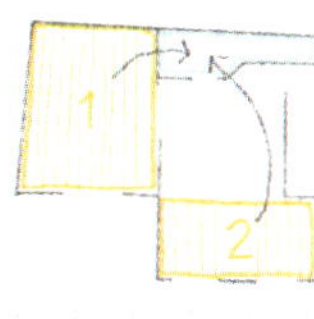

5

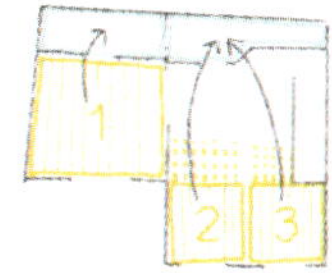

6

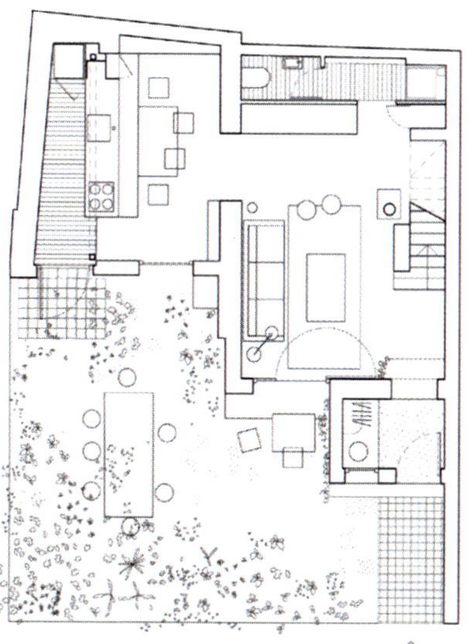

Proposal GL

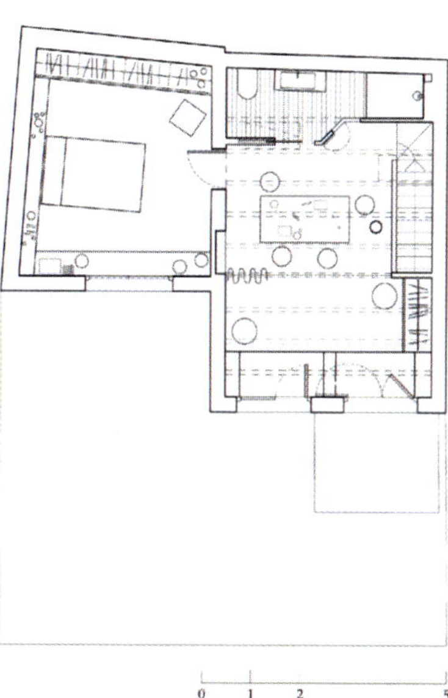

Proposal 2nd floor

ARCH
4041/5051
+ 6041/6051

Research Studio

UG
+ GR

FA23

APPROPRIATION & MODIFICATION

Swiss Models of Regeneration of Buildings, Urban Space, and Constructive Technique

Wendeline Redfield [C]
Iñaki Alday

The studio explores the underlying prerequisites of architectural sustainability in its most holistic and comprehensive sense. How, and perhaps more importantly. Why are certain objects, buildings, urban spaces, and ways of making sustained while others are discarded? Why do some endure—modified, maintained, and updated for evolving purpose—whileothers are abandoned and forgotten? What inherent material characteristics, or alternatively what societal priorities bestow value on certain objects, places, and ways of doing and making things such that they are loved sufficiently to be saved?

While these questions are cultural and theoretical in nature, they have profound global, climactic implications for human survival and quality of life. No cutting-edge technology can conserve or replace energy or natural resources more efficiently than meeting the needs of multiple generations by building fewer things very rarely, and very well. But durability requires something more, namely the ingenuity and commitment to cultivate ways of updating old buildings, places, and methods to meet changing needs and expectations of performance.

The work of contemporary Swiss architects, notably the offices of Peter Zumthor and Herzog & De Meuron, includes many pertinent precedents at a variety of scales and modes of making. Swiss culture is inherently conservative. It values quality, durability, adaptability, and a certain kind of frugality—things are built to last requiring them to be constructed very well, using high quality, durable materials. Perhaps the root of Swiss values with respect to material production stems from the region's scant native resources due to geographical isolation. Switzerland's lack of access to coastal or historical on-ground trade routes, paucity of mineral resources, and the predominance of its dispersed, rural-centered communities limited local building materials to timber from alpine forests and stone quarried from its mountainous terrain. These material limitations are countered by the ingenuity and impeccability of Swiss craft traditions.

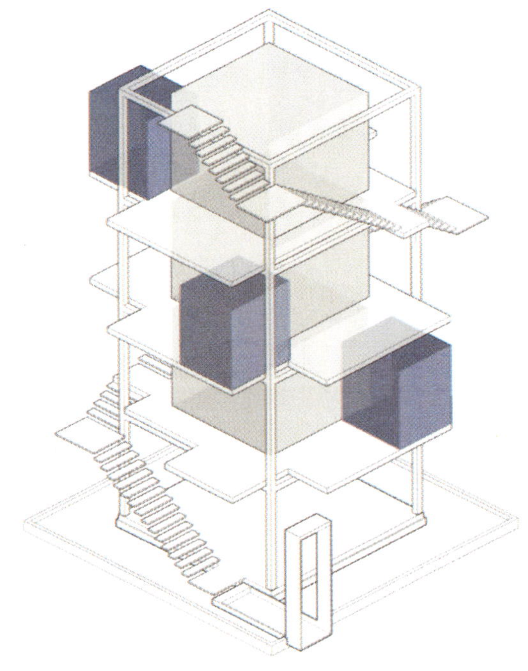

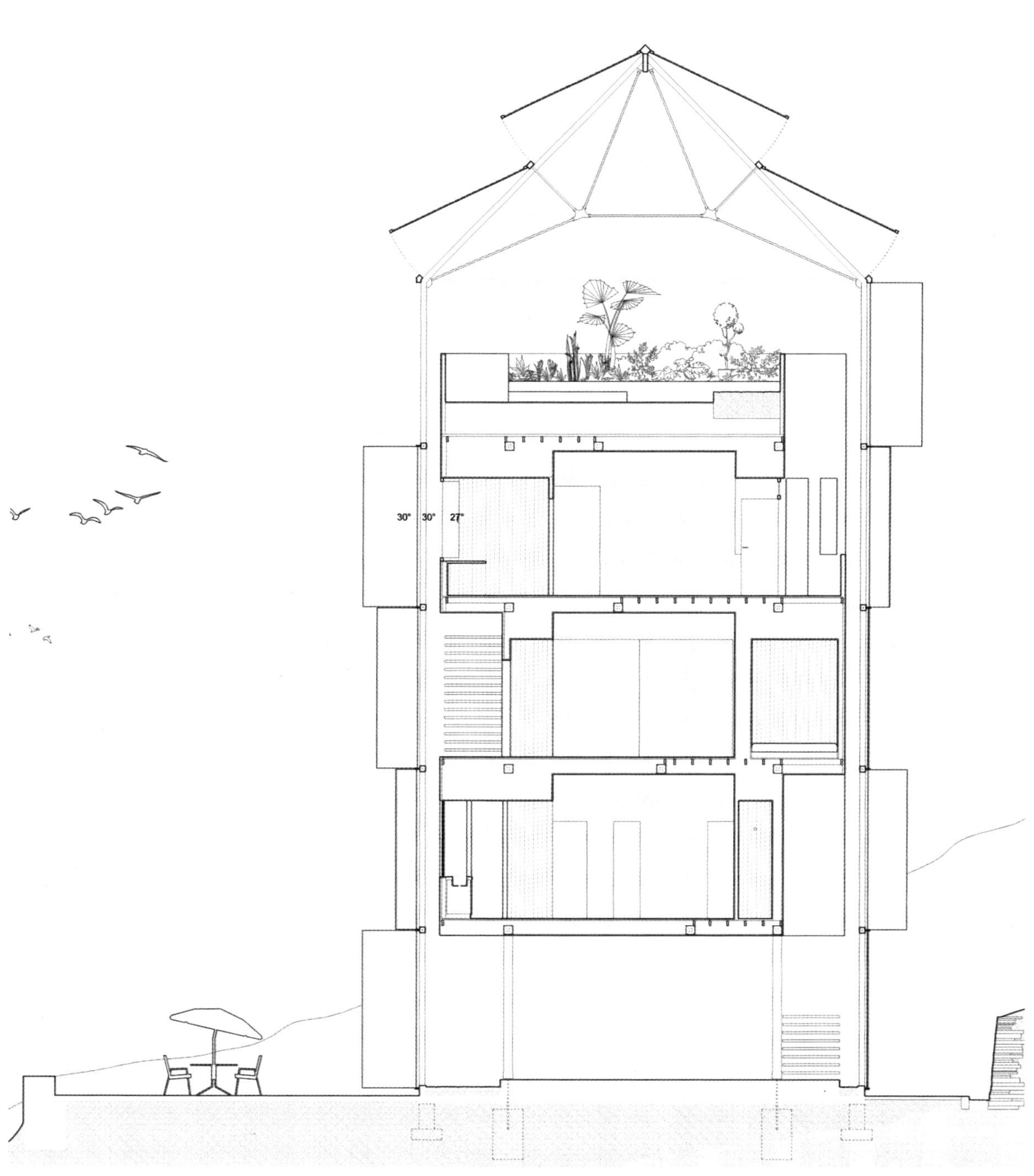
30°
30°
27°

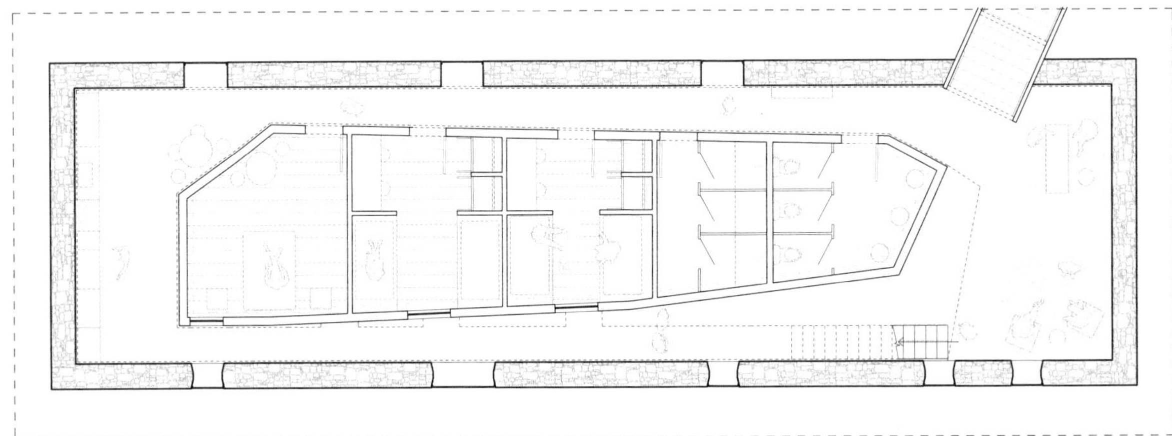

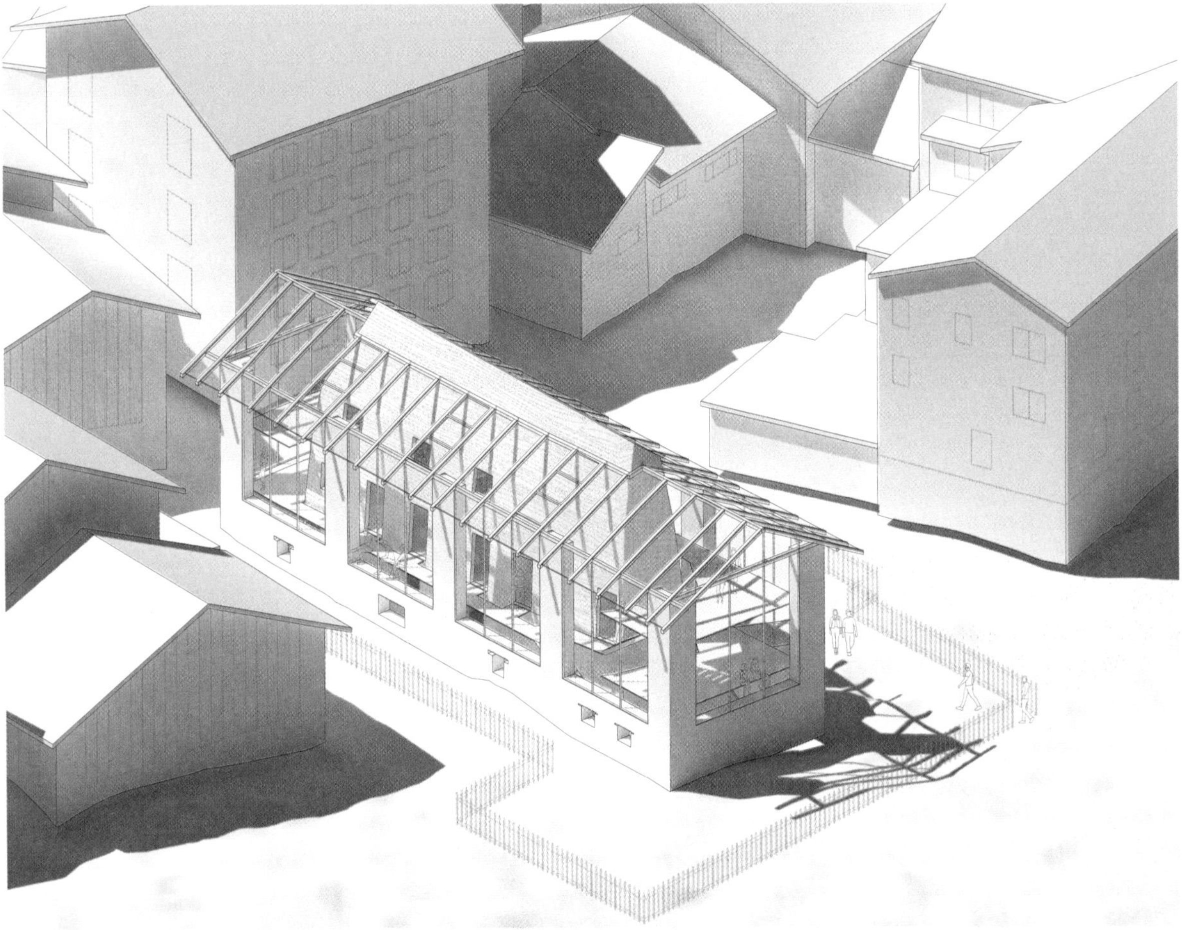

s> Cassie Kaddish

i> Wendy Redfield, Iñaki Alday

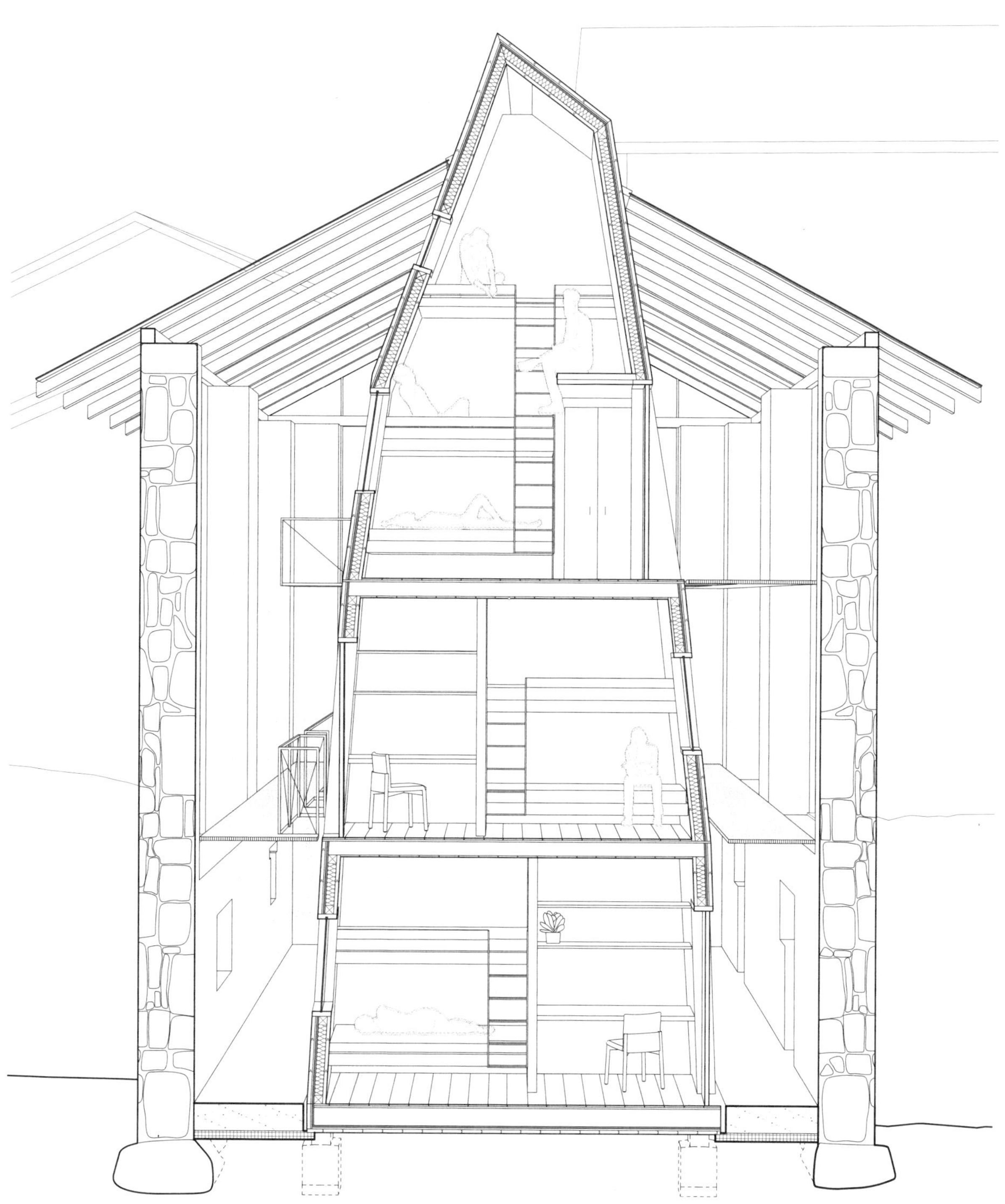

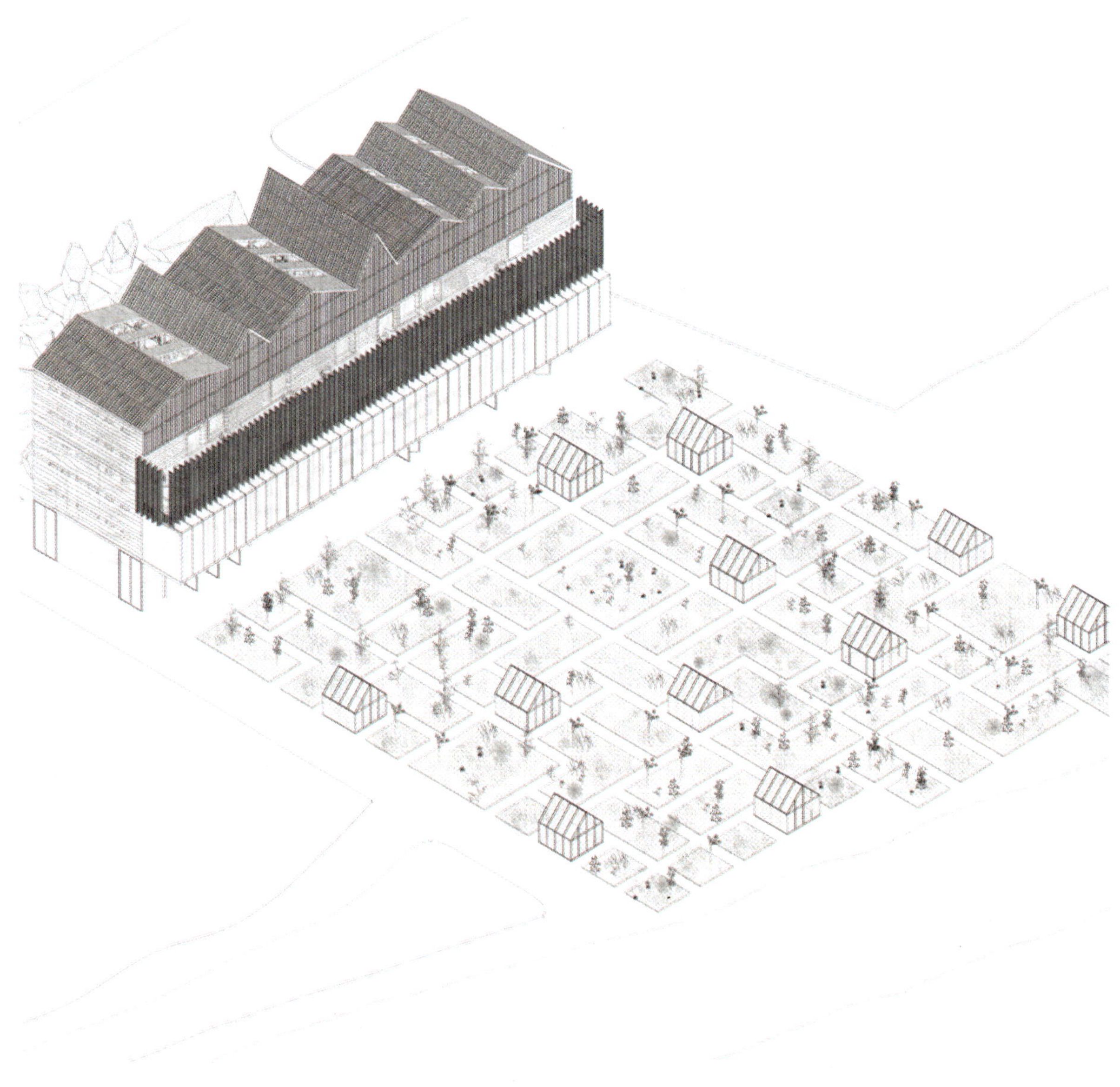

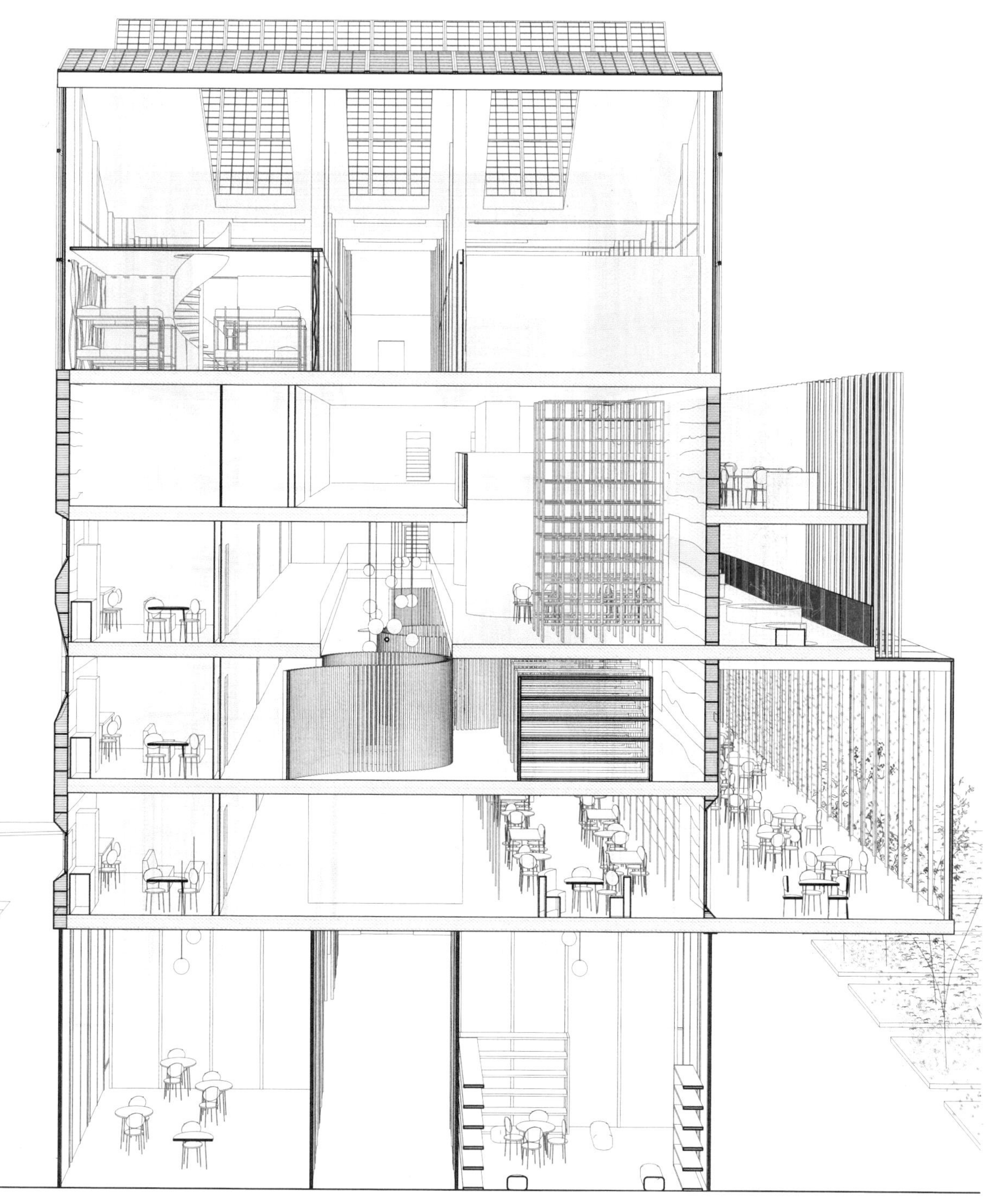

URBAN RESILIENCE

Los Angeles

Ruben Garcia Rubio[C]
Irene Kiel
Angela Morton
Catherine Sckerl

Students in Tulane School of Architecture and Built Environment third year design studio studied the urban scale and its integration with the architectural one as well as the metabolic and territorial scale used by architects and urbanists. This studio focused on the integration of the urban and architectural design through the understanding of the intermediate scale. Students developed an architectural design that acted as a catalyst for a previously designed part of Los Angeles based on a specific program.

Firstly, students investigated, analyzed, and synthesized the city's major urban systems transversely and across multiple scales. Secondly, students identified urban issues and opportunities and proposed a resilient urban design for a specific part of the city, focusing on the architectural dimension of urban design. They also analyzed significant urban precedents during this phase. Thirdly, students developed an architectural design that acts as a catalyst for the previously designed part of the city based on a specific program.

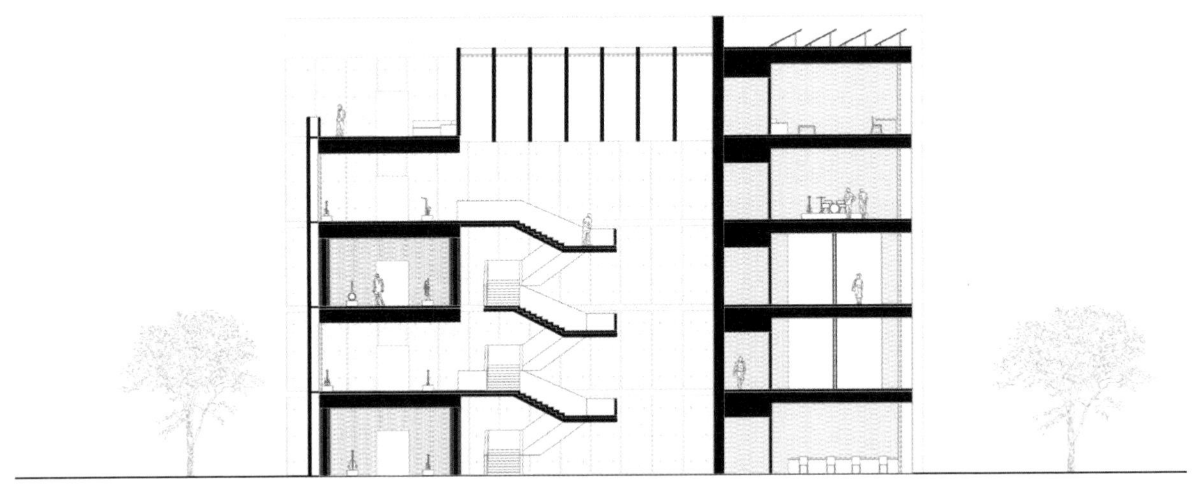

s> Brian Harris, Francesca Lubega

i> Ruben Garcia Rubio

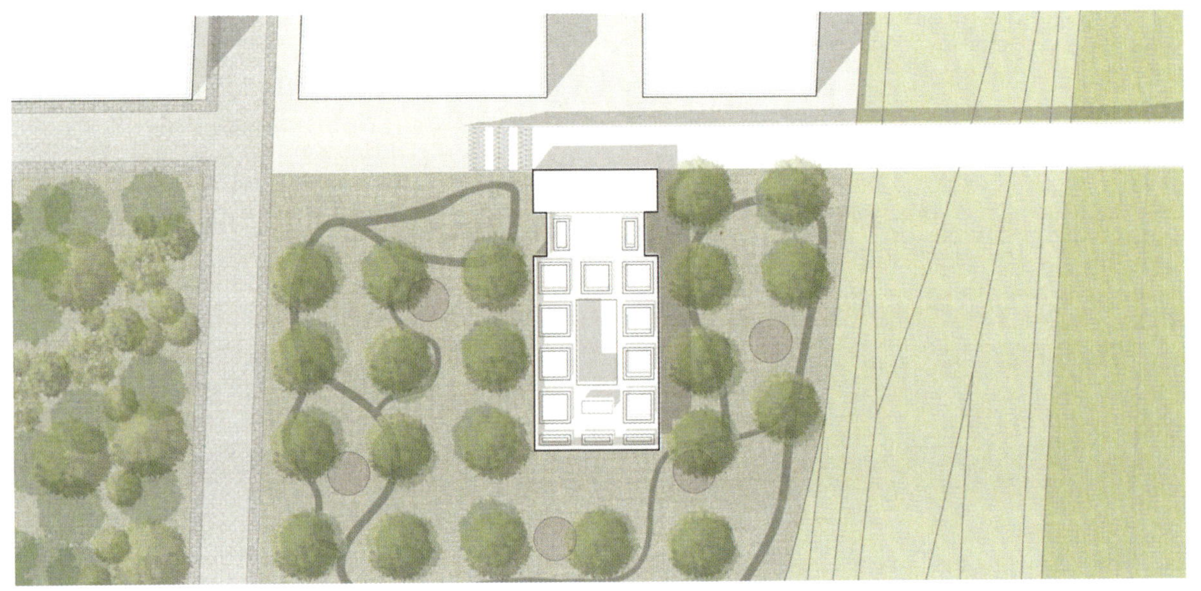

s> Nicole Waxman **i>** Catherine Sckerl

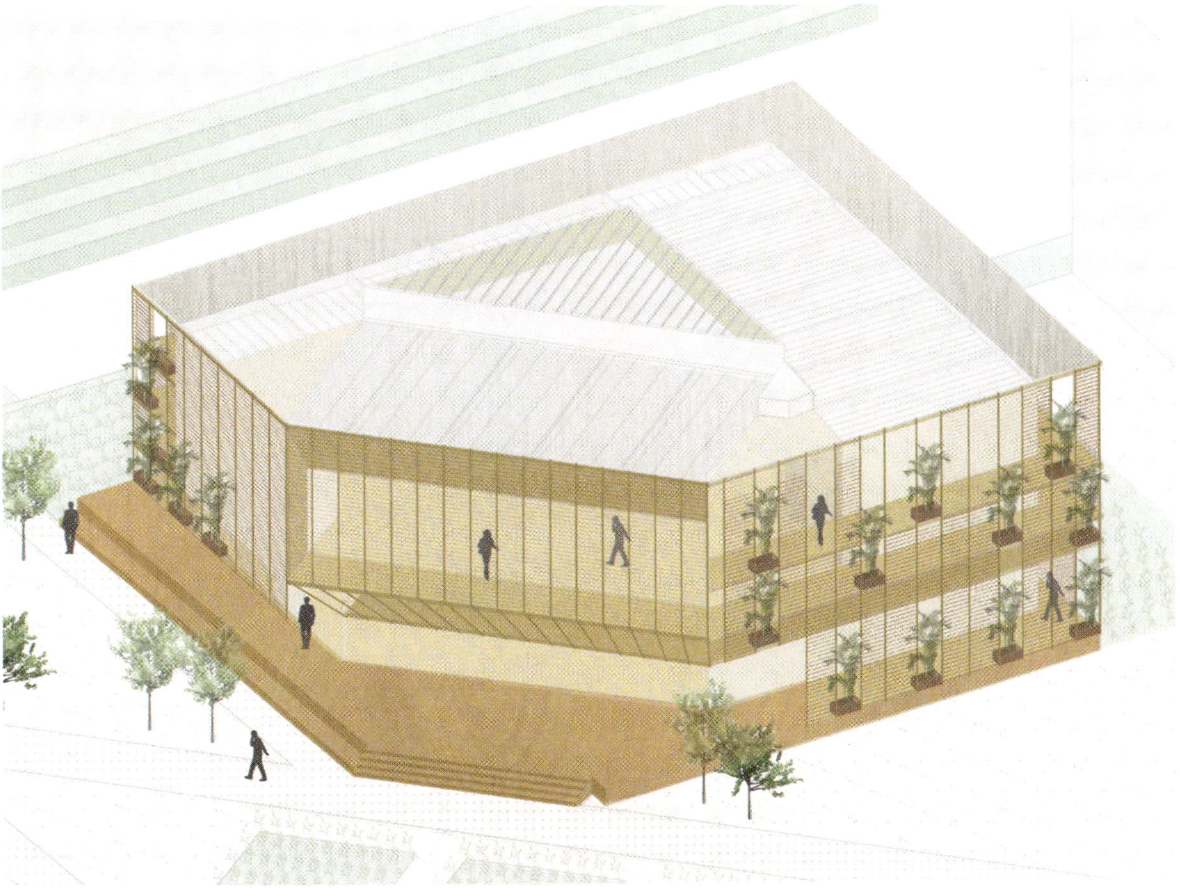

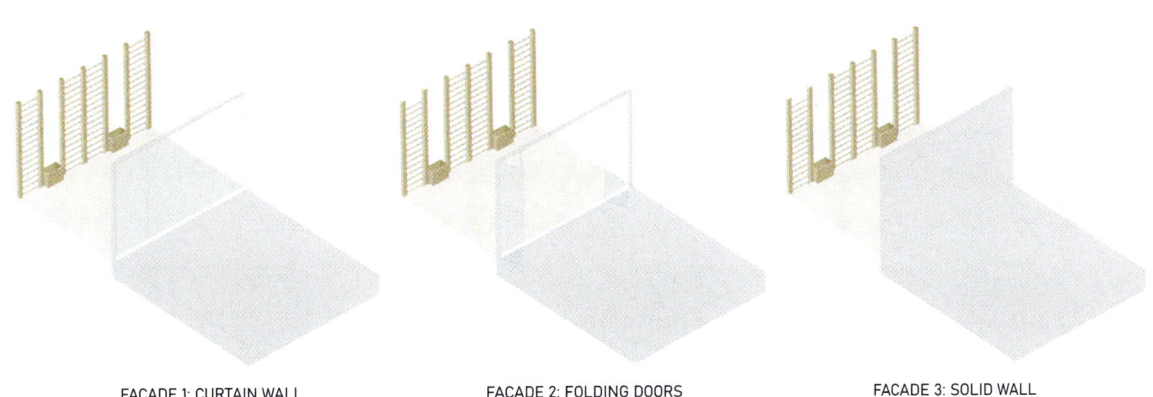

FACADE 1: CURTAIN WALL

FACADE 2: FOLDING DOORS

FACADE 3: SOLID WALL

6
5
4
14
ALABAMA
10
MISSISSIPPI
LOUISIANA
18
se Varela Castillo

13

INFRASTRUCTURES

AS COMMON GOOD

INFRASTRUCTURES AS A PUBLIC GOOD

Addressing Societal Needs in a Changing Climate

By Liz Russell
Professor of Practice in Architecture
Tulane School of Architecture and Built Environment

Infrastructure—roads, bridges, power and water systems, communication networks, and public services—forms the backbone of modern society. It is easy to take these systems for granted, assuming that they will continue to function seamlessly. However, as the impacts of climate change become more apparent, the invisible nature of infrastructure's everyday functionality is being exposed. Extreme weather events, rising sea levels, and shifting precipitation patterns are revealing the vulnerabilities of systems that were often designed with limited foresight into future environmental and societal challenges. This reality forces us to confront how these systems are maintained, upgraded, and reimagined to meet the dynamic needs of society.

The most basic and fundamental components required for a society to thrive—such as roads, bridges, energy, and water systems—are not merely functional; they represent shared investments that support collective well-being. From the first investments made as geographies became settled to the complex systems we depend on today, infrastructure functions as a communal investment that enables societal growth. As colonial and post-colonial systems took form, infrastructure projects such as levees, roads, and sewage systems were established to mitigate risks, manage resources, and facilitate economic opportunity. These systems allowed people to live together in larger, more interconnected communities by addressing critical needs such as hygiene, transportation, and energy access.

However, the benefits of these infrastructural systems extend far beyond their functional purposes. They lay the framework for social and economic opportunities, creating the conditions necessary for growth, mobility, and quality of life. Water and sanitation systems improved public health, transportation infrastructure connected rural areas to cities, and energy systems powered homes and industries. When designed and implemented thoughtfully, infrastructure serves as a conduit for shared societal progress.

Yet, even in the most developed societies, these essential systems often go unnoticed until they fail. Many residents in the Western world, for example, assume that roads will remain smooth, water will always flow from taps, and energy will always be available. However, these systems are increasingly in decline, with decades of underinvestment in maintenance and renewal. The very idea of maintenance—ensuring that systems continue to operate effectively over time—has become an invisible aspect of infrastructure management, one that politicians often fail to prioritize in their short electoral cycles. Without regular upkeep, the longevity and resilience of these systems cannot be guaranteed.

The changing climate is pushing existing infrastructure systems beyond their original capacity. As cities expand, so too does the pressure on transportation, energy, and drainage systems. In many cases, infrastructure development is happening in areas where the risks of flooding, heat, and other climate-related events are rising. For example, new developments are often permitted in floodplains without considering the long-term impacts on stormwater drainage systems or the increased risk of flooding. These systems, originally designed for different climate conditions, can no longer meet the demands of a warmer, wetter world.

At the same time, the demand for infrastructure is growing as populations swell, particularly in urban areas. In cities across the globe, traffic congestion increases as roads, bridges, and public transportation networks fail to keep up with rapid population growth. Schools become overcrowded, healthcare facilities are stretched thin, and infrastructure systems struggle to handle the compounded effects of climate change and urban sprawl. This growing pressure exposes the limitations of our existing systems and challenges our capacity to invest in new solutions.

The question then becomes: how do we create and maintain infrastructure that is not only responsive to current needs but also anticipates the challenges of a rapidly changing world? How do we ensure that investments in infrastructure continue to benefit the public and address the evolving realities of climate change, population growth, and social inequality?

In response to these challenges, there is a growing recognition that infrastructure should be viewed as a tool for transformation, rather than simply a set of static systems. Investment in infrastructure must move beyond reactive maintenance to proactive innovation, incorporating climate resilience, sustainability, and inclusivity into design and planning. This requires a shift in how we conceptualize infrastructure—as a dynamic, evolving entity that must adapt to the changing needs of society, rather than something fixed in time.

The need for reinvention is particularly urgent as we confront the social, environmental, and economic consequences of climate change. Sea level rise, more frequent and intense storms, and shifting precipitation patterns are just some of the forces that demand new forms of infrastructure—systems that can absorb shocks, accommodate growth, and function sustainably over time. This includes investments in flood-resistant drainage systems, renewable energy grids, green building technologies, and resilient transportation networks that can withstand extreme weather events.

However, these investments cannot be made by isolated individuals or organizations. Just as infrastructure has historically been a shared investment, so too must future investments be communal. The “tragedy of the commons,” a scenario where individuals exploit shared resources to their detriment, highlights the importance of collective responsibility in maintaining and upgrading infrastructure. It is only through shared commitment and investment that we can reimagine infrastructure systems that serve the collective good while addressing the risks and opportunities presented by climate change.

As we face the increasing demands of a changing climate, our approach to infrastructure must be one of reinvigoration, reimagination, and transformation. No longer can we afford to treat infrastructure as a set of static systems designed for the past. We must invest in resilient, adaptable systems that can meet the needs of a rapidly evolving world. This requires bold leadership, long-term thinking, and a commitment to shared investment in infrastructure as a public good—one that benefits society today while preparing for the challenges of tomorrow. Only by rethinking how we design, build, and maintain our infrastructure can we ensure a more sustainable, equitable, and prosperous future for all. ■

ARCH 5990 | **FINAL THESIS** | UG | **SP24**

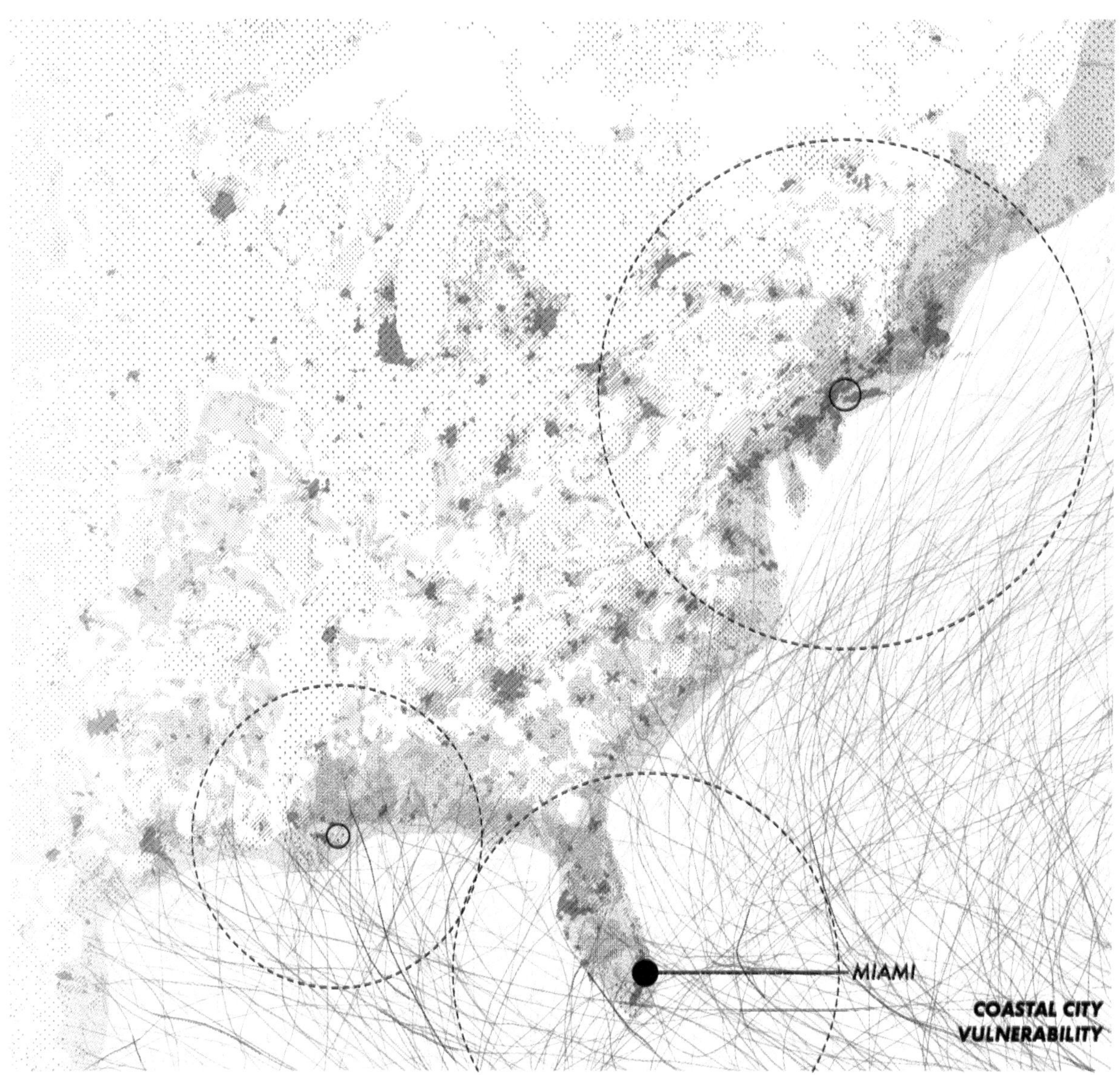

Max Kronengold + Jeremy Goldberg

EDGE OF TOMORROW:

A Replicable Model for Floor Protection

ARCH 5990 Instructors:
Cordula Roser Gray + Todd Erlandson

s> Max Kronengold + Jeremy Goldberg

i> Cordula Roser Gray, Todd Erlandson

Since the start of the 20th century, sea levels have risen about 9 inches. Additionally, increasing global temperatures have caused 28 trillion tons of ice to melt just between 1994 and 2017. A seemingly ever growing amount of water on our planet is putting human settlement at great risk. Coastal cities such as New York, Tokyo, Mumbai, Miami, and countless more are the most vulnerable. In fact, it is estimated that around 650,000 parcels of land across 4.4 million acres of land are projected to fall below tidal boundaries by 2050.

Sea level rise and the increasing frequency of natural disasters will drastically impact urban coastlines, and redefine how millions of people interact with the threshold between water and land. Current flood mitigation infrastructure predominantly relies on impenetrable, uninhabitable forms. These projects often lack the essential components for adaptive solutions. This thesis explores an alternative approach to flood management by advocating for the development of a modular, deployable architectural system that prioritizes permeability and inhabitability.

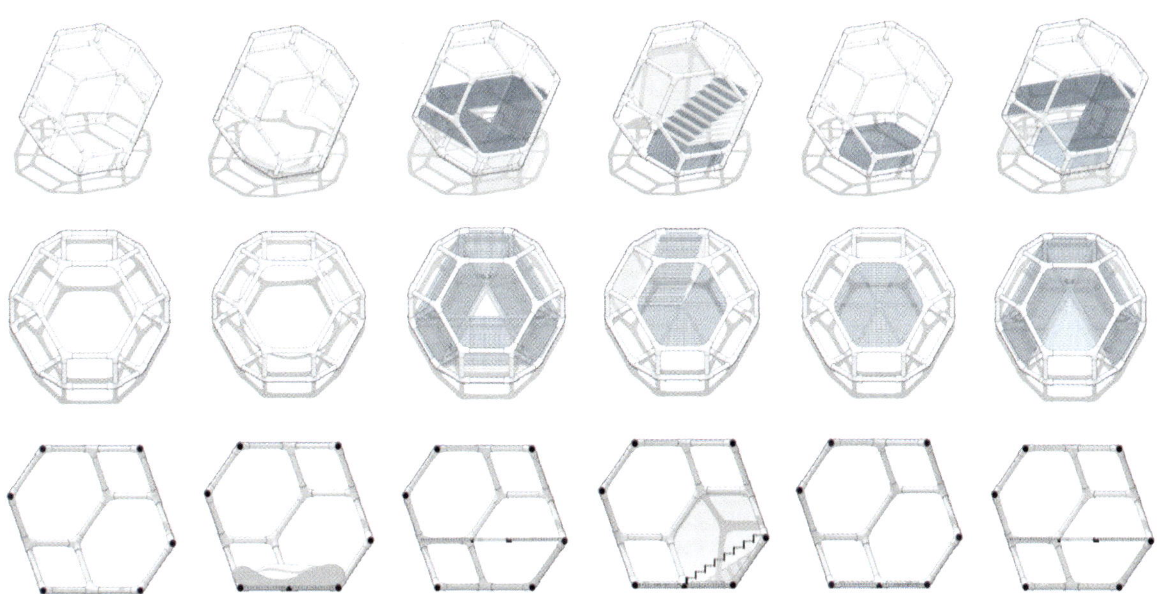

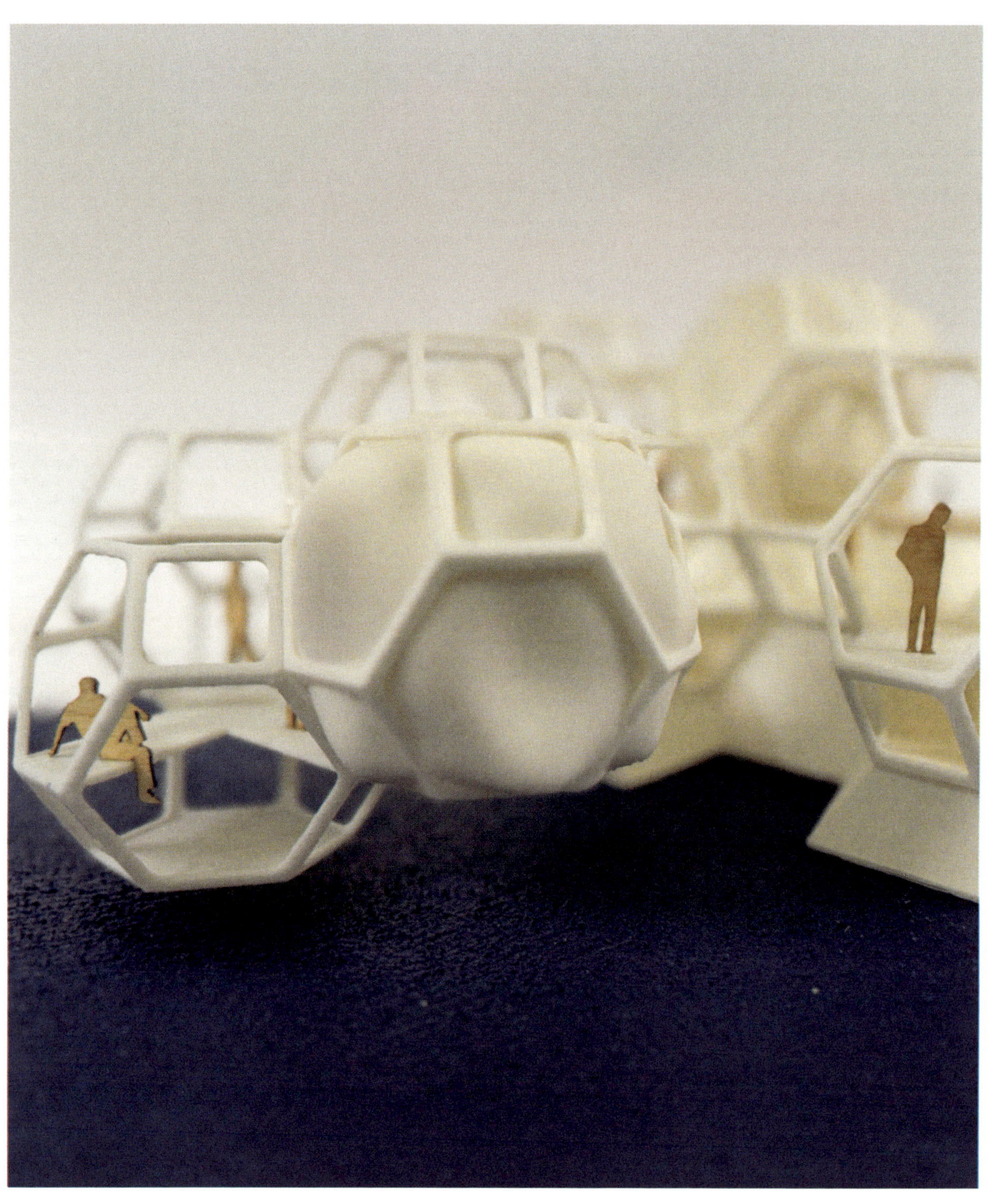

s> Max Kronengold + Jeremy Goldberg

i> Cordula Roser Gray + Todd Erlandson

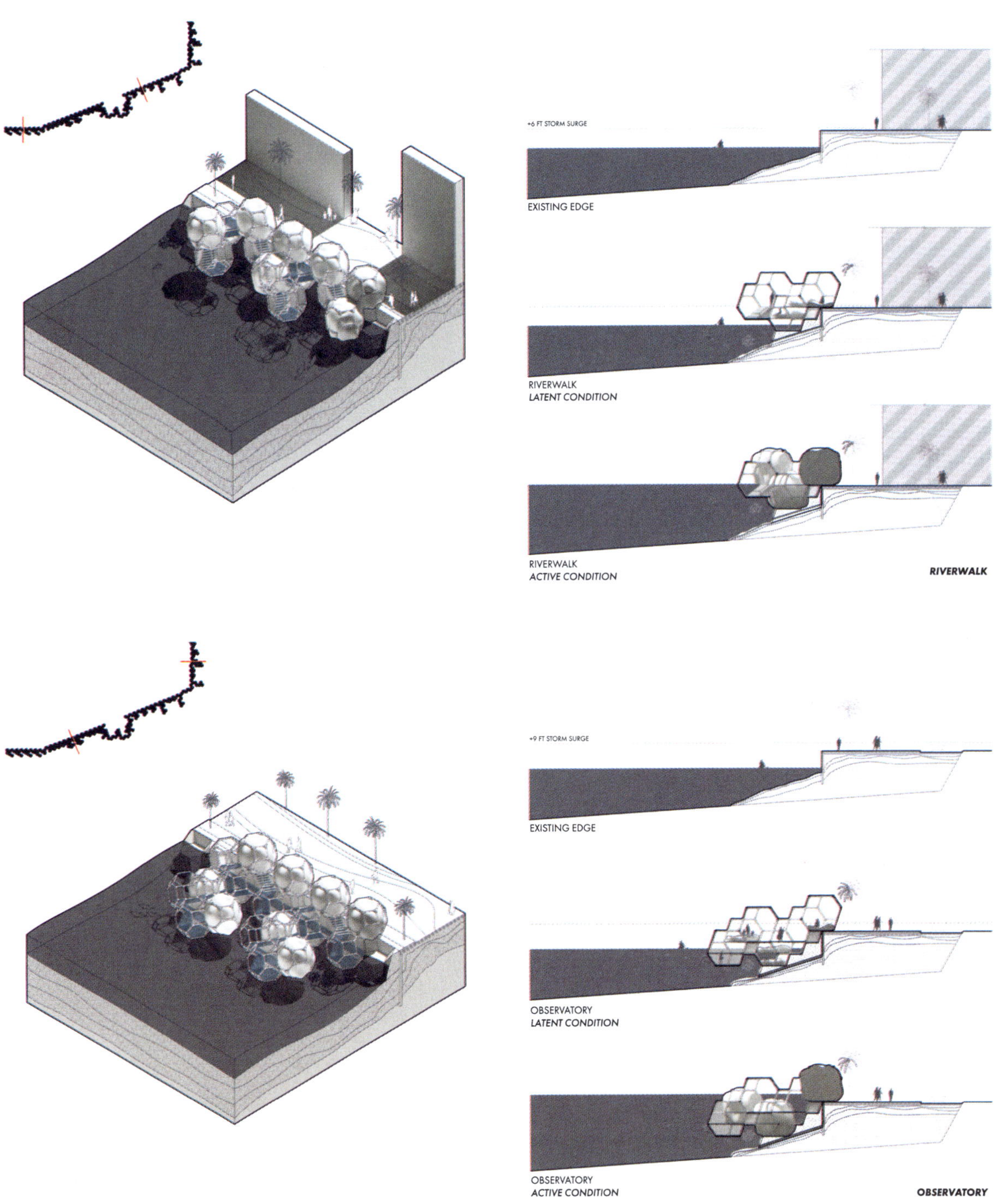

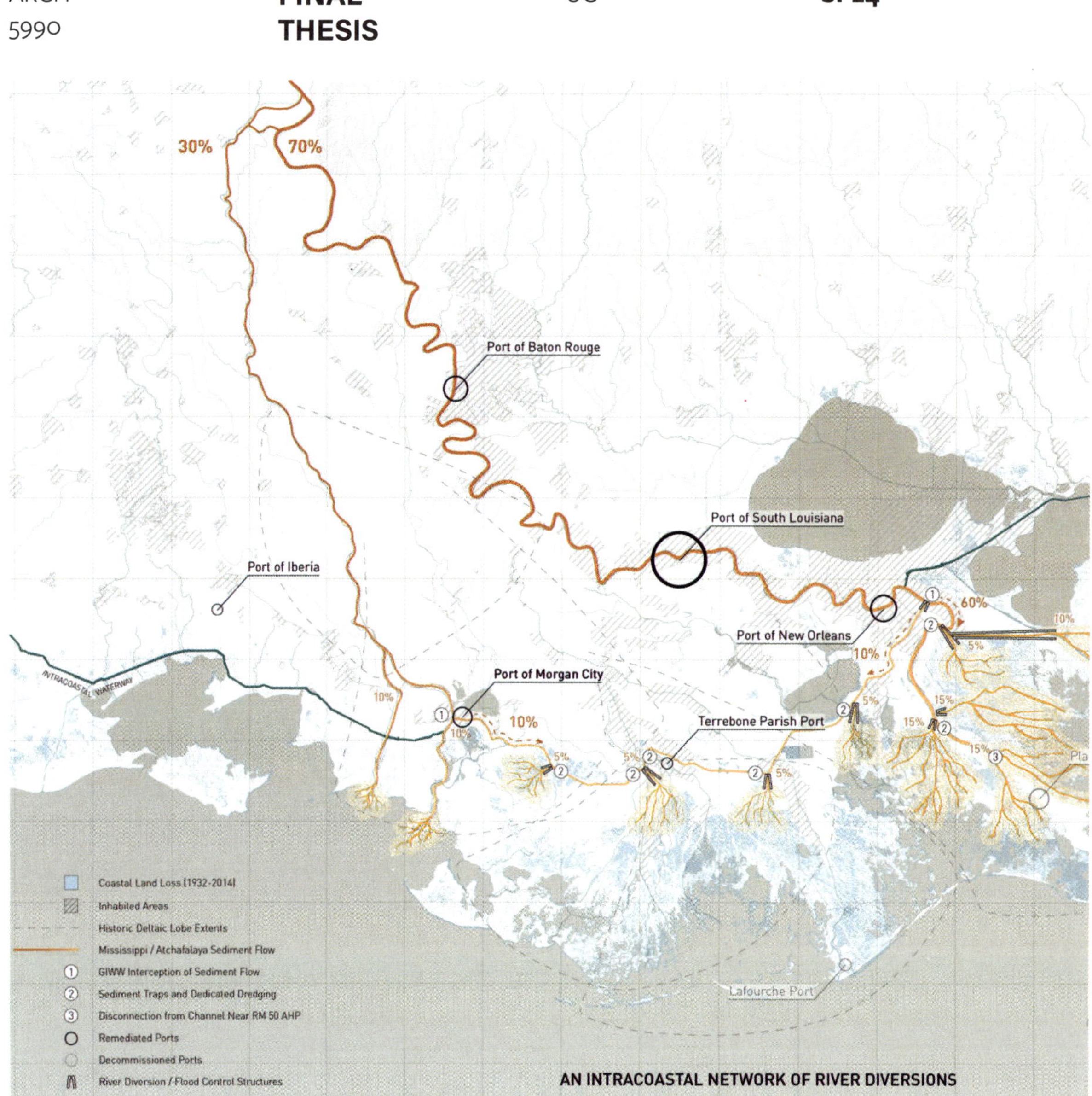

Jose Varela + Frank Taylor

ALLUVIAL CITY:

Port Towns as Catalysts
for Regenerative Industrial Landscapes

ARCH 5990 Instructors:
Cordula Roser Gray + Todd Erlandson

s> Jose Varela + Frank Taylor

i> Cordula Roser Gray + Todd Erlandson

Using Morgan City, LA as a Case Study, this thesis proposes a methodology of urban design that moves past stylistic and compositional strategies but derives built form from the active ecological and cultural systems of the site. Through this process of carving and shaping the land, it aims to transition Morgan City into a town of flattened hierarchies, allowing for symbiotic relationships between community, industry, and ecology to evolve.

In 1964 Fumihiko Maki argued for an architectural theory of collective group form. His reasoning was based on architectural strategies that respond to society's dynamic change rather than static, predictive urban design strategies that generate fragmented urban conditions. Through this theory, Maki critiqued compositional form found in projects such as Bernard Tschumi's Park de La Villette that relied on the overlay of points, lines, and grids to delineate a new layer of public programs. Maki claimed that compositional form valued graphical composition rather than a societal response. Similarly, mega-form strategies found in the masterplans of modernism, while provocative, relied on an often significant one-time investment where an unknown future can change the value of the project to its context.

Despite its critiques of Tschumi, Maki's conceptual framework fails to move past a graphical argument when implemented. Tschumi and Maki's methodologies create a generic urbanism that lacks an adaptive capacity to their cultural context. Therefore, this thesis recenters Maki's theory and adds a technical dimension grounded on site ecology and culture, producing a responsive architecture molded off human and non- human systems. This approach is applied to Morgan City, LA, where urban hierarchies have created a built environment maximized for industrial efficiency and Capitolgenic logic despite the region's proud connection to its surrounding ecology. Using time-based strategies that move beyond a graphical approach, architecture becomes a cultural and ecological catalyst. This process ultimately aims to transition Morgan City's past extractivist cultural underpinnings into a site of flattened hierarchies, allowing for symbiotic relationships between community, industry, and ecology to evolve.

In order to move past the hard boundaries that define Morgan City's industrial maximization, urban conditions are sequentially generated, first by carving the river edge through the dredging of sediment and then by the natural dynamics of the river. The re-scaping results in a blurred gradient of wetlands, elevated industrial zones, and recreational structures. Buildings are built over time based on cultural needs, creating idiosyncratic objects that share a context but respond to varying needs delineated by the time they are built.

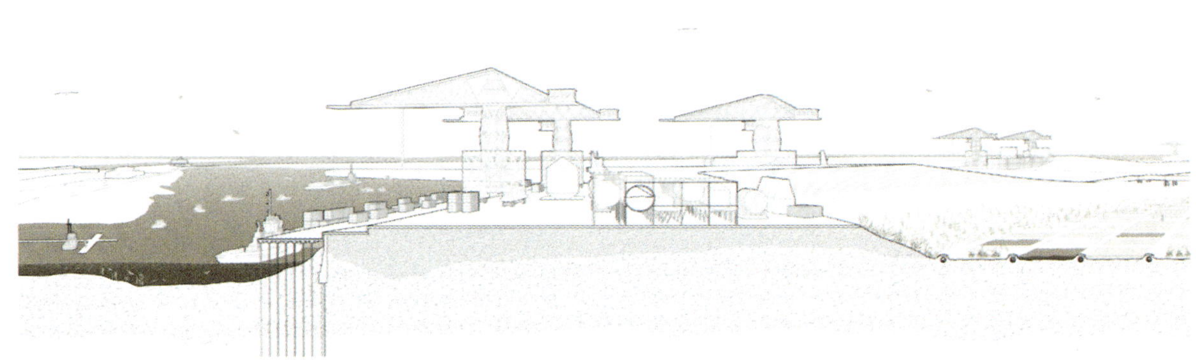

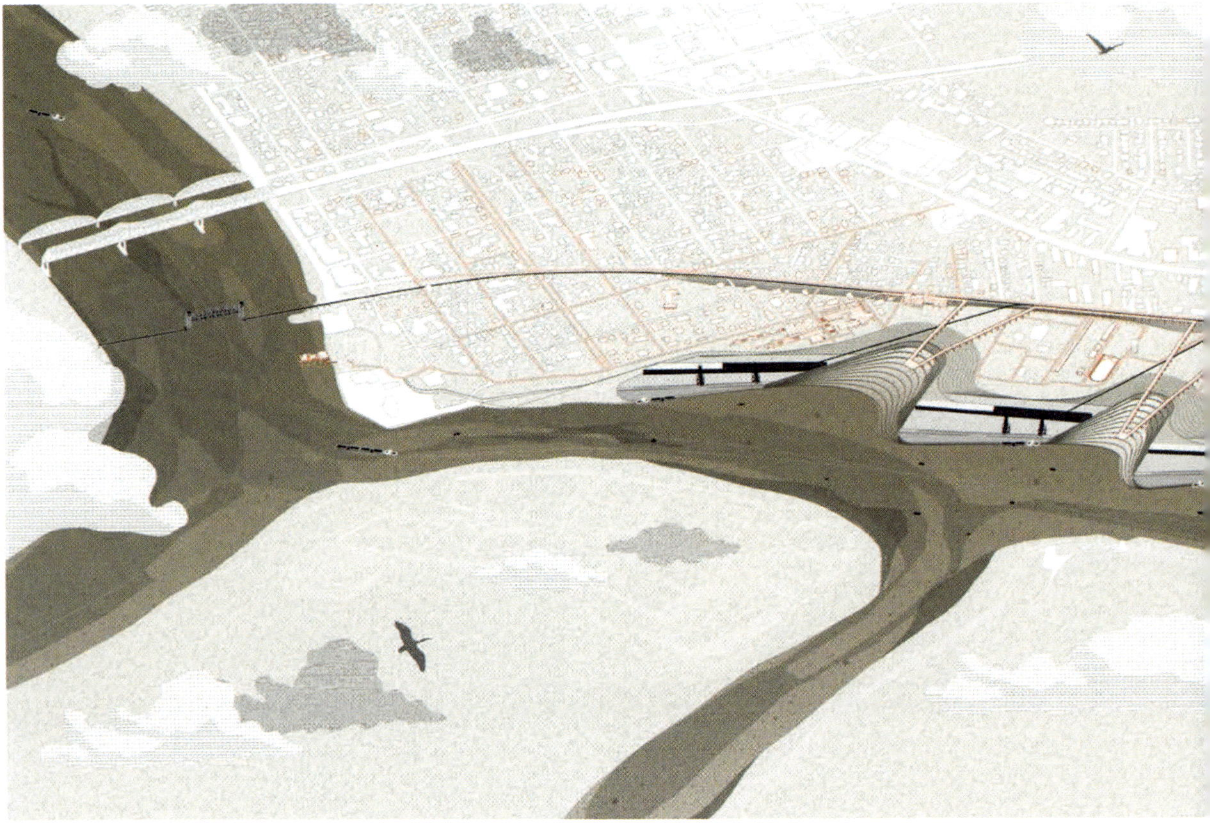

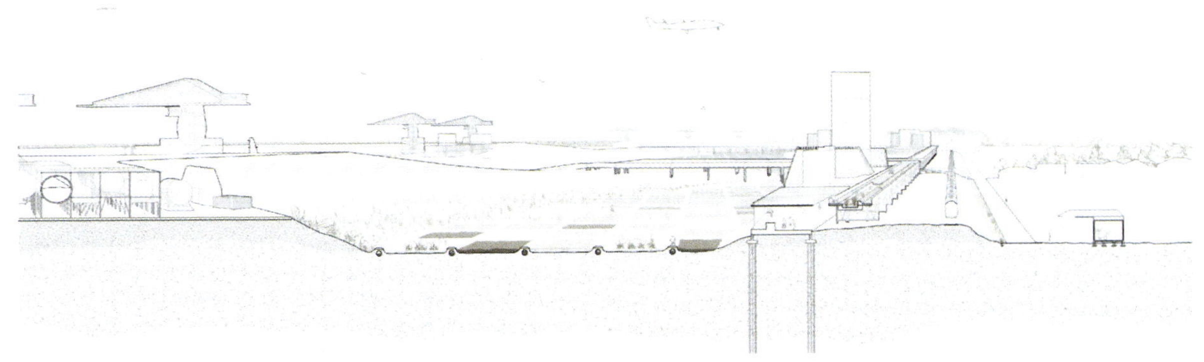

DIRECTED RESEARCH

Casius Pealer [C]

In this course students will conduct an original investigation in order to acquire new knowledge within a framework set by a client in practice. The primary goal of this research class is to deepen students' personal understanding of a particular topic or issue in real estate development. A key secondary goal is to build students' skills and confidence to make succinct public presentations of complex material. Students will be assessed both on your final work product (written and oral) as well as students' professional client communication along the way.

IS COMMUNITY SOLAR A PATH TO NEIGHBOR-HOOD RESILIENCY?

An Analysis of Community Solar Development in the United States and its Impact on Community and Disaster Resilience

Marissa Brown

Resilience, defined as the ability to withstand and recover from shocks, is crucial in the context of climate change. The increasing frequency and severity of natural disasters, driven by rising global temperatures, necessitates robust resilience strategies for communities. Climate change exacerbates various environmental and socio-economic issues, disproportionately affecting underserved communities that contribute minimally to greenhouse gas emissions. The primary concern is to mitigate these impacts through sustainable and community-centric solutions.

Community solar, as defined by the U.S. Department of Energy, involves solar projects where the generated benefits are shared among multiple customers, including individuals, businesses, and non-profits. These projects typically range up to five megawatts and can be installed in rural, suburban, or urban areas, often on unused land. Community solar addresses the accessibility barriers of traditional rooftop solar, providing renewable energy to those who cannot install personal solar panels due to financial or logistical constraints.

Community solar projects can be financed through ownership-based or subscription models. In the ownership model, customers purchase rights to a portion of the solar panels, receiving credits for the generated energy. The subscription model involves leasing panels or purchasing power at a fixed rate lower than utility prices, often without upfront costs but with ongoing maintenance fees. Successful community solar projects often involve anchor tenants like local schools or businesses, which enhance the project's financial stability and community benefits.

Community solar projects enhance resilience by reducing living costs, fostering community engagement, creating jobs, and providing educational opportunities. In regions like the Gulf Coast, where energy burdens are high due to poor housing quality, community solar can make living more affordable by lowering utility costs. This financial relief allows communities to invest in energy efficiency and housing improvements, further enhancing resilience.

Community engagement is vital for the success of shared solar projects, involving collaboration among residents, organizations, and local governments. This engagement fosters a sense of ownership and pride in shared developments. Additionally, community solar projects can repurpose brownfield sites, transforming contaminated or underused land into productive solar farms, thereby revitalizing neighborhoods and contributing to environmental cleanup.

The DOE Solar in Your Community Prize Challenge showcases various successful community solar projects across the United States. These projects target low-to-moderate income (LMI) households and underserved markets, demonstrating the potential of community solar to enhance resilience. For instance, projects in Kerrville, Texas, and Burlington, Vermont, have effectively integrated LMI participants and created substantial community benefits.

In Baltimore, Maryland, the Power52 Foundation developed a 2.5 MW community solar project specifically for LMI individuals, while in Brooklyn, New York, the Gowanus Grid & Electric project focused on LMI residents in multi-family housing. These projects not only provide renewable energy but also foster job creation and community development.

Community solar represents a promising path to enhancing neighborhood resiliency by addressing both energy and socio-economic challenges. Through innovative financing models and strong community engagement, these projects can provide affordable, clean energy to underserved populations, reduce environmental impacts, and foster community pride and involvement. As climate change continues to pose significant threats, the expansion of community solar can play a crucial role in building more resilient and sustainable communities.

"Linspiration" Font Design, by Professor Meghan Saas

14

REPRESENTATION & NARRATIVES

AS COMMON GOOD

THE ARCHITECTURE OF DATA

Digital Representation as a Tool for The Common Good

By Austin Lightle
Visiting Assistant Professor
Tulane School of Architecture and Built Environment

> "As architects, we've long considered the ecological impact of our built work—but have we stopped to examine the digital landscapes we're creating in its wake?

Render by Professor Austin Lightle

Architecture and ecology have long been discussed, from the primitive hut to HVAC systems and megastructures. In recent years, however, the ecological issue has expanded on two fronts. While the impact of architecture on the built environment is empirical and rightly the main topic of discussion, the digital impact is often overlooked, almost a blip on the radar of architectural history. Since the integration of Building Information Modelling, architecture and adjacent industries have taken a sharp digital turn. In many cases, the use of paper has been eliminated. At first glance, the elimination of paper appears to be a good thing, but it is a sign of a new era of digital representation. With this new era comes a new shadow to contend with: data.

While digital representation brings with it the caveat of data, it also brings with it a new potential for awareness that holds a mirror up to society. You could say it is a war on two fronts: a battle against man-made climate change, but also a war with its own dark data.

In recent years, a new term has emerged: digital sustainability. As an industry, we have become more aware of the environmental impact of our buildings, but have we realised the impact of our data? Every project we work on is often made up of multiple programs, ranging from Revit, Rhino and Autocad to Adobe. Each file we create stores data on our computer, and each of these files stores backup data that is separate from the file. We often back up or copy files on a regular basis to prevent loss of work. It is a rather mindless and seamless process. Working as a designer for Pelli Clarke Pelli Architects, we backed up our files daily. I'd often work on competitions and create countless iterations that would never be built. All these projects live on as pure data, with most projects running into several terabytes. Where does the data go and what do we do with it? Our data no longer lives on our computers, but on servers or "the cloud" (iCloud, Drive, Box, etc.). But does it really exist in a cloud? Unfortunately it does not, it exists in one of 10,978 data centers worldwide (as of December 2023).

The number of data centers is growing exponentially; in fact, it is one of the most commonly built architectural typologies in the world. It is an architecture built not for people, but for our information trail. It is often an architecture built without an architect. Perhaps calling it an architecture is a stretch; the average size of each of the 10,978 data centers is 1.07 million square feet. The largest is over 10.7 million square feet. The monumental size of these projects is just the beginning; they require a significant amount of energy to keep the data racks cool.[1] Data center construction is growing at an average of 6.5% per year and is expected to reach $131.8 billion per year by 2030. We have seen firms like Superuse Studios in Rotterdam begin to upcycle physical architecture, but how do we become sustainable with our data? Is there a new exploration of digital up-cycling that needs to take place?

While we need to be aware of the data we create in our digital representations, we cannot downplay the tremendous benefit it brings. As architects, we have developed unique ways of thinking and conceptualizing. Our way of thinking creates new opportunities to communicate through a variety of digital media. In terms of ecology, perhaps the best examples are the current works of Liam Young and Jennifer Chen. Trained as architects, they are now devoting their careers to raising awareness of climate activism through architectural representation. Much like Super Studio, Archigram, and Constance did in their day, critical digital projects allow architects to reflect on society. For example, Liam Young's "Planet City" is a critical project that imagines a future Earth devastated by climate change. Humans must live in a singular city to allow the rest of the earth to heal. He uses architecture and animation to tell this story. He creates a new architecture that responds to unimaginable population density as a means of staging emotions that mere data from scientists could not. Similarly, in her exhibition "No Evil," Jen Chen imagines a future world saved by geoengineering. Like Liam, she does this by creating new architectures and machines to tell the story of life after geo-engineering. It serves as a critical response to our current way of life, and even architectures' current attitudes towards climate change.

Digital representation, paired with the unique thinking of architects, allows for new ways to communicate with those who might not otherwise be reached. It allows us to create work that speaks for itself and engages on a personal level. It offers the opportunity to speculate on a future that could be the result of a present neglect.■

[1] The amount of energy consumed in data centers grew from 4.9 gigawatts to 7.4 gigawatts between 2022 and 2023, roughly enough to power 6,482,400 homes in the U.S. Google's newest data center in Iowa, soon to be the largest data center campus in the world, is on pace to surpass $5 billion in construction costs.

Emerging technologies of design and production have transformed the role of drawings within the contemporary design process from that of design generators to design products. As architectural design has shifted from an analog drawing-based paradigm to that of a computational model-based paradigm, the agency of the drawing as a critical and important form of design representation has shifted. *Drawing Codes: Experimental Protocols of Architectural Representation* examines the effects of this transformation on the architectural discipline and explores how architects have critically integrated procedural thinking into their drawing process.

The book contains 96 commissioned drawings by a diverse range of architects that investigate how rules and constraints inform the ways architects document, analyze, represent, and design the built environment. Each drawing responds to a shared conceptual prompt developed by the authors and conforms to a standard size and format. The intent is for this consistency to elicit a wide range of approaches to questions of technology, design, code, and representation. The book documents how computational processes such as procedural drawing, digital simulation, automated production, and machine learning can contribute to a new understanding of what drawings are and how they are created.

DRAWING CODES: Experimental Protocols of Architectural Representation

BOOK
Applied Research + Design, 2024

Credits
Andrew Kudless and Adam Marcus

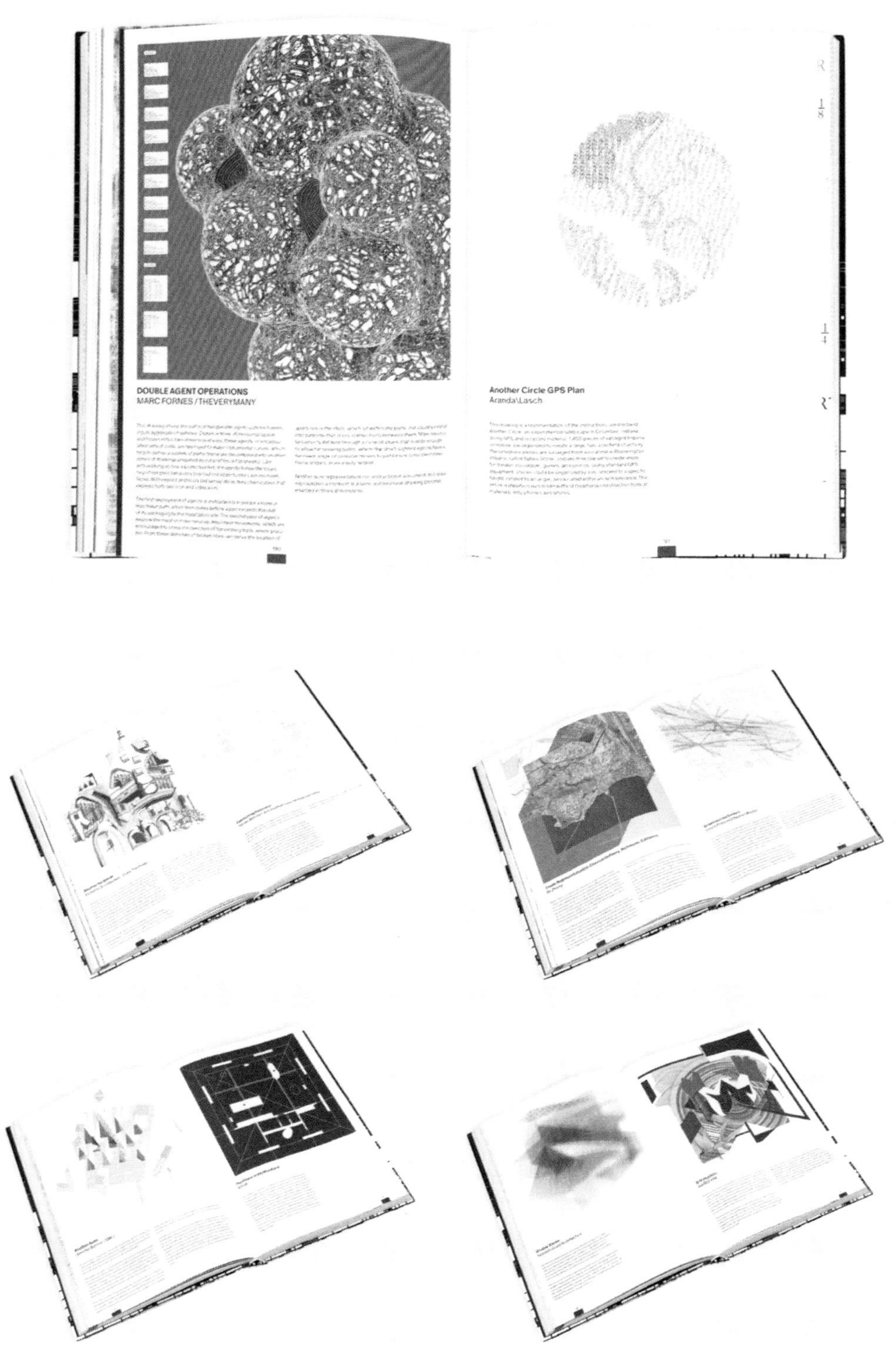
DOUBLE AGENT OPERATIONS
MARC FORNES / THEVERYMANY
Another Circle GPS Plan
Aranda\Lasch

Lauren Beach

ARCHITECTURAL SPECULATION AND THE POETICS OF REPRESENTATION

A Case Study on Bryan Cantley

The thesis "Architectural Speculation and The Poetics of Representation: A Case Study on Bryan Cantley" delves into the unique and complex world of Bryan Cantley's architectural drawings. Cantley's work, rooted in both historical traditions and contemporary innovations, represents a significant contribution to the field of architecture, particularly in the realm of speculative and representational drawing.

Historically, architectural drawings were primarily utilitarian, meant to convey exact forms and dimensions of buildings to be constructed. From the Renaissance to the 19th century, these drawings were precise and devoid of embellishment. However, various artistic movements and socio-political changes in the 20th century, including Expressionism, De Stijl, and Constructivism, among others, began to transform architectural drawings into more dynamic and interpretative artworks.

This shift in drawing practices coincided with a broader change in architectural discourse, moving away from strict representation towards a more speculative and interpretive approach. The advent of digital technology in the 1980s and 1990s further revolutionized the field, allowing architects to explore new forms and representations that were previously unimaginable.

Bryan Cantley, born in 1965, emerged as an influential figure during this pivotal period of transformation in architectural drawing. His education at the University of North Carolina at Charlotte and the University of California, Los Angeles, laid the foundation for his experimental approach to architecture. In 1992, he founded Form:uLA Dimension Laboratory, a platform to explore the boundaries of architecture and representation.

Cantley's work is heavily influenced by both historical and contemporary figures in architecture, including Peter Cook, Perry Kulper, and Thom Mayne. However, unlike many of his contemporaries, Cantley provides acces-

ARCH 6990 Instructor:
Ammar Eloueini [D]

sible pathways for non-architects to engage with his spatial drawings. His use of a machinic aesthetic and graphic notation style creates a unique visual language that invites subjective interpretation and exploration. Cantley's drawings are characterized by their intentional ambiguity and multi-layered complexity. They blur the lines between physical and virtual environments, challenging conventional notions of architectural representation. Central to his work is the concept of the "post-liminal fuzz," a term he uses to describe the space between the physical subject and the drawn object, enriched by notational elements. This "fuzz" creates a dynamic interplay that requires active engagement from the viewer, akin to a call-and-response in jazz music.

His drawings often incorporate elements from non-architectural sources, such as farm equipment and martial arts, further enriching the interpretative possibilities. This cross-disciplinary inspiration adds depth and layers of meaning to his work, prompting viewers to explore beyond the immediate visual impact.

Cantley's 2023 publication, "Speculative Coolness," is a significant compilation of his projects and thoughts. Edited by Peter J. Baldwin, the book includes essays that provide context and guidelines for engaging with Cantley's work. Baldwin's editorial techniques, such as bracketing and playful syntax, mirror the complexity and multi-faceted nature of Cantley's drawings, offering readers multiple entry points for interpretation.

The thesis examines Cantley's work through two lenses: Draw (noun) and Draw (verb). The former investigates the mediums, compositions, and clarity of Cantley's drawings, focusing on their static qualities. The latter speculates on the dynamic processes of directing, worldmaking, and bounding within his drawings. This dual approach highlights the intricate balance Cantley maintains between tradition and innovation, static representation, and dynamic speculation.

Bryan Cantley's work exemplifies the transformative potential of architectural drawing. By synthesizing historical traditions with contemporary innovations and personal vision, his drawings transcend conventional boundaries and invite viewers into a world of endless spatial possibilities. As architecture continues to evolve, Cantley's work stands as a testament to the enduring power of imagination and innovation in shaping the built environment.

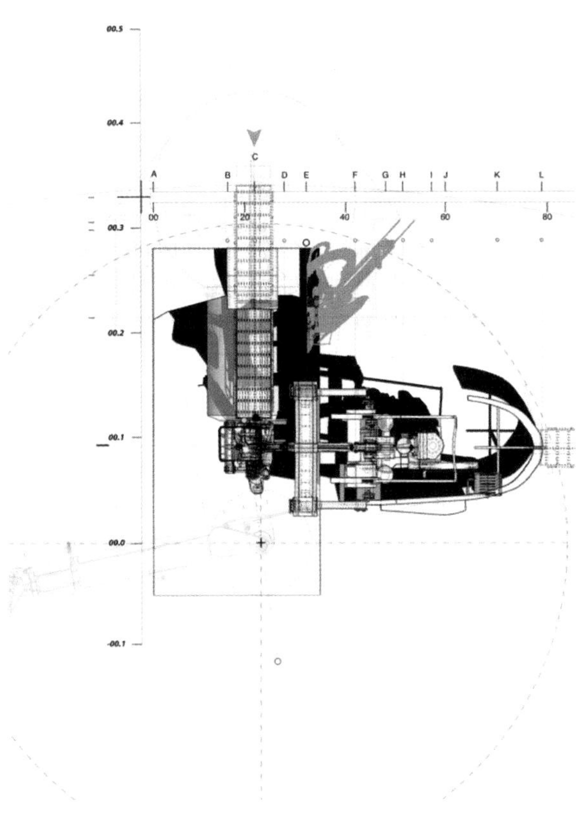

Cantley's approach to architectural drawing challenges viewers to engage deeply with the work, decoding its layers and exploring its meanings. His blend of analogue and digital media under a cohesive theoretical framework pushes the boundaries of what constitutes inhabitable space, blurring the lines between reality and imagination. His work, thus, remains a critical reference point for understanding the future directions of architectural representation and speculation.

ARCH 4042 + 6042 | **Research Studio** | UG + GR | **SP24**

CREATING VALUE THROUGH PRODUCTIZATION

BJ Siegel [C]

The "ARCH 4042 Research Design Studio" course at Tulane School of Architecture and Built Environment is structured to foster creativity and innovation in the architectural design process. It operates on a studio-based learning model, which encourages hands-on, exploratory learning. The primary focus is on integrating theoretical knowledge with practical design skills to address complex architectural challenges, particularly through a case study approach for housing.

Students are expected to engage deeply with the design process, utilizing knowledge from previous coursework while developing new skills. The course emphasizes the importance of understanding user needs, domestic life experiences, and the role of productization in architecture. Assignments include creating photorealistic and abstract self-portraits, developing detailed user personas, and visualizing domestic life moments. Additionally, students will research component manufacturing and create a comprehensive database, exploring innovative construction methods like off-site and prefabrication. The course aims to equip students with the skills and knowledge to create value-driven, user-centered architectural designs.

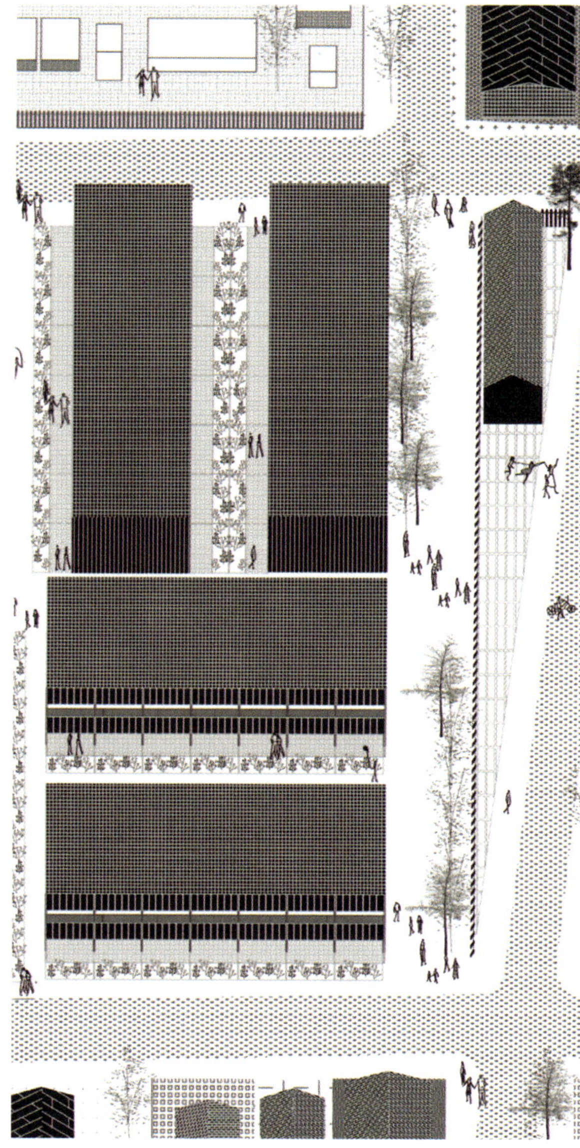

Want to see pictures of the final reviews?

s> Charlotte Love **i>** BJ Siegel

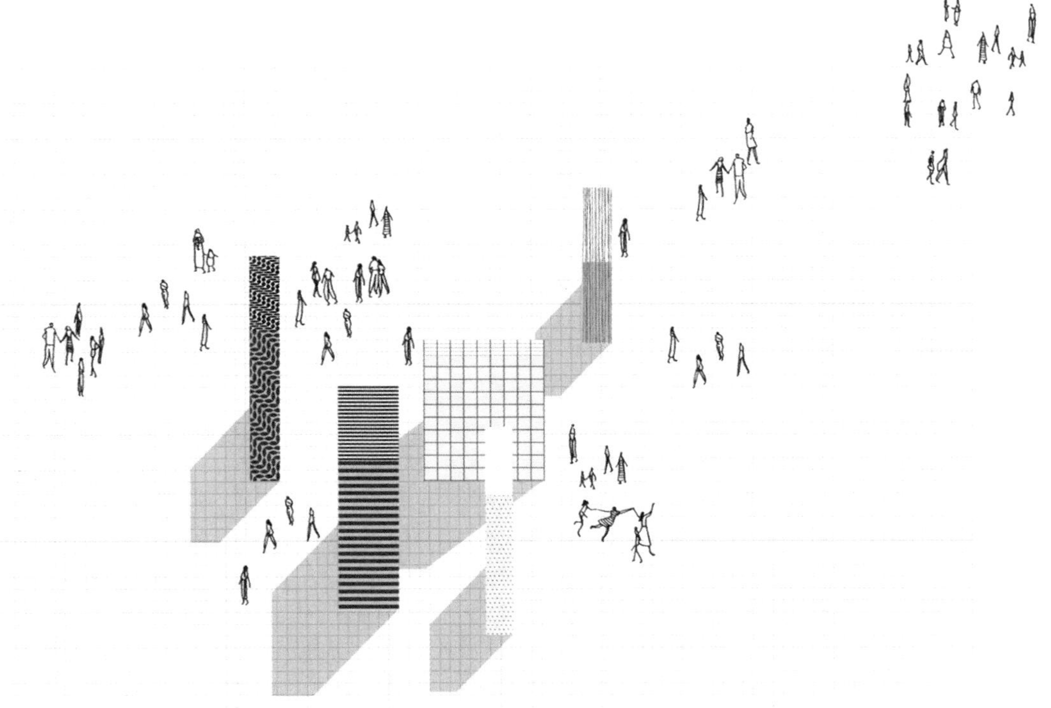

s> Charlotte Love, Ethan Meisler   i> BJ Siegel

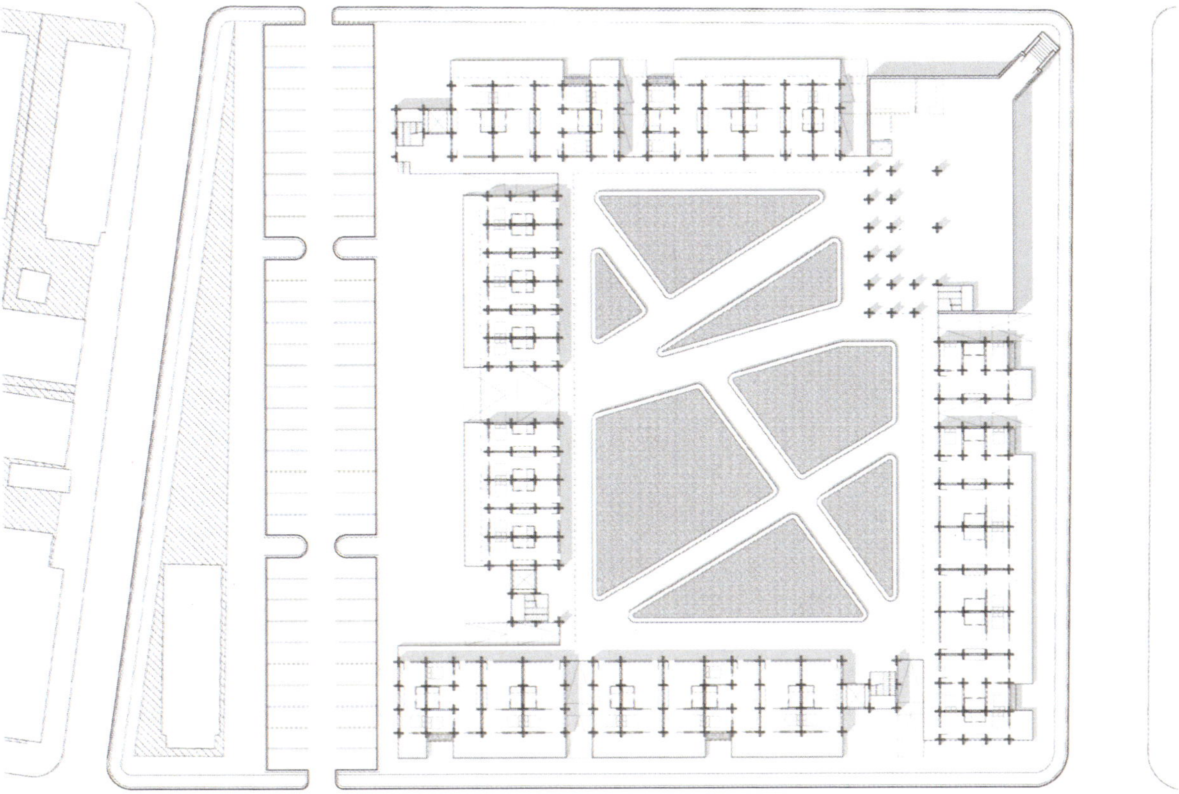

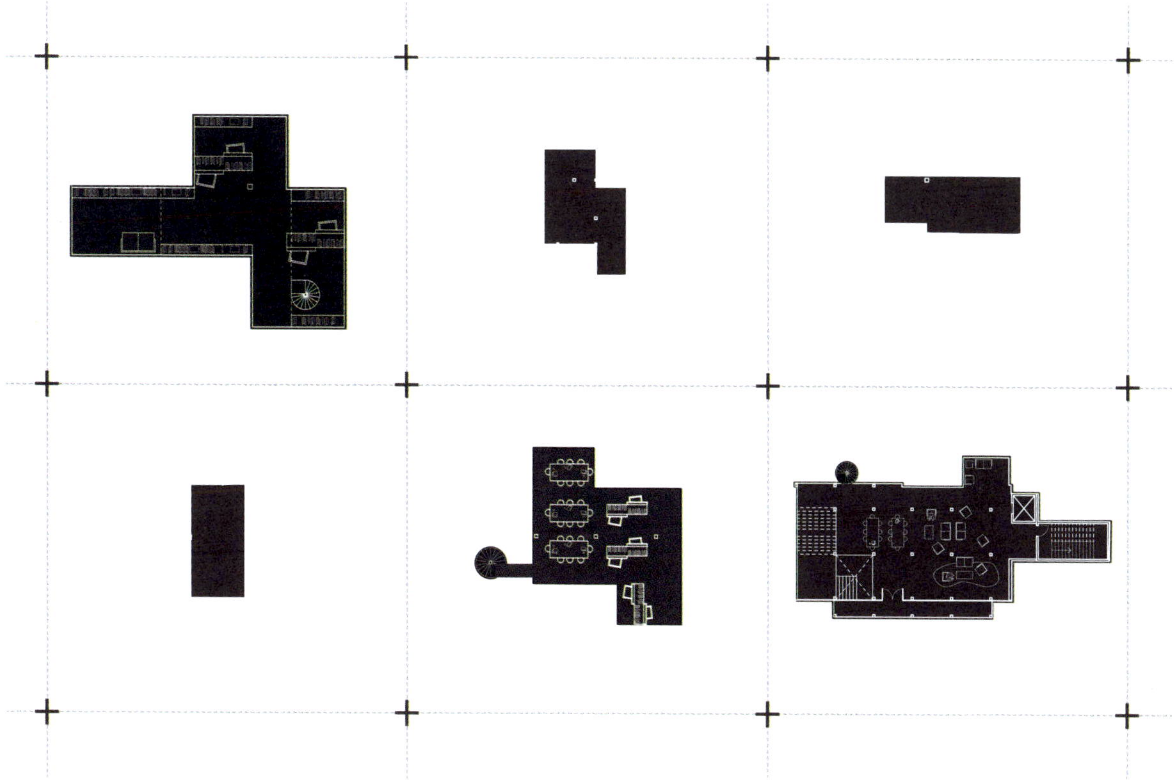

s> Livi Bowers

i> BJ Siegel

CULTURE:
From Concepts to Program

Andrea Bardón de Tena [C]
Juan Medina Revilla

This design studio is the introduction of the new master students to the architectural culture. It is an introduction at various levels so that they acquire the basic working tools to be able to approach the design of architectural proposals. To this end, during these first four intensive weeks, the methods of representation, the analysis of existing architectural projects, and the working culture of the studio are addressed.

Starting from a case study, each student goes through a process of extraction, abstraction, exploration, relocations and reprogramming, to arrive at their proposal integrated into the urban fabric of New Orleans. The use of diagrams, catalogs, 2D orthongonal representation—plans, sections, elevations, axonometric projections and perspectives help them in this process while learning the main representation strategies.

"Culture" is the first half of a two-studio sequence for the new graduate students enrolled in the summer courses. The main goal of the course is to help the new students build the foundational skills of the design and graphic process and to learn the nature of studio work. This becomes the first step of the largest goal during their 3.5-year program: to become "visual thinkers" who transform their ideas into spatial organizations.

Through analysis and transformation of a case study, the students explore the relationship between concepts, spatial schemes, and programs. This process helps them understand the importance of clarity on the architectural scheme, by working with the "front of the house" and the "back of the house" in different typologies: one public museum or gallery, and one private housing project.

From public to private. From private to public. From diverse contexts to the urban fabric of New Orleans.

The methodology encourages the class to develop their proposals using both general thinking—to work with clear ideas—and specific thinking—to contextualize them in the real context and needs.

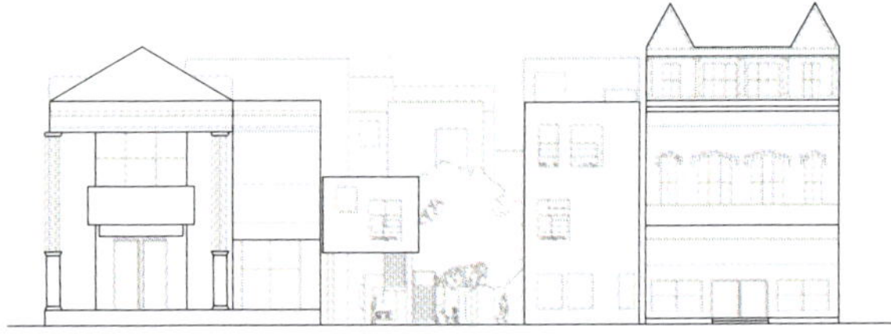

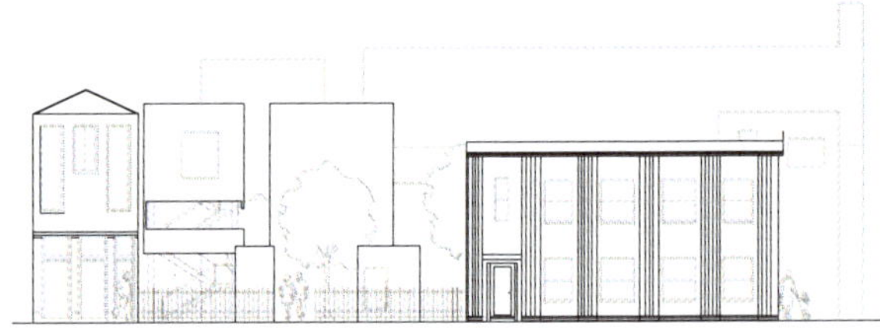

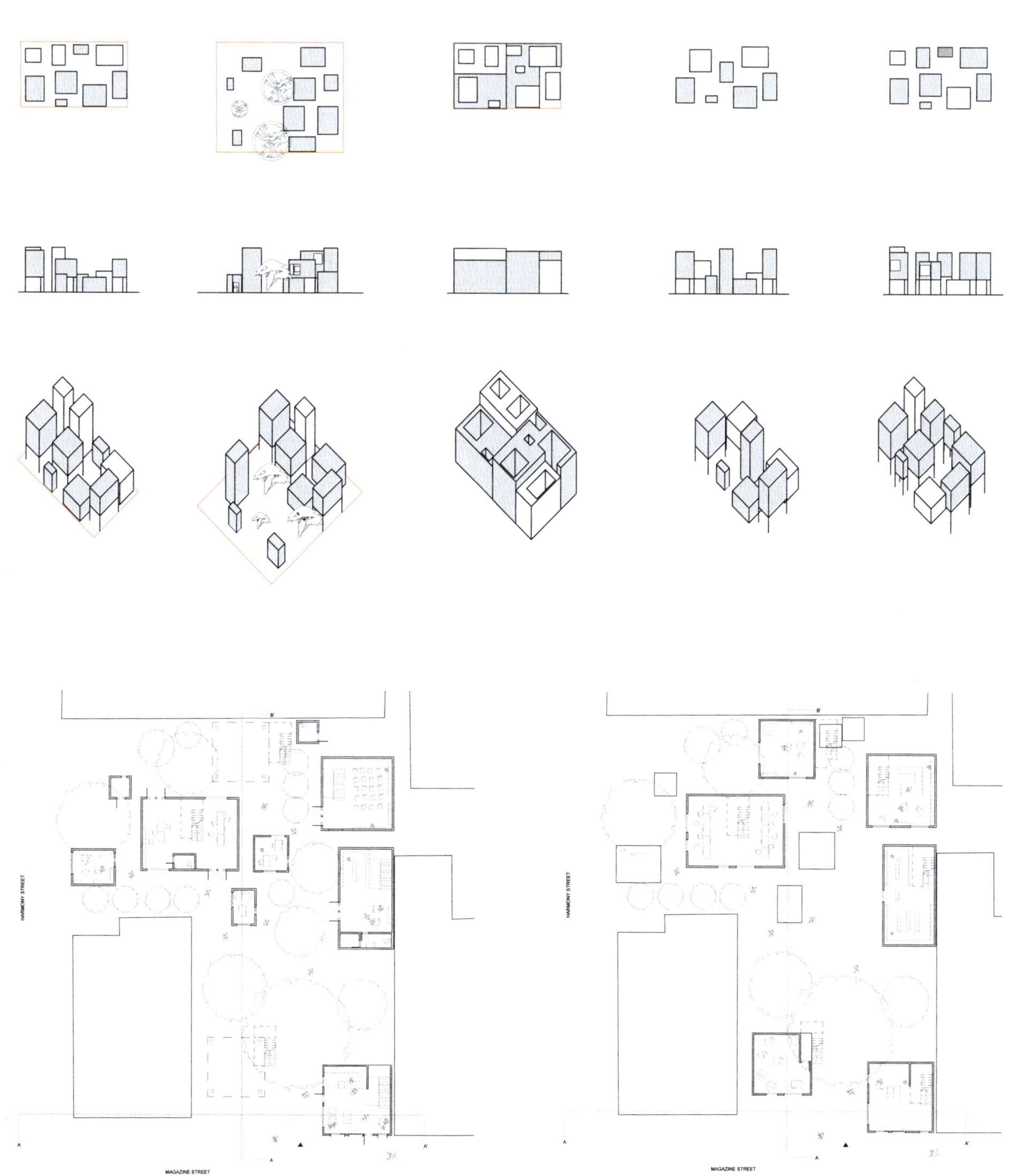
HARMONY STREET
MAGAZINE STREET
HARMONY STREET
MAGAZINE STREET

MATERIALITY:
Tech-Shelter

Andrea Bardón de Tena [C]
Juan Medina Revilla

This course takes the history of the Eames House (Case Study No. 8, Los Angeles, 1949) as a possible exercise hypothesis. Charles and Ray Eames, having the materials of their house already in place, decided to rethink their project to configure a different space with the same construction of pieces. The students, over the next four weeks, found themselves in a similar situation.

In this case, we imagine that each student "lands" in a specific territory [a national park in the United States] with a load of materials from a building [a 20th-century case study]. The starting point is twofold. On the one hand, they will study the assigned case study, specifically, its most significant materials and construction systems to understand how they work and use its material in their project proposals: a shelter in nature. This is a new challenge. The use of smaller scales (1:50, 1:40, 1:20) both in models and drawings prompt students to get closer to working with detail, with materiality.

The main goal of this course is to get familiarized with the construction systems, material properties, and scale of one of the structures. The main objective for the students is to become "visual thinkers." During this course, the students explore different representational scales: the territory scale, to analyze and understand the problems and challenges of the placement through mapping, and the small scale to explore the structural systems and construction details.

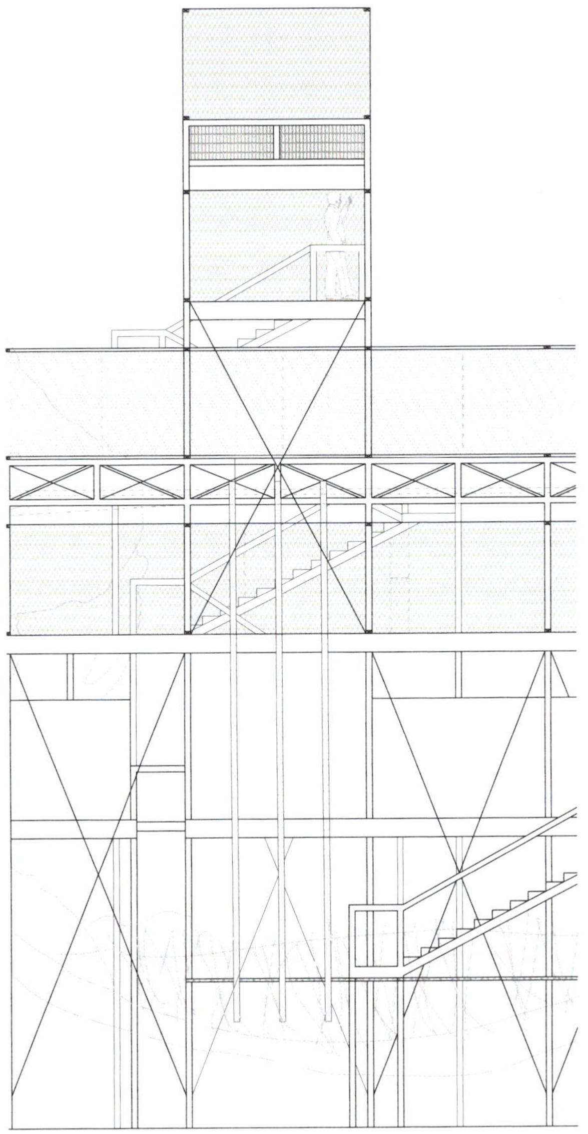

s> Brooks Barrios   i> Andrea Bardon de Tena, Juan Medina Revilla

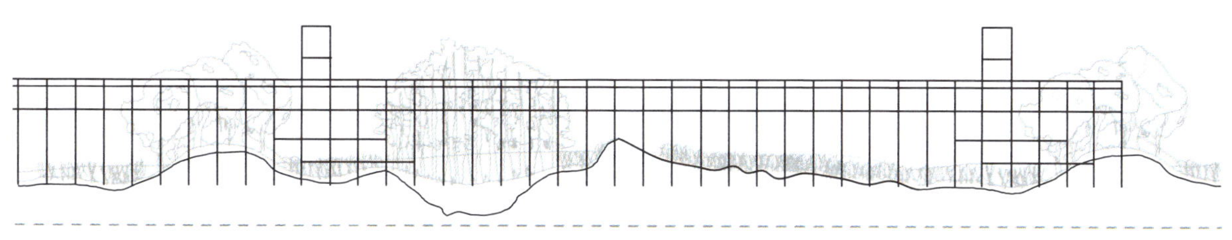

HB-ZSU

ACTS OF TRANSLATION

Zaid Kashef Alghata[C]
Austin Lightle
Ira Concepcion
Jason Blakenship
Ken Schwartz
Tucker van Luewen-Hall

This studio engaged in architectural acts of translation, advancing an understanding of how the shift from modes of representation produces new understandings. By leveraging conventions of architectural notations germane to the discipline, such as diagrams and orthographic drawings, students learned how to describe conceptual framework using the building as the medium. The project challenged the direct translation of a precedent from the diagram to the drawing, the drawing to the model, and the model to the image of the building.

The studio pursued a combination of digital and analog design and fabrication techniques, considering how these methods affect the production of buildings. Louis Sullivan's axiom, "form follows function," was applied directly, and in reverse, "function follows form," creating productive friction to challenge conventional building types. Students developed their perception of scale and order through spatial investigation of massing and interiority.

The studio asked questions such as: Does the performance only occur on stage? What is the audience-performer relationship? How does the building perform on the site? The answers to these questions will be made visible through representational arguments in the form of diagrams, drawings, models, and renderings.

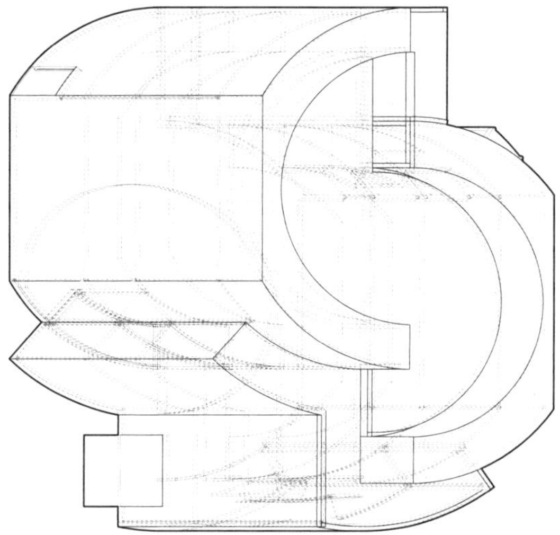

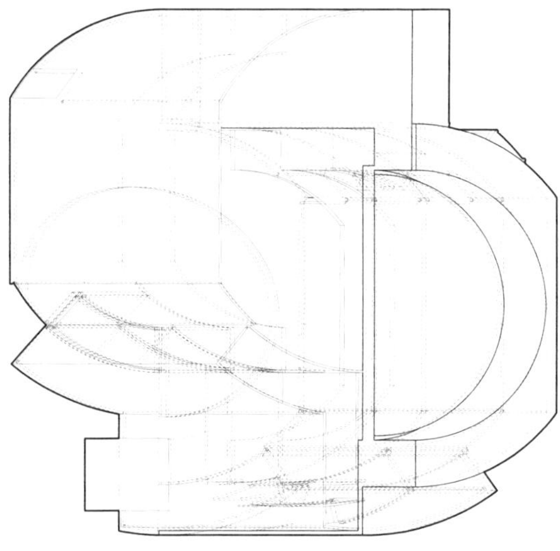

Want to see pictures of the final review?

s> Kay Tober, Dean Behrend **i>** Austin Lightle, Ira Concepcion

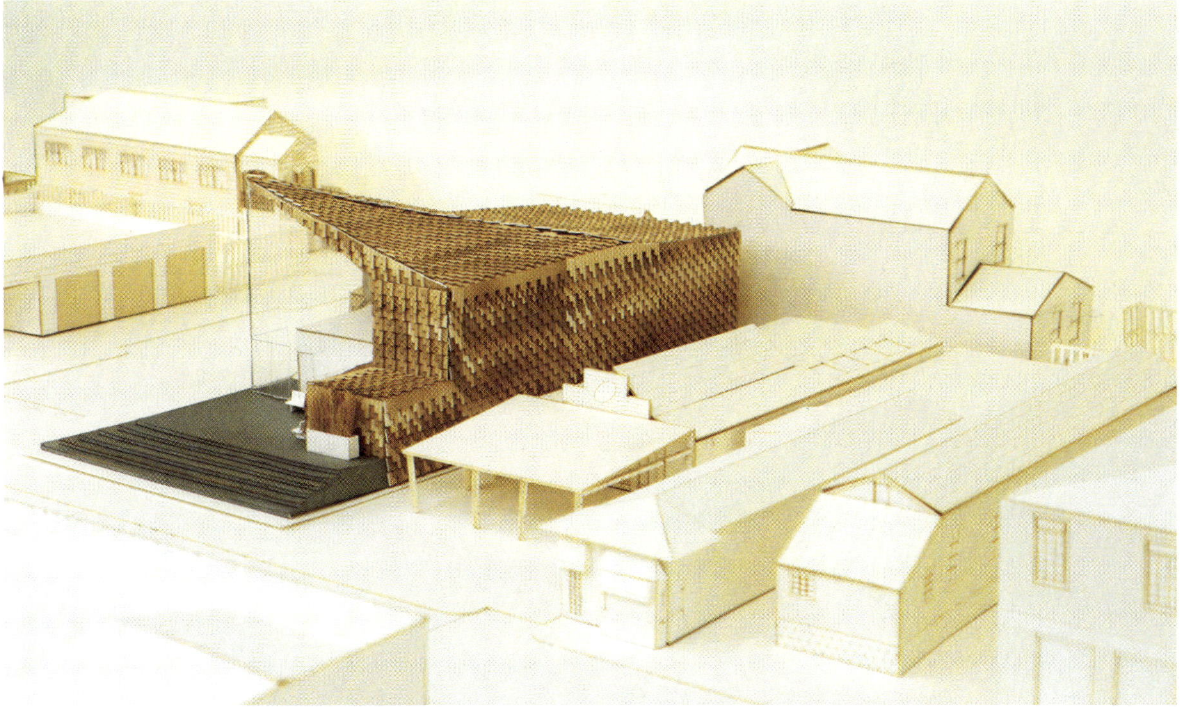

s> Mila Waske, Annika Jones, Maria Erzini **i>** Ira Concepcion, Zaid Kashef Alghata

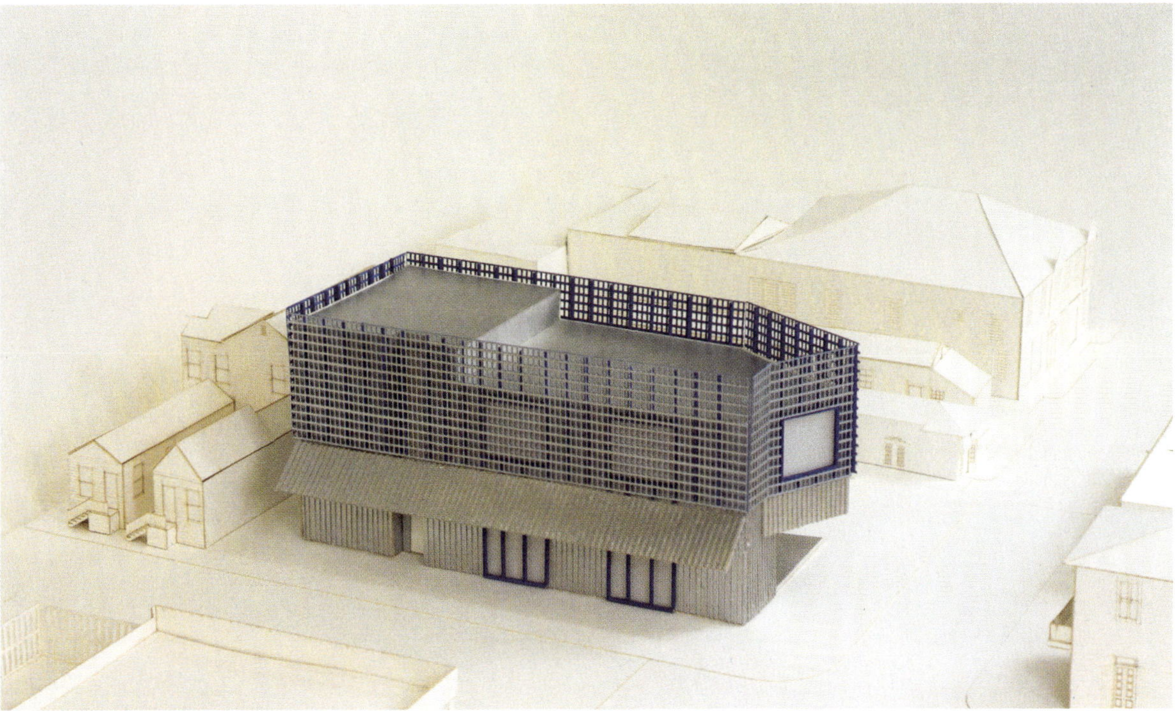

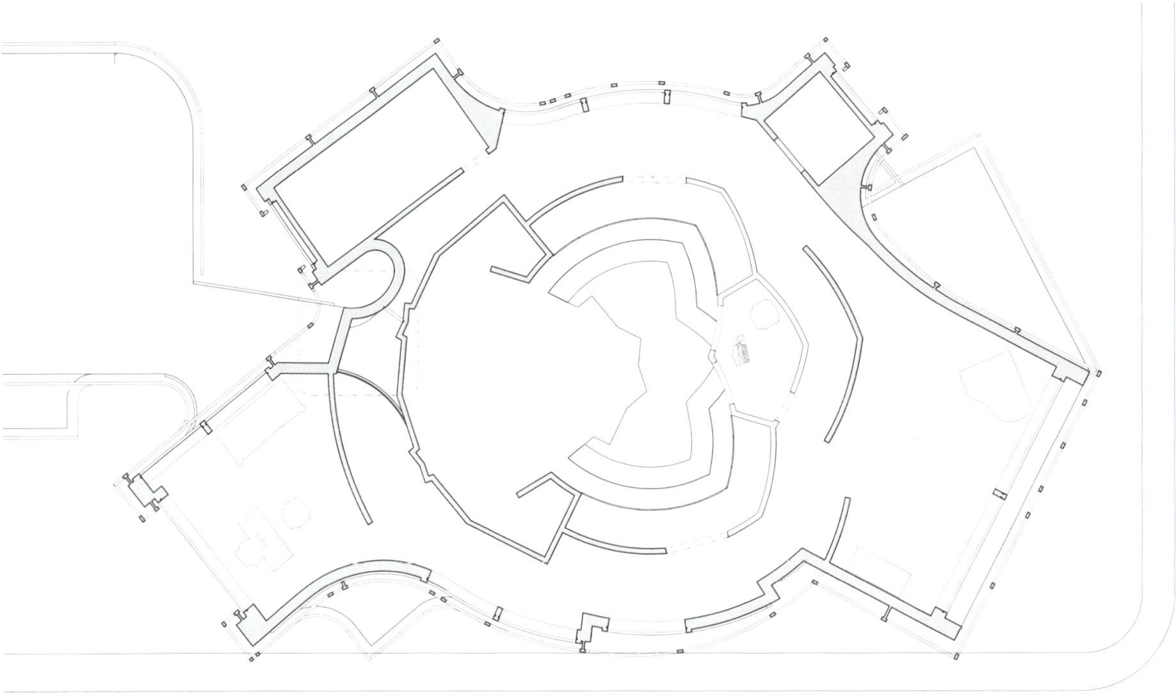

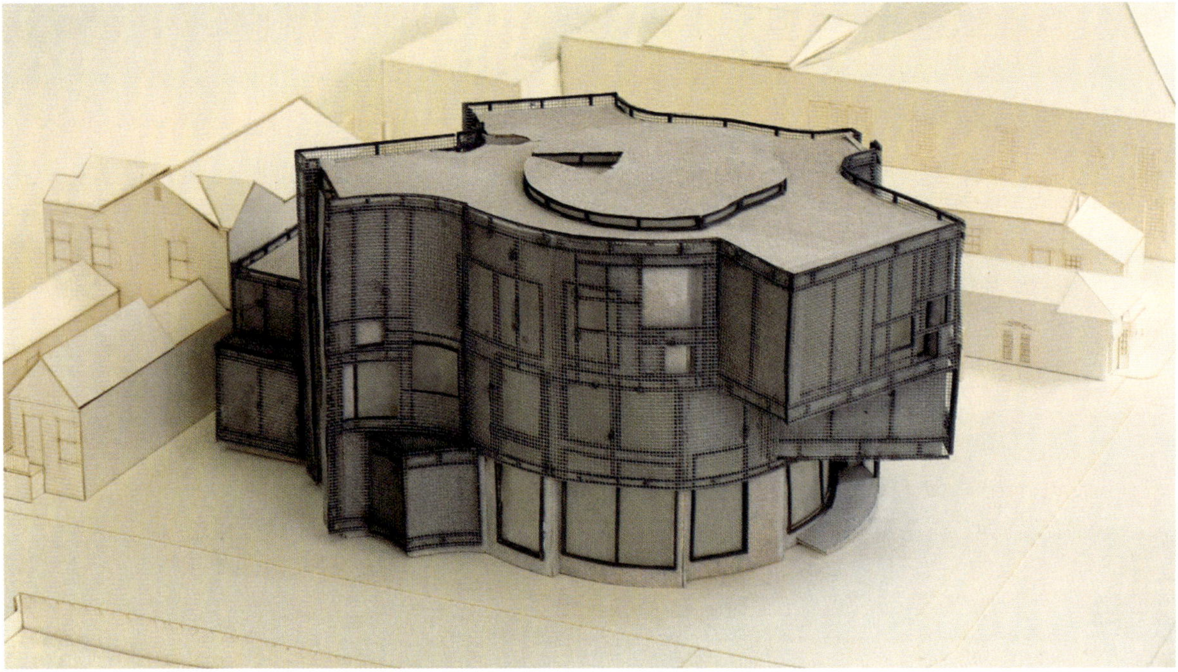

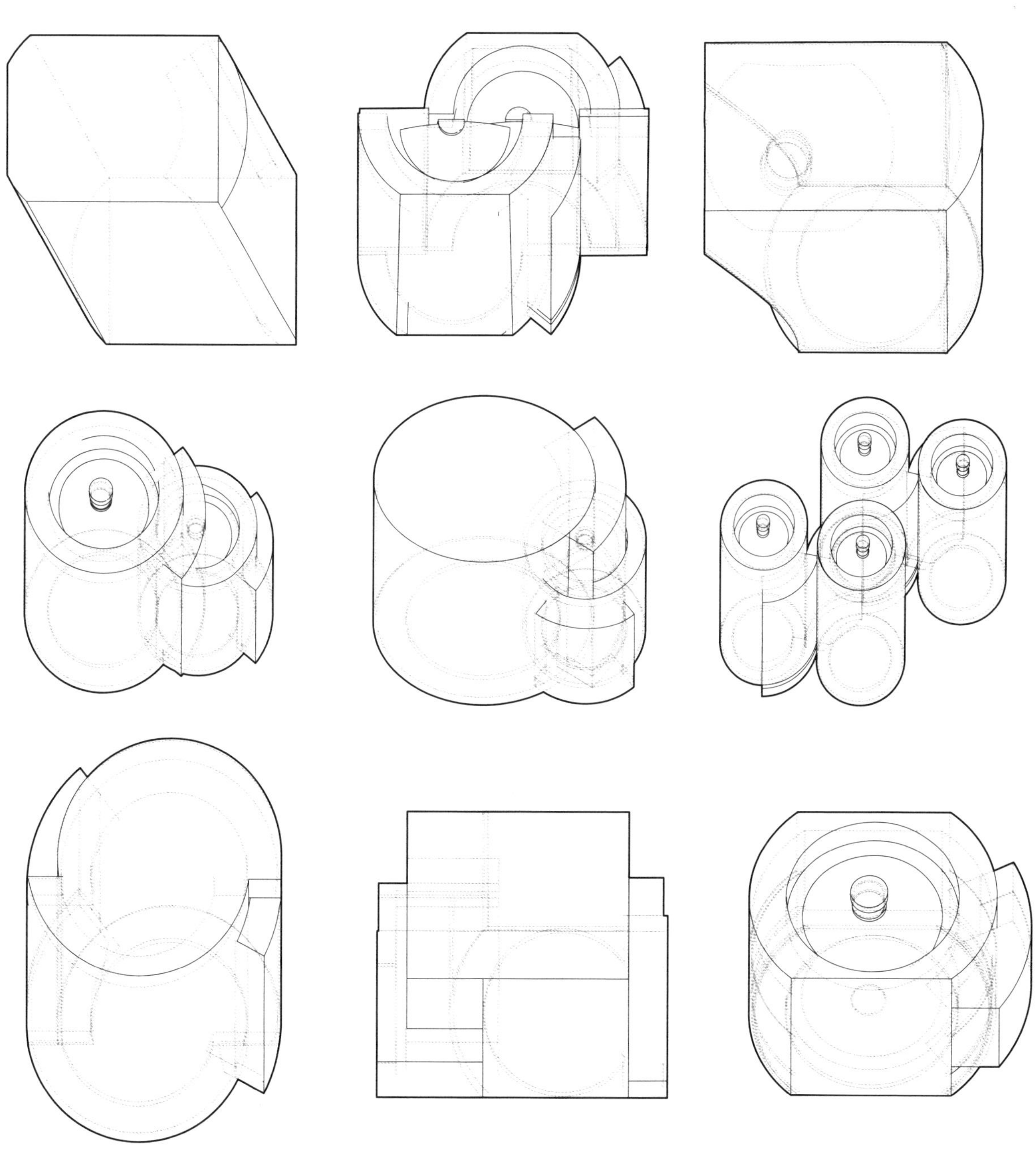

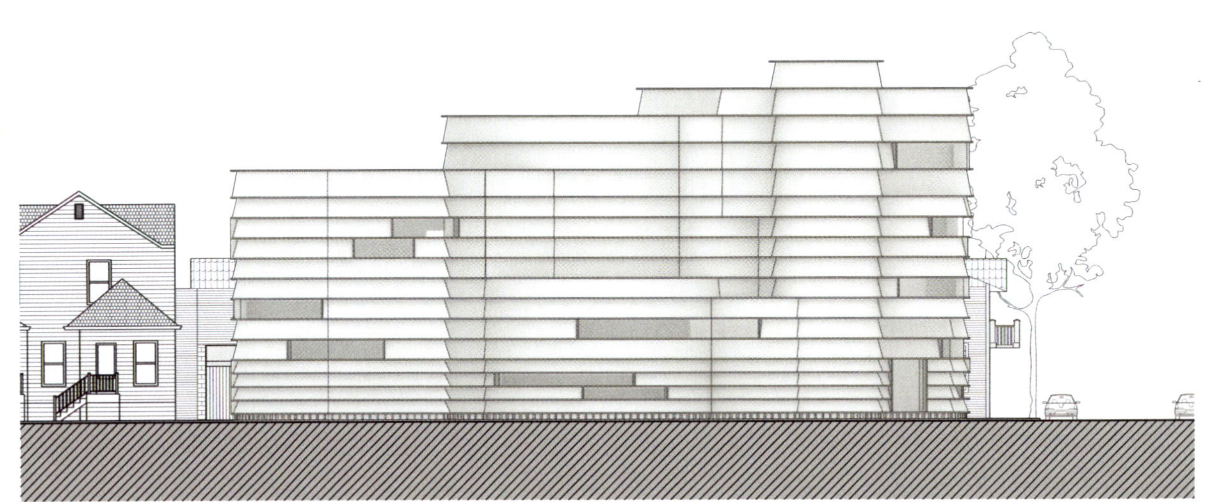

s> Marcus Flory, Lorelei Schmitzer-Torbet **i>** Zaid Kashef Alghata, Ken Schwartz

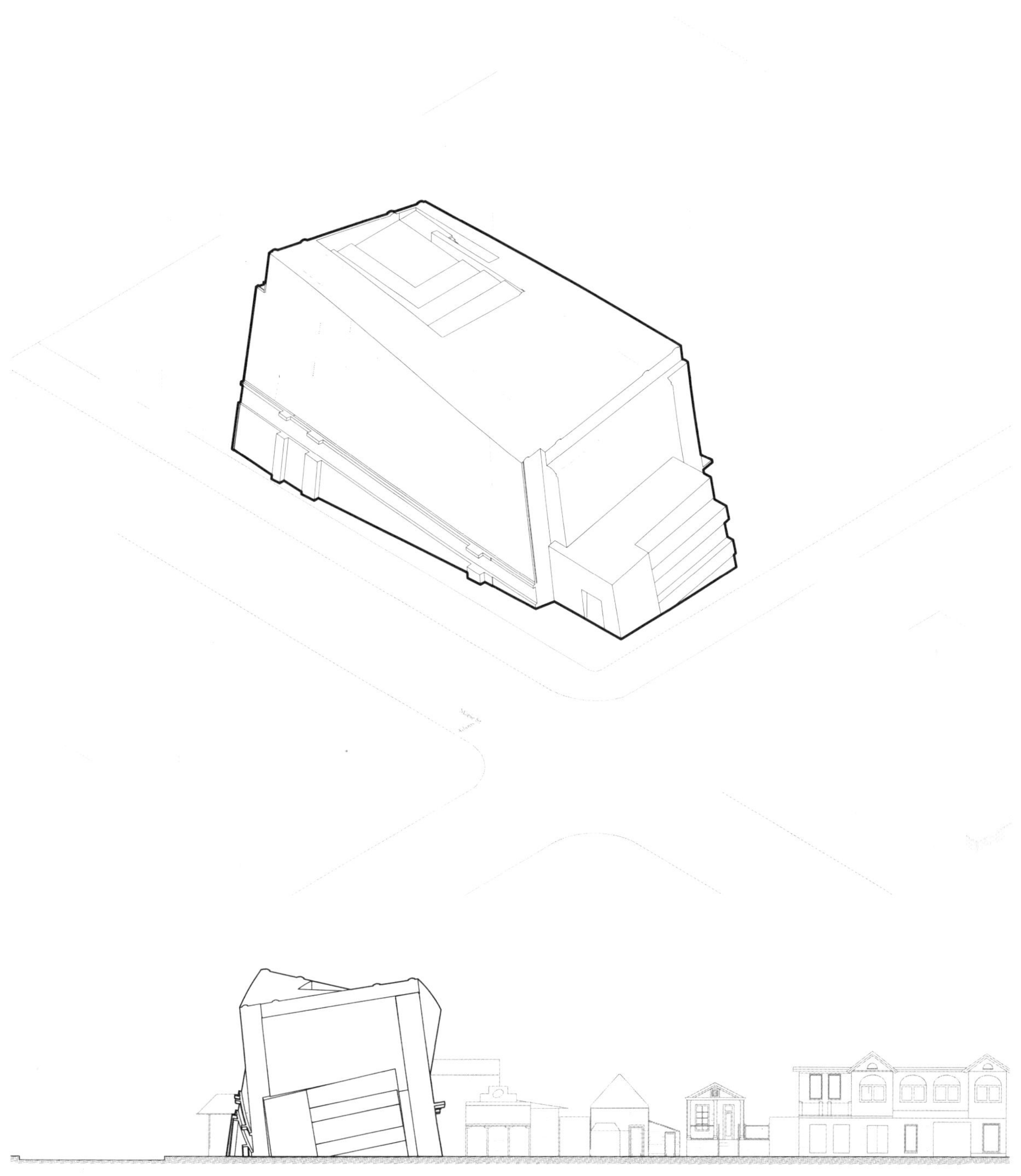

SPACE

Ira Concepcion[C]
Charles Jones

Core studio 1012 explores fundamental methods and principles of architectural design, pushing students to conceive, analyze, and represent architectural form and space. The course introduces various forms of architectural representation and discipline-specific terminology, enabling students to communicate ideas with increasing skill and precision both visually and verbally. Students develop critical thinking skills through project-based learning and experimentation.

The role of form in architecture and design is a key component of the studio. Form is an expansive term that involves shape, configuration, arrangement, manifestation, type, operative sequence, and performance state. In architecture and design, form is closely related to geometry through position, orientation, size, proportion, and pattern. This studio explores the role of form in the construction of objects and space, while also considering form in drawings and images.

The semester pedagogy is intended to advance representational skills, introduce new tools for managing complexity, and expand design vocabularies. Over the course of the semester, projects scale up progressively in size, intricacy, and complexity. "Scaling up" provides an entry point for exploring fundamental architectural problems such as tolerance, fidelity, and resolution.

Computer-aided design (CAD) software is introduced as a new tool for drawing and modeling, with Rhino as the primary tool for almost all work. Greater proficiency with Rhino expands design possibilities, reduces production time, and promotes a deeper understanding of the role of form in architecture and design.

s> Syd Van Slyke, Ari Solomon

i> Ira Concepcion, Charles Jones

s> Charlotte Ertmann

i> Ira Concepcion, Charles Jones

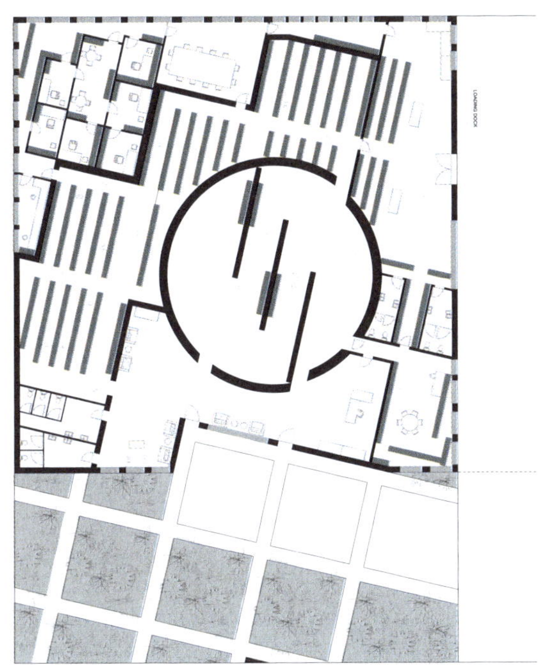

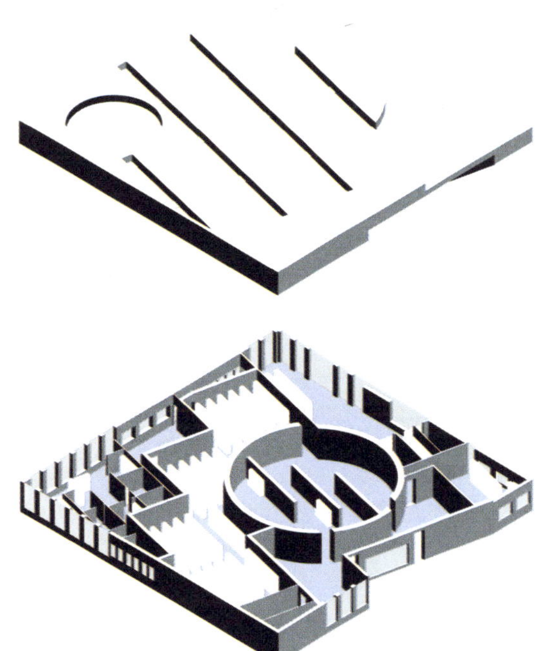

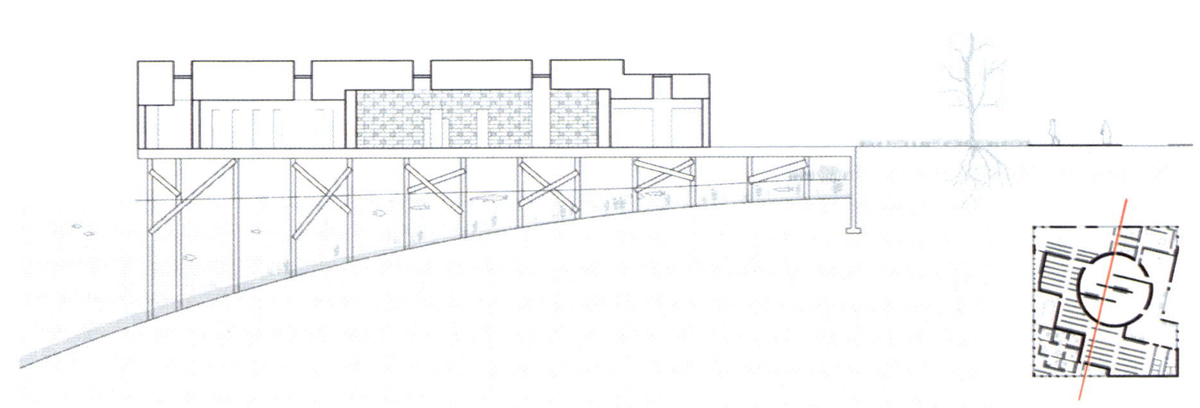

VIN
SE

s> Syd Van Slyke, Jay Martin

i> Ira Concepcion, Charles Jones

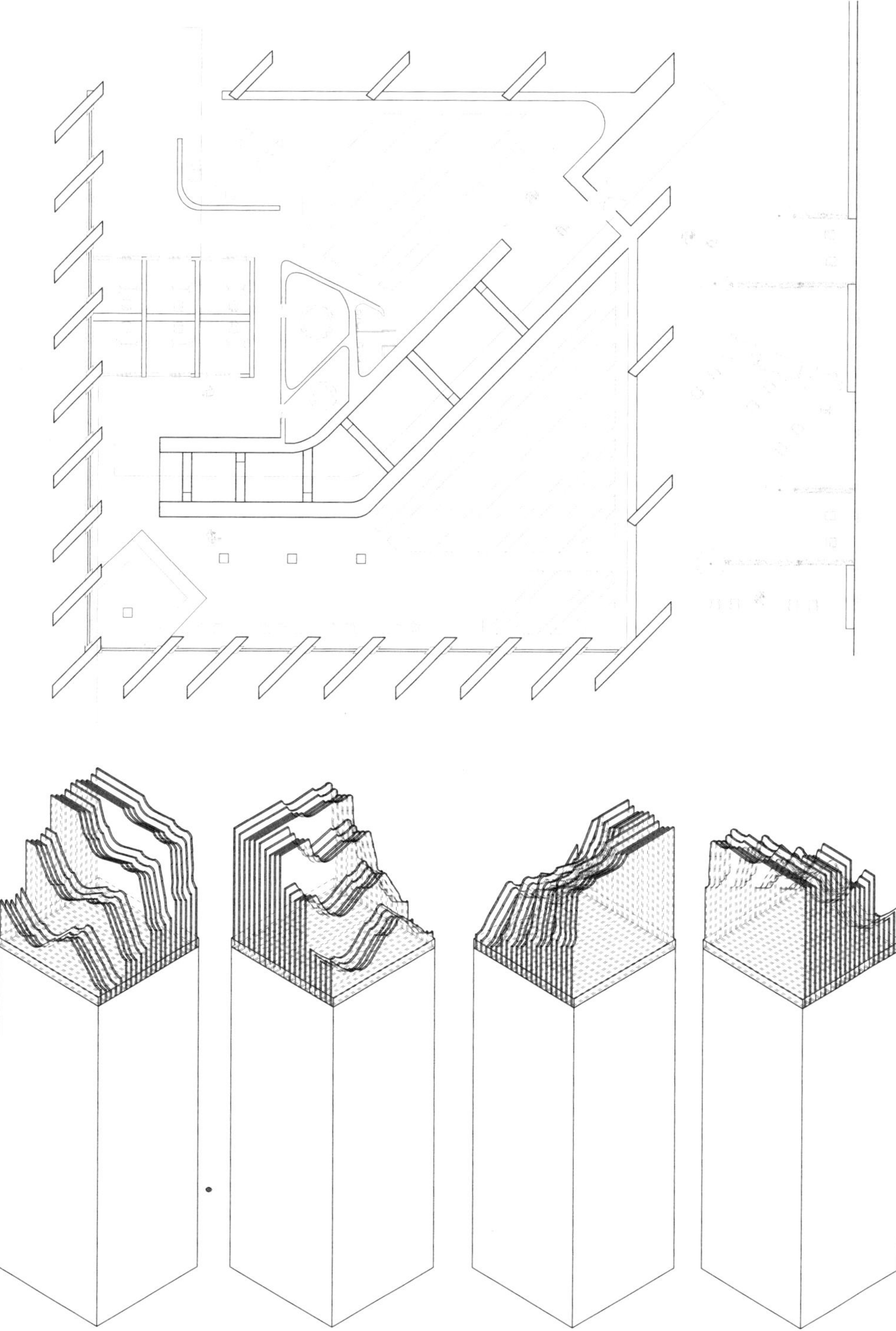

COMMON OBJECTS

having no name or classification

Austin Lightle[C]

This seminar will question the viable models of permanence as a mode of thinking and producing, by addressing architecture's in-flux nature through the development a project in the medium of animation.

The commission of an architectural project begins with a program. This methodology creates an association of form, program and function. Thus developing a naming problem in architecture.

The course will explore the in-flux nature of architecture, questioning our understanding of how program and function have become synchronous with the form of the building. It will begin with research and discussions on the topics of architecture, language, and narrative.

Simultaneously, tutorials will be given on how to animate using Cinema 4D. Each student will start designing morphologies such as the room, stack, shell, nest, etc. The vagueness of morphologies allows for each student to embed a personal identity into their work. As they design, they will begin forming an asset library of found digital waste. Using this library, they will contextualize their morphologies in order to interpret the performative qualities of each object at a multitude of scales. The students will then work to develop new environments for their morphologies to become developed in. They will work to animate the development of these objects into architecture elements existing within their environments. It is up to the student to decide the scale and function of their objects.

Precedents are often held up as exemplars from certain historical lineages, extracted from their original contexts, erased of their ideological and cultural underpinnings, and deployed to make current their anachronisms and to develop a relationship of relevancy to the current problem at hand. Architecture is a field that remains in constant flux, but the current pedagogical models of architecture do not address this problem.

The discourse of this studio will focus on questioning the use of naming, function and scale in architecture and will seek to develop new objects that take on the production of new vocabulary that rides between the camps of ontology and epistemology.

Want to see the videos the students created?

s> Frank Taylor **i>** Austin Lightle

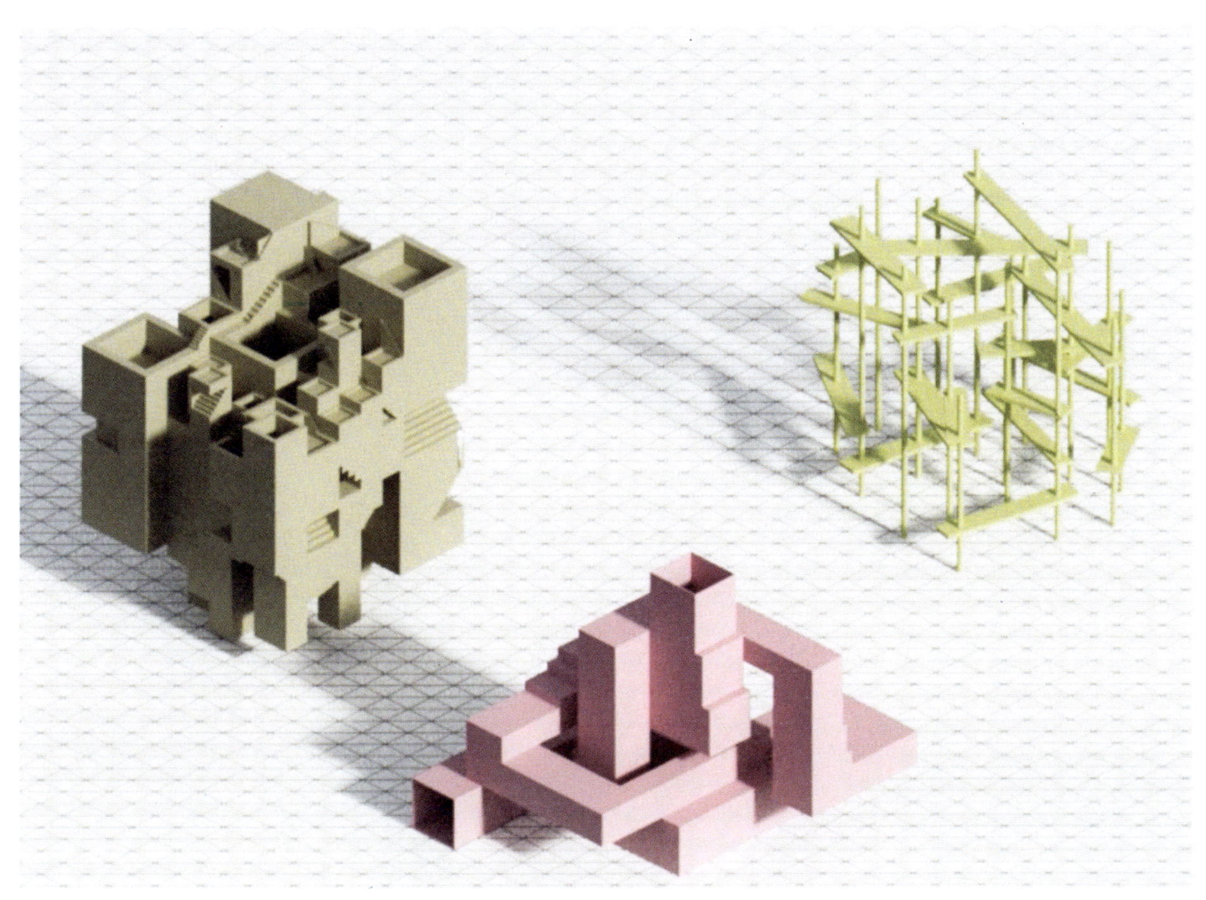

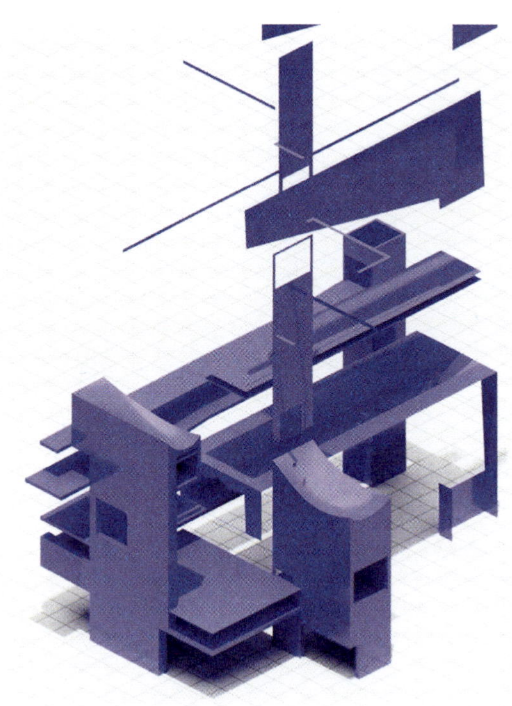

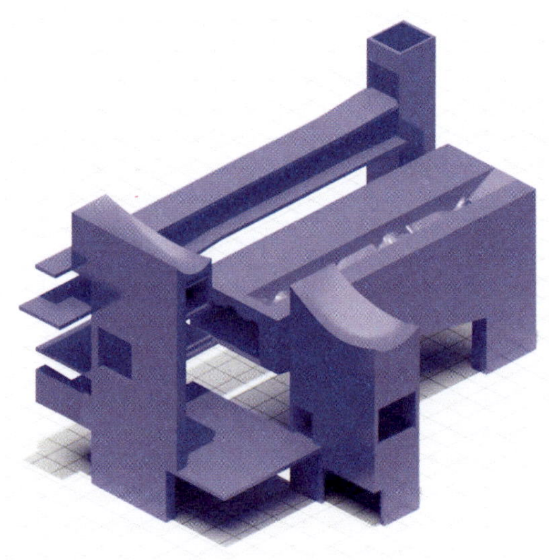

s> Anthony Gagliano i> Austin Lightle

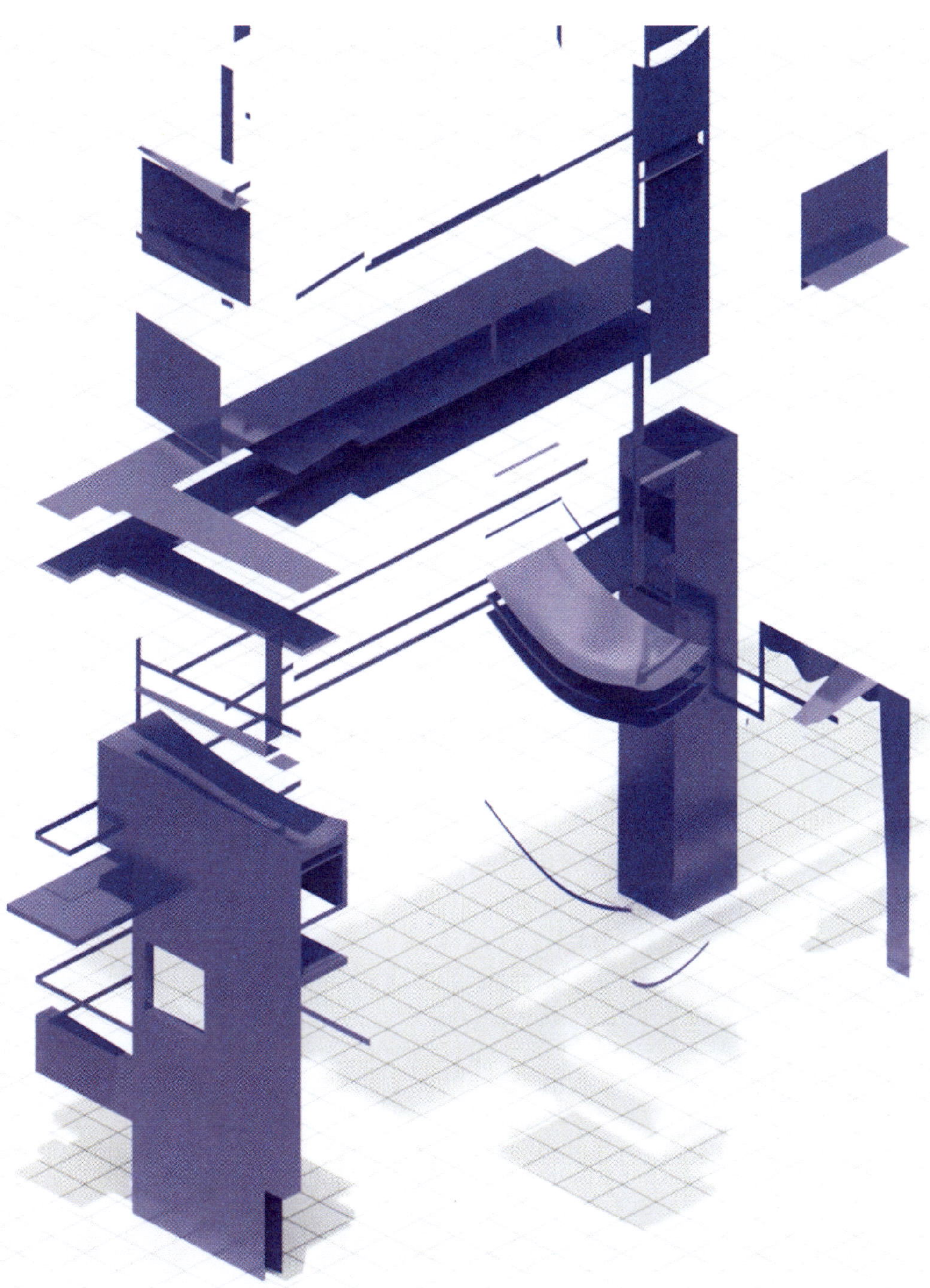

MEMORIAL

LANE SCHOOL OF
CHITECTURE
BUILT ENVIRONMENT
2023-2024

LECTURES

Lecture Series: Thinking Out Loud

Margarita Jover
[October 2023]

Mónica Ponce de León
[October 2023]

Jaqueline Shaw
[November 2023]

Maggie Tsang
[March 2024]

Felecia Davis
[April 2024]

Weiping Wu
[April 2024]

Other lectures

Class of 1973 Student Travel Fellowship Lecture
[October 2023]

Real Estate Lecture: "Green Banks: Financing the Transition to Clean Energy in the Built Environment" led by Bert Hunter; Patnership between TuSABE's Real Estate Development Program, Finance New Orleans, and the AIA New Orleans Committee on the Environment.
[November 2023]

Historic Preservation Lecture: "Preservation as Conversation" led by Jorge Rigau, FAIA
[November 2023]

Historic Preservation Lecture: "Olmsted's Riverside: The History and the Implementation of America's First Planned Community"
led by Charlie Pipal, AIA
[November 2024]

TuSABE GradSchool Night. Image by Akhil Singh

EVENTS & WORKSHOPS

Career Days
A multi-day career and professional development event organized by Tulane School of Architecture and Built Environment's Career Services.
[January 2024 - February 2024]

An Evening with Maurice Cox
[March 2024]

Graduate Colloquium
Organized by Tulane School of Architecture and Built Environment's Graduate Government.
[April 2024]

Symposium: Architecture's Ecological Restructuring, Part II
Speakers: Debbie Chen, Rebecca Choi, Liz Gàlvez, Mae-Ling Lokko, Antoine Picon, Meredith Tenhoor
[April 2024]

"Confronting America's Housing Crisis: Solutions for the 21st Century"
Sponsered by the Murphy Institute's Center for Public Policy Research, the Federal Reserve Bank of Atlanta, and Tulane University School of Architecture and Built Environment and its Real Estate Development Program, and AB Freeman School of Business; Keynote Speaker: Rephael Bostic
[April 2024]

Design Symposium 2024: Future Form
Organized by Tulane School of Architecture and Built Environment Student Government and workshop leaders: Kathy Guo, Joshua Vermilion, Adam Marcus, Maria Yalonina, Kory Bieg
[April 2024]

EXHIBITIONS & INSTALLATIONS

Small Center Exhibit: "Play it Louder: Amplifying Carceral Realities and Abolitionist Futures"
[October 2023 - December 2023]

Sukkah 15
Eric Chesebrough, Lauren Liroff, and Cole Schwabacher
[October 2023]

Small Center Exhibit: "DON'T STAND ALONE: Black Labor Organizing in New Orleans"
[March 2024 - May 2024]

Seminar Exhibit: "May Home is in the Delta"
Students in the seminar, led by Rebecca Choi
[April 2024]

Design Showcase + Fashion Show
More than 100 Students in the Design Program
[May 2024]

TuSABE Career Days 2024. Image by Catherine Restrepo

FACULTY

2023-24. Regular and full-time faculty

Fallon Samuels Aidoo
Assistant Professor in Real Estate Development and Historic Preservation, Tenure Track

Iñaki Alday
Richard Koch Chair Professor in Architecture
Dean

Mostafa Akbari
Assistant Professor in Architecture, Tenure Track

Scott Bernhard
Associate Professor in Architecture
Associate Dean for Academics

Andrea Bardón de Tena
Assistant Professor in Architecture, Tenure Track

Hannah Berryhill
Professor of Practice in Design
Curriculum and Outreach Coordinator

Will Bradshaw
Professor of Practice in Real Estate Development

Edson Cabalfin
Associate Professor
Associate Dean for Faculty Affairs
Program Director, SISE

Richard Campanella
Mintz Senior Professor of Practice
Associate Dean for Research

Liz Camuti
Assistant Professor in Architecture, Landscape Architecture, Tenure Track

Rebecca Choi
Assistant Professor in Architecture, Tenure Track

Cynthia Dubberly
Professor of Practice in Architecture

Steve Dumez
Professor of Practice in Architecture

Patti Dunn
Professor of Practice in Design

Ammar Eloueini
Professor in Architecture
Director, Graduate Programs in Architecture

Sean Fowler
Research Assistant Professor in Architecture

Ruben Garcia Rubio
Assistant Professor in Architecture, Urbanism
Associate Director in Sustainable Urbanism

John Huppi
Professor of Practice in Real Estate Development
Associate Program Director, Real Estate Development

Aarthi Janakiraman
Assistant Professor in Historic Preservation, Tenure Track

Margarita Jover
Professor in Architecture and Landscape Arch.
Program Director, Landscape Architecture and Engineering

Jesse Keenan
Favrot II Associate Professor in Real Estate
Director, Center on Climate Change and Urbanism

Irene Keil
Senior Professor of Practice in Architecture

Judith Kinnard
Professor in Architecture
Harvey-Wadsworth Chair in Landscape Urbanism

Tiffany Lin
Favrot V Associate Professor
Program Director, Design

Adam Marcus
Associate Professor in Architecture, Tenure Track
Research Director, Center on Climate Change and Urbanism

Carol McMichael Reese
Favrot IV Professor in Architecture
Director, Sustainable Urbanism

Juan Medina Revilla
Professor of Practice in Architecture

Jesús Meseguer Cortés
Research Assistant Professor in Architecture

Wes Michaels
Associate Professor in Architecture, Landscape Architecture, Tenure Track

Byron Mouton
Lacey Senior Professor of Practice in Architecture
Director, URBANbuild

Casius Pealer
Senior Professor of Practice in Real Estate

Nick Perrin
Professor of Practice in Design

Wendy Redfield
Associate Professor in Architecture

John Renne
Shane Professor
Director, Real Estate Development Program

Liz Russell
Professor of Practice in Architecture

Daniela Rivero-Bryant
Professor of Practice in Real Estate Development

Cordula Roser Gray
Senior Professor of Practice in Architecture

Meghan Saas
Professor of Practice in Design
Associate Director, Design

Kenneth Schwartz
Professor in Architecture
Michael Sacks Chair in Civic Engagement and Social Innovation, Director of Phyllis M. Taylor Center for Social Innovation and Design Thinking

Catherine Sckerl
Professor of Practice in Architecture, Managing Director, Center on Climate Change and Urbanism

Sergi Serrat
Professor of Practice in Architecture

Versé Shom
Professor of Practice in SISE, Curriculum Coordinator

FACULTY

Jill Stoll
Professor of Practice in Design

Jonathan Tate
Professor of Practice in Architecture

Emilie Taylor-Welty
Favrot III Associate Professor in Architecture, Tenure Track
Program Director, Architecture
Director of Design-Build Small Center

Kentaro Tsubaki
Favrot Associate Professor in Architecture
Associate Dean for Equity, Diversity and Inclusion

Sonsoles Vela Navarro
Assistant Professor in Architecture, Tenure Track

Heather Veneziano
Professor of Practice in Historic Preservation
Associate Director, Historic Preservation

Ann Yoachim
Professor of Practice
Director, The Albert & Tina Small Center for Collaborative Design

2023-24. Visiting faculty

Tyler Antrup
Visiting Assistant Professor in Real Estate Development

Ben Bolz
Visiting Assistant Professor in Real Estate Development

Emek Erdolo
Architecture Fellow

Abel Fernandez Villegas
Pre-Doctoral Fellow in Architecture

Patricia Fraile
Pre-Doctoral Fellow in Architecture

Hannah Kenyon
Visiting Assistant Professor in Architecture, Design
Director of Explorations in Architecture and Design

Austin Lightle
Visiting Assistant Professor in Architecture

Andrew Liles
Visiting Assistant Professor in Architecture
Curriculum Coordinator

Javier Marcano
Visiting Assistant Professor in Architecture and Real Estate Development

Cristobal Molina
Visiting Assistant Professor in Architecture

Xenia Stoumpou
Pre-Doctoral Fellow in Architecture

Kelly Tierney
Visiting Assistant Professor in Design

Alper Turan
Design and Architecture Fellow

Isabel Verhaeghe
Pre-Doctoral Fellow in Architecture

Stone Stitching Reviews. Images by Catherine Restrepo

FACULTY

2023-24. Adjunct faculty

Sienna Abdulahad
Adjunct Lecturer in SISE
Dwan Adams
Adjunct Lecturer in SISE
Richelle Allen
Adjunct Assistant Professor in Real Estate Development
Allison Anderson
Adjunct Lecturer in Architecture
Jacob Alter
Adjunct Lecturer in Architecture
Margie Tillman Ayres
Adjunct Lecturer in Design
Erinn Banks
Adjunct Lecturer in TYLR
Stephanie Barksdale
Adjunct Lecturer in SISE
Alex Barthel
Adjunct Lecturer in Historic Preservation
Alon Barzilay
Adjunct Lecturer in Real Estate Development
Megan Bell
Adjunct Lecturer in Architecture
Jason Blakenship
Adjunct Lecturer in Architecture
Francois Boudreaux
Adjunct Lecturer in Design
Erika Bradford
Adjunct Lecturer in TYLR
Bryan Bradshaw
Adjunct Lecturer in Design
Jada Buckner
Adjunct Lecturer in TYLR
ZoAnn Campana
Adjunct Lecturer in Historic Preservation
Robert Cangelosi
Adjunct Lecturer in Historic Preservation
Bear Cheezem
Adjunct Lecturer in Real Estate Development
Annie Clark
Adjunct Lecturer in Real Estate Development
Page Comeaux
Adjunct Lecturer in Architecture
Ira Concepcíon
Adjunct Lecturer in Architecture
John Coyle
Adjunct Lecturer in Architecture
Allison Cruz
Adjunct Lecturer in Historic Preservation
Jacquelyn Dadakis
Adjunct Assistant Professor in Real Estate Development
Michael Dalle Molle
Adjunct Lecturer in Architecture
Matthew DeCotiis
Adjunct Lecturer in Historic Preservation
Ben Derlan
Adjunct Lecturer in Architecture
Miriam T. Fair
Adjunct Lecturer in Architecture
Maille Faughnan
Adjunct Lecturer in SISE
Marion Forbes
Adjunct Lecturer in Design
Victor Franckiewicz
Adjunct Assistant Professor in Real Estate Development
Darryl Glade
Adjunct Lecturer in Real Estate Development
Kyle Goggans
Adjunct Lecturer in Real Estate Development
Hugh Jackson
Adjunct Lecturer in Architecture
Emma Jasinski
Adjunct Lecturer in Architecture
Nick Jenisch
Adjunct Lecturer in Architecture

Courtney Jones
Adjunct Lecturer in Architecture
Dasjon Jordan
Adjunct Lecturer in Architecture
Regina LaMacchia
Adjunct Lecturer in Real Estate Development
Julia Lang
Adjunct Lecturer in SISE
Casey Last
Adjunct Lecturer in Architecture
Joseph Latson
Adjunct Lecturer in Real Estate Development
Wendy LeBlanc
Adjunct Lecturer in TYLR
Leonardo Leiva Rivera
Adjunct Lecturer in Architecture
Blake Lewis
Adjunct Lecturer in TYLR
Alex Lopez
Adjunct Lecturer in Historic Preservation
Abigail Lukens
Adjunct Lecturer in TYLR
Eric Lynn
Adjunct Lecturer in Architecture
Smith Marks
Adjunct Lecturer in Architecture
MC Matucheski
Adjunct Lecturer in Architecture
Andrew Mayronne
Adjunct Lecturer in Real Estate Development
Anna Monhartova
Adjunct Lecturer in SISE
Fred Neal
Adjunct Assistant Professor in Real Estate Development
Adam Newman
Adjunct Lecturer in Design
Becky Otten
Adjunct Lecturer in SISE
Martha Pearson
Adjunct Lecturer in Design
Emily Riemer
Adjunct Lecturer in TYLR
James Rolf
Adjunct Lecturer in Historic Preservation
Sofia Romeo
Adjunct Lecturer in Architecture
Marguerite Sheffer
Adjunct Lecturer in SISE
Lloyd Shields
Adjunct Professor Historic Preservation
Michael Shoriak
Adjunct Lecturer in Historic Preservation
LeShawn Simplis-Barnes
Adjunct Lecturer in TYLR
Allison Slomski
Adjunct Lecturer in Architecture
Miguel Sotos
Adjunct Lecturer in Architecture
Shaina Spector
Adjunct Lecturer in TYLR
Jesse Toohey
Adjunct Lecturer in Design
Nichole Valenzuela
Adjunct Lecturer in TYLR
Valerie Vides
Adjunct Lecturer in Historic Preservation
Megan Weyland
Adjunct Lecturer in Architecture
Bruce White
Adjunct Lecturer in Architecture
Joy Willig
Adjunct Assistant Professor in Real Estate Development
Thomas Wimberly
Adjunct Lecturer in Design
Sarah Woodward
Adjunct Lecturer in SISE
Rosie Yates
Adjunct Lecturer in TYLR

EMERITI

Errol Barron
Emeritus Professor of Architecture

Eugene D. Cizek
FAIA, Emeritus Professor of Architecture and Historic Preservation

Geoffrey Baker
Emeritus Professor

Karen Kingsley
Emerita Professor

John P. Klingman
Emeritus Professor of Architecture

John Stubbs
Emeritus Sr. Professor of Practice

Ellen Weiss
Emerita Professor

Food Truck Friday. Image by Catherine Restrepo

STAFF

Alexandria Andara
Program Manager, Faculty Employment

Skyler Choice
Financial Services Specialist

Christy Crosby
Assistant Dean for Administration and Operations

Allison Cruz
Assistant Dean for Academics

Michael J. Cusanza
Assistant Director of Admissions

Naomi King Englar
Communications and Marketing Director

Victor Garcia
Technology Manager

Alvin Green Jr.
Building Manager

Sean Huff (†)
Executive Administrative Assistant

Nick Jenisch
Associate Director, Small Center

Joshua Johnson
Academic Advisor

Kristen Jones
Director, Student Affairs

Angelle Keller
Associate Director, Academics

Nick LiCausi
Director of Fabrication

Philip Lopez
Director of Finance and Budgets

Andrew Lorelli
Associate Director, Student Success

Hailey Mathieu
Administrative Program Coordinator, Student Affairs

Beth Nazar
Associate Director, Faculty Affairs

Ben Neal
Executive Administrative Assistant

Keyoka Nelson
Program Manager, Office and Student Employment

Abraham Passman
Administrative Program Manager, Landscape Architecture and Engineering

Nick Poché
Assistant Director, Tulane Center on Climate Change and Urbanism

Catherine Restrepo
Visual Design Manager

Jazmine Smith
Web Developer I

Brandon Surtain
Assistant Director, Community Engagement, Small Center

Jesse Toohey
Fabrication Labs Manager